WRITING ASSESSMENT AT
SMALL LIBERAL ARTS COLLEGES

WRITING PROGRAM ADMINISTRATION
Series Editors: Christopher Carter and Laura R. Micciche

The series provides a venue for scholarly monographs and projects that are research or theory-based and that provide insights into important issues in the field. We encourage submissions that examine WPA work broadly defined and thus not limited to studies of first-year composition programs.

BOOKS IN THE SERIES

Writing Assessment at Small Liberal Arts Colleges, edited by by Megan O'Neill and Genie Nicole Giaimo (2024)

Emotions and Affect in Writing Centers edited by Janine Morris and Kelly Concannon (2022)

The Framework for Success in Postsecondary Writing: Scholarship and Applications edited by Nicholas N. Behm, Sherry Rankins-Robertson, and Duane Roen (2017)

Labored: The State(ment) and Future of Work in Composition edited by Randall McClure, Dayna V. Goldstein, and Michael A. Pemberton (2017)

A Critical Look at Institutional Mission: A Guide for Writing Program Administrators edited by Joseph Janangelo (2016)

A Rhetoric for Writing Program Administrators edited by Rita Malenczyk, 2nd ed. (2016). First ed., 2013.

Ecologies of Writing Programs: Program Profiles in Context edited by Mary Jo Reiff, Anis Bawarshi, Michelle Ballif, & Christian Weisser (2015)

Writing Program Administration and the Community College by Heather Ostman (2013)

The WPA Outcomes Statement—A Decade Later, edited by Nicholas N. Behm, Gregory R. Glau, Deborah H. Holdstein, Duane Roen, & Edward M. White (2012). *Winner of the CWPA Best Book Award*

Writing Program Administration at Small Liberal Arts Colleges by Jill M. Gladstein and Dara Rossman Regaignon (2012)

GenAdmin: Theorizing WPA Identities in the 21st Century by Colin Charlton, Jonikka Charlton, Tarez Samra Graban, Kathleen J. Ryan, and Amy Ferdinandt Stolley (2012). *Winner of the CWPA Best Book Award*

WRITING ASSESSMENT AT SMALL LIBERAL ARTS COLLEGES

Edited by Megan O'Neill and
Genie N. Giaimo

Parlor Press
Anderson, South Carolina
www.parlorpress.com

Parlor Press LLC, Anderson, South Carolina, USA

© 2025 by Parlor Press
All rights reserved.

Printed in the United States of America
S A N: 2 5 4 - 8 8 7 9

Library of Congress Cataloging-in-Publication Data on File

978-1-64317-487-7 (paperback)
978-1-64317-488-4 (pdf)
978-1-64317-489-1 (epub)

1 2 3 4 5

Writing Program Administration
Series Editors: Christopher Carter and Laura R. Micciche

Cover art by Yotuya at iStockphoto.com. Used by permission.
Cover and interior design by David Blakesley.
Copyediting by Fran Chapman

Printed on acid-free paper.

Parlor Press, LLC is an independent publisher of scholarly and trade titles in print and multimedia formats. This book is available in paper and ebook formats from Parlor Press on the World Wide Web at https://parlorpress.com or through online and brick-and-mortar bookstores. For submission information or to find out about Parlor Press publications, write to Parlor Press, 3015 Brackenberry Drive, Anderson, South Carolina, 29621, or email editor@parlorpress.com.

Contents

Acknowledgments   *vii*

Foreword
   Writing Assessment at Small Liberal Arts Colleges:
   Sites for Visibility and Collaboration   *ix*
      Jill Gladstein

Introduction   *xv*

Section I: Methods and Models   *1*

1 Questions and Answers from Writing Assessment:
   Methods and Reporting at SLACs   *3*
      Megan O'Neill

2 The Possibilities and Challenges of WEC-
   Driven Writing Assessment   *21*
      Crystal Fodrey

3 Assessing a First-Year Writing Seminar at a Small Women's
   College: Practices and Opportunities   *39*
      Sarah E. Polo

Section II: Alliance Building and Collaboration   *67*

4 A Data-Driven Model of Collaborative Assessment:
   Harnessing Writing Program and Writing Center Data for
   Continuous Improvement of Writing Support   *69*
      Bryan A. Lutz and Justine Post

5 "We've always done it this way, so why change it?" Navigating
   Change in a First-Year Writing Program   *98*
      Nicole Weaver

6 Amplifying Student Voice in Writing Program Assessment
   through Mutual Mentoring and Students as Partners   *119*
      Hannah Bellwoar and Abby Madar

Section III: Equity/Justice in SLAC Writing Programs *153*

7 Assessing an Honor Code: What "Authorized Aid" Signals to Learners and Educators About the Writing-Collaboration Process *155*
   Genie Giaimo

8 Subverting Elitism with Equitable Assessment at a New England SLAC *173*
   N. Claire Jackson, Gabriel Morrison, and Hayley C. Stefan

9 Developing Anti-Racist Assessment of First-Semester Writing Seminars to Support Students from Historically Underrepresented Groups *202*
   Diane LeBlanc and Bridget Draxler

Section IV: Complicated/Complicating Assessment *227*

10 This Will Never Be 20/20: What Reflection Teaches Us about Assessment *229*
   George Cusack, Julie Christoph, Kara Wittman, and Bridget Fullerton

11 Percentages, Averages, and Exclamation Points: Parsing Assessment, Evaluation, and Research in the Writing Center *255*
   Kristina Reardon

12 Layered Conversations: Methodologizing Lore as a Scholarly Assessment Practice *273*
   Sarah Kosel Agnihotri, Holly Blakely, Matthew Fledderjohann, and Kim Fahle Peck

Coda: What Comes Next? The Future of SLAC Research and Assessment *295*
   Genie Giaimo and Megan O'Neill

Contributors *297*

Index *301*

About the Editors *313*

Acknowledgments

The editors, Megan O'Neill and Genie Giaimo, are indebted to the work of our colleagues in the production of this collection. The SLAC writing administrator world is a small one, filled with inventive people whose jobs include much more than writing assessment, and we recognize the contributions of time, energy, and labor from people already taking on substantial teaching, administration, and service work at their institutions.

We thank each of our contributors for their willingness to share their stories. Critical to the success of this collection were the peer reviewers, including Allison Carr (Coe College), who offered suggestions and affirmations of the book's value. The support of David Blakesley, leader of Parlor Press, was invaluable from the start in getting this book into your hands. We also thank Fran Chapman for copyediting work and Richelle Braswell for offering early guidance on the book's format.

Megan and Genie also acknowledge the work of our historical peers in the field, many of whom served long and faithfully at their institutions to make their programs significant and successful. Among them, Megan includes Carol Rutz (formerly of Carlton College), Andrea Scott (Pitzer College), Noreen Lape (Dickinson College), Duane Roen (Arizona State University), and Scott Whiddon (Transylvania University). Genie thanks colleagues at Middlebury (especially Shawna Shapiro) and in the larger field (Liz Egan, Kristina Reardon, Dan Lawson, Dana Driscoll) for sharing their professional and academic experiences, for encouraging this project, and for encouraging connection with the amazing SLAC WPA organization.

The support for this work included those who picked up additional work on campus while we were working. Megan offers deep appreciation for Leigh Ann Dunning, director of the Stetson University writing center, for her ongoing, unflagging support.

Finally, we wish to thank, most sincerely, Jill Gladstein and Dara Rossman Regaignon, whose landmark work *Writing Program Administration at Small Liberal Arts Colleges* was significant, inspiring, and reassuring to both of us. Jill's foreword to the current collection is a generous donation of her time and expertise.

Foreword
Writing Assessment at Small Liberal Arts Colleges: Sites for Visibility and Collaboration

Jill Gladstein

Writing assessment and the sharing of it makes the work of a site of writing visible by providing opportunities for collaboration and reflection. Due to the size and structure of most small liberal arts colleges (SLAC), site of writing administrators (SWA)[1] seek out others to collaborate with on the design, implementation, analysis, and application of an assessment project. At SLACs where many take a writing across the curriculum (WAC) and writing in the disciplines (WID) focus, assessment provides opportunities for faculty conversations around the teaching of writing and creates a space for the SWA to explore questions from their practice. These conversations and explorations raise awareness of the work of a particular site of writing. In this context, assessment shifts from bean counting to pedagogical development.

When assessment arrived at my previous institution, I remember the overwhelming response-resistance. I use the phrasing arrived because assessment practices began after the accreditation agency called out the institution for a lack of assessment practices. As a private institution with a strong sense of faculty governance and a culture of intellectual rigor, where faculty have the autonomy to decide what and how they teach, many faculty perceived assessment as unnecessary and intrusive. Initiatives comparable to assessment tended to come out of carefully built faculty consensus rather than top down from the administration or an outside entity. Faculty may

---

1. I use the term site of writing administrator (SWA) to be more inclusive than the commonly used WPA. More about this switch in terminology can be found in Gladstein (2023). *Revising the Terminology and Frames around WPA work to Uncover Networks of Sites of Writing Administration.* In Graziano, Halasek, Hudgins, Miller-Chochran, Napolitano, and Szymanki (2023). *Making Administrative Work Visible: Data-Driven Advocacy for Understanding the Labor of Writing Program Administration.* Utah State University Press.

have asked pedagogical questions in conversations, but few performed any kind of assessment including a course evaluation.

On the other hand, writing studies scholars see assessment as an opportunity for collaboration and to make our work visible. Assessment at SLACs provides spaces to highlight the SWA's expertise and identity as a researcher. It has the potential to break down silos. SLACs due to their size should lack silos; however, even though individuals may engage with each other, some SLACs retain institutional structures and institutional memory to keep the intellectual work of writing siloed and undervalued. Through assessment, the SWA pushes back against these norms by providing opportunities using structured analysis to help an institution name its embedded practices or challenge its perceptions about the role of writing in the curriculum. Rather than seeing the teaching of writing only as instrumental for success at the institution and future work in a graduate program, assessment extends the role or definition of writing to include it as a site of pedagogical inquiry.

When Dara Regaignon and I wrote *Writing Program Administration at Small Liberal Arts Colleges in the early 2010s*, we set out to answer the simple question of "What does WPA work look like at a SLAC?" We wanted to name and better understand the different sites of writing in order to increase visibility of this work both on our campuses and in the field. At the time the narratives presented in publications, at conferences and on list-servs did not line up with our experiences as sites of writing administrators at small liberal arts colleges. Not only did we not read or hear about our experiences from authors and presenters, but at the CWPA conference we found few people in attendance from SLACs. This lack of a SLAC presence led Dara and me in collaboration with Lisa Lebduska to host a meeting with our peer administrators. We had one goal—to create a community for those doing this work at SLACs so we could learn from each other about what's happening around writing at SLACs and in some way increase the visibility of writing at this type of institution. This meeting served as the genesis for the SLAC-WPA consortium.

The generosity and kinship of the consortium made the book possible. As stated in the final line of the text:

> The SLAC-WPA consortium emerged from the same impetus as this research process and the two have continued to sustain one another. It is our hope that *Writing Program Administration at Small Liberal Arts Colleges* helps that community of SLAC-WPAs continue their work for local change, just as the knowledge of SLAC-ers has galvanized this research. (Gladstein and Regaignon 2012, 211)

The generosity, intellectual engagement, responsiveness to current conditions, and community building begun at the first SLAC-WPA meeting continues in this collection on writing assessment. By focusing on writing assessment, this collection increases the visibility of how SLACs teach writing and support writers. Each chapter invites readers into the author's assessment processes and helps us to understand how a chosen methodology for a particular driving question allowed the author to learn about their local context and own experiences. Reading these individual accounts (though some chapters include more than one author) creates a community of assessment scholars. SLACs may be too small to have a data set large enough to impress others; however, the collective voices of this collection provide a wealth of examples of the kinds of questions being asked about writing. As Kosel Agnihotri, Blakely, Fledderjohann, and Fahle Peck (this volume) argue, these independent assessment projects may meet the objectives for institutional assessment on a given campus, but when we put these projects or narratives in conversation with each other as done in their work and more broadly with this collection, we begin to learn about assessment itself and join in conversation with others about this important work. In many of the pieces in the collection, assessment provided a chance for conversation around writing.

This collection sheds light on the diversity and importance of the work of the SLAC SWA. In the WPA @ SLACS text, we set out to name the different leadership configurations at SLACs to illustrate how these configurations tell a story about the ecosystem of writing at an institution. For example, at some institutions the person with the title writing center administrator maintains similar job responsibilities to those administering a first-year writing program at other campuses. For these institutions the writing center serves as the explicit site of writing responsible for cultivating a culture of writing by supporting both faculty and students. The authors in this new collection represent different leadership positions and configurations and through their assessment projects we learn more about the varied positionalities and responsibilities of each SWA. Through these different positionalities we also learn a host of assessment methods from interviewing departmental faculty as a method to create buy-in for change to a first-year writing program (Weaver) to the sharing of data between a writing center and writing program to understand the student writing process (Lutz and Post) to analysis of assessment methods through an antiracist lens (LeBlanc and Draxler; Cusack, Christoph, Witman, and Fullerton.) The authors in this text explore questions similar to those discussed in other contexts beyond SLACs and therefore their methods can be applied at a myriad of institution types.

Several authors in this collection share the limitations of their assessment project, often referring to the small size of their data set or what they perceive as unique aspects of their institution. Differences do exist between SLACs and other institutional types; however, this collection underscores that SLAC assessment has much to contribute to the discussions in the field of writing studies around understanding how writing is taught, supported, administered, and assessed. Due to the breadth and depth of the SLAC SWA's responsibilities and their positionalities on campus, the SLAC SWA provides an intersectional perspective on the ecosystem of writing. At some SLACs this occurs because the SWA is the only writing professional on campus and even if their institutional home resides in a writing center or learning commons, the boundaries of the sites of writing within the ecosystem of writing are more fluid than a larger institution. This provides the SLAC SWA with opportunities to not only reflect and ask questions about one site of writing but it also provides opportunities to look at how students and faculty transverse between different sites of writing.

In SWA positions at SLACs where some are non-tenure track or staff positions, where research is not an expected part of the position, assessment provides a space for intellectual engagement within the confines of job responsibilities. Institutions call on an SWA to account for the work of their site of writing. We see throughout this collection examples of how the SWA called on faculty, students and other members of the community and invited them to assist with the assessment process. Through these engagements, SWAs sometimes can push past faculty resistance by modeling how assessment can be used for pedagogical change rather than as an obligation to gain accreditation.

Writing assessment at SLACs is about visibility more than accountability. It allows sites of writing administrators to work beyond the box that their institution or the field of writing studies may have defined for them. It creates spaces for pedagogical conversations. Throughout this volume we see how SLAC SWAs continue to ask questions related to their practices teaching writing and supporting writers and faculty. Because of its size, assessment encourages work across institutions. It creates spaces for the SWA to follow questions of inquiry that may not be a part of their job responsibilities.

My initial experiences with writing assessment come from the positionality of someone who engaged with the literature and conversations from the field of writing studies but found these conversations often did not understand the SLAC context. Now I'm at an R1, with its own uniqueness, and I see how my approach to assessment is informed from my time as an SWA at a SLAC. As I read through this edited collection, I saw the potential for replicating methods in my own context, and I plan to take advantage of the generosity that SLACs continue to exude through the many resources shared throughout this volume.

Introduction

This collection is a follow-up to Jill Gladstein and Dara Regaignon's 2012 Parlor Press text *Writing Program Administration at Small Liberal Arts Colleges*, which brought national attention to the work done at liberal arts colleges (SLACs). Gladstein and Regaignon collected critical data from over one hundred SLACs in the United States, including how and by whom writing programs are directed, how directors are compensated, what responsibilities are shared, how "writing program" is defined, what kinds of writing curricula are in place, and more. Their book identifies a taxonomy and a framework offering a common infrastructure in which all SLAC writing administrators could find themselves and locate their institutions. Such data had not been collected before, and the book thus surfaced the intricate and sometimes complicated and/or inequitable labor structures that affect quality writing assessment. Their collection has allowed SLAC writing administrators to improve processes, to enhance transparency, to create more equitable labor conditions, and to bolster reporting to upper-level institutional administrators who require us to answer the question "What are our peer institutions doing?" This collection extends—and updates—that highly influential work by asking long overdue questions about assessment practices and policies.

SLACs have rich writing traditions (teaching through writing about writing, first-year seminar, organic and interconnected writing curricula, linguistic social justice and activism work, etc.) that are unique to the size and culture of a liberal arts institution. Writing assessment is a substantial part of any writing administrator's work. For the writing administrator at a SLAC, where the typically small faculty body means that the writing administrator is frequently the only faculty member trained in rhetoric, composition, or writing center studies, the work is often done solo or by leading and training allied faculty in assessment work. These situations often position the writing program administrator (WPA) or writing center director (WCD) (which this text often collapses into one term, WPA, although we applaud Gladstein's use of a more inclusive term—SWA—in the foreword to this text) in ways that allow for innovative, highly contextualized, and broadly impactful thinking and practice about assessment of writing. We hope this collection provides SLAC WPAs and teachers of writing with approaches to and questions about that work that are both suitable and useful.

Engaging with This Book

While the topic of this book is writing research and writing assessment at SLACs, we hope that readers from a broad array of institutional backgrounds find meaningful material in this collection. We hope, of course, that those who currently work as WPAs or WCDs at SLACs and those who are interested in working at SLACs will find valuable information that reflects their own lived realities.

But this text is also useful to any new writing administrator as well as to graduate programs in English, writing and rhetoric, which increasingly offer courses in writing program administration. In this way, this book offers those who enjoy a certain amount of flexibility and innovation in their approaches—and those who are interested in conducting cross-institutional assessment between SLACs and other kinds of educational institutions—guidance on how to get started on this work. Smaller schools, as this collection demonstrates, can often exercise considerably more creative and comprehensive approaches than larger schools, and this under-explored facet of SLAC writing assessment offers lessons for colleagues at larger institutions. Additionally, this book teaches us a lot about bringing stakeholders into processes around assessment, research, and curricular innovation. Just about every contributor details the networked constellation that SLAC WPAs build up to do their jobs effectively and ethically. We hope that these lessons are not lost on our counterparts at larger institutions; we are, after all, a profession built on coalition building. SLACs have a lot to teach the discipline about bringing in outside stakeholders and promoting student-faculty research partnerships.

Thus, the new WPA—who may have little if any experience with a SLAC before starting their position, who may be in a rotational leadership arrangement, and who may not be a writing studies or composition specialist—will find theory, methods, plans, results, and innovations in this book. The experienced WPA will benefit from the perspectives carefully marshalled to add weight to proposals about curriculum, assessment, and a variety of program types from which to draw ideas and potentials. The WPA who has no specific training in running a writing program or writing center will benefit from the viewpoints and experiences of formally trained and experienced professionals in the field and will ideally offer starting points for additional study as they settle into the work. These chapters each offer substantial and influential resources for further inquiry for a range of audiences and needs, from upper administration to non-writing studies colleagues who benefit from—or want to benefit from—faculty development and training from professionals. In the absence of SLAC-specific journals in which to publish, an edited collection demonstrating the array of assessment methods can speak to both SLAC institutions and larger research-based colleges and universities. That array of methods is as wide as the imagination of a writing administrator and their colleagues. This collection shows the same range and imagination as we see in writing administrators and their organizations.

The articles in this collection cover areas of vital interest to SLAC writing administrators:

- current SLAC institutional context,
- SLAC methods of writing assessment;
- writing center assessment;
- workload and labor distribution of assessment work at SLACs;
- engaging students and allies in the work;
- theorizing writing assessment; and
- conducting more inclusive and equity-based assessment, including grading.

Why SLAC Writing Programs and Writing Centers?

The institutional context of a SLAC is unique among higher education institutions but is rarely defined clearly or comprehensively. We can think about the question of identifying a SLAC as one with two potential answers: the "by definition" answer and the "spirit of SLAC" answer. The difficulty of finding ourselves in the ways institutions of higher education identify us makes it easy to see why much of the work done by the institution's writing program leaders is invisible to outsiders.

If we ask the "by definition" question, we are faced with conflicting and sometimes elusive data. Of the over 1000 colleges and universities in the United States, approximately 10 percent are considered SLACs, although differences in classification strata make the exact number difficult to define. For example, the Carnegie Classification of Institutions of Higher Education does not offer a SLAC category. Instead, the category that might best describe small liberal arts colleges is "baccalaureate," meaning that they offer a four-year course of study. That classification breaks down into "arts and sciences focused" or "diverse fields." If we assume that "liberal" means "primarily arts and sciences," we may then be asked about what "small" means. While the Carnegie classification identifies kinds of institution, the American College on Education (ACE) offers more categories of size: very small, small, medium, and large. ACE, like the Carnegie classifications, does not offer a category for small liberal arts colleges. The Integrated Postsecondary Education Data System (IPEDS) size categorizations include "<1,000" and "1,000–4,999," aligning with ACE descriptions; however, the range between "fewer than 1,000" and "up to 4,999" does not allow for fine cutting of data. Thus, some sources report a total of 220 SLAC institutions (Latham, Stiles, and Wilcox 2016), while others identify a number closer to 238 (The National Census of Writing 2017–2018). Such definitional data does little to enlighten us or to inform the field of WPA; to do that, we must ask the more relationally-oriented question: what is the "SLAC spirit"?

The "SLAC spirit" can be easily described, as the SLAC-WPA organization website articulates: "The central mission of SLAC-WPA is to support the teaching of writing at small liberal arts colleges where *size, residentiality, curriculum, and faculty structure* present unique opportunities for teaching writing." These institutions typically provide small class sizes (an average of eighteen students in a class), which allows for mentoring and forming closer relationships with faculty and classmates. Further, most of these institutions are residential, with many students living on campus for the four years of a typical undergraduate education. Residential communities provide a sense of belonging and place, a sense of the person as being more than a student identification number. In addition, SLACs are well-known for their supportive, "high touch" learning environments, bolstering the mission of the SLAC, which is historically grounded in a liberal arts goal of engaged citizenship, social justice, and high-quality education around critical thinking, engagement, and rhetoric. SLACs emerge from the national picture of higher education because they carry forward a traditional educational mission centered on students as they are and not just for the career they may move into.

Less administratively heavy and more focused on faculty and shared governance, these small schools often function through informal networks and decades of shared experience, practices, and history. Because of these circumstances, WPA work is unique insofar as it is not uncommon for a very small group of people—or just one person—to be responsible for the wide variety of writing curricula and writing support services at the institution. Yet the ways that the curricula and support services are structured—as many of the chapters in this collection note—vary widely from institution to institution and often rely on precedent rather than field-specific best practices for its functioning. It is these highly localized and specific features that we believe contribute to the fact that, to date, there is very little published research about SLAC writing administrator work that might describe a "typical" writing program at a SLAC, or indeed "best practices in writing at SLACs." Writing centers, which seem ubiquitous at SLACs, may be the single common element across SLAC writing leadership, but even here we face complex questions: we know that students who seek tutoring in writing benefit from those sessions, but assessable, reportable results may be challenging to identify in concrete and replicable ways. For this collection, writing studies, rhetoric and composition, and writing center professionals—the appropriate disciplines for such work—contribute expert reporting from those trained in the field, who can then contribute to the national data record represented by publication.

We recognize and value the research studies that include or feature SLACs (Bromley, Northway, and Schonberg 2013, 2016; Lape 2019). However, these studies often use SLACs as a research site rather than as specific institutional type with a unique set of features. In other words, research about writing programs and writing centers at SLACs often does not distinguish itself much from other institutional types. This kind of flattening of WPA work across different institutional types ignores the very specific contexts in which this labor is done. Thus, instead of journal articles on assessment and empirical work in SLAC-focused writing programs and centers, writing directors at SLACs tend to publish program interventions (O'Neill 2014; Lape 2019) or current challenges in writing administration and teaching work (Shapiro 2020; Giaimo 2020). Research and assessment work, then, is shared at the field's two major conferences: The Council of Writing Program Administrators (CWPA) and the more narrowly targeted conference known as the Small Liberal Arts College Writing Program Administrator Consortium (SLAC WPA). These primarily relational opportunities for exchange of experiences, practices, and results reflect the nature of our work and how we operate. These values also permeate the one or two long-established list-servs that serve the university writing community. Thus, this collection is a first of its kind, offering not just an engaging set of topics specific to SLAC-focused practitioners and scholars but also advancing an underexplored area rich in complex methodological and theoretical approaches: the assessment of student writing in a liberal arts college setting.

Our rationale for such a project was in part driven by the fact that the gap in published research does not reflect the true vibrancy of SLAC writing program research that is currently being produced and shared in more internal and localized spaces like departmental meetings, accreditation reports, and annual small conferences. The chapters in this collection frequently detail the complications of publishing such research and assessment work. Some contributors note their contingent status as visiting or contract instructors (Jackson, Morrison, and Stefan), while others note the ways in which assessment can go awry despite the best of intentions (Cusack et al.; LeBlanc and Draxler; Reardon). And while this field of practice is often concerned with the nuances of assessment and research work and recognizes the need for more inclusive and intentionally anti-racist assessment projects, we do not often recognize or highlight the ways in which such work makes a positive (but very localized) impact on a college or particular population.

Yet for each one of these projects, as our contributors note, many assessment projects are upended—despite the best of intentions—by rogue inter-raters, intransigent faculty colleagues, or experimental design flaws and other challenges (Cusack et al.; Fodrey; Reardon; LeBlanc and Draxler; Giaimo). These projects, then, not only show a number of outcomes from assessment work: they also provide roadmaps to more ethical, thoughtful, and at times novel, methodological approaches to writing administration work at SLACs. Furthermore, many of these chapters are particularly concerned with inclusion efforts and anti-racist approaches to assessment— from the ways in which writing placement is carried out (Weaver) to how one might measure metacognitive development through reflective writing (Cusack et al.) to the efficacy of grading systems, honor codes, and writing program assessment models (Jackson, Morrison, and Stefan; Giaimo; LeBlanc and Draxler). Ultimately, assessment and research work is getting done at SLACs by writing administrators, but the labor conditions under which these authors are conducting their research range widely from tenured and tenure-track faculty to contract faculty and staff members. So, in addition to methodological considerations, material conditions of labor are also heavily featured in these chapters.

This work, however, is not only driven by gaps in our field's scholarship, but also by what the editors see as the need for guidance on novel and more inclusive assessment practices. One editor, Megan, is a twenty-two year writing program director at a small liberal arts college in Florida, while the other, Genie, is a mid-career writing center director with WPA (writing program administration) and WAC (writing across the curriculum) responsibilities at a different liberal arts college in Vermont. Megan has worked at a SLAC for decades, while Genie took up their position right before the start of the pandemic, though they also earned a BA at a SLAC as a scholarship kid. From our unique professional vantage points, we believe that writing assessment at SLACs needs to be updated for the twenty-first century. When Genie took up their position, *Writing Program Administration at Small Liberal Arts Colleges* (Gladstein and Regaignon 2012) was already nearly a decade old. When Megan picked up her copy of the Gladstein text shortly after it was published, she was seeking data to substantiate a move to an embedded, multi-course writing requirement, replacing an unsuccessful ENGL 101 program; she was challenged at multiple administrative points about what other "schools like us" were doing before revising the university writing requirement (a successful initiative, she is proud to say). Both of us, then, found the book invaluable in our own professional development and also to our programs' successes.

However, given the seismic shifts in how we work, learn, and teach—shifts including the Black Lives Matter movement of 2013 and widespread BLM protests in summer 2020, as well as the COVID-19 pandemic—our collective interest in student and faculty well-being, as well as racial justice, has found new life and new directions. Equitable approaches to grading student writing—for example, the "ungrading" approach—have been advanced, establishing pathways toward institutional adoption of these more equitable practices. Thus, we believe it is time to return to our field's work and take stock of where we are as researchers and practitioners laboring in this unique institutional context, often at the forefront of inclusive and meaningful (if unpublished) writing work. Inherent to this conversation, of course, is all the assessment and research work that foregrounds diversity, equity, and inclusion—values that are part of the missions of many of the SLACs featured in this collection.

SLACs are unique among institutions of higher education, given that there are so many of these institutions but so few published writing studies deliberately situated in these institutional sites. Much of the framing for this collection, then, comes from our lived experience, given the dearth of published material from these colleges. In fact, readers will notice that many of the chapters situate their research and assessment first through personal and autobiographical narratives. Some then conduct rhetorical analysis around the everyday documents of writing program work or institutional documents governing policies around writing work (honor codes, grading policies, placement policies, accreditation reviews, etc.) (Giaimo; Jackson,

Morrison, and Stefan; Weaver; Fodrey). Others refer to reports and findings previously shared only internally with administrators, faculty, and other stakeholders of specific colleges (O'Neill). In this way, institutional ethnography, past data, and other forms of qualitative research are pivotal to assessment work among SLAC writing administrators.

Below, and expanding the foundational work of Gladstein and Regaignon (2012), we detail the ways in which SLACs are qualitatively different from other institutional types such as two-year colleges, Research 1 institutions, etc.

The Institutional Mission of Liberal Arts Colleges

The writing instruction and assessment work done at SLACs tends to be invisible to all but the individual institutional program leaders and directors. Yet SLACs are a deep site of engaged learning. These institutions are historically devoted to liberal study, civic engagement, and social and global justice. Wide variations in how the institutional mission is stated and carried out, however, exist, and can be seen in articles in this collection, whose authors work within these institutional contexts: Le Moyne College's mission statement is rooted in the Jesuit tradition, as is the statement of the College of the Holy Cross, focusing on these roots as supporting a dialogue about the moral character of learning and teaching, finding meaning, and identifying obligations humans have to each other. St. Olaf, while "nourished by" Lutheran tradition, offers a focus on a "meaningful vocation in an inclusive, globally engaged community." Ohio Northern University, influenced by the United Methodist Church, prepares students for success, community service, and personal growth in truth, beauty, and goodness. And Cedarville, too, has roots in the Christian tradition, overtly identifying their mission as a way to "use your in-demand skills and high Christian character to make a difference for Jesus Christ."

More overtly secular SLACs represented in this collection include Carleton College, which offers a relationship-rich environment meant to encourage intellectual curiosity, and Moravian University, which prioritizes reflection and transformative leadership. Juniata College, too, is a relationship-rich institution, focused on community, mutual benefits, and mutual respect. York College encourages students to develop their passion for and engagement with their potentials as global citizens; similarly, Wayne State University prepares students to thrive in a diverse set of local and global communities. Pomona College prioritizes inquiry and creative learning to guide students to leadership. Cottey College is a women's college, focused on leadership development and the growth that comes from a required international experience for each student. Middlebury College focuses on immersive learning as a pathway to "engaged, consequential, and creative lives," while the University of Puget Sound offers an education that seeks to "liberate each person's fullest intellectual and human potential." Stetson University describes itself as an institution "where learning and values meet," fostering qualities of "mind and heart." Amherst College commits to learning through a purposely small and highly diverse population seeking to promote inquiry and experience. Bates College prioritizes the "emancipating potential" and transformative power of difference.

SLAC mission statements, then, typically focus on enrichment of relationships, an emphasis on inclusion and engagement, and high academic expectations intended to build quality of the individual mind and person. Within those mission statements, SLACs typically offer a classical breadth curriculum and, specifically, a "writing about writing" (WAW) approach; in contrast, in the research university at large, the WAW pedagogy emerged in 2007 with the publication of "Teaching About Writing, Righting Misconceptions: (Re)Envisioning 'First Year Composition' as 'Introduction to Writing Studies'" by Elizabeth Wardle and Doug Downs. That is to say, many of the ideas coming from institutions that set the bar for the national data record—R1s, primarily—are not new to institutions whose operating systems, priorities, and accomplishments do not appear in that national data record.

Furthermore, the particular mission of SLACs—while often focused on a traditional liberal arts education, civic engagement, and justice—also vary widely, as the authors of these chapters note. They represent religious institutions, a women's college, and secular institutions, all of which have different takes on how one might engage in social justice and ethics. Additionally, many of these schools might be classified as "elite" (most often meaning highly selective) and boast multi-billion-dollar endowments and wealthy student enrollees, which comes with its own mission-related tensions (as Jackson, Morrison, and Stefan note) while others are more regional, rural, or urban institutions with a local mission where the language of "elite" is not in regular use.

Student Enrollment

The comparatively small population at a SLAC opens opportunities for us to study what can happen when institutions are small enough to respond to complex problems; to reflect on how robust writing curricula impacts student learning; and to assess qualitative differences in student writing and related assessment processes. "Small" usually means fewer than 3000 students, although the Carnegie classification system and IPEDS offer a range from "less than 1000" to "up to 5000." Regardless of student enrollment, the small liberal arts school typically prioritizes small class sizes, mentorship, undergraduate research, a writing intensive general education core and major curricula, and a specific kind of student and faculty who are drawn to the small residential college atmosphere. These institutions are teaching-focused and often ask faculty across the disciplines to teach first-year and upper-level writing courses, as well as advise incoming students. So, SLACS are, in many ways, unique among higher education institutions not only for mission, demographic make-up, and a focus on the liberal arts, but, also, faculty expectations around student advisement and the teaching of writing.

A key difference between SLACs and R1 institutions is that more than 80 percent of SLAC WPAs and WCDs who responded to Gladstein and Regaignon's surveys describe their writing programs as multiple, embedded, or disciplinary. That is, most SLACs do not require a formal "first-year writing course" as its only writing requirement, requiring the WPA or WCD to develop and offer training and development opportunities to colleagues teaching courses with writing expectations. Nearly all the WPAs and WCDs lead these faculty development and training opportunities that support the required multiple points of contact or "sites of writing" for a student writer, including writing intensive courses across disciplines, courses for writing in the major, seminar-style first-year courses that prioritize writing skills, and often a capstone or senior research project. In addition, a student writer's experience will often include frequent encounters with advisors (especially before and moving through the first two years of a student's education) and wrap-around mentorship (peer-to-peer, professional, and specialist), which is arguably less common at larger schools. And, finally, while some elite SLACs do not perform regular assessment, most do—and assessment is how the WPA learns what faculty want and need to do in order to improve student writing. Lending professional expertise to all stakeholders on a campus—students, colleagues, and high-level administrators—ensures a standard of quality for teaching and assessing writing that larger institutions may find unmanageable or unnecessary.

Simply put, size matters: a smaller school offers rich territory for student learning because the writing culture of SLAC institutions is often more distributed, more localized, and heavily dependent upon personal relationships and institutional history. Many of our contributors talk about the importance of faculty-student research collaborations and partnerships among different programs and stakeholders as keys to successful writing program outcomes (Bellwoar and Madar; Fodrey; Lutz and Post; O'Neill; Weaver). Several chapters (LeBlanc and Draxler; Lutz and Post; Polo; Weaver) detail the unique challenges and affordances of first-year writing seminars at liberal arts institutions.

Writing Administration and Assessment Labor at SLACs

The assessment work done by SLAC writing program directors is largely unrecognized, not just for many of our colleagues at SLACs, who often inherit traditional thinking about writing centers and writing programs as vehicles for "improving" student writing, but also in the field at large. While it is, as many of our colleagues at SLACs are aware, typical for a SLAC writing administrator to devote far more time to teaching, assessment, and administration than to scholarship, what is not as well understood are the subsequent sets of labor conditions around compensation, tenure, and promotion.

As Gladstein noted in 2012, some 30 percent of SLAC writing center directors are not only NTT but also hold neither a terminal nor "in field" degree. In 2017, according to the National Census of Writing (also developed by Gladstein with Brandon Fralix), 62 percent of the responding institutions indicated that the writing center director held a PhD, but only 28 percent of them were on a tenure line and 24 percent were NTT/FT. Writing program administrators in 2017 reported that 87 percent held the PhD, while 63 percent were on a tenure line. From this data, we might think about the reality that on many small residential campuses, the writing center is the most visible facet of the writing program; many small colleges do not have a writing program *per se* but instead rely on a writing center to perform WAC (writing across the curriculum) and WID (writing in the disciplines) professional development and support work. Many writing center directors and writing program directors are attached to departments of English or communication or independent departments of writing and rhetoric—but many are not. Again, the many ways in which not just we ourselves but our institutions value our work make seeing our commonalities clearly a challenge—but also a point of interest to surface through a collection like this, which makes visible a variety of common concerns around labor, tenure, and promotion that are connected to assessment work.

Further, because our leadership positions may not prioritize publication for advancement or promotion, the ways in which we do our work remain fugitive, available only through relationship-building across SLAC institutions, in discussion on email lists, or by way of internal reports to faculty and upper administration. Such private conversations obscure a wider, more visible understanding of the range of SLAC writing practices around assessment. Additionally, how SLAC institutions distribute the work of assessment is critical to understanding more deeply the working conditions and labor expectations, but without broader dissemination of existing data, equity issues remain invisible. In this collection, several authors discuss the difficulties of conducting writing research and assessment, which includes challenges based on one's faculty or staff status (Jackson, Morrison, and Stefan), but, also, lack of resources for continued programmatic and assessment work with faculty across the disciplines (Fodrey).

Diversity of Assessment Processes and Goals

Writing assessment processes at SLACs are as diverse as writing program administrative structures. At Swarthmore College (Pennsylvania), for example, virtually no writing assessment is done at the institutional level, although individual faculty assessment of student writing is of course a natural part of classroom instruction (National Census of Writing, n.d.). At Moravian University (Pennsylvania), attempts at writing assessment initiated a writing in the disciplines (WID) program that operates with significant program-level and general education (first-year seminar) involvement (Fodrey et al. 2019). At Middlebury College (Vermont), assessment is done at the program level and in partnership with other institutional programs, such as directed self-placement (since 2020) through a writing center director-led partnership between the writing and rhetoric program, the writing center, and the first-year seminar program. At Stetson University (Florida), writing is assessed at both the general education and program levels and "fed" back into the system in an aspirational model of continuous improvement. Assessment methods are as varied as the programs and people who carry out these initiatives. As the table of contents indicates, the wide range of assessment methods includes qualitative (interviews, artifact collection, rubrics, classroom grading, etc.) and quantitative (surveys, linguistic analysis, institutional ethnography, rhetorical analysis, etc.).

Similarly, the methods often include time-specific factors such as longitudinal studies, classroom interventions, and program-specific interventions. SLACs—because of their wide array of support systems (e.g., writing fellows, professional tutors, summer bridge programs, among others), and their manageable population sizes—present several unique opportunities for assessment that contributors want to unpack and share. However, this rich array of experiences and histories is not widely known, discussed, or systematically shared. Genie, for example, has found that assessment on specific elements of first-year seminar student outcomes or impacts of peer writing tutoring on student learning had been conducted in the past but was lost to time in moments of transition. So, this project attempts to collect the kind of work that might otherwise disappear with time and turnover. This is one advantage of a common structure at SLACs: one person oversees a program for the entirety of their career. This is the situation for Megan, who has written and preserved program and assessment documentation for over twenty years—a situation which, as she approaches retirement, raises questions of succession, passing on of institutional memory, and explicit follow-up on pedagogical initiatives. Several of the chapters in this collection grapple with the complexities of carrying forward past research or inheriting programs and assessments that might no longer fit institutional needs.

Linguistic and Social Justice

As one additional example of the adaptive and responsive nature of small liberal arts college writing programs and writing centers, social justice and its attendant movements, such as linguistic justice, are paramount in our institutional missions, which often promote global and social justice, ethics, and community engagement. While institutions themselves may engage in anti-racism activism by enriching faculty expertise or focusing on curricular or co- curricular options, writing directors are typically positioned to intervene in how academic writing is taught and, further, how responding to student writing can be made more inclusive, nurturing, and respectful. In brief, a writing administrator at a SLAC is often in the position of encouraging anti-racist pedagogies that align with the college's mission, as one can see from the table of contents and the chapters on these particular interventions.

Yet these pedagogical interventions (and assessment approaches) get at the subsequent questions of privilege, power, and authority that SLAC writing administrators confront —often alone—in their day-to-day work.

While not a new area of research, there is renewed urgency around issues of social justice in higher education, particularly around writing center work (Haltiwanger Morrison and Nanton 2019; Faison and Condon 2022; Lockett 2019; Giaimo 2020; García 2017) and WPA work (Inoue 2012; Poe and Cogan 2016; Martinez 2016). Yet, there is little to no research that focuses on this work in SLAC writing programs and writing centers, though some SLAC writing center directors write about social justice separate from this institutional context (Bell and Hewerdine 2016). Most of the contributors to this collection detail the importance of equity and inclusion in the policies, research and assessment practices, and curricular interventions that writing administrators contend with at SLACs. Jackson et al. discuss the tension between traditional grading and mental health crisis among student writers. Giaimo discusses the ways in which the honor code shuts down informal networks of writing support and care in favor of prescriptive writing trajectories. LeBlanc and Draxler use anti-racist pedagogy to develop a first year seminar assessment. Polo discusses Cottey College's centralized and shared oversight of a first-year writing seminar that echoes the mission and values of a women's college. Weaver discusses ways to bring stakeholders into conversations around changing long-held but inequitable placement practices, and Cusack et al. identifies how we might teach faculty to be fairer and more compassionate reviewers of students' reflective writing.

It's important to note that while WPAs typically direct a program's goals and assessment of achievement of those goals, faculty grading practices are only infrequently discussed. Faculty classroom autonomy does not often invite WPA intervention. WPAs assume—usually with good reason—that their colleagues are doing good work and, if they find issues in their own grading practices, will adapt and improve accordingly. But it must be said that grading writing is definitely a form of assessment of student writing; in fact, questions about building anti-racist writing pedagogy most often find answers in individual classroom practice and only then are elevated, after testing and refining, to institutional practice. The recent developments in ungrading and contract or labor-based grading took their original shapes in individual classrooms, caught momentum, and then spread themselves broadly over the writing programs of some of our peers. Thus, the chapter by Jackson et al. on challenging the perception of equitable grading practices is both instructive and appropriate for many faculty at SLACs. In most of our work, these days, we are concerned with equity and inclusion because SLACs have continued to recruit and attempt to retain BIPOC and first-generation students. Writing administrators, of course, recognize that recruitment and retention mean little if the writing curricula (and our assessment of it) are racist and classist.

A Note on the Organization of *Writing Assessment at Small Liberal Arts Colleges*

Below, we offer a structure that shows the breadth of research, assessment, and pedagogical work taking place at SLACs. We also want to draw attention, however, to the complexity of focus in each of these chapters even beyond assessment and research work. As we found out, this work cannot be all or nothing when considering issues of equity and inclusion around race and class alongside methodologies and assessments. Labor considerations, of course, make their way into these chapters, too, because of the breath and complexity of the positions that many contributors hold at their institutions.

We break the chapters down thematically by topics that include methodologies, alliance building, equity and social justice, and complicated/complicating assessments. This structure arose organically and elegantly as we looked at our contributors' work. It seemed natural to us to begin with a discussion about the methods we use at SLACs, since asking "how" is a vital part of any assessment question. Thus, we offer chapters that review common concepts and offer specific questions to guide the development of assessment (O'Neill), open the discussion on how a specific writing curriculum can provide specific directions for assessment (Fodrey), and offer an example of assessing a very common first-year course at a SLAC: the first-year seminar (Polo).

The only way to enact some of the methods is to join forces with our faculty and administrative colleagues, which primed the second section on alliance building. Most SLAC writing directors rely on the institutional community to do the work that calls to us because on our campuses, there are rarely more than one or two specialists in our field, and of course, creating a cohort of program allies ensures an institutional commitment populated by the colleagues who, like us, take student writing very seriously. Chapters in this second section focus on alliances between writing programs and writing centers (Lutz and Post); building collaborations between writing faculty and the rest of the college faculty (Weaver); and hearing student voices in an alliance between teachers and learners (Bellwoar and Madar).

This section segues well into our third section on equity and inclusion, as programs and their allies frequently bring their own learning about anti-racism and inclusivity to the writing program's concerns. All stakeholders can be invested and engaged in making our programs and assessment more inclusive, and sometimes the areas of inequity are not immediately obvious. To explore these questions, we include a chapter on the underlying equity tensions in university honor systems (Giaimo); a chapter discussing the values of "elitism" as they contrast with "equity" in assessment (Jackson,

Morrison, and Stefan); and a chapter prioritizing the development of assessment methodologies that seek to level the playing field for underrepresented groups (LeBlanc and Draxler).

The final section addresses something that surprised us with its honesty and transparency: the recognition that assessment—in part or in total—can fail. Many of these chapters (Agnihotri et al.; Cusack et al.; Reardon) detail the ways in which assessment projects needed to be re-done, reimagined, and recontextualized. We believe these chapters to be some of the most exciting because they show how writing administrators are creative, innovative, and concerned with equity and social justice, in how they develop and carry out assessment work. We believe any reader can learn from this last section by understanding the assumptions and practices underlying good assessment and what to do when best-laid plans do not work out.

While we structured this book in four parts, most of these chapters move, unsurprisingly, between most if not all of these themes. Several chapters detail interventions and assessments of first-year writing programs that include both methodologies and assessment plans. Other chapters engage in rhetorical analysis and institutional ethnography with a focus on challenging how we do more inclusive writing work while facing gatekeeping and non-inclusive structures such as timed placement processes, stifling honor codes, and unequal grading practices. Most authors write about WPA labor and the work it takes to maintain ethical and well-managed writing programs; some talk about their contingent status and the issues and consequences of pushing back against institutional elitism.

In short, the work we do as a profession is complex and multifaceted. It is no different at liberal arts colleges. Here, we finally get to witness how complex this work can be.

Bibliography

Bell, Katrina, and Jennifer Hewerdine. 2016. "Creating a Community of Learners: Affinity Groups and Informal Graduate Writing Support." *Praxis: A Writing Center Journal* 14, no. 1. http://www.praxisuwc.com/links-page-141-final.

Bromley, Pam, Kara Northway, and Eliana Schonberg. 2016. "Transfer and Dispositions in Writing Centers: A Cross-Institutional, Mixed-Methods Study." *Across the Disciplines* 13, no. 1: 1–15.

Bromley, Pam, Kara Northway, and Eliana Schonberg. 2013. "How Important Is the Local, Really? A Cross-Institutional Quantitative Assessment of Frequently Asked Questions in Writing Center Exit Surveys." *Writing Center Journal* 33, no. 1: 13–37. https://doi.org/10.7771/2832-9414.1755.

Faison, Wonderful, and Frankie Condon, eds. 2022. *Counter Stories from the Writing Center.* Logan: Utah State University Press.

Carnegie Classification of Institutions of Higher Education. n.d. "About Carnegie Classification." Accessed November 1, 2022. https://carnegieclassifications.acenet.edu/.

Downs, Douglas, and Elizabeth Wardle. 2007. "Teaching about Writing, Righting Misconceptions: (Re)Envisioning 'First-Year Composition' as 'Introduction to Writing Studies.'" *College Composition and Communication* 58, no. 4 (June): 552–84.

Downs, Douglas, and Elizabeth Wardle. 2011. *Writing about Writing: A College Reader.* New York: Bedford/St. Martin's.

Fodrey, Crystal N., Meg Mikovits, Chris Hassay, and Erica Yozell. 2019. "Activity Theory as Tool for WAC Program Development: Organizing First-Year Writing and Writing-Enriched Curriculum Systems." *Composition Forum* 42 (Fall). https://compositionforum.com/issue/42/moravian.php.

García, Romeo. 2017. "Unmaking Gringo-Centers." *Writing Center Journal* 36, no. 1: 29–60. https://www.jstor.org/stable/44252637.

Garcia, Lisa D., and Chiara C. Paz. 2009. "Evaluation of Summer Bridge Programs." *About Campus* 14, no. 4: 30–32. https://doi.org/10.1002/aca.299.

Gladstein, Jill M., and Dara Rossman Regaignon. 2012. *Writing Program Administration at Small Liberal Arts Colleges.* Anderson: Parlor Press.

Gladstein, Jill M. 2017. National Census of Writing. https://writingcensus.ucsd.edu.

Giaimo, Genie. 2020. "Laboring in a Time of Crisis: The Entanglement of Wellness and Work in Writing Centers." *Praxis: A Writing Center Journal* 17, no. 3: 3–15. http://dx.doi.org/10.26153/tsw/9568.

Haltiwanger Morrison, Talisha, and Talia O. Nanton. 2019. "Dear Writing Centers: Black Women Speaking Silence into Language and Action." *The Peer Review* 3, no. 1 [Special Issue: (Re)Defining Welcome]. https://thepeerreview-iwca.org.

Inoue, Asao B. 2012. "Racial Methodologies for Composition Studies: Reflecting on Theories of Race in Writing Assessment Research." In *Writing Studies Research in Practice: Methods and Methodologies*, edited by Lee Nickoson and Mary P. Sheridan, 125–39. Carbondale: Southern Illinois University Press.

Kodama, Corinne M., Ceon-Woo Han, Tim Moss, Brittany Myers, and Susan P. Farruggia. 2018. "Getting College Students Back on Track: A Summer Bridge Writing Program." *Journal of College Student Retention: Research, Theory & Practice* 20, no. 3: 350–68. https://doi.org/10.1177/1521025116670208.

Lape, Noreen. 2019. "From English-Centric to Multilingual: The Norman M. Eberly Multilingual Writing Center at Dickinson College." *Composition Forum* 41 (Spring). https://compositionforum.com/issue/41/dickinson.php.

Latham, Michael, Randall Stiles, and Kaitlin Wilcox. n.d. "Thriving at the Liberal Arts College: Best Practices in Operations and Research." *Proceedings of the 12th Annual National Symposium on Student Retention.* 441–51. Grinnell College.

Lockett, Alexandria. 2019. "Why I Call It the Academic Ghetto: A Critical Examination of Race, Place, and Writing Centers." *Praxis: A Writing Center Journal* 16, no. 2. http://dx.doi.org/10.26153/tsw/2679.

Martinez, Aya Y. 2016. "Alejandra Writes a Book: A Critical Race Counterstory about Writing, Identity, and Being Chicanx in the Academy." *Praxis: A Writing Center Journal* 14, no. 1 http://hdl.handle.net/2152/62610.

McCurrie, Matthew Kilian. 2009. "Measuring Success in Summer Bridge Programs: Retention Efforts and Basic Writing." *Journal of Basic Writing* 28, no. 2 (Fall): 28–49. http://www.jstor.org/stable/43443880.

O'Neill, Megan. 2014. "A Force for Educational Change at Stetson University: Refocusing Our Community on Writing." *Composition Forum* 30 (Fall). https://compositionforum.com/issue/30/stetson.php.

Poe, Mya, and John Aloysius Cogan. 2016. "Civil Rights and Writing Assessment: Using the Disparate Impact Approach as a Fairness Methodology to Evaluate Social Impact." *Journal of Writing Assessment* 9, no. 1. https://escholarship.org/uc/item/08f1c307.

Shapiro, Shawna. 2020. "Inclusive Pedagogy in the Academic Writing Classroom: Cultivating Communities of Belonging." *Journal of Academic Writing* 10, no. 1: 154–64. https://doi.org/10.18552/joaw.v10i1.607.

SLAC-WPA. n.d. "About." https://slacwpa.org/. Accessed July 2023.

Wardle, Elizabeth, and Doug Downs. 2013. "Reflecting Back and Looking Forward: Revisiting 'Teaching About Writing, Righting Misconceptions' Five Years On." *Composition Forum* 27 (Spring). https://compositionforum.com/issue/27/reflecting-back.php.

Section I: Methods and Models

1 Questions and Answers from Writing Assessment: Methods and Reporting at SLACs

Megan O'Neill

Abstract: This chapter identifies many of the most critical concepts and audiences in developing successful assessment processes at a small liberal arts college, using the author's twenty-plus years as the first and only writing program director at Stetson University in Florida. The chapter first articulates the essential questions to be asked and ways to understand the deeper contexts influencing the questions, then describes the process at Stetson University using these questions, and concludes with a discussion of the reporting processes that are essential to administrative leadership, with an eye to embedding knowledge practices into what may otherwise be a *pro forma* expectation of an institutional leader.

Assessment methodologies around writing are easy to find but often not easy to implement to the satisfaction of all stakeholders. Provosts and presidents seek different data than faculty, who are often interested in results that differ from those that writing program administrators and writing center directors develop. Much of the implementation of an assessment plan grows organically from existing structures at the institution, especially SLACs: a solo writing program administrator (WPA) or writing center director (WCD) may implement assessment differently than the methods available to a writing across the curriculum (WAC) team, an interdisciplinary writing committee, or a departmental committee utilizing (or providing to other departments) a writing enriched curriculum (WEC) assessment model.

Moreover, the assessment question differs according to institutional priorities. For example, questions concerning student achievement of learning outcomes shape different assessment approaches than questions about retention of those skills, which differ from questions about student learning in first year versus learning done in upper level and capstone writing courses. And, as alluded to earlier, the institutional type, the student population, and any state (or, less often, federal) funding situations will all also affect assessment priorities. Two-year colleges and larger four-year colleges, for example, may be more concerned with retention and degree completion/ transfer rates than private liberal arts colleges like the ones contributing to this collection. These wide potentials for exploration of learning gains can be distilled down to a handful of directive questions, which I provide here from the institutional context of a small liberal arts college (SLAC).

By showing how each assessment question can be approached, providing a case study, and identifying shifts and changes in reporting approaches depending on a variety of factors, I provide a model that people in SLAC WPA or WCD positions often need but may struggle to enact: a clear assessment plan. A new WPA or WCD can start with this chapter (and many other excellent sources) to get assessment started, but it will also be useful for those WPAs (a term I intend to include writing center directors) who are tasked with educating their colleagues about assessment that matters. I start with a description of institutional roles and lines of reporting, which establishes assessment leadership, then move to a discussion of what questions to ask at individual SLAC institutions, offer methods used successfully at my institution, and discuss the specifics of my reporting lines and audiences. At the conclusion, I offer what I hope are helpful resources for starting, completing, and making meaning from assessment work.

As the introduction to this collection makes clear, the work of SLAC WPAs—that is, in institutions that operate in the relational realm and not always in the transactional arena—is often hidden. One way to surface that work is by creating the institutional and program history embodied in reports. Often considered *pro forma* and sometimes irritating expectations, reports are also a hidden gem of narrating successes and preserving institutional history.

My Background at a SLAC

At my own institution, Stetson University in Florida, I act as the writing program director, the first and only one in over twenty years. Over time, my role has changed as curriculum and institutional missions have worked together for improvement. I began as director of the first-year English program—the general education writing requirement that was handled solely through courses offered by the English department. I reported only to the chair of the English department and the dean of the College of Arts and Sciences. Over time, that set of courses and the writing requirement itself evolved and then moved outside the department and indeed the college as the university began to incorporate high-impact practices more intentionally, including the writing intensive course (WI) and the first-year seminar (FSEM) (O'Neill 2014). With those curricular changes, my title, responsibilities, and lines of reporting changed accordingly.

Now, as the university writing program director, my responsibilities include the faculty- and administration-facing work of shaping and reporting on assessment primarily across two required writing-intensive courses in the core curriculum—the first-year seminar (FSEM) and junior seminar (JSEM)—as well as over 110 individual program-based WI courses, from psychology to accounting to music history. The writing program also supports and to some extent finances the student-serving arm of the writing center, led by a director overseeing tutors and project-based, course-embedded tutors. The writing center director, who also holds an administrative title in the program itself, reports to me, as WPA. My own line of reporting now goes directly to the provost; the writing program at my institution now operates and reports at the university level and is no longer homed in the English department or in the College of Arts and Sciences, meaning that it is separate from the typical faculty, program, and college lines of reporting. Together, the writing center director and I set our own assessment goals (e.g. studying student visits to the writing center, tutor training efficacy, and faculty engagement in writing enhanced courses), and we provide extensive faculty development and education around writing instruction. Objective assessment of student writing is also coordinated through me, in collaboration with a free-standing university general education committee (UGEC). Reporting on that work is typically a joint effort between me and the chair of UGEC. At other SLACs, similar (and dissimilar) systems evolve depending on the nature of the institution, the number of administrative leaders in the writing program or writing center, and the institutional commitment to nourishing writing.

I am also a member of UGEC, in that I oversee the vertical and horizontal coherence of critical skills instruction. Finally, I direct the university's accreditation mandate, the quality enhancement plan, which focuses on teaching information literacy skills. This breadth of service and administration—required when the institution has a limited number (often one) of WPAs—is also typical of SLACs where WPAs and WCDs are often engaged in work that does not directly relate to writing but that reaches into many spaces on campus: academic affairs, student life, institutional research, etc. At other SLACs, WPAs report being involved in admissions decisions, handling department chair responsibilities, directing first year seminar programs, and coordinating student research initiatives like senior project or capstone courses. We wear many hats but are often also the lone writing expert in our schools, which can provide an extraordinary autonomy but may come at the cost of our own professional goals when the single voice trained in the field is shouted down by other, more robust groups.

The SLAC Institutional Context

All of this description is to say that my institution represents some of the ways in which SLAC writing programs typically operate much differently than those at larger or public institutions: many WPAs direct their own programs (separate from English) and they often set their own assessment priorities and outcomes. WPAs also tend to have fewer formally articulated job responsibilities, while administrative duties accumulate over time because so few people share the required expertise and interest in rhetoric and composition/WPA work. An introductory writing course at a larger college (ENGL 101 or something like it) is often taught by graduate students; a SLAC's model is more likely to be multiple courses prioritizing writing via a range of multidisciplinary instructors in first-year seminars and other courses offered through disciplinary programs (Gladstein and Regaignon 2012). Everyone at a SLAC teaches writing to some extent, which means the job responsibilities of the WPA and/or the WCD are numerous and intensive. For example, some SLACs have writing programs without faculty development, without training, and/or without colleague support; some SLACs have no formal writing program at all; some SLACs create structures of leadership to account for the reality that the one or two people who have WPA/writing/ rhetoric experience get leaned on to a disproportionate degree. A different set of institutional expectations may lead to a vibrant program, loved and nourished by its leadership and well-resourced by its institution, whose multiple administrative leaders can collaborate on assessment projects they find interesting and productive. These differences—radical, embedded, unsupported, well-loved—create a range of approaches to assessment models and can also challenge workload assumptions, enable burnout and turnover, and test the limits of our creativity.

Assessment models at SLACs are often qualitatively different from those at larger or public universities. Models can typically be designed by the WPA, or by a faculty group organized from across the institution, whereas at a larger or public university, assessment goals and methods can be mandated by an institutional committee, accreditation requirements, or offices of institutional research. Larger schools may also opt for outside methods of assessment to handle large data loads, for example the third-party commercial packages that use computer readers to score responses to a set of standardized questions, a situation unlikely in the smaller, close-knit communities of SLACs. The goals of assessment processes at larger schools often focus on improvements in first-year writing; at SLACs, given the particular nature of the school in question, assessment goals can range more widely: senior capstone courses, disciplinary writing courses, and courses in methods and practices, as official sites of writing practice, are excellent choices for this kind of work.

Even among SLACs, we can see differences in approach as Gladstein (2012) notes. Not all SLACs have a formalized writing program, but all SLACs seem to have a writing center, typically staffed by peer tutors with an administrative leader. Some SLACs offer a course resembling ENGL 101, but it is rarely the stand-alone model that's most familiar to a general academic audience. Instead, most SLACs offer some form of multi-course writing expectation, whether that is a WAC, WID, or WEC curriculum. Staffing and program leadership in SLAC institutions are typically a combination of tenure-stream and non-tenure track people. Gladstein's 2012 data from over one hundred SLACs showed that WPAs at SLACs are more likely to be in tenure-track lines, while WCDs are likelier to be in NTT or staff positions. These data reveal potential issues of faculty advancement, long-term leadership, and equity; authority and power differentials, too, are important to consider. It is challenging on a number of social and institutional levels to expect a non-tenurable faculty member or a staff member to intervene in faculty development around writing or to spearhead assessment efforts, particularly if the institutional culture around assessment is under-developed.

Faculty Engagement in Assessment Work

Faculty engagement in the assessment process at a SLAC is essential and likely to be more intensive, and, at the same time, potentially more contentious than at a larger institution, because it is often driven by accreditation mandates. SLAC faculty are, by the nature of the institution, fiercely independent and often likely to resist assessment mandates, but faculty who resist writing assessment can be drawn in during the critical process of building allyships from the writing program or writing center out to faculty and students.

The resistance to assessment SLAC WPAs and WCDs might feel from a subgroup of faculty is natural. There is much less movement within the faculty body at SLACs, perhaps because of their specialized and often privileged structure, which places a lot of emphasis on faculty autonomy, small class sizes, interdisciplinarity, and residential living. If instructors have been teaching at the same small institution for twenty-plus years (a common situation), it can be challenging to convince them that assessment will bring something novel to the pedagogical table. Other instructors might believe that the assessment results make no difference to their teaching (or, worse, could impinge on their academic freedom). So, given many of the reasons why faculty might be skeptical or dismissive of assessment, SLAC WPAs need to convince them why assessment matters.

One way to do this convincing is to bring faculty into the assessment conversations by asking them their levels of satisfaction with student writing. In my own experience, asking this question brought a surprising buy-in when faculty immediately said their students "couldn't write" and, when pressed, identified skills and abilities that they assumed other courses (and other faculty) would or should teach. This conversation was very useful when my next questions were "what does good writing look like for you?" and "what models do students have to work with?" These discussions led organically to faculty education and development around teaching writing and responding to student writing in ways that support and suggest rather than criticize. Improvement in student writing typically results from improvement in instruction, and that takes work, investment, time, and energy from faculty who are, because of the nature of SLACs, already doing close, engaged, intensive work with students. And because many SLACs have writing programs and writing centers whose work is distributed throughout the college (taught by a multi-disciplinary faculty), issues of governance and academic freedom also arise in the assessment process. At a larger or public institution, such improvements can often be mandated or handled through an outside process; at SLAC institutions, collegiality and community are often better forms of assessment currency, which can be invested in relationships rather than transactions. Recognizing and then building on established structures offers opportunities for faculty development that in itself may constitute or initiate engagement in the assessment process. Clearly, at a SLAC, the faculty are not only vital in the work of assessment but are close colleagues whose delivery of instruction is likely to be qualitatively affected by the relational surround. Faculty drive the SLAC curriculum, and they are essential allies in any writing program or writing center assessment.

The Questions That Drive Writing Assessment

Regardless of the particular SLAC and its individual program structure, culture, and engagement with assessment, choices about writing assessment at SLACs are driven by a series of questions. I do not make the claim here that larger institutions are not driven by the same questions, but I hope that the discussion that follows each question allows a SLAC WPA to take advantage of the small school "surround" to ensure a healthy practice.

1—What Are the Sites of Writing?

Depending on how the institution delivers writing instruction, these sites might include individual courses marked with specific learning goals about writing, general education or other required courses, or disciplinary writing instruction handled within programs and departments. Writing centers and embedded tutor programs known as writing fellows or writing associates are sites of writing as well. Unofficial or extracurricular sites of writing include community writing projects, creative writing spaces, and digital writing projects that may be student-run or club-based. There may also be professional writing spaces such as departmental colloquia, thesis workshops, or career centers run by programs in student affairs rather than academic affairs. Knowing the sites of writing enables the WPA to know what kinds of questions can be, or should be, asked to drive assessment and improvement in the areas around those sites. When a learning goal is set and artifacts are being identified, already knowing the map of writing sites saves a great deal of time.

2—What Is Being Assessed?

This is the question that should drive writing assessment work: what do we want to learn? Generally, the answers are in the areas of student performance, student retention, transfer of knowledge, student engagement, student perceptions, and/or faculty engagement/perceptions. More specifically, the WPA might want to learn about other vital questions:

- student abilities to revise;
- the efficacy of a program's disciplinary writing curriculum;
- student traffic in writing centers and their relationship to a given course;
- the impact of student visits with a writing fellow;
- student mastery of conventions at a given level;
- student retention of learning from first year to senior;
- amount of class time faculty spend talking about writing;
- effective assignment design; or
- student use of academic support services.

Each of these potential questions and answers are purposeful, intentional, focused, and yield usable data for program improvement. Each answer also provides indications of where potential artifacts might be located.

3—What Would a Successful Outcomes Assessment Look Like?

This question, asked broadly with input from institutional communities and including students, is where the needs of stakeholders are likely to be seen. Positive outcomes from assessment will look different in different institutional contexts, depending on whether state standards exist, on whether stakeholders like a provost or other administrative body have set goals, or whether the institutional curriculum bodies have specific questions or goals. These goals may be in the questions above: student performance, student retention, transfer of knowledge, student engagement, student perceptions, and/or faculty engagement/perceptions about the desirable outcomes.

Successful outcomes assessment goals might look like students' scoring at or above a specific level on a writing assessment rubric; additional success markers might look like sufficiently high percentages of faculty engaged in learning about writing pedagogies. Some stakeholders will expect at least one of the success measures to be grammatically correct writing (which is a contentious issue given a rapidly diversifying, often multilingual student body and raises the question of the use of digitized, third-party writing software such as Grammarly). At the senior level, success might look like consistently effective use of disciplinary writing and research; at the developing level, success might look like students accessing and understanding documentation conventions and uses of appropriate databases. For example, a pre-and-post survey of student confidence about writing and revision skills conducted in a critical course, while limited in its usability, can be useful in concert with a faculty survey about what skills they have been focusing on in that class.

4—What Methodologies Should I Choose for Assessment?

Many methodological approaches to doing assessment exist. Some of these are **qualitative** (case studies, interviews, focus groups, ethnography, etc.) and some are **quantitative** (surveys, student test scores and grades, attrition, and completion rates, etc.). Some are **formative**, meant to identify something about an intermediate step in an ongoing process; some are **summative**, intended to report at the close of a process or teaching unit. Some are **indirect** assessments, for example syllabus review or student self-reporting; more are **direct** assessments of student writing samples read for proficiency, which, as William Condon (2001) has pointed out, was happening in SLACs with WAC programs before larger, public institutions fully adopted writing assessment as a form of accountability.

Each method has built-in limiting factors: the kinds of artifacts or samples available in the greater pool being assessed or the kinds of data that best connect with the assessment questions and outcomes. For authentic, embedded writing samples, the courses being sampled must already assign that kind of work to be collected. Examples within a WID program's artifacts would include some product of a disciplinary nature; a literature review or annotated bibliography, then, might make an effective artifact if the question is to learn if students can research effectively. In contrast, writing centers have long concerned themselves with how to measure efficacy through data, through "customer satisfaction surveys," through student perceptions and engagement or through faculty engagement. Yet tension exists between those who use qualitative and quantitative assessment models and many in the field resist replicable, aggregable, and data-supported approaches (even though they can be either quantitative or qualitative because they are often framed within the realm of the numeric in the literature) in favor of ethnographic methodologies in writing center assessment. The questions we ask about what we want to learn via assessment, some idea of what success would look like, and the methods used in assessment help to identify some of the artifacts or samples that will be suitable for the process.

5—How Will the Results Be Used?

Perhaps the most difficult part of writing assessment is deciding what to do with the data once it's available. No matter the assessment question, methods, success image, artifacts, and scoring, which constitutes a great deal of work in itself, data on its own does nothing except provide something to report. Thus, one more step in the process is necessary.

Generally known as "closing the loop," the steps after the assessment results come in are what to do with them, how to use them to improve instruction and results, and—most importantly—whether and how the faculty can usefully deploy them for improvement of learning and teaching. "Closing the loop" procedures tend to be phrased very generally: "work to improve," as most of the recommendations seem to boil down to, is not as helpful as it might be. Part of the issue is that any writing program or writing center is necessarily highly specific to its institutional mission, needs, students, and faculty, and so specific steps "to improve" at one institution may not be appropriate at another.

Some methods WPAs might try to achieve actionable engagement with assessment results are more successful than others. For example, stakeholders who have been engaged from the start can be approached for their suggestions, their insights, and their needs. Students can be empowered to engage with their own education and make suggestions about how best to assess what they are learning. Faculty who participated in a writing assessment might already be making suggestions for improvement during and after the assessment, and part of any healthy assessment process is the post-assessment discussion among the readers or scorers. (I have included an appendix at the end of this chapter describing the steps in an assessment process that relies on educating readers to be formative in the closing-the-loop process.)

Faculty who were less involved in assessment processes may better understand the results and the suggestions for improvement if they're shown data that certain methods (or better alignment of artifacts to learning goals) improve student learning outcomes and in fact make teaching, if not easier, then more effective. Closing the loop can be persuasively described for faculty in a number of ways:

- as a return on the investment of time and energy;
- as a way to create a stronger program;

- as a way to create happier faculty and students;
- as a way to increase collegiality and integration; and
- as a way to improve writing program outcomes.

Fundamentally, the communication of assessment results is critical to any assessment process: faculty who do not know about the assessment, including "closing the loop" processes, can't be asked to participate in it or care about findings or interventions. In general, assessment as a mandate can be disastrous; done well, assessment is a living, evolving, organic process. Closing the loop is not the end of the process; it is simply the identification of next steps.

Writing Assessment at Stetson University: A Case Study

Because the writing program at my institution is housed in the university-level general education program (not in the English department), our writing assessment processes have settled into a four-year schedule (O'Neill 2014) that aligns with the institutional commitment to assess all general education learning goals on a four-year cycle. It is in fact the writing assessment, which took priority in the general education learning outcomes, that set the organizational pattern for the general education learning outcomes the university regularly assesses. The way the institution uses assessment in general is to improve student learning via improving faculty instruction, which suggests that a natural focus for our now standardized assessment processes is on faculty engagement. In this section, I offer the example of Stetson University and its responses to the questions outlined above.

- **Sites of writing** include the FSEM, the JSEM, and other WI courses offered as part of the general education program; the senior capstone experience; the writing center and other student support resources; and faculty education and development opportunities.
- **What we want to assess** is determined partly by faculty teaching the courses and partly by my professional responsibility to support and reinforce ongoing improvement. In the last ten years, during which the general education program underwent a significant rebuilding, our assessment question has been mapped onto a writing rubric we modified from the AAC&U written communication rubric: what percentage of student samples meet or exceed mid-range expectations? (AAC&U) This quantitative result is, admittedly, easy to

chart, easy to read, and fairly simple to repeat year after year to show trajectories that may or may not require a degree of intervention.
- **What success looks like** at my institution is a set of numbers demonstrating a trajectory of improvement over time; specifically, the institution wants to see an increasing percentage of sampled students scoring at "meets expectations" or "exceeds expectations." The modified written communication rubric lends itself to easy reporting, and this analytical rubric allows more granular assessment and helps to identify elements students may not be consistently demonstrating. While I often take on specialty assessment projects that cannot be easily reduced to a set of numbers, the institution does prefer a quantifiable frame.
- **The appropriate samples and artifacts**, per instructional faculty, are typically authentic and embedded final essays written for a specific writing-intensive general education course that demonstrates content and skills mastery. These artifacts, perhaps not surprisingly, are from assignments that carry the most weight in a given class and, again not surprisingly, are the easiest ones for faculty to submit for assessment. (Ease of procuring suitable artifacts is an important factor in SLAC assessment success.)
- **How the results are used** includes capitalizing on the typical SLAC focus on high- quality teaching and close relationships with students. "Closing the loop" procedures at Stetson University have, over time, come to focus on specific faculty-engagement strategies that honor best practices in writing assessment. Writing program leaders and the UGEC ask those faculty whose classes or students are being assessed for writing to help read, score, and discuss the writing samples, thereby forming over time a series of cohort groups who year after year become more deeply engaged in improving their writing instruction by seeing what students are doing with it. Cycling through various faculty groups has produced a level of engagement and understanding that has contributed to our steadily improving writing outcome assessments. I would also say that taking this approach has nourished and created a culture of writing across the campus while never overtly agitating for it.

Reporting: A Variety of Stakeholders

Reporting the results of assessment is determined by levels of accountability for results. I include reports here because of the deep knowledge required to produce them, knowledge that comes from experience in the field, the research being published, and, most importantly, the empirical and institutional history. Thus, reports are rich storehouses of data, lore, and research that is often hidden unless intentionally made visible.

Lines of reporting, as I mentioned above, determine the first and often the most deeply detailed report. Depending on the stakeholders, first reports might go to a provost or university-level administrator, typically those who fund the program or assessment. Alternatively, first reports might go to an assessment committee. The position and needs of the stakeholder(s), in other words, dictate the shape of the report. Here, I identify four broadly identifiable groups of stakeholders to whom SLAC WPAs might report the results of writing assessment, with follow-up discussion about each:

- upper level administration,
- assessment committees,
- faculty groups, and
- students/parents.

Reporting to the top administrator typically justifies the work done and the results achieved, with discussion of how the work supports the mission of the institution, its strategic map, and/or its essential student learning outcomes. These discussions provide accountability for the substantial investments that are made in writing assessment or assessment initiatives writ more largely. Details include the personnel involved, the kinds of preparation that were entailed, the best practices employed, a summary of any budget expenditures supporting assessment (meals, for example), sets of numbers or other evaluative measures, an interpretation of these measures and provision of institutional or program context, discussion of areas to be studied further or places for intervention, and often some of the next steps planned in assessment. A report of longer than four to five pages typically starts with an executive summary, crafted so as to outline the detailed nature of the discussion to follow. These top-level reports can be intricately referenced, if such background scholarship is institutionally valued for this work. (At my institution, where I report directly to the provost, a recent writing assessment report ran to seventeen pages, exclusive of the graphics showing improvements from the previous assessment effort and exclusive of the three references pages.)

Reports to committees overseeing widespread assessment initiatives tend to be highly contextualized with previous assessment efforts so as to provide a panoramic view of the learning gains as they relate to the communally established goals. Committee readers have a range of needs determined by the SLAC institution, but it is worth the investment of time and careful consideration to determine those needs; committees, too, report upward and to other stakeholders, and the WPA report will often be included or excerpted. Report writers should remember, in addition, that existing Faculty Senate bodies often have an academic affairs subcommittee, who may take writing assessment results in context with wider academic quality initiatives. At my institution, my typical report to an assessment committee consists of several transactional pages describing faculty involvement, scores, initial interpretations and directions to take, and a history of the assessment initiatives to date.

Reporting to faculty depends on which faculty groups are identified as needing to know. WPAs might issue a report to the entire faculty, for example, in ways that justify and support the program's efforts and reinforce the importance of the work being done, perhaps ending with appreciation for the community's support for excellence in student writing. These full-faculty reports act to create spaces in which the entire teaching community can engage as they wish.

In contrast, reports to the faculty who were particularly engaged (supplying samples, reading and scoring, reflecting on next steps) are usually focused more on student learning and areas of specific interest to those faculty. Because these faculty have invested time, energy, intellectual work, and reflection on their own teaching practices, a report providing language that appreciates their work is a return on that investment. Too, these reports to a group of faculty tend to offer specifics: reports might include contextualizing data about a specific set of courses or discussion of the impact of recent faculty-centered teaching initiatives.

Next steps in the assessment process are commonly expected in both kinds of faculty reports. At my institution, which consists of about 200 instructional faculty, nearly all of whom teach writing to some extent, I report to the faculty at large every year while reserving particular care for the report I share with the engaged and invested faculty.

Reports to students and their parents (who are also stakeholders) is not a universal expectation, although parents increasingly expect accountability in return for the substantial investments of time and money they are often making in their children's future. These reports, tailored to a specific kind of audience, might be most useful if they detail the relationship between learning gains and specific curricular or pedagogical features of the institution or program. That is, if the institution has a new WAC program, students might read reports to understand why they take so many classes prioritizing writing; their parents might be more interested in the whys of such a curriculum change and may expect to see improvements in student learning as a result. For such audiences, reporting might underscore sustained successes in student writing as it relates to future employment; reports might also offer praise or encouragement for specific pedagogical approaches or suggest reasons for students to take the initiative for seeking additional support through the writing center or a writing fellows program. At my institution, reports to students and parents takes the form of a new item on the Writing Program website, which is publicly available (that is, not behind the institutional wall) and thus readily accessible for students and parents researching various colleges.

Reporting, as I mentioned at the beginning, is accountability. The report, like "closing the loop" practices, is a public document of institutional effectiveness and its work on continuous improvement in student writing goals as articulated in outcome statements or other kinds of mandates. Done with sophistication and forethought, reporting practices become a living record that provides evidence for a number of claims WPAs make about their SLACs: the value propositions around writing that WPAs make to ourselves, our administrative leaders, our faculty colleagues, and to our students.

Writing assessment is an engaging and ongoing conversation, which—done appropriately and effectively—can draw in all elements of an institution. The essential questions of writing assessment, designed for the institutional character of a SLAC, are critical for the portfolio of any WPA or WCD's responsibilities. Other chapters in this collection speak to questions of application, a range of sites of writing assessment, the thorny issues of assessment of "standard English" among our diverse student populations, and challenges of leadership and privilege; here, I hope, I have established a baseline for my SLAC colleagues to transform for their own complex institutional situations.

Bibliography

AAC&U (American Association of Colleges and Universities). n.d. "VALUES Rubrics." https://www.aacu.org/initiatives/value-initiative/value-rubrics. Accessed July 2023.

Condon, William. 2001. "Accommodating Complexity: WAC Program Evaluation in the Age of Accountability." In *WAC for the New Millennium: Strategies for Continuing Writing Across the Curriculum Programs*, edited by Susan H. McLeod, Eric Miraglia, Margot Soven, and Christopher Thaiss, 28–51. Urbana: National Council of Teachers of English.

Giaimo, Genie. 2007. "Counting Beans and Making Beans Count." *Writing Lab Newsletter* 22, no. 1. https://wlnjournal.org/archives/v22/22-1.pdf.

Gladstein, Jill M., and Dara Rossman Regaignon. 2012. *Writing Program Administration at Small Liberal Arts Colleges*. Anderson: Parlor Press.

Kixmiller, Lori A. S. 2004. "Standards without Sacrifice: The Case for Authentic Writing." *English Journal* 94, no. 1 (September): 29–33. https://doi.org/10.2307/4128844.

Lape, Noreen. 2012. "The Worth of the Writing Center: Numbers, Values, and the Rhetoric of Budget Proposals." *Praxis: A Writing Center Journal* 10, no. 1. http://www.praxisuwc.com/lape-101.

Miley, Michelle. 2017. "Looking Up: Mapping Writing Center Work through Institutional Ethnography." *Writing Center Journal* 36, no. 1. https://www.jstor.org/stable/44252639.

National Census of Writing. n.d. https://writingcensus.ucsd.edu.

O'Neill, Megan. 2014. "A Force for Educational Change: Refocusing Our Community on Writing." *Composition Forum* 30 (Fall). http://compositionforum.com/issue/30/stetson.php.

Stetson University. n.d. "List of Writing Intensive and Writing Enhanced Courses." Writing Program. https://www.stetson.edu/other/writing-program/resources/writing-intensive-courses/list.php. Accessed July 2023.

Appendix A: Template Schedule for Assessment

Here, I share the specific steps I take at this institution to ensure quality assessment and engage with faculty more persuasively. I developed this list for sharing in the 2019 SLAC-WPA conference workshop on difficult questions of assessment.

1. Notify faculty and other stakeholders of the upcoming assessment (pre-fall semester for the year in which the assessment is scheduled).

2. Institutional research (IR) provides a random sampling of students enrolled in the course(s), and instructors are notified which students in their sections have been selected.

3. Midterm reminders to faculty to provide the artifacts and a reminder for the samples to be rendered anonymous. (A separate document, kept by the director of the writing program, identifies the student, the student identification number, and the sample provided. This document becomes useful should a longitudinal study develop.)

4. Faculty are asked to choose the best example of the students' writing from the latter half of the semester. (This approach underscores faculty judgment about writing but presumes that the best sample is one demonstrating a semester of learning.)

5. The collected samples are scored by a faculty group consisting of instructors in those classes. Faculty are recruited and incentivized with meals and gift cards.

6. Discussion **before** the scoring session serves to orient or "calibrate" a sample (or two) using the rubric, with clearly articulated guidelines for addressing strong disagreement on a score. (Options here include deploying a third reader, but I prefer that strongly disagreeing colleagues find their way to an agreement themselves.) Discussion **after** scoring focuses on impressions from the reading, suggestions for improving any and all parts of the assessment process, and ways to close the loop to enact change.

7. The director, in concert with IR, performs data analysis and summarizes the results for the faculty who taught the courses that were sampled. The faculty are then expected to contribute to closing-the-loop procedures. Useful questions:
   - What observations did you have about the process?

- What do you wish you had known before reading the samples?
- Where could we change our process to make things easier, simpler, more effective, shorter?
- How useful was the rubric in establishing descriptions of levels of achievement?
- What similarities and differences across samples did you notice?
- Were there many samples that could not be scored on the rubric? Why?

8. The assessment report is formally submitted to programs that participated, faculty who taught the classes, IR, and administration (including deans and provost). Reports are made widely available on the institutional intranet and all faculty at the institution are invited to read and comment.

2 The Possibilities and Challenges of WEC-Driven Writing Assessment

Crystal Fodrey

Abstract: This chapter describes the writing-enriched curriculum (WEC) model and shares why and how WEC provides an ideal approach to WPA-supported faculty-driven disciplinarily-situated assessment of writing at small private colleges and universities. The potential problem of WEC program sustainability is addressed through a narrative of a short-lived WEC initiative at Moravian University—a small private college in northeastern Pennsylvania transitioning from a primarily undergraduate-serving liberal arts college to a regional comprehensive university, with an undergraduate student population of ~2000 and a graduate population of ~700. The elements necessary for a sustainable WEC program at a SLAC are reinforced through this cautionary tale.

The writing-enriched curriculum (WEC) model of faculty-driven campus-wide disciplinarily situated writing curriculum development and assessment is particularly well suited for small liberal arts colleges (SLACs). This may seem counterintuitive given that the model was first developed and refined at the University of Minnesota and North Carolina State University, two large public research-intensive institutions. However, as Jill Gladstein and Dara Regaignon (2012, 205) note in their conclusion to *Writing Program Administration at Small Liberal Arts Colleges,* "[m]ost small college faculty believe in the importance of writing, and, at the very least, assign it regularly. The challenge for small college WPAs, then, is not just to identify their institutions' sites of writing and writing instruction, but to also uncover the practices informing them." WEC directly addresses this SLAC WPA challenge by sharing oversight of the process of identifying and uncovering writing across local disciplinary contexts, "putting control of writing instruction and assessment into the hands of the people best positioned to make informed, locally relevant decisions about instruction and assessment—namely, a department's faculty" (Flash 2021, 17). The model encourages writing across the curriculum (WAC) and writing in the disciplines (WID) WPAs to relinquish curricular control of discipline-situated writing or writing-intensive designated courses and serve more as a WAC consultant, working with faculty liaisons from WEC-opted departments to assist in the production and iterative revision of writing plans (see Appendix A for Moravian's writing plan prompt). As described on the University of Minnesota WEC FAQ webpage, in a writing plan "faculty members within undergraduate academic units define and characterize writing in their discipline, name the writing abilities with which they would like students to become proficient, map these abilities into undergraduate curricula, and plan for relevant writing assessment and instructional support."

WEC has already been adapted for and implemented within SLAC contexts. Of the first three SLACs to pilot WEC programs between 2014 and 2016, Colby College's program is still going strong, Hobart and William Smith's was stalled in 2020 even though WEC is embedded in their new general education program, and Moravian University's program, which I oversaw, has been on hiatus since the start of the pandemic for reasons I discuss later in this chapter. Smith, which began WEC in 2018, now appears to have a robust grant-funded program (based on their "Writing Enriched Curriculum" website), and Goucher College has redesigned and reframed elements of the WEC model to work at their institution (based on their "Writing Enriched Curriculum" website). Other SLAC writing programs and writing specialists have considered starting WEC on their campuses, as evidenced by the many represented at the May 2022 Writing-Enriched Curriculum Institute—"a virtual two-day event in which WAC/WID professionals, faculty members, researchers, and educational administrators [came] together to discuss practical and theoretical aspects of the WEC approaches and models" (WEC Institute, n.d.)—hosted online by the University of Minnesota.

Through my experience leading a WEC initiative at Moravian from 2016 to 2020 as well as through my engagement with the international WEC community of scholar-administrators, I, like so many others, have come to understand WEC through its many positive attributes and possibilities to improve the scaffolding, teaching, and evaluation of writing as well as enhance overall student learning in courses across the disciplines at postsecondary institutions. WEC can be a set of meaningful, collaborative curricular reform practices that rely upon analysis of locally sourced data (Fodrey et al. 2019; Fodrey and Hassay 2021). It can be a dynamic and recursive coalition-building exercise with the potential to enhance a campus's culture of writing (Scafe and Eodice 2021). It can be a process through which departments of faculty dialogically articulate the nuances of their tacit writing knowledge (Anson 2021; Sheriff 2021) via "structured conversations [led by a WAC consultant] that can challenge and change faculty assumptions and behaviors about teaching writing" (Luskey and Emery 2021, 118). The hope is that the WEC process, regardless of how exactly it manifests in a particular institutional context, leads to enriched curricular experiences around writing for students *and* faculty.

I say "the hope is" not because of a lack of evidence illustrating the positive effects of WEC on postsecondary curricula; WEC is proven to be effective and encouraged by accrediting agencies (see, for example, "2014 SERU Results for Writing Enriched Curriculum Participants" [2015]; see also Appendix B for feedback Moravian received in 2018 from the Middle States Commission on Higher Education in praise of WEC). I say "the hope is" because to start and maintain this deeply reflective and collaborative assessment-oriented process takes time as well as consistent administrative and financial support, at least one dedicated WAC consultant with a sufficient portion of their administrative workload dedicated to WEC, faculty willing (and, ideally, encouraged and incentivized) to engage, and an institutional commitment to effective student learning assessment practices. These are all resources that are often in short supply in the current higher education landscape.

The WEC model, designed for long-term sustainability, uses an intentionally slow and methodical process that typically asks an academic department or program (hereafter, "unit"), led by an appointed faculty liaison from that unit, to work with a WAC consultant to do the following:

1. Study and map their curriculum based on data from student, faculty, and, if relevant, professional affiliate surveys[1] as well as document analysis (e.g., assignment prompts, grading rubrics, student writing samples, etc.)

---

1. Note: Qualtrics is the best program to use for these surveys.

2. Reflect upon their curriculum and teaching as it relates to writing, responding to data from curricular study in structured meetings led by a WAC consultant

3. Develop an evidence-informed and faculty-responsive writing plan (Appendix A)—usually written by the department liaison—often making a concerted effort to connect the writing plan to equity and accessibility-focused campus goals and initiatives, general education, and other relevant departmental and institutional outcomes and priorities

4. Implement the writing plan, which often calls for revision of the unit's curriculum, including course-level writing instruction approaches, assignments, and assessments

5. Develop an assessment rubric and/or other relevant assessment instruments using faculty-generated criteria that can be used to measure discipline-relevant writing outcomes and other WEC and broader student learning goals (e.g., criteria to be used to review writing prompts)

6. Iteratively—that is, repeating on a schedule that makes sense for the unit and/or WAC consultant—assess student writing artifacts using the locally designed assessment instruments(s)

7. Iteratively make revisions to the writing plan and curriculum based on the results of those assessments.

The initial WEC process in a unit—from planning between WAC consultant and department liaison to data collection to WAC consultant-led discussions to first edition writing plan development to implementation to assessment to development of second edition writing plan to assessment—is meant to happen over a period of three to five years per unit, with multiple new units starting the curricular data collection phase of the process each academic year. The number of new units able to engage in the WEC process each year, starting on a concurrent timeline, is largely dependent on time and resources available to those serving in the consultant role and liaison role at a given institution. At the beginning, the program might allow only one or two units to participate. As WEC efforts scale up and more academic units opt in and engage with the process, the administrative "caseload" increases for the WAC consultant(s) who will need to balance serving in different roles for units—data gatherer and organizer, meeting discussion leader, writing plan drafting coach, implementation advisor, or assessment specialist—depending on where a given unit is in the process. WEC program implementation leads to a different yet equally valuable sort of program administration for a SLAC WPA than any of the then-representative administrative models shared by Gladstein and Regaignon over a decade ago.

The WEC approach to supporting and sustaining writing across the curriculum activity at postsecondary institutions is relatively systematic and may appear to be a tad rigid or overly bureaucratic, which may seem incompatible with perceptions of what faculty autonomy—*vis a vis* student learning assessment and assessment-responsive curriculum revision—should look like at a SLAC. However, while WEC does entail a series of WAC consultant-supported steps that units need to progress through, it is important to remember that faculty liaisons within each WEC-opted department are meant to guide the work within this system. The WAC consultants are primarily providing the WEC infrastructure through which faculty move as well as writing specialist knowledge as needed. In addition, the minutiae of WEC practices can and should be adapted to specific institutional contexts. For example, unlike the University of Minnesota that publishes all unit writing plans on their website, Moravian faculty decided to keep their writing plans private within their departments and programs since curricular revisions detailed in writing plans at small institutions often connect with the work of individual faculty who do not want to feel like their course revision plans might be publicly scrutinized.

Detailed examples and analyses of the WEC model in action at both large public institutions and small private ones—Colby and Moravian—are available in the 2021 open access collection *Writing-Enriched Curricula: Models of Faculty Driven and Departmental Transformation* edited by the model's creators, Chris M. Anson and Pamela Flash. The writing at Moravian (WAM) team has published elsewhere about how WEC fit into our writing program's plans to combine all sites of curricular, faculty, and student writing support on campus (Fodrey et al. 2019). In addition, a fairly comprehensive starter kit of resources is available from the University of Minnesota's WEC team on their website (https://wac.umn.edu/wec-program). The elements of the model will therefore not be the focus of the remainder of this chapter. Instead, I take this opportunity to critically reflect on WEC at Moravian University to explore "the interconnected web of writing [and other student learning] goals, mandates, programs, initiatives . . . resources" and ideologies (Galin 2021, 193), especially those related to direct assessment of student learning outcomes at the institution.

Perhaps aspects of the themes that emerge from my institutional context will ring true for those at other small private postsecondary institutions as well. Perhaps not. Either way, I share the story of WEC at Moravian University to illustrate potential challenges of transitioning to and maintaining this worthwhile model supporting departmentally designed writing assessment and then make challenge-responsive recommendations to SLAC WPAs and other administrators considering the WEC model.

Resource Obstacles to a Sustainable WEC Program

Moravian University is a small private postsecondary institution in Bethlehem, Pennsylvania, that enrolls approximately 2100 undergraduate and 600 graduate students and has about 160 full time faculty as of summer 2022. As my colleagues have written elsewhere, "while we identify as a liberal arts college with the addition of preprofessional programs and graduate programs, we are increasingly looking like a masters comprehensive institution" (Traupman-Carr, Dunn, and Wetcher-Hendricks 2021). During the 2021–2022 academic year, Moravian officially transitioned from "college" to "university" in name; we hired a new provost, we dissolved our two-school structure and underwent a reorganization, and we passed a new general education program in which writing and other foundational literacies will play a key role. In recent years—especially since the start of the COVID pandemic, which has had a marked impact on undergraduate retention—most initiatives connected with improving the undergraduate educational experience have been under-resourced and underfunded at our tuition-reliant institution, at least in comparison to pre-pandemic years. This includes the WAM program, of which WEC became a part in 2016.

The WAM program, which was awarded a Conference on College Composition and Communication Writing Program Certificate of Excellence in 2022, has long aspired to develop the infrastructure for a vertical writing transfer curriculum (Melzer 2014) "using an application of activity theory to produce a . . . vision that guides [the program's] work" (see Fodrey et al. 2019 for details). WAM defines writing through a multimodal lens as any form of multimodal communication (i.e., as communication in which audio, visual, spatial, gestural, and/or alphanumeric textual components convey meaning) and encourages writing transfer "not just from first-year writing to courses in the disciplines but at every stage of a student's college writing career" (Melzer 2014, 83). One of the many perceived benefits of WEC within this vertical writing transfer curricular system is that the work of promoting writing transfer within the majors would be discipline-relevant, decentralized, and therefore implemented and assessed in ways reliant upon unit faculty consensus, not WPA mandate.

During the relatively well-supported years that the WEC program existed at Moravian, WAM also included first-year writing taught by faculty across the disciplines; the writing center; the writing fellows program; upper division writing-intensive course approval and assessment; faculty writing workshop series development and leadership[2]; and cohorts of undergraduate writing researchers who studied various aspects of writing on our campus[3] and with our local community, the results of which informed the iterative improvement of other activities within the institution's writing ecologies. Once WEC got off the ground and grew in popularity during the 2016-2017 academic year, the WAM program was then given a part-time twenty-hour per week staff assistant and a ten-hour per week education graduate assistant from the Master of Arts in Teaching program dedicated entirely to WEC starting in fall 2017. Between 2016 and 2019, the WEC team worked with over ten academic units spanning the humanities, social sciences, natural sciences, and health sciences. All of these units got through at least step two of the seven steps listed earlier (reflecting on data from the curricular study of writing). However, despite understanding what the WEC process was meant to entail, when no compensation or reassigned time was available for the liaisons in the first cohort of academic units, two of the three liaisons asked the WAC consultants to co-write the writing plan with them (the work of step three, meant to be completed by the liaison in collaboration with unit faculty), which we agreed to do despite the fact that it set an unsustainable precedent and went against WEC principles of faculty

---

2. To support the program's writing transfer-oriented mission, WAM-developed faculty workshop series tend to focus on, among other things, the knowledge domains from which successful writers draw (Beaufort, 2007), threshold concepts of writing (Adler-Kassner and Wardle, 2015; Adler-Kassner and Wardle, 2019), critical reading strategies (e.g., Carillo, 2016); antiracist/inclusive/accessible teaching and assessment practices (e.g., Browning, 2014; Inoue, 2019; Young, 2020; "Antiracist WAC Toolkit," n.d.), public and community-engaged writing (e.g., Holmes, 2016; House, 2015); and multimodal WAC assignment design (Fodrey and Mikovits, 2020).

3. See *Young Scholars in Writing* article "Understanding the Learned Conceptions of Writing that First-Year Students Bring to College" by recent undergraduate researcher Gabrielle Stanley (2020) as an example.

autonomy, decentralization, and the privileging of discipline-situated writing knowledge over WPA-situated writing knowledge. We should not have complied. Only one unit from that group made it as far as step four (implementing the curricular revision goals set in their writing plan).

At the beginning of the 2019–2020 academic year, for austerity-related reasons, the WAM program lost the graduate assistant line and our staff assistant line was cut from twenty to ten hours a week (it has since been eliminated). I appealed to our provost at the time with a data-filled proposal to scale up our WEC efforts at the institution and hire a full time WEC program coordinator to oversee the majority of the administrative tasks given how many more units wanted to engage with the WEC process, but to no avail even though the institution had invested quite a bit between 2016 and 2019 to launch and maintain the program.[4] By this time I was not only overseeing the WEC program, but as director of WAM, I was also running the first-year writing seminar program largely on my own, co-coordinating an undergraduate writing studies research group, teaching multiple undergraduate writing courses, and collaborating with an interdisciplinary team of faculty to revise the general education program. The biggest obstacles to maintaining WEC at Moravian were, therefore, a lack of resources and time; however, I can see now how the lack of official policy-level articulation between assessment within and assessment outside of the WEC structure played an important role in its lack of sustained institutional support, which I address in the next section.

After the start of the pandemic, the WAM program made the hard but necessary decision to put WEC on hiatus—at which time no unit had made it to steps five through seven (developing a unit-specific assessment rubric,

---

4. Between summer 2016 and spring 2019 Moravian invested approximately $51,750 (an average of $17,250 annually) beyond faculty salaries to support the development and beginning implementation of the WEC program. This support included but was not limited to: one-time internal grant support from Moravian's Student Opportunities for Academic Research (SOAR) program for summer 2016; one-time financial support from the office of the provost to fund WEC creator Pamela Flash's consultation visit to Moravian in September 2016; funding for five representatives from Moravian to travel to the University of Minnesota's WEC Institute and Symposium in 2018 to present as a featured WEC institution; student worker funding from the Education Dept. to support an undergraduate WEC team member over winter break 2016; and an MAT Fellowship offered to a graduate student fall 2017 through spring 2019 funding ten hours per week of WEC support. No additional institutional support has been offered for WEC since spring 2019.

assessing student writing, and planning for assessment data-responsive curricular revisions). Yet I will note, because of the decentralized nature of WEC, the many academic units at Moravian with whom we already worked continued to use the data from that process and their drafted writing plans (if they got that far in the process) to make curricular changes in support of improved student writing in their disciplines. This is, indeed, programmatic assessment work in line with the purpose and spirit of WEC, but not necessarily programmatic assessment work recognized by the institution or understood by unit faculty as such. However, only one department (to my knowledge) connected the WEC process with the institutional mandate for sharing annual unit-level assessment activity with stakeholders outside of the department; therefore, the two processes and the policies surrounding them, which have the potential to articulate well together, developed concurrently but separately and, while promoted by the writing program as compatible, were not widely understood as such.

As of August 2022, the WAM program exists within the center for academic excellence—a student and faculty academic support hub—where I serve as executive director, and the administration of WAM is supported by a small, dedicated team of faculty that, at present, are most concerned with using the limited time and resources available to maintain the writing center and writing fellows program, and oversee the transition to the new general education foundational literacies seminar program. I am currently trying to figure out how we might restart WEC at Moravian in a way that works within the program's time and budgetary constraints as well as within the institution's wider assessment requirements and culture. To do this, I look to the institution's department and program-level *assessment ecologies*—referring to the idea that assessment is and exists within a complex system "bound up in, influenced by, and relational to spaces, places, locations, environments, and the interconnections among the entities they contain" (Reiff et al. 2015, 3).

Assessment Ecology Obstacles to a Sustainable WEC Program

Moravian University's process implemented during the 2016–2017 academic year for iterative academic unit-level assessment of student learning outcomes (SLOs), lauded by the Middle States Commission on Higher Education and highlighted in *Exemplars of Assessment in Higher Education: Diverse Approaches to Addressing Accreditation Standards,* allows each academic unit to "employ a method of assessment that they deem appropriate for their program" (Traupman-Carr, Dunn, and Wetcher-Hendricks 2021). Consistency across the institution comes not in how SLOs are to be assessed but instead in how and when SLO assessment data is reported to administration using a form with consistent prompts to be addressed each year such as "[explain and justify your chosen] measurement technique" and "[describe] department faculty's perceptions regarding what [that year's collected] data indicate about the extent to which students fulfilled [that year's targeted] SLO" (Traupman-Carr, Dunn, and Wetcher-Hendricks 2021). The decision to approach annual unit assessment in this way is in response to the expressed wishes of Moravian faculty, who, like many faculty at small private colleges, "expect significant autonomy in their teaching and scholarly endeavors" (Gladstein and Regaignon 2012, 20) and who would likely balk at department or program-level assessment if they felt as though the process was a top-down mandate "being imposed upon them," which, as Traupman-Carr, Dunn, and Wetcher-Hendricks (2021) explain, could lead faculty to view the practice as invasive, overwhelming, and potentially detrimental to tenure and promotion even when it is not intended to be any of those things. Instead, with faculty autonomy and academic freedom comes faculty buy-in. At Moravian that was certainly part of the initial appeal of WEC (documented in Fodrey and Hassay 2021), which, as noted earlier, supports shifting the locus of control for discipline-situated writing course/instructional oversight and assessments from the WPA to faculty within academic units. WEC, however, necessarily leads to direct assessment of student writing in the disciplines, which is, in general, an unfamiliar practice for most faculty at my institution.

My observation has been that while Moravian faculty and administrators may have a growing understanding of assessment thanks to processes described in the *Exemplars of Assessment in Higher Education* chapter mentioned above (Traupman-Carr, Dunn, and Wetcher-Hendricks 2021) that have developed largely in response to accreditation requirements over the last decade, the institution has historically lacked a culture of supporting robust *direct* assessment practices or using credible evidence from such practices to inform strategic planning and resource allocation decisions. By "direct assessment" in this instance, I specifically mean assessment in which direct evidence found in student learning artifacts is analyzed and scored by local stakeholders using an agreed-upon and consistently applied context-sensitive rubric or other locally informed tool/metric to measure and longitudinally track students' knowledge and skills at the programmatic or departmental level in order to support iterative evidence-responsive faculty-driven revisions of curricula and teaching practices. Instead, indirect student learning assessment data tends to be deemed acceptable and therefore relied upon more frequently for curricular decision-making purposes, which includes evidence such as course grades (e.g., DFW rates), retention/graduation rates, student surveys and focus groups, faculty self-reporting of student learning outcome attainment, and other important but overall "less compelling evidence of student learning," as Linda Suskie (2018, 26) refers to it in *Assessing Student Learning: A Common Sense Guide*. Without a culture and corresponding institutional infrastructure promoting direct evidence from student artifacts analyzed collaboratively and systematically by faculty, and integrated purposefully into institutional decision making practices and policies, members of an institution may not think to, know how to, support the time required to ask, or privilege the answer to, for example, important equity-oriented questions like: does pre-/post- data illustrate that X curricular change had a disparate impact on a specific student learning outcome (SLO) for Black, Indigenous, and other students of color/multilingual students/ first-generation students, etc.? If so, why and also how, and with what resources, should the disparity be addressed? The WEC process can play a major role in this sort of work at the academic unit level (Anson 2021; Scafe and Eodice 2021), but only if WEC can be sustained and understood as supportive of unit-level direct assessment of SLOs.

When it comes down to it, direct assessment designed and implemented to effectively and equitably measure student learning is a complex and logistically difficult undertaking that some small institutions may lack the resource capacity to support. This could mean a lack of financial resources to pay portfolio scorers, but just as often it means that the institution lacks any or all of the infrastructure put in place to support folks with dedicated time and/or expertise to help faculty within or across academic units do the following:

- develop outcomes informed by both (inter)national disciplinary and local context-specific values and student learning goals;
- align curricula and course activities with outcomes;
- create rubrics and/or other measurement tools using context-sensitive criteria developed using a justice-oriented framework[5];

---

5. By "justice-oriented framework" I mean that the assessment tools and approaches are designed with the intention to "disrupt . . . systems of oppression . . . not eradicate, students' cultures, languages, and ways of knowing/being" (Inoue, 2015 paraphrased in Randall et al., 2022, p. 3). See "Disrupting White Supremacy in

- design a process using digital portfolios or other means for collecting and de-identifying relevant student learning artifacts;
- engage in normed scoring practices using sample artifacts;
- score and record observations about collected artifacts (which can be an excellent form of faculty development!);
- write up data in a report responsive to stakeholder needs;
- take action to address what is learned from the data; and
- maintain a historical record of scores, qualitative observations, and actions taken as the assessment is repeated.

If such a direct assessment-supporting infrastructure is not in place or generally encouraged for academic units that are not beholden to discipline-specific accreditors (as they typically are for preprofessional units), a critical mass of faculty and administrators may not know what it is, how it works, how data from such assessment activity should be interpreted and inform institutional decision-making, or why the practice may be valuable in the first place. Therefore, when well-intentioned instructional designers or WPAs with assessment knowledge offers their services in this domain, faculty and administrators may not see a need for such a robust assessment method (like WEC supports) to be prioritized or utilized at all, especially if, as noted above, the normalized practice has been for administrators to encourage members of academic units to design their own unit-level assessment methods, or go through assessment motions without generating useful data, or do no assessment at all.

Without administrative encouragement and without incentives—financial, time, or otherwise—why would an academic want to go all the way through the WEC process during which time locally-developed rubrics are used to assess only writing-related SLOs within the unit? What would unit faculty need to understand about the importance of ongoing effective writing instruction and writing transfer for that to be understood as valuable enough to maintain long term? When learning assessment is not particularly well understood and it is not being particularly well supported, and writing in the disciplines can be assessed indirectly through student responses to survey questions about writing outcomes attainment on course evaluations from writing-intensive courses (as has been the case at Moravian historically), the faculty in an academic unit would need to have collective intrinsic or

---

Assessment: Toward a Justice-Oriented Antiracist Validity Framework" by Randall et al. (2022) for details on how to approach assessment design in a justice-oriented way.

extrinsic (e.g., accreditor-inspired) motivation to go the extra mile and stick with the WEC process.

As of summer 2022, WAM has most recently revised aspects of the program in response to the pandemic and urgent calls for writing programs to address the social inequities, regulation, and racism perpetuated in/through writing and writing instruction/assessment. With limited resources, the program has prioritized faculty development at the intersection of writing threshold concepts and social justice. If Moravian restarts WEC, the hope is that, for example, elements of critical language awareness writing pedagogies (Shapiro 2022) discussed in campus-wide faculty development workshops will find their way into writing plans and that more assessment tools will be designed using a justice-oriented framework.

Toward Sustainable WEC Assessment Ecologies

For a WEC initiative to be sustainable, Jeffrey R. Galin argues that it needs "permanent funding, stable leadership, and established policies, procedures, and practices" developed to facilitate the work in the local context (2021, 198). Attempts to start a WEC initiative without sufficient funding, attempts to rush the WEC process within a department, and/or attempts for a writing specialist with significant additional teaching, administrative, and/or scholarship- producing responsibilities beyond WEC to undergo the WEC process with multiple departments simultaneously are not recommended. I'll add to Galin's list that for WEC to work at any small liberal arts institution, administrators and the institutional infrastructure itself must recognize and privilege the connection between assessment, faculty development, knowledge production, and curriculum design because the WEC approach is a comprehensive approach that takes those connections as a given. If they are approached and dealt with in silos, in different offices with folks who do not regularly collaborate or communicate with each other, then priorities in those areas will likely not align and WEC will likely not be supported well. A slight reframing of the WEC model, one that connects WEC to *all* or at least *most* academic unit-level assessment and highlights the prioritizing of discipline-relevance and faculty autonomy, could be a way to bring all of those areas together better at SLACs. Given writing's powerful connections with thinking and learning, that is certainly a possibility worth exploring. All in all, small private colleges and universities need sustainable systems of curricular improvement and accountability, and what WEC provides has great potential to offer such a system as a WPA-supported framework within which faculty can take the lead in decision-making and evidence-responsive change.

Bibliography

Adler-Kassner, Linda, and Elizabeth Wardle. 2015. *Naming What We Know: Threshold Concepts of Writing Studies*. Logan: Utah State University Press.

Adler-Kassner, Linda, and Elizabeth Wardle. 2019. *(Re)Considering What We Know: Learning Thresholds in Writing, Composition, Rhetoric, and Literacy*. Logan: Utah State University Press.

Anson, Chris M. 2021. "WEC and the Strength of the Commons." In *Writing-Enriched Curricula: Models of Faculty-Driven and Departmental Transformation*, edited by Chris M. Anson and Pamela Flash. WAC Clearinghouse: University Press of Colorado. https://doi.org/10.37514/PER-B.2021.1299.1.3.

Beaufort, Anne. 2007. *College Writing and Beyond: A New Framework for University Writing Instruction*. Logan: Utah State University Press.

Browning, Ella R. 2014. "Disability Studies in the Composition Classroom." *Composition Studies* 42, no. 2 (Fall): 96–117.

Carillo, Ellen C. 2016. "Engaging Sources Through Reading-Writing Connections across the Disciplines." *Across the Disciplines* 13, no. 1. https://doi.org/10.37514/ATD-J.2016.13.2.06.

Flash, Pamela. 2021. "Writing-Enriched Curriculum: A Model for Making and Sustaining Change." In *Writing-Enriched Curricula: Models of Faculty-Driven and Departmental Transformation*, edited by Chris M. Anson and Pamela Flash. WAC Clearinghouse: University Press of Colorado. https://doi.org/10.27514/PER-B.2021.1299.2.01.

Fodrey, Crystal N., and Chris Hassay. 2021. "Piloting WEC as a Context-Responsive Writing Research Initiative." In *Writing-Enriched Curricula: Models of Faculty-Driven and Departmental Transformation*, edited by Chris M. Anson and Pamela Flash. WAC Clearinghouse: University Press of Colorado. https://doi.org/10.27514/PER-B.2021.1299.2.07.

Fodrey, Crystal N., Meg Mikovits, Chris Hassay, and Erica Yozell. 2019. "Activity Theory as Tool for WAC Program Development: Organizing First-Year Writing and Writing-Enriched Curriculum Systems." *Composition Forum* 42 (Fall). https://compositionforum.org/issue/42/moravian.php.

Fodrey, Crystal N., and Meg Mikovits. 2020. "Theorizing WAC Faculty Development in Multimodal Project Design." *Across the Disciplines* 17, no. 1-2: 42–58. https://doi.org/10.37514/ATD-J.2020.17.1-2.04.

Galin, Jeffrey. 2021. "Theorizing the WEC Model with the Whole Systems Approach to WAC Program Sustainability." In *Writing-Enriched Curricula: Models of Faculty-Driven and Departmental Transformation,* edited by Chris M. Anson and Pamela Flash. WAC Clearinghouse: University Press of Colorado. https://doi.org/10.27514/PER-B.2021.1299.2.08.

Gladstein, Jill M., and Dara Rossman Regaignon. 2012. *Writing Program Administration at Small Liberal Arts Colleges.* Anderson: Parlor Press.

Goucher College. n.d. "Writing Enriched Curriculum." Accessed December 18, 2022. https://www.goucher.edu/learn/curriculum/writing-program/writing-enriched-curriculum.

Holmes, Ashley J. 2016. *Public Pedagogy in Composition Studies.* Urbana: National Council of Teachers of English.

House, Veronica. 2015. "Community Engagement in Writing Program Design and Administration." *WPA: Writing Program Administration* 39, no. 1: 54–71.

Inoue, Asao B. 2015. *Antiracist Writing Assessment Ecologies: Teaching and Assessing Writing for a Socially Just Future.* Anderson: Parlor Press.

Luskey, Matthew, and Daniel L. Emery. 2021. "Beyond Conventions: Liminality as a Feature of the WEC Faculty Development." In *Writing-Enriched Curricula: Models of Faculty-Driven and Departmental Transformation,* edited by Chris M. Anson and Pamela Flash. WAC Clearinghouse: University Press of Colorado. https://doi.org/10.27514/PER-B.2021.1299.2.04.

Melzer, Dan. 2014. "The Connected Curriculum: Designing a Vertical Transfer Writing Curriculum." *WAC Journal* 25: 78–91. https://doi.org/10.37514/WAC-J.2014.25.1.04.

Randall, Jennifer, David Slomp, Mya Poe, and Maria Elena Oliveri. 2022. "Disrupting White Supremacy in Assessment: Toward a Justice-Oriented, Antiracist Validity Framework, *Educational Assessment* 27, no. 2: 170–78. https://doi.org/10.1080/10627197.2022.2042682.

Reiff, Mary Jo, Anis Bawarshi, Michelle Ballif, and Christian Weisser. 2015. "Writing Program Ecologies: An Introduction." In *Ecologies of Writing Programs: Program Profiles in Context,* edited by Mary Jo Reiff, Anis Bawarshi, Michelle Ballif, and Christian Weisser. Anderson: Parlor Press.

Scafe, Robert, and Michele Eodice. 2021. "Finding Writing Where It Lives: Departmental Relationships and Relationships with Departments." In *Writing-Enriched Curricula: Models of Faculty-Driven and Departmental Transformation,* edited by Chris M. Anson and Pamela Flash. WAC Clearinghouse: University Press of Colorado. https://doi.org/10.27514/ PER-B.2021.1299.2.11.

Shapiro, Shawna. 2022. *Cultivating Critical Language Awareness in the Writing Classroom.* Abingdon, Oxfordshire: Routledge.

Sheriff, Stacey. 2021. "Beyond 'I know It When I See It': WEC and the Process of Unearthing Faculty Expertise." In *Writing-Enriched Curricula: Models of Faculty-Driven and Departmental Transformation,* edited by Chris M. Anson and Pamela Flash. WAC Clearinghouse: University Press of Colorado. https://doi.org/10.27514/PER-B.2021.1299.2.06.

Smith College. n.d. "Writing Enriched Curriculum." Accessed December 18, 2022. https://www.smith.edu/academics/jacobson-center/writing-enriched-curriculum.

Stanley, Gabrielle M. 2020. "Understanding the Learned Conceptions of Writing that First-Year Students Bring to College." *Young Scholars in Writing* 17 (January): 89–101. https://youngscholarsinwriting.org/index.php/ysiw/article/view/303.

Suskie, Linda A. 2018. *Assessing Student Learning: A Common Sense Guide.* 3rd ed. San Francisco: Jossey-Bass.

Syracuse Writing across the Curriculum. n.d. "Antiracist WAC Toolkit." Accessed July 2023. tps://thecollege.syr.edu/writing-studies-rhetoric-and-composition/writing-across-curriculum/antiracist-wac-toolkit.

Traupman-Carr, Carol, Dana. S. Dunn, and Debra Wetcher-Hendricks. 2021. "One Institution's Journey to Annual Program Assessment." In *Exemplars of Assessment in Higher Education: Diverse Approaches to Addressing Accreditation Standards*, edited by Jane Marie Souza and Tara A. Rose. Sterling: Stylus.

University of Minnesota. n.d. "Frequently Asked Questions." Accessed December 18, 2022. https://wac.umn.edu/wec-program/wec-faq.

University of Minnesota Office of Institutional Research. 2015. "2014 SERU Results for Writing Enriched Curriculum Participants." https://wac.umn.edu/sites/wac.umn.edu/files/2019-09/seru_2014.pdf.

WEC Institute. n.d. "2022 WEC Institute." Accessed December 18, 2022. https://sites.google.com/umn.edu/2022wecinstitute/home?authuser=0.

Young, Vershawn Ashanti. 2020. "Black Lives Matter in Academic Spaces: Three Lessons for Critical Literacy." *Journal of College Reading and Learning,* 50, no. 1: 5–18.

Appendix A

Moravian University's WEC writing plan prompt — modeled closely after but not exactly the same as the one created for the University of Minnesota:

- **Writing plan narrative**—*For what reason(s) did this academic unit become involved in the WEC project? What key implementation activities are proposed in this edition of its writing plan and what, briefly, is the thinking behind these proposed activities? What, if any, plans are proposed for disseminating content from this writing plan?*
- **Section 1**—Discipline-relevant writing characteristics—*What characterizes writing in this academic unit? This explanation can include but need not be limited to audiences, purposes, genres and genre conventions, and commonly used media that define writing in the discipline(s) this academic unit represents.*
- **Section 2**—Desired writing abilities—*What writing abilities should students demonstrate proficiency in by the time they graduate? How do these abilities synergize with your student learning outcomes?*
- **Section 3**—Integration of writing into unit's curriculum—*How is writing instruction currently positioned in this academic unit's curriculum (or curricula)? What, if any, structural plans does this academic unit have for changing the way that writing and writing instruction are sequenced across its course offerings? With what rationales are changes proposed and what indicators will signify their impact?*
- **Section 4**—Assessment of student writing—*How does this academic unit currently communicate writing expectations (see sections #1 and #2) to students? What do these expectations look like when they are translated into assessable criteria? How does/will faculty in this academic unit assess that students have met these expectations?*
- **Section 5**—Summary of implementation plans and requested support—*Based on above discussions, what does the academic unit plan to implement during the period covered by this plan? What forms of instructional support does this academic unit request to help implement proposed changes? What are the expected outcomes of named support? What kinds of assessment support does this academic unit need to help assess the efficacy of this writing plan? What are the expected outcomes of this support?*
- **Section 6**—Process used to create the writing plan—*How, and to what degree, were stakeholders in this academic unit (faculty members,*

instructors, professional affiliates, students, others) engaged in providing, revising, and approving the content of this writing plan?

Appendix B

In the Middle States team report to the Commission on Higher Education regarding then Moravian College from March 2018, the following was said about the then newly piloted WEC at Moravian:

- "The establishment of assessment procedures within the Writing-Enriched Curriculum program is a step towards broader assessment of academic programs."
- "The Writing-Enriched Curriculum that situates writing in the disciplines is an excellent example of ongoing attention to skill development beyond the initial first- and second-year core courses."
- "Writing program rubrics are well developed and emphasize authentic writing within the disciplines as well as in the first-year writing program."
- "Moravian College demonstrates its commitment to educational effectiveness assessment by . . . the Writing-Enriched Curriculum that assist[s] students in improving their learning."

3 Assessing a First-Year Writing Seminar at a Small Women's College: Practices and Opportunities

Sarah E. Polo

Abstract: This chapter examines the first-year writing seminar program at Cottey College, a private women's liberal arts and sciences college in Nevada, Missouri. Situated within a unique women's institution (one with a nonsectarian status and a small size), this writing program is also noteworthy in the ways it is designed to tie to the college's threads and embody the college's women's college culture, particularly its community-building emphasis. This chapter describes the interlinking, defining features of the program, placing special emphasis on how its curricular advisory board strives to measure the program's successes via its assessment practices. Likewise, this chapter provides resources and reflects on areas for development that may be useful to other SLACs seeking to institute or update their FYWS programs.

First-year writing seminars (FYWS) are by no means uncommon forms of writing programs at small liberal arts colleges. In fact, in their 2012 study in *Writing Program Administration at Small Liberal Arts Colleges*, Gladstein and Regaignon find that FYWS are the most common form of explicit writing requirements utilized at small colleges, with forty-five schools in their data set using this model (97, 101). Other scholars have remarked on the benefits of FYWS structures, such as their frequent emphasis on writing across the curriculum structures (Moon 2003) and their promotion of academic literacy (Brent 2005).

Despite the prevalence of FYWS at small colleges, it would be incorrect to assume that these colleges—and their FYWS programs and assessment practices—are identical and homogenous. Much can be learned by examining FYWSs in their unique contexts. In this chapter, I describe the context, features, and assessment practices of a relatively new FYWS program: the one at Cottey College.

In addition to Cottey's somewhat unique status as a nonsectarian women's college and its small size, Cottey's FYWS program is also noteworthy in the ways it is designed to tie to the college's threads (guiding themes articulated in the college's mission and vision statement that run throughout its curriculum) and embody the college's women's college culture, particularly its community-building emphasis. In this chapter, I describe the interlinking, defining features of this program, placing special emphasis on how the program's curricular advisory board strives to measure the program's successes via our assessment practices. Additionally, as the current writing program administrator (WPA), I reflect on challenges and areas for expansion and development in our program itself and in its assessment practices, with the hope that these reflections may be useful to other SLACs seeking to institute or update their FYWS programs.

Institutional Context and Women's College Culture

Cottey College is a private women's college located in rural Southwest Missouri, mid-way between Kansas City and Joplin, Missouri. Like many women's colleges, Cottey prides itself on its long history. The college was opened in 1884 by Virginia Alice Cottey. In 1927, Cottey was purchased by the women's education organization, the P.E.O. Sisterhood. Connections to Cottey's history and its founder, as well as to the long-standing P.E.O. Sisterhood, are prominent features of social and academic life at Cottey, as seen through many of the ongoing school traditions, annual celebrations of Virginia Alice Cottey's birthday, scholarships and care packages from P.E.O. chapters, and much more.

Cottey's current mission is as follows:

> Cottey College, an independent liberal arts and sciences college, educates women to be contributing members of a global society through a challenging curriculum and a dynamic campus experience. In our diverse and supportive environment, women develop

their potential for personal and professional lives of intellectual engagement and thoughtful action as learners, leaders, and citizens. (Cottey College 2021b, 10)

Cottey's mission is thus focused on helping students develop global perspectives and empowering them to meaningfully contribute to the world. Further, Cottey prides itself on its small size and its ability to provide a close-knit, supportive environment, yet also on its ability to help students grow in their understanding of culturally different others. For instance, in the 2021–2022 academic year, students from seventeen distinct countries attended Cottey (Cottey College 2021a, 6). Additionally, Cottey provides an international trip for all second-year students each year over spring break, helping students to further experience new environments and cultures.

After spending many years as a two-year institution, Cottey College offers both associate and bachelor's degrees, with its first four-year degrees granted in 2013. In fall 2021, Cottey's total student FTE enrollment, which is all undergraduate, was 302.4[1] (Cottey College 2021a, 5). Cottey's first-time, full-time student population in fall 2021 was primarily white (79.71 percent), followed by Hispanic (16.67 percent) and Black (5.07 percent) (4). In fall 2021, 7.92 percent of Cottey students were international students (5). The number of international students has unfortunately declined each year since the COVID-19 pandemic began, with 12.89 percent in 2019 (5). In fall 2021, the college had a student/faculty ratio of 6:01 and an average class size of seven students (12).

Cottey's long history, small size, close-knit community, and supportive environment for students, coupled with its emphasis on growing students' global perspectives, make up crucial parts of the culture it strives to exemplify and market to prospective students and donors, elements likewise embodied by other women's colleges.

Program History

The writing program at Cottey, which I serve as WPA, is a first-semester general education course called the first-year writing seminar (FWS) (FWS 101). It was first piloted in 2017, initiated by a writing faculty member at the

---

1. According to Cottey's 2021 Factbook, "The full-time equivalent (FTE) of students is a single value providing a meaningful combination of full- and part-time students. The part-time equivalent for private four-year colleges is estimated by multiplying the part-time headcount by a factor of .39287. The full- and part-time headcounts are added together to determine FTE" (5).

college with support from other faculty. The faculty voted to adopt FWS 101 as part of an overhaul of the general education requirements. Currently, FWS 101 is part of a two-course sequence of required writing courses in Cottey's general education core, the second course being Writing 102: College Writing (WRI 102). Although these two courses are part of a sequence, FWS 101 has its own course designation and programmatic structure, and it will be my chief focus in this chapter.

The current course description for FWS 101 is as follows:

> FWS is a foundational course for Cottey students for both writing and content. Students will be introduced to the benefits of women's-only education, Cottey history, leadership, social responsibility, and global awareness through the practice of thoughtful reading, analysis, and writing within a liberal arts context. This course provides students the opportunity to connect with the institution while also building community among themselves. (Cottey College 2021b, 137)

With the exception of students who transfer to Cottey already having obtained an associate's degree, every student who enrolls at Cottey takes FWS 101, most often during their first semester. The course is currently only offered in fall semesters. We offer approximately nine to ten sections each fall with each section capped at fifteen students.

Program Profile and Defining Features

Before moving to a discussion of the FWS program and course itself and its defining features, it is important to explain how it is administered.

FWS Administration

I began at Cottey as a tenure-track assistant professor of English in 2019, at which time I also became coordinator of the FWS program. As depicted in the organizational chart in Figure 1, the FWS coordinator also chairs and collaborates with a faculty standing committee called the FWS Curricular Advisory Board (CAB). Of committee-based writing program leadership, Gladstein and Regaignon write that "Committees provide a way to share leadership and governance of writing while also capitalizing on the kinds of expertise we believe are needed and best embodied in a professional writing administrator." Further, "the centrality of committee governance at small colleges provides a mechanism through which oversight of writing is simultaneously centralized and shared" (Gladstein and Regaignon 2012, 63). This is certainly present in Cottey's FWS program, with the CAB largely comprised of the instructors who teach the course, though also a college administrator and any other faculty or staff who have interest in the program.

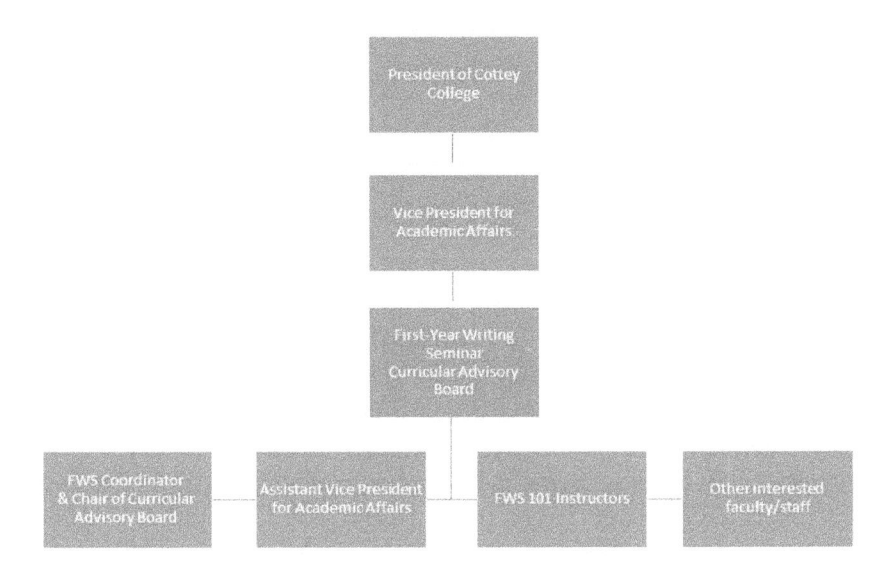

[Organizational chart showing hierarchy: President of Cottey College → Vice President for Academic Affairs → First-Year Writing Seminar Curricular Advisory Board, which connects to: FWS Coordinator & Chair of Curricular Advisory Board, Assistant Vice President for Academic Affairs, FWS 101 Instructors, Other interested faculty/staff]

Figure 1. Organizational chart depicting the current structure of Cottey's First-Year Writing Seminar Program in relation to college administration. Figure created by the author.

FWS Instructors

Importantly, sections of FWS 101 are taught by faculty from across the college's four academic divisions: humanities, social sciences, math and sciences, and fine arts. For example, in fall 2021, the sections of the course were taught by instructors from anthropology, international relations, writing, physics and astronomy, French and Francophone, and music. One instructor is a staff member who also has adjunct status for their teaching of the course; all other instructors who have taught FWS thus far are tenured or tenure-track faculty. I elaborate on instructor recruitment practices below.

Due to the makeup of the instructors and the procedures in place to guide their teaching of the course, this program aligns with Gladstein and Regaignon's observations in their study of *Writing Program Administration at Small Liberal Arts Colleges* in that it embodies a writing across the curriculum (WAC) structure. Gladstein and Regaignon write that FWS programs often have a WAC-rich context, which may actually "[push] their faculty to make their values more explicit as they came to consensus across (rather than within) disciplines" (2012, 102). Instructors in Cottey's FWS 101 program shape how the course teaches writing by bringing their unique discipline's writing conventions and genres to the table; conversely, instructors also regularly articulate how teaching the course improves their abilities to teach writing in their discipline-specific courses, something some have even publicly discussed in welcome videos created for incoming students in 2020 and 2021, which were created in attempts to help students transitioning to college after finishing high school during the early months of the COVID-19 pandemic.

For instructors preparing to teach FWS 101, there are two major forms of instructional support and professional development in place: First, instructors who plan to teach FWS 101 in the upcoming fall semester participate in training sessions during the preceding spring semester. These sessions, which I discuss further below, focus on both course content and writing pedagogy, as well as serving as opportunities to develop and revise the course for the upcoming fall semesters. While attendance at these sessions is uncompensated, the sessions serve as valuable professional development opportunities that are also open to all faculty and staff at the college. In recent years, Cottey's faculty personnel committee has even periodically recommended to candidates undergoing mid-tenure reviews in recent years that they take advantage of these sessions to improve elements of their pedagogy.

Second, during the fall semesters, which is when FWS 101 is taught, we hold weekly or bi-weekly fifty-minute meetings for current FWS instructors actively teaching the course (though these are also open to others). These meetings primarily provide support for the instructors. For example, we hold norming sessions to assist in grading upcoming major assignments, discuss in-class activities, and troubleshoot any issues.

FWS Curriculum

In the Council of Writing Program Administrators' 2019 statement on "Evaluating the Intellectual Work of Writing Administration," two of the major categories of intellectual labor engaged in by WPAs described are those of "program creation" and "curricular design." These are areas in which the ongoing efforts of the CAB have been concentrated. In this section, I elaborate on the threads, guiding documents, course assignments,

Common Reader, and special events utilized in FWS 101, all of which continue to be refined each year. These components, some of which have small-scale assessment components built in, work together to provide an interwoven, dynamic, and community-building structure to FWS 101 that is in keeping with this small women's college's culture.

Outcomes, Threads, and Guiding Documents. In terms of course content and student learning outcomes, FWS 101 chiefly teaches writing, aligning each semester with the college's learning outcome of "communicates effectively." However, FWS 101 does so in a particular way, which is through teaching connections between writing and three threads of Cottey College. Those three threads, which are guiding themes that run throughout the college's curriculum, are articulated in the college's vision statement. They are: social responsibility, women's leadership, and global awareness (Cottey College 2021b, 10).

When the FWS program was initially piloted in 2017, the goal was to introduce all three threads each fall semester; by the time I arrived in 2019, the instructors and CAB had determined that this was too much content to incorporate into a single semester. As a result, the course now primarily focuses on a single thread at a time, and the threads are rotated through on a two-year basis.[2] Thus, in addition to the overarching outcome of "communicates effectively," there is an additional outcome each year which we tie to the specific thread of emphasis.

However, because the college as a whole does not have explicit definitions for each of these threads, learning and defining what they mean and determining how to meaningfully incorporate them into the course have been areas on which our curricular design has been particularly focused. This has led to the need to create clear learning outcomes and guiding documents to aid both instructors and students in defining the threads. In fall 2019 and fall 2020, the thread of focus was social responsibility; for this, we were fortunate to be able to draw on the American Association of Colleges and University's (AAC&U) document "Character Traits Associated with the Five Dimensions of Personal and Social Responsibility." In fall 2021 and fall 2022, when our focus was the thread of global awareness, the CAB collaborated with other college faculty and staff to develop our own document modeled after the AAC&U's, which we titled "Character Traits Associated

---

2. It is important to recognize that FWS 101 is intended to *introduce* students to these Cottey threads and that they will be emphasized throughout their Cottey experience; there is no expectation that students will be able to fully enact the threads in their first semester.

with the Four Dimensions of Global Awareness." In addition to serving as course readings and guiding texts throughout the semester, these documents likewise play direct roles in some of the major course assignments.

Common Reader. Another important defining characteristic of FWS 101 that allows us to combine the writing emphasis with the college's threads is the usage of a common reader, a shared text selected each year to be read by all FWS students. This text aids in creating a shared experience for all first-year students at Cottey, regardless of the specific FWS 101 section in which they are enrolled.[3] The common reader was a feature of the program from its inception; thus far, all instructors teaching the course have expressed nothing but support for its usage.

The selection process for this text is a multiphase process. To briefly summarize, members of the Cottey community submit nominations using an online form in the preceding fall semester. The CAB reviews the nominations and narrows them down to a list of finalist texts. These are divided among the group members to read and assess using a collaboratively developed rubric. A copy of the rubric used to select the 2022 common reader is included in Appendix B. The completed rubrics then aid discussion and voting among the group, and the top two finalists are then sent to college administration for final feedback. The new common reader is announced to the campus community in approximately January or February, and the entire campus is likewise invited to read along with the FWS 101 students during the fall semesters. A list of common readers selected to date appears in Appendix A.

To date, selected common readers for each year of the FWS 101 program have included: *The Immortal Life of Henrietta Lacks* by Rebecca Skloot, *A Path Appears* by Nicholas Kristof and Sheryl WuDunn, *Killers of the Flower Moon* by David Grann, *Just Mercy* by Bryan Stevenson, *The Girl Who Smiled Beads* by Clemantine Wamariya and Elizabeth Weil, and *A Mind Spread Out on the Ground* by Alicia Elliott.

Course Assignments. FWS 101 is able to fuse writing instruction with instruction in Cottey's threads in another major way, which is through the course's major assignments. These have undergone several adjustments since FWS 101's 2017 inception, and the current assignment sequence seems to lend itself well to adaptation and modification to match each year's thread

---

3. In addition to the common reader, we also employ an open-access writing textbook as well as various online resources to help teach some of the more writing-content-based skills to students.

of emphasis, as well as each year's new common reader, though we will continue to refine this sequence as needed as the program continues. As with the common reader, the notion of having a shared curriculum was established when the program was first piloted, and I have yet to experience any resistance to it from the instructors teaching the course. This may be in part due to the faculty's early buy-in when the course was established. In addition, having shared assignments reduces the workload for instructors.

The course is currently divided into four major units with the following guiding emphases:

- Unit 1: Reading, understanding, and analyzing texts
- Unit 2: Supporting arguments using your personal experiences
- Unit 3: Advocating for social issues
- Unit 4: Reflecting on the course

Each unit has a specific major project: Project 1 entails rhetorical analysis of a text. Students select from a list of text options, all of which connect to either the semester's specific thread, common reader, or the college's history. Project 2 asks students to script and record a podcast episode in the style of a "This I Believe" essay. Their episode argues for the importance of one of the dimensions of the thread of emphasis in the guiding document (for instance, one of the dimensions of global awareness), using the students' experiences as evidence. Project 3 is a multi-phase collaborative project in which groups of students create infographics about a social issue of their choosing, directed to audiences of their choosing. Other sub-steps in Project 3 include the creation of a group contract, proposal, cover letter, and group member evaluation. Project 4 is a reflective letter directed to future FWS 101 students that explains how writing and the semester's specific thread are connected (for example, what is the relationship between writing and global awareness?). This final project requires ample reflection on the course and its content and serves as our major tool for programmatic assessment.

Special Events. Finally, understanding of FWS's curriculum is also aided by understanding its usage of special events. These likewise tie together writing and the college's threads and promote a sense of community among first-year students. FWS 101 students are required to attend specific special events each fall semester; though these have shifted and changed somewhat in the program's six years, the two major events that have been maintained include Films for Changemakers[4] and We Who Wow.[5] Each of these required events, as well as other optional events,[6] are held in collaboration with and aided by funding from Cottey's Serenbetz Institute for Women's Leadership, Social Responsibility and Global Awareness. As with the common reader, a small-scale form of assessment is in place to help assess the effectiveness of these special events: Cottey's director of leadership development in the Serenbetz Institute, Denise Carrick Hedges, regularly conducts online post-event surveys of the FWS 101 students and shares the results with the CAB, allowing us to continually gauge how well students self-report to value and engage with the events.

In addition to discussions at these events themselves, students engage in writings and discussions regarding them in their individual FWS 101 sections, and they are encouraged to use them as components of the Project 4 reflective letters when explaining the relationship between the college thread and writing. Holding these events is not without its challenges; in particular, scheduling the events to avoid conflicts with other student activities is always difficult. However, the post-event surveys, class conversations with students, and conversations among FWS instructors in our meetings suggest that these out of class experiences are highly worthwhile elements of Cottey's FYWS that promote shared experiences and a sense of community among first-year students that is in line with Cottey's women's college culture.

Program Assessment Practices

Having described Cottey College's FWS 101 program and its defining features, some of which have assessment measures incorporated already, I now move in this section to a discussion of the larger assessment practices cur-

---

4. Students attend screenings of documentary films and participate in discussion led by the faculty/staff discussion leaders. All films feature topics or individuals striving to enact change, and film options tie to the specific semester's thread (and often the specific common reader).

5. This is an event in which panelists describe the activism and change initiatives in which they are engaged (as well as what led them along their specific personal and professional trajectories) and answer questions from students.

6. For instance, students have the option to have their groups' Project 3 infographics displayed in Cottey's college-wide academic showcase. In recent years, students have also had opportunities to apply to participate in immersion trips that are loosely connected to each year's common reader.

rently in place to assess the success of the program, particularly in aligning with the college's threads.

Program Assessment

Although classroom assessment—in the form of major and low-stakes assignments—is an ever-ongoing component of the FWS 101 sections, the major form of systematic assessment I discuss here takes place at the program level.

The fourth and final project in FWS 101 is a reflective letter in which students synthesize the content of the course to produce a letter to future FWS 101 students in which they explain what the connection is between writing and their semester's thread of focus, and students taking the course the next year do actually see samples of these letters. To develop their letters, students draft, peer review, and receive instructor feedback and grades for this project, as they do for all major projects. However, this project is also used as a tool for assessing the program as a whole, particularly each semester's two outcomes: the college "communicates effectively" outcomes that every year's FWS 101 sections strive to achieve and the college outcome tied to the specific thread of that year's FWS 101 sections. For both social responsibility and global awareness, the two threads we have focused on individually thus far,[7] the college outcome has been "acts responsibly," which it describes as either "A Cottey student is reflective and acts ethically as a personally and socially responsible member of global, national, and local communities" or "A Cottey student respects diversity, is attentive to cultural context, and demonstrates ethical reasoning and action."[8]

The procedure the CAB and I have followed to perform this annual assessment is as follows: First, if one is not already in place, we develop a rubric that will be used to assess the outcome that corresponds closely to the sub-outcomes listed on the course syllabi. For "communicates effectively,"

---

7. During the first two years of FWS 101, in which all three threads were taught simultaneously, the CAB assessed for the "recognizes the role of women" outcome. In this chapter, I focus on the assessments we have performed when working with singular threads.

8. These slightly differing definitions are due to changes in the outcomes that occurred at the college level. Originally, our goal had been for FWS 101 to align each thread with a different college learning outcome; global awareness was going to be tied to an outcome of "respects diversity." In fall 2021, however, the Cottey faculty body voted to condense to a fewer number of total learning outcomes, and "respects diversity" became folded into "acts responsibly."

we have thus far drawn on a rubric already in use by several other Cottey departments. For "acts responsibly," the CAB has collaboratively developed two rubrics: one for the social responsibility thread and one for the global awareness thread. Samples of these rubrics are contained in Appendix C. The rubric criteria all include a four-point scale (4 being "exceptional," 3 being "good," 2 being "acceptable," and 1 being "below average"). Not only will we develop a new rubric when we move to the thread of women's leadership (which will align with the outcomes of "recognizes the role of women"), but we will almost certainly continue to adapt and modify our rubrics to perform our assessments most effectively.

Once we have a rubric in place, we then gather twenty-five random samples of student Project 4s that were completed during a given fall semester. These samples are anonymized and coded. In my time as WPA, I have served as the sole coder. Additionally, I collect at least three additional Project 4 examples that can serve as the basis for our norming sessions. I set up these materials and spreadsheets for norming and scoring (including each scorer's assigned sample numbers) in advance.

Regarding the timing of this annual assessment, our program is fortunate that Cottey has a specific day each spring semester called assessment day, in which classes are cancelled so that the college and individual programs and departments can perform assessment-related activities. We typically have a two-hour meeting block for our FWS 101 work, and this is when we have thus far held our norming and the beginnings of the actual scoring for one outcome. Any remaining work is completed individually. As for the procedure in the meeting, the sessions begin by reviewing the rubric, discussing the individual criteria, and addressing questions. We then spend time norming two to three pre-prepared example projects, discussing each in turn and arriving at collective understandings of the criteria.

After the norming session, the official samples are scored by two pre-assigned readers using the rubric. Once all scoring is completed, the scores for these criteria are averaged to provide an overall score for each of the two readers. Then, the average of these two overall scores provided the final score for each sample. In instances where the overall scores diverge by more than one point, a third reader scores the sample.

I analyze the results and complete Cottey's assessment document called an assessment implementation matrix to describe the findings, which the CAB then helps to revise. Some of the data we focus on includes average scores for each criterion and distribution of scores. This is then compared to previous years' scores to determine if and where changes are occurring. Importantly, the final piece of the matrix involves making recommendations to improve student learning. Appendix D is an example of an assessment implementation matrix, which analyzes data from the fall 2020 iteration of FWS 101 for "acts responsibly" and compares it to data from fall 2019. This example matrix demonstrates ways in which we are reflecting on the program's successes, yet also critically reflecting on potential reasons for some decreases in student scores (such as the COVID-19 pandemic).

At this time, our goal is to continue this procedure annually until we have assessed each outcome twice (as we move through the threads on a two-year rotating basis). This allows us to adjust our curriculum and teaching of the course most effectively as we more fully establish the program. After this, we plan to evaluate whether to continue with an annual assessment or move to a less frequent assessment timeline. Last, I will briefly mention that the second general education writing course at Cottey, WRI 102: College Writing, is likewise engaged in a system of assessing the "communicates effectively" outcome to determine how student scores are changing across this two-course sequence.

Training Session Assessment

Programmatic assessment is the most expansive form of direct assessment in which FWS 101 is currently engaged, and the findings after our six-year rotation through all three threads will certainly be used to shape the program going forward. Another smaller yet important form of assessment the program is engaged in is related to the training sessions for FWS 101 instructors that take place during the spring semesters. Their primary goal is to help prepare instructors—particularly those new to the program—to teach the course. As such, the three major areas our sessions focus on include course content (the actual writing and rhetorical skills the course teaches, as well as elements related to the threads that we will be teaching students), writing pedagogy (with topics such as facilitating peer review and class discussions, commenting on student work, and more), and course planning (making decisions about the course schedule, syllabus policies, and major assignment revisions).

To both plan and revise these training sessions, in the three years I have conducted the training, I have asked for input on the sessions from the FWS instructors, most often via an anonymous post-training survey at the end of the spring semester. I also encourage instructors to provide feedback directly to me if they wish. A copy of the survey questions administered following the spring 2022 sessions is included in Appendix E. These surveys have been beneficial for both measuring effective components on the sessions and for determining what changes to make. Assessment work, therefore, improves the program, not only by influencing the curriculum but also by shaping the training of the program's instructors.

Looking Forward: Areas for Growth and Exploration

Cottey's FYWS program has been successful since its 2017 piloting. In this section, I explore some of those successes, while also offering areas where the program can continue to grow and explore.

WAC, Collaborations, and Instructor Recruitment

Chiefly, Cottey's FWS 101 program does indeed promote a WAC mindset and model, particularly in its utilization of instructors from across the academic disciplines to teach the course. These instructors shape the curriculum by bringing with them their discipline-specific writing knowledge, while also using their increased writing content and pedagogy knowledge obtained by teaching FWS 101 to improve their abilities to teach writing in their other courses.

Further, as an early-career faculty at the college, I have been particularly struck by the program's embodiment of the fourth WAC program goal, as outlined in the 2014 Statement of WAC Principles and Practices from the International Network of WAC Programs (INWAC): this program most definitely helps to "create a community of faculty around teaching and student writing." INWAC writes of this goal that "WAC seeks to break down the silos that can divide disciplines by creating common ground through its focus on teaching and learning, often accomplished through cross-disciplinary faculty development programming" (International Network of WAC Programs 2014, 2). Though difficult to quantify, there is a palpable sense in our FWS fall meetings and spring training sessions of collaboration, camaraderie, and shared desire to improve our abilities to teach writing, despite our differing academic disciplines. This speaks to the ways Cottey's culture of community-building is not just for students, but also is an ingrained part of the experience of instructors who choose to teach FWS 101. A goal moving forward is to continue expanding this community beyond the FWS instructors themselves. We have engaged in several practices to do so, but there is still room for improvement, and here I provide a few key examples.

First, some community-building practices relate to the spring training sessions. We invite any faculty or staff who teach or use writing in their work to participate in the spring training sessions, and we have experienced some success with this. Additionally, we strive to make said training sessions more collaborative; they are designed to allow experienced FWS 101 instructors to share their experiences and expertise (a "teach the teacher" model of professional development), and we have even recently invited specific academic departments to lead particular training sessions (such as having education faculty lead sessions related to facilitating class discussions).

Second, we actively collaborate with other already-established campus constituencies, particularly the Serenbetz Institute for Women's Leadership, Social Responsibility and Global Awareness, with whom we work and benefit from funding to continue enacting the FWS 101 special events. There may be additional room to create further collaboration with the Cottey writing center; this is an area where we can explore further.

Third, a major way we strive to increase collaboration and increase this community is by involving individual faculty and staff with the program. For instance, we invited and were successful in having non-FWS faculty and staff join us in the 2022 common reader selection process (and recall that the entire campus is already encouraged to submit nominations and to actually read the chosen text each year) and in developing the guiding document we created for the global awareness thread (something we will likely do again as we approach revisiting the women's leadership thread with our current assignment sequence).

Behind each of these efforts to continue developing a "community of faculty around teaching and student writing" also lies the INWAC goal of creating a "campus culture that supports writing," which at Cottey seems particularly connected to the issue of instructor recruitment to teach FWS 101 (International Network of WAC Programs 2014, 2). Currently, instructors can opt in to the program if interested; there is no requirement that faculty at Cottey participate. Most of the current instructors have been teaching sections of the course since it first piloted in 2017, so these are folks who have a demonstrated commitment to the work of FWS 101 and clearly want it to succeed.

But how do we continue to recruit new instructors? As WPA, I strive to promote awareness of the program and teaching opportunities in it via presentations, emails, and other larger-scale tactics. Recruitment of new instructors seems to have been most successful thus far through individual conversations and networking, whether by me or by the other FWS instructors/CAB members. But these smaller-scale interactions do take more time and relationship-building. As an added complication at a small college, faculty are already burdened with significant service expectations and full teaching loads (not to mention the stresses of an ongoing global pandemic), so there is likewise no guarantee that an instructor who joins FWS 101 will be able to continue teaching it long term. Further, even the FWS instructors who have been with the program since its inception may experience changes in their teaching availabilities, service commitments, etc.

While we have not yet encountered a shortage of FWS instructors, we may encounter it in future semesters. Our challenges thus far have certainly been eased by developing the program using a WAC structure and beginning with strong campus buy-in.

Assessment and Retention

In addition to the areas of WAC, collaboration, and instructor recruitment, I end by pointing to an area of potential growth for Cottey's FWS 101 program where assessment may play a crucial role, which is retention. Like many colleges, Cottey experienced a decrease in retention because of the ongoing COVID-19 pandemic (for instance, Cottey had 75 percent retention from fall 2019 to fall 2020; there was 58 percent retention from fall 2020 to fall 2021) (Cottey College 2021a, 8). We believe that the community-building emphasis that FWS 101 promotes for first-year students through features like a shared common reader, special events, clear connections to Cottey's threads, WAC, and more contribute to students' success and desire to matriculate. However, we do not yet have a system in place for determining the specific impacts the FWS 101 program has on student retention. The CAB and I hope to do more work to study scholarship on writing programs and retention and seek out models (for example, Ruecker et al.). This is an important area of assessment that may likewise aid us in sustaining the program and recruiting new instructors moving forward, allowing the program to continue to promote meaningful connections between writing and the college's threads and to carry out the community-building emphasis (for faculty, staff, and students) that Cottey values as a women's institution.

Bibliography

AAC&U (American Association of Colleges and Universities). n.d. "Character Traits Associated with the Five Dimensions of Personal and Social Responsibility." Accessed July 2023.

Brent, Doug. 2005. "WAC (Again): The First-Year Seminar and Academic Literacy." *College Composition and Communication* 57, no. 2 (December): 253–76.

Cottey College. 2021a. *2021-2022 Cottey Facts*. June 30, 2021. https://cottey.edu/wp-content/uploads/2022/06/2021-22-Cottey-Facts.pdf.

Cottey College. 2021b. *Cottey College Catalog 2021–2022*. September 27, 2021. https://cottey.edu/wp-content/uploads/2022/07/Catalog_2021-2022.pdf.

Cottey College First-Year Writing Seminar. 2021. "Character Traits Associated with the Four Dimensions of Global Awareness." Nevada: Cottey College.

Council of Writing Program Administrators. 2019. "Evaluating the Intellectual Work of Writing Administration." http://wpacouncil.org/aws/CWPA/pt/sd/news_article/242849/_PARENT/layout_details/false.

Gladstein, Jill M., and Dara Rossman Regaignon. 2012. *Writing Program Administration at Small Liberal Arts Colleges*. Anderson: Parlor Press.

International Network of WAC Programs. 2014. "Statement of WAC Principles and Practices." https://wac.colostate.edu/docs/principles/statement.pdf.

Moon, Gretchen Flesher. 2003. "First-Year Writing in First-Year Seminars: Writing across the Curriculum from the Start." *WPA: Writing Program Administration* 26, no. 3 (Spring): 105–18.

Ruecker, Todd, Dawn Shepherd, Heidi Estrem, and Beth Brunk-Chavez, eds. 2017. *Retention, Persistence, and Writing Programs*. Logan: Utah State University Press.

APPENDIX A: LIST OF SELECTED COMMON READERS

- 2017: Skloot, Rebecca. 2010. *The Immortal Life of Henrietta Lacks*. New York: Broadway Books.
- 2018: Kristof, Nicholas D., and Sheryl Wudunn. 2015. *A Path Appears: Transforming Lives, Creating Opportunity*. New York: Vintage Books.
- 2019: Grann, David. 2018. *Killers of the Flower Moon: The Osage Murders and the Birth of the FBI*. New York: Vintage Books.
- 2020: Stevenson, Bryan. 2014. *Just Mercy: A Story of Justice and Redemption*. New York: Delacorte Press.

- 2021: Wamariya, Clemantine, and Elizabeth Weil. 2019. *The Girl Who Smiled Beads: A Story of War and What Comes After.* New York: Broadway Books.
- 2022: Elliott, Alicia. 2020. *A Mind Spread out on the Ground.* New York: Melville House.

Appendix B: "Global Awareness" Rubric Criteria for Common Reader Selection (for Fall 2022)

This text:

- Provides exposure to and meaningful engagement with culturally different others
- Promotes empathy by allowing readers to see themselves as "members of a world community, knowing that we share the future with others" (from the AAC&U's "Intercultural Knowledge and Competence VALUE Rubric")
- Promotes readers' abilities to practice "perspective taking": "the ability to engage and learn from perspectives and experiences different from one's own and to understand how one's place in the world both informs and limits one's knowledge. The goal is to develop the capacity to understand the interrelationships between multiple perspectives, such as personal, social, cultural, disciplinary, environmental, local, and global" (from the AAC&U's "Global Learning VALUE Rubric")
- Demonstrates relevance for first-year students (recency in terms of publication year; relevance in terms of content or ability to apply to issues happening now, etc.)
- Provides content for thoughtful reflection, dialogue, and intellectual growth
- Provides potential connections to other writing-related topics covered in FWS 101 (analyzing rhetorical situations and appeals, such as kairos, transitions, evaluating sources, using evidence from sources, etc.)
- Is challenging but not overwhelming to entering first-year students
- Is not typically read in high school
- Has precedence for use as a common reader, based on comparison with other institutions

Appendix C: Example Assessment Rubrics

Acts Responsibly: Social Responsibility

	Exceptional (4)	**Good (3)**	**Acceptable (2)**	**Below Average (1)**
Striving for Excellence:	The student thoroughly understands the value of taking time to revise and improve their writing; makes specific connections between their actions and success; fully demonstrates an understanding of the work involved in doing one's very best.	Has a good understanding of the value of taking time to revise and improve their writing; demonstrates some understanding of the connection between their actions and success; demonstrates an understanding of the work involved in doing one's very best.	Has some awareness of the value of taking time to revise and improve their writing; includes some understanding of the connection between their actions and success; partially demonstrates an understanding of the work involved in doing one's very best.	Has minimal awareness of the value of taking time to revise and improve their writing; includes little to no understanding of the connection between their actions and success; does little to demonstrate an understanding of the work involved in doing one's very best.
PSR: Student's definition of PSR is connected to course readings/events/assignments and demonstrates change over the course of the semester.	Thoroughly understands the characteristics of PSR; fully demonstrates learning about themselves as it relates to a reinforced and clarified sense of PSR.	Has a good understanding of the characteristics of PSR; demonstrates some learning about themselves as it relates to a growing sense of PSR.	Has some awareness of the characteristics of PSR; demonstrates little learning about themselves as it relates to a growing sense of PSR.	Has minimal awareness of the characteristics of PSR; demonstrates no learning about themselves as it relates to PSR.
PSR and Writing: Student clearly identifies the link between PSR and their writing	Thoroughly understands the link between PSR and their writing, provides strong evidence	Has a good understanding of the link between PSR and their writing, provides some evidence	Has some awareness of the link between PSR and their writing; provides little evidence	Has minimal awareness of the link between PSR and their writing; provides no evidence

Acts Responsibly: Global Awareness

	Exceptional (4)	Good (3)	Acceptable (2)	Below Average (1)
Global Awareness: Student defines global awareness in ways connected to course readings/events/assignments and articulates change/reinforcement of their understanding of global awareness over the course of the semester.	Has a **thorough understanding and definition** for global awareness connected to course readings/events/assignments; **fully articulates** change/reinforcement of their understanding of global awareness over the course of the semester.	Has a **good understanding and definition** for global awareness connected to course readings/events/assignments; **articulates some** change/reinforcement of their understanding of global awareness over the course of the semester.	Has **some understanding and definition** for global awareness connected to course readings/events/assignments; **articulates little** change/reinforcement of their understanding of global awareness over the course of the semester.	**Has minimal or no understanding and definition** for global awareness connected to course readings/events/assignments; **articulates no** change/reinforcement of their understanding of global awareness over the course of the semester.
Dimensions of Global Awareness: Student enacts **character traits of the four dimensions of global awareness:** Cultivating self-awareness and integrity Striving to learn Demonstrating empathy and respect for difference Collaborating and contributing to a global society	**Effectively** enacts **multiple** (3-4) character traits connected to the four dimensions of global awareness.	**Adequately** enacts **multiple** (2-4) character traits connected to the four dimensions of global awareness.	**Somewhat adequately** enacts **some** (1-4) character traits connected to the four dimensions of global awareness.	**Inadequately** enacts or **does not** enact character traits connected to the four dimensions of global awareness.
Global Awareness and Writing: Student clearly identifies a link between global awareness and writing and provides evidence to support that link.	Has an **excellent understanding and articulation** of a link between global awareness and writing; provides **strong** evidence to demonstrate that link.	Has a **good understanding and articulation** of a link between global awareness and writing; provides **some** evidence to demonstrate that link.	Has **some awareness and articulation** of a link between global awareness and writing; provides **little** evidence to demonstrate that link.	Has **minimal or no awareness or articulation** of a link between global awareness and writing; provides **no** evidence to demonstrate that link.

Appendix D: Example Assessment Implementation Matrix, Adjusted from Table Format

COTTEY

Assessment Implementation Matrix

Student Learning Outcome/Program Goal: A Cottey student acts responsibly: "A Cottey student is reflective and acts ethically as a personally and socially responsible member of global, national, and local communities."

Data Analysis Group: FWS Curricular Advisory Board Members

Direct Assessment of FWS 101 Student Final Projects from Fall 2020 + Comparison to Fall 2019

Assessment Activity: What method was used to gather the data?
Students in all sections of FWS 101 completed a reflective letter assignment for their final course project in fall 2020. Twenty-five random samples of these projects were gathered, coded, and anonymized.

After holding a norming session, these samples were scored by two readers using the attached rubric. These rubric criteria, which were scored on a four-point scale (4 being "exceptional," 3 being "good," 2 being "acceptable," and 1 being "below average"), included "striving for excellence," "personal and social responsibility" and connections between "personal and social responsibility and writing."

The scores for these criteria were averaged to provide an **overall score** for each of the two readers. Then, the average of these two overall scores provided the **final score** for each sample.

In instances where the overall scores diverged by more than 1 point, a third reader scored the sample.

The results were also compared to the fall 2019 assessment project.

Results: Summarize the results of the assessment activity.
Of the twenty-five samples, only four contained overall scores from the two initial readers that diverged by more than one point, indicating a high level of inter rater reliability.

The average final score of all samples was 2.30. The lowest final score in the range of scores was 1.08; the highest was 3.92. The full list of scores is included below, as well as a comparison to fall 2019.

Regarding the three rubric criteria, according to the two initial readers' scores, the average scores for each criteria included:
- "Personal and social responsibility and writing": 2.25 (-0.37 from 2019)
- "Striving for excellence": 2.44 (-0.19 from 2019)
- "Personal and social responsibility": 2.45 (-0.34 from 2019)

Analysis: Analyze the results. What does the data tell us?
Overall, these results indicate that the outcome is being met. However, there are overall decreases in outcome achievement from fall 2019.

The fact that the average final score for the full set of twenty-five samples was 2.30 indicates that students are achieving this outcome at a level between "acceptable" and "good." Three students are reaching this outcome at a level of "good," and one (3.92) is very near "exceptional."

In comparing the final scores to 2019, the lowest final score received for a 2020 sample, 1.08, was lower than that received in 2019; however, the highest score for a 2020 sample, 3.92, was also higher than 2019.

Regarding the three rubric criteria, the average scores for the three criteria (which were each lower than in 2019) were very close together, with "personal and social responsibility" the highest, just slightly above "striving for excellence." Like 2019, the lowest average criteria is "personal and social responsibility and writing." This was also the area of least improvement across the two years. This may suggest that students are still more likely to understand the concept of personal and social responsibility and be able to strive for excellence, but less likely to understand personal and social responsibility's connection to writing.

Recommendations for Improving Student Learning: Based on the analysis, what recommendations are we making to improve student learning?

Although this outcome is being met with an average final score between "acceptable" and "good," student scores show room for improvement. For example, no students received a final score of fully "exceptional," and nine students' work was "below average" (up from only one student in 2019). Additionally, the decrease in scores from 2019 bears consideration.

As background, after the 2019 assessment and in preparation for the fall 2020 semester, we revised many of the lower-stakes, daily writing assignments ("GRQs" or response writings), as well as replaced the first two major writing projects with ones that more directly connect PSR and writing. This was done based on our assessment results with the goal of allowing students to build this understanding earlier and more solidly in the course.

How, then, do we account for the overall decrease in both final scores and individual criteria scores experienced in 2020, as well as the wider range in scores? We believe that this may be attributed to the COVID-19 pandemic. While in 2019 we had a traditional, face-to-face structure for all FWS sections, in 2020 we employed a hybrid structure in all sections to account for the presence of online-only students, as well as the movement of non-online students in and out of quarantine and isolation. As such, it is difficult to determine whether the revisions to the lower-stakes and major assignments were effective.

We recommend continuing with the current major assignments and lower-stakes assignments that were revised after 2019 and that the overall assessment practices described in this AIM continue. A more longitudinal view is needed to determine the long-term impacts of the pandemic.

Appendix E: Example Spring Training Session Survey Questions (Spring 2022)

Feedback on Spring 2022 FWS Training Sessions

Please provide feedback on the spring 2022 training sessions held for instructors in Cottey's first-year writing seminar program.

If you have questions or other feedback to share, please email Dr. Sarah Polo (spolo@cottey.edu).

1. Which of the following training sessions did you attend?
   - Jan 13, 2022: Reflection on fall 2021; student evaluations of teaching
   - Jan 20: 2022: Course planning
   - Jan 27: 2022: Course planning
   - Feb 10: Content training—reading, annotating, and summarizing texts; understanding the rhetorical situation; understanding rhetorical appeals
   - Feb 17: Content training—understanding genre; understanding writing processes; understanding rhetorical appeals
   - Feb 24: Content training—writing thesis statements; structuring arguments; using textual evidence
   - March 3: Pedagogy training—responding to student writing
   - March 24: Pedagogy training—facilitating peer review; facilitating discussions
   - March 31: Pedagogy training—"What if..." classroom scenarios, led by faculty in Cottey's education department
   - April 7: 2022 course planning
   - April 14: CAB business meeting
   - April 21: FWS assessment
   - April 28: FWS assessment
   - May 5: 2022 course planning

Training in Writing Pedagogy

Based on the sessions you attended, please evaluate their coverage of the following pedagogical topics. In particular, how effectively do you feel these topics were covered in the training sessions in order to equip you to teach FWS? (1 = This topic was not effectively covered in the training sessions; 5 = This topic was covered very effectively in the training sessions)

If you did not attend the session in which a particular topic was covered, please skip the corresponding question(s).

1. Topic: Responding to student writing (local vs. global issues; methods for responding and assessing, etc.)
2. Topic: Facilitating peer review
3. Topic: Facilitating class discussions
4. Topic: "What If . . . " classroom scenarios
5. Please use this space to provide explanations for your responses in this section or provide any other feedback you have regarding the coverage of writing content knowledge topics in this year's spring training sessions
6. Please identify any other specific writing content knowledge topics you would like to see added to next year's spring training sessions

Training in Writing Content Knowledge

Based on the sessions you attended, please evaluate their coverage of the following writing content knowledge topics. In particular, how effectively do you feel these topics were covered in the training sessions in order to equip you to teach FWS? (1 = This topic was not effectively covered in the training sessions; 5 = This topic was covered very effectively in the training sessions)

If you did not attend the session in which a particular topic was covered, please skip the corresponding question(s).

1. Topic: Reading, annotating, and summarizing texts
2. Topic: Understanding the rhetorical situation
3. Topic: Understanding genre
4. Topic: Understanding writing processes
5. Topic: Writing thesis statements, structuring arguments, and using textual evidence
6. Please use this space to provide explanations for your responses in this section or provide any other feedback you have regarding the coverage of writing content knowledge topics in this year's spring training sessions

7. Please identify any other specific writing content knowledge topics you would like to see added to next year's spring training sessions

Training Session Format

Based on the sessions you attended, please provide your feedback regarding their format/structure. In particular, how effective were each of the following components? (1 = This component was not effective; 5 = This component was very effective)

1. Holding training sessions approximately every Thursday throughout the spring semester, a meeting time determined by FWS faculty availability
2. Making the training sessions open to all Cottey faculty/staff
3. Providing readings that instructors were asked to complete in advance of training sessions
4. Providing other tasks that instructors were asked to complete in advance of training sessions and posting these as resources on the T: Drive (for example, for Feb 17, instructors shared examples of activities, resources, etc. useful for teaching genre or writing processes to students)
5. Structuring training sessions to be discussion-based and placing emphasis on the writing instruction instructors are engaged in in FWS and non-FWS courses and programs
6. Reserving several training sessions for making plans for the upcoming fall semester
7. Reserving several training sessions for completing FWS assessment projects
8. Inviting Cottey Education faculty to lead a session on general, effective classroom pedagogy practices ("what if..." classroom scenarios)
9. Please use this space to provide explanations for your responses in this section or provide any other feedback you have regarding the format/structure of this year's spring training sessions. Additionally, identify any other specific changes you would like to see to the format/structure of next year's spring training sessions

Final Questions

1. What was the MOST valuable component of the spring 2022 training sessions?
2. What was the LEAST valuable component of the spring 2022 training sessions?
3. Please share any other feedback you have about ways the FWS spring training sessions should be adapted in the future.

Section II: Alliance Building and Collaboration

4 A Data-Driven Model of Collaborative Assessment: Harnessing Writing Program and Writing Center Data for Continuous Improvement of Writing Support

Bryan A. Lutz and Justine Post

Abstract: Writing program administrators at SLACs strive toward the continuous improvement of support for students' writing. In first-year writing programs, we collect direct and indirect measures of students' achievement of course outcomes, including student and instructor surveys, rubric scores, essays, and grades. In writing centers, we track faculty and students' perceptions of, utilization of, and satisfaction with writing center services. These efforts drive improvement. But while data gathering and analysis is common, the field is still discovering ways to assess student success at the confluence of first-year writing and writing centers. This chapter chronicles our efforts and offers a replicable model for collaborative assessment. We combine previously discrete data sets—first-year writing students' tutoring appointment data, tutoring session drafts, tutoring session recaps (written by tutors), final drafts submitted in class, and direct assessments of students' drafts—-to model a combined assessment that creates a robust view of students' writing needs and successes.

A goal of writing program administration (WPA) is the continuous improvement of support for students' writing development. Administrators of writing programs and writing centers commonly pursue this goal using data-driven methods of assessment. In writing programs, we collect direct and indirect measures of students' achievement of course outcomes, including student or instructor surveys, rubric scores, essays, and grades (Gladstein and Fralix 2017; Fodrey and Hassay 2021; Olinger 2021). In writing centers, we track faculty and student perceptions of, utilization of, and satisfaction with writing center services (Okuma 2013; Cheatle and Bullerjahn 2015; Giaimo 2017; Aldohon 2021). Our data analysis drives changes—from developing instructor resources to tutor training workshops—that aim to better meet the writing needs of students across campus.

The field is still discovering ways to define student success around the role of writing and a writing center's place in supporting that success. While data gathering is common, the majority of approaches rely on indirect measures such as surveys, interviews, and observations. While indirect measures generate valuable insights, we want to show that direct measures offer a grounding and perhaps a fuller picture of students' successes and opportunities for growth. The problem, then, is how to efficiently conduct such studies using data we have because of significant labor demands at institutions of higher learning generally (Swaak 2022) and on WPAs specifically (Anson 2021; Fodrey and Hassay 2021), and for the purpose of creating replicable models (Giaimo 2017) that can be adapted to other colleges and universities.

As Gladstein and Regaignon (2012) showed, WPA work can take many forms at small liberal arts colleges (SLACs). Collaboration most often occurs between WPAs, faculty, and staff tasked with teaching courses within their program. Despite their shared goals and similar approaches, the challenges that WPAs regularly face create substantial barriers. At siloed institutions, administrators must work hard to develop the kinds of interdisciplinary relationships that foster cross-campus collaboration (Holly-Wells, Jamieson, and Sanyal 2014). Our institution is Ohio Northern University, a SLAC situated in rural Ohio with approximately 3,000 students each year and an endowment of about $160 million. As two experienced administrators with backgrounds coordinating first-year writing (FYW), supporting writing across the curriculum (WAC) duties, and directing the writing center (WC) at our SLAC, we feel collaboration between WPAs is a necessary element of assessment efforts in the dynamic context of SLACs of similar size.

This chapter offers a model for collaborative assessment that leverages direct and indirect measures to increase the insights generated from writing-program and writing-center assessment. By aligning data collection methods and leveraging data regularly gathered in both the writing center and the writing program, we demonstrate one model for measuring student success that connects the work of a writing center and writing program. This model enables administrators to generate robust direct measures of outcomes in each space, creating a more holistic view of students' writing needs and successes across campus. In bringing together previously discrete data sets—which in our case included first-year writing students' tutoring appointment data, tutoring session drafts, tutoring session recaps (written by tutors), final drafts submitted in class, and direct assessments of students' drafts—this study demonstrates a collaborative approach to assessment that holds promise for those working at SLACs.

Models of WPA Structures and the Importance of Leadership, Collaboration, and Data

When Gladstein and Regaignon (2012) compared one hundred SLACs to find similarities and differences in administrative configurations among and between *programs*, broadly defined, as sites where writing instruction is a focus (43), they struggled to categorize leadership configurations because liberal arts colleges "pride themselves on their uniqueness" (44). In this tradition, faculty have tremendous freedom to conduct their classes while also fulfilling heavy service loads and participating in shared governance. The climate results in a "tension between faculty governance and faculty autonomy, [which] leads to a philosophical preference for leadership over administration" (21). All the SLACs surveyed by Gladstein and Regaignon involved the appointment of faculty leading first-year writing (FYW), writing across the curriculum (WAC), and a writing center (WC). Since any homogenizing of curricula that happens at an administrative level can feel stifling to faculty who expect to be involved in decision making and who expect freedom to teach their subject according to their expertise, *leadership* is what makes writing programs work.

Holly-Wells, Jamieson, and Sanyal (2014) describe writing program administration as *stochastic,* referring to a variable process where the outcome involves some randomness and has some uncertainty. The administration of writing tutors at their institution, they argue, involves collaboration between WAC and the writing center codified through a synergistic training program for writing fellows. While they acknowledge that they followed a writing fellows model "without realizing that there are other, possibly more appropriate" models at smaller colleges, they combined their efforts to solve several problems for their SLAC. First, tutors were often siloed apart from the contexts where writing occurs (Holly-Wells, Jamieson, and Sanyal 2014, 54–55); second, embedded tutors informed tutees with knowledge contrary to the lessons taught by faculty (59); and third, half of the writing fellows were not trained in the same methods as WC tutors (62).

They argue that they solved these issues by leading a "vertical WAC curriculum" guided by a liberal arts philosophy for combining writing-to-learn and learning-to-write into topics-based, introductory seminars taught by experienced and appropriately trained faculty from across the curriculum (Holly-Wells, Jamieson, and Sanyal 2014, 82). The training was made possible by collaboration between leaders: the director of WAC, two FYW coordinators, and the assistant director of the WC, two of whom were tenured faculty and two of whom were staff. These leaders created context-specific training scenarios that foreground concepts and skills valued by faculty and used rubrics that were agreed upon by faculty teaching the course. Key to its success, they show, is how the tutors themselves also assumed leadership roles, creating an interdisciplinary writing course "guiding not only weaker writers, but a whole class" in the development of foundational academic writing skills (64–65).

Under various leadership configurations, two key issues arise. First is devising methods to assess the impact of writing support such as tutoring in academic writing courses; second is understanding how to lead sustained improvement of writing support across campus. But approaches to these two goals reflect the varied leadership and administrative structures among SLACs and involve managing the substantial labor required to collect and analyze data and determine how to improve practice.

In her published keynote address for the 2012 IWCA conference, Lauren Fitzgerald (2013) suggests that the task of continuous improvement can be delegated to undergraduate tutors. Tutors at her own institution become "tutor-authors" who strengthen the practice of tutoring by studying how tutors work while enacting the role of tutor. Fitzgerald observes how "tutors often put a spotlight on the more authentic gaps they encounter—between themselves and the people they work with" (24). Regarding impact, Fitzgerald suggests that tutors who research and write can foster their own critical praxis, and that WPAs can "take advantage of their [tutors] perspicacity at the end of every semester with a meeting on what works and doesn't in our center" (25). In this way, Fitzgerald positions tutors as researchers of their own tutoring practices and highlights the role they play in collaborating to support the assessment process for continuous improvement.

Like Fitzgerald, Hatem Aldohon (2021) offers a model of enriching assessment by collaborating with writing tutors. Aldohon gathers data about how tutors approached their sessions with writers to improve tutoring in his WC. He observed how "little attention has been given to tutor perceptions and actual practices, particularly *vis-à-vis* writing conferences" (Aldohon 2021, 554). By conducting interviews with tutors about how they approach sessions and then observing tutors as they worked with students, Aldohon "compared the perceptions and actual practices of two experienced tutors with respect to one-on-one tutoring sessions in the writing centre [British spelling]" (554). He found discrepancies between what the tutors thought they were doing and how they conducted themselves during conferences, as tutors were much more inclined to "fix" lower-level concerns such as citation and punctuation than they were to coach higher-level concerns of analysis and synthesis. The analysis enabled Aldohon to gain greater insight into the effectiveness of the writing center and led him to coach tutors on how to better reach their own ideal form of tutoring that balances feedback between high and low-level concerns.

While Fitzgerald and Aldohon saw success by collaborating with tutors, Joseph Cheatle and Margaret Bullerjahn (2015) highlight the benefits of collaborating with faculty in support of continuous improvement efforts. They surveyed undergraduates to understand how the primary stakeholders of writing center effectiveness—the students—had their expectations met. They found that students primarily viewed the WC as a service necessary only for first-year and international students despite efforts to market WC services directly to upper-level students. To persuade students that the WC is beneficial for students at every level and thus improve WC utilization on campus, Cheatle and Bullerjahn emphasize the need to collaborate with faculty in promoting the WC. They theorized that faculty would be more effective to set expectations for the benefits of the WC, writing, "while not all faculty members will be on board with our message, one-to-one outreach is the best opportunity to get our faculty to support our center" (Cheatle and Bullerjahn 2015, 26).

Fodrey and Hassay (2021) show how fostering a writing-enriched curriculum model, or WEC, involves a departmental and program-based integration of writing and writing instruction that requires support for the substantial labor assumed by WPAs. In their case, this initiative was collaboratively led by a FYW coordinator and a WAC director (Fodrey and Hassay 2021, 168). As a data-driven process of codifying faculty expectations, the FYW coordinator and WAC director conducted short interviews coupled with larger department meetings about writing issues, which were transcribed so that data could be easily collected for further review. They asked faculty questions about what qualities and criteria for effective writing were important to faculty to "reveal the tacit assumptions about writing English faculty embedded within their assignments and by extension enacted across the curriculum (171).

They acknowledge that such collaboration invokes contemporary concerns about labor at a time when service commitments are higher than years past, particularly for the pre-tenured FYW coordinator "who was expected to develop and teach new rhetoric and writing studies courses, produce scholarship, and administer most aspects of the writing program minus the writing center" (Fodrey and Hassay 2021, 170). So in response, their department approved additional language in their tenure and promotion plan, stating that "administrative contributions that promote intellectual growth could count as scholarly production toward tenure and promotion" (169). Fodrey and Hassay include supporting language in their notes so that others may successfully argue for department support of faculty-driven programmatic writing curriculum development to be codified within their tenure and promotion plan.

Across this literature, a clear theme is that WPAs need to design data-driven methods of assessment in ways that are attentive to their institutional context and that leverage the relationships they have built across campus to carry out this work. As Gladstein and Fralix (2017, 22) show, writing supports a liberal arts education and is an activity and skillset sought by "every program and department," so it is important to name all writing practices and work to optimize them for the purpose of "improved student outcomes." They demonstrate that writing program leadership, data gathering, assessment, and continuous improvement can be made possible within a collaborative, writing-enriched curriculum model that "affords practitioners the opportunity to make context-informed modifications to the methodology," one suited for "sustainable effectiveness; department-retained agency; and substantial, meaningful, goal-driven conversation about writing and the teaching of writing" (167). As the remainder of this chapter will demonstrate, these considerations drove our efforts to develop our own collaborative model, one that aimed to minimize the labor involved in these efforts by harnessing data sets we were already collecting in our FYW program and the WC.

Context for Collaboration

Our collaborative assessment model was shaped by conditions common across many SLACs. Although our writing center was not the first tutoring center on campus, it was founded as a replacement for a much more expensive communication skills center that had been staffed by paraprofessionals. When that center was closed, it was replaced with a writing center directed by a newly hired tenure track faculty member and staffed by undergraduate and graduate student peer tutors. This meant that much of the institutional knowledge that predated the writing center was lost. The financial exigencies that led to the establishment of the WC also contributed to an unsustainable administrative workload, as the new WC director was hired as the sole WPA at the university. In addition to performing service and scholarship responsibilities as a tenure track faculty member, the WC director also served as the first-year writing coordinator and taught two courses a semester.

During the same timeframe, the university began placing an increased emphasis on assessment. The WC's inaugural assessment was conducted at the end of its first year and by the time that study took place, a robust process for collecting, analyzing, and reporting on student utilization of and satisfaction with WC services was well established. Then in 2017, our administration pushed for assessment of the first-year writing curriculum. However, given the WPA's dual administrative roles, heavy service load, and tenure-track responsibilities, a data-driven approach to continuous improvement of first-year writing was difficult to achieve. The timing of this issue was fortunate, as it coincided with the retirement of a tenure track English faculty member. After discussing possible directions for the position, the English faculty agreed that converting the line into a new WPA position that made it possible to split the administration of the writing center and the first-year writing curriculum across two roles was the best course of action for the department. With support from a sympathetic dean, a new first-year writing coordinator (FYW) was hired in 2018, also with heavy teaching, service, and scholarship obligations as well as additional writing across the curriculum responsibilities.

When the new FYW coordinator joined the university, the previous coordinator (and current WC director) had developed a plan for assessing FYW but had not yet implemented it. This plan included an instructor survey that captured an indirect measure of students' achievement of the course's eight learning outcomes and a rubric instructors could use to directly measure course outcomes. Instructors' survey responses, rubric scores of students' essays, and students' first and final drafts of that essay were collected as assessment data. At the time of this pilot, the instructor survey, rubric, and collection method for gathering student essays had been in place for three years; however, compliance with the assessment process was uneven across instructors due to an institutional restructure and the COVID-19 pandemic. The writing center assessment had been in place for eight years and was supported by the director who had recently received tenure and a part-time administrative assistant.

This institutional history directly informs the model of collaborative assessment reported here. The WC director's prior experience as the FYW coordinator meant there was shared knowledge about the procedures for collecting and analyzing FYW data. Although a number of obstacles delayed the level of collaboration we describe in this chapter, the conditions created by our intersecting roles within our SLAC and our shared goal to be careful and measured about how to sustain the improvement of writing support at our institution ultimately enabled this collaboration.

Data Collection and Assessment: First-Year Writing

Like Holly-Wells, Jamieson, and Sanyal (2014), our institution is likewise stochastic, where faculty specializing in creative writing, language arts education, literature, and rhetoric and composition all teach our FYW course alongside adjunct faculty. Since faculty have varying ways of meeting the outcomes of this course, course guidelines were developed that allow for a considerable amount of flexibility in assignment design while also establishing key consistencies across sections. For instance, all FYW instructors are required to teach the same five major assignments: an annotated bibliography, critical analysis, formal letter, researched persuasive argument, and synthesis essay. These five major assignments were negotiated twelve years ago before either author of this chapter joined our SLAC. At that time, an ad-hoc committee interviewed faculty from our five major colleges. From those interviews, the ad-hoc committee determined letter-writing, documentation, synthesis, and a fully researched argument to be the toolkit necessary to prepare students for writing in their respective majors. The ad-hoc committee brought their findings to faculty in the English program, who found consensus on the core curriculum. While the full scope of the negotiations is buried in our SLAC's history, the product was codified guidelines kept on a secure server and distributed to all faculty members at the start of each school year. These guidelines remain as a resource for all faculty and staff, and they define our FYW program.

Our English program has around eight tenure-track faculty and between two to five adjunct faculty teaching all sections of FYW. Beyond the negotiated guidelines for each assignment, facility and staff have a considerable amount of freedom in determining the scope, scaffolding, and structure of their class. The FYW coordinator regularly meets with faculty and staff as needed to support their teaching. Further supporting this balance between standardization and flexibility is a class observation process. Tenured faculty observe adjunct and tenure-track faculty once a year and write a formal letter that both praises faculty for what was done well and offers suggestions for improvement. For tenure-track faculty, the observation letters are compiled into annual reviews for their tenure and promotion binder. For adjunct faculty, the formal letter is kept on file in the dean's office. Conversations are genuinely collegial and supportive of both the instructor and the curriculum, though our program continues to revise the structure of observations to be as efficient and equitable as possible.

The most highly regimented of FYW assignments is the researched persuasive argument (RPA), a six-to-eight-page essay that serves as the culminating assignment to the course. This assignment is taught by all faculty and staff. It comprises 35 percent of students' final grade for the FYW course and serves as the primary artifact for programmatic assessment. To facilitate our course assessment, students submit rough drafts and final drafts of this essay to a website hosted on our learning management system. Each semester, approximately 200 rough drafts and final drafts of researched persuasive argument essays are collected from students through this system.

Like Fodrey and Hassay (2021), a standard rubric was developed that aligned with the course's eight learning outcomes and that clarifies the qualities that comprise successful achievement of these outcomes (see Appendix A for the version of this rubric used in this study). This rubric offers criteria that can accommodate the variations across instructors' assignments while maximizing flexibility and confidence that every student who completes the FYW course has suitably met the outcomes. For FYW assessment, the rubric is applied to all students' submissions of the researched persuasive argument essay (RPA) every semester by all faculty and staff who teach the course. Each faculty member assesses their own students. While not all faculty use the rubric when calculating their students' grades, every instructor is required to assess the RPA essays using an online version of the rubric developed with Qualtrics software.

The scores are then aggregated by the writing seminar coordinator into an annual FYW assessment report that combines direct assessments with an indirect survey of instructors' impressions of how well their students met the outcomes of the first-year writing course. It takes approximately one week at the end of the semester to export these data into spreadsheets and sort these data into tables organized around the course outcomes. An additional week is spent analyzing data and writing the FYW year-end assessment report. The course outcomes that are scored lowest by direct and indirect measures are marked as opportunities for the continuous improvement of first-year writing at our SLAC.

Data Collection and Assessment: Writing Center

Our WC uses the commercial scheduling tool *WCOnline* to facilitate students' tutoring sessions. This system schedules and tracks in-person and online tutoring sessions, hosts online sessions, houses forms that tutors complete to record and communicate their feedback to students after their sessions, and automatically distributes and collects students' responses to post-session satisfaction surveys. On their satisfaction surveys, students provide Likert scale ratings of the helpfulness of their tutoring session, their likelihood to attend another session, and the ease with which they were able to schedule their tutoring sessions. They are also asked open-ended questions about the strengths and weaknesses of their tutoring session and their suggestions for improving the writing center. Student satisfaction surveys play a key role in the writing center's assessment process, but because they are anonymous, they are not linked to students' appointment data and therefore could not be utilized in the collaborative assessment we describe here.

Other data, however, could be utilized. When students create their writing center account, for instance, they report their year (freshman, sophomore, etc.), major, college, and strongest academic language, among other details. This personal data is then linked to the tutoring appointments they schedule. When students seeking help (tutees henceforth) sign up for writing center appointments, they provide information about the class and instructor they are writing for (or audience for non-academic writing tasks), the genre, assignment guidelines, citation style, and any major concerns they have or aspects of their writing they want to work on with their tutor. Tutees are also invited to upload assignment sheets, rubrics, and drafts of their writing for the tutor to review during their session. This data capturing method enabled us to collect information from FYW students about their RPA drafts and, in some cases, to collect the rough drafts that students submitted prior to their tutoring sessions, enabling us to directly measure the impact of their tutoring sessions.

In addition, *WCOnline* also captures data from the tutors who work with students. After each session, tutors complete a post-session tutor report form that includes three checklists that capture an overview of the feedback the tutor offered during the session (see Appendix B for an example of the data the report generates). The form includes a list of common higher-order concerns (e.g., global revisions like organization or thesis), a list of common lower-order concerns (e.g., local revisions like grammar or mechanics), and a list of common recommendations for tutees to follow up on after the session (e.g., attend another session, talk with your instructor). The forms also include a space for notes where tutors are instructed to summarize the tutoring session and suggest next steps for the tutee as they continue revising their draft. Tutors can attach files to their post-session client report forms, which could include a helpful resource for a student or a draft with the tutor's comments. The report is largely used to support tutor training efforts in our WC. The reports are also shared with students' instructors if the student requests that the WC share their tutor's feedback.

Both FYW assessments and WC assessments are sent to the dean of arts and sciences, the vice president of student success, and the leadership in our English program. The results of each report are used for our accreditation with the Higher Learning Commission. It was always assumed that faculty-led committees will take the results of the report and use them for continuous improvement of writing support, but these separate assessments were stymied by repeated university restructures and the COVID-19 pandemic. It wasn't until the fall of 2022 that the FYW assessment finally reached its intended stakeholders for discussion for the first time.

Method: Combining Data Sets and Building a Collaborative Corpus for Assessment Across WPA Contexts

Our method—and our model—utilizes our already robust data collection methods for FYW and the WC, but for the expressed purpose of tracing a first-year writer's revision process from the time they receive help from the WC to the time they submit a final draft of the researched persuasive argument essay. Our sample of students came from the fall 2021 semester. That fall, the writing center conducted 693 tutoring sessions with 464 students, or 14.9 percent of the 3,116 students enrolled in the university (see Table

1). Concurrently, 295 students completed FYW. Although writing center utilization was strong university-wide, utilization among first-year writing students was disproportionately low. Only 4.7 percent of FYW students (14 students) attended a writing center tutoring session for their researched persuasive argument essays during the fall semester. These 14 students serve as our sample population for our pilot because we could trace their writing processes across our separate assessments.

Table 1. Fall 2021 writing center utilization

Population served	% students served	# students served	Total student population
University-wide	14.9	464	3,116
FYW	4.7	14	295

Table 2 provides an overview of our data collection and analysis. Looking across the datasets we were already capturing in our FYW program and our WC, we found immediate opportunities to enhance the direct measures of student learning captured in each space. For instance, while the FYW coordinator collects first and final drafts of students' RPAs, the assessment plan did not capture the feedback that students received in-between those drafts to help illuminate the effectiveness of students' revising process. Final copies of the RPA were submitted by students to a shared site hosted on our learning management system created with Moodle software. Likewise, while the WC regularly captured students' drafts and tutor feedback, the revisions that students completed after tutoring sessions were inaccessible.

Table 2: Overview of Fall 2021 data collection and method of analysis

Area	Collection tools	Data collected	Assessment methods
WC	WCOnline	Tutee-submitted rough drafts of students' researched persuasive argument essays (RPAs)	Direct with RPA rubric, normed between the WC director and FYW coordinator
		Tutor session notes	Indirect qualitative
FYW	Moodle	Student-submitted final drafts of students' researched persuasive argument Essays (RPAs)	Direct with RPA rubric, normed between the WC director and FYW coordinator

By merging our data sets, we were able to create a corpus of first drafts, tutor feedback, and revised drafts that enabled us to measure how FYW students responded to feedback and the extent to which their writing improved following their writing center tutoring sessions. We used students' names to identify which students had scheduled a tutoring session and submitted a rough draft through *WCOnline* and also submitted a final draft to Moodle for the FYW assessment. There were fourteen total rough drafts collected from students who sought help from tutors in the WC. Some rough drafts were too incomplete to assess with a direct measure. Some rough drafts were attainable from the tutoring session, but their final copies were not submitted to the shared site on Moodle. Thus, a sample of five participants was winnowed from the fourteen possible participants identified. Even with a large corpus of texts collected through our FYW assessment and our WC session notes, our sample for this study was small due to the disproportionately low utilization of the writing center by FYW students. Our small sample size demonstrates that the amount of usable data can be small even when collection methods are as large and sweeping as those collected for our WC and FYW assessments. Before we even began analyzing our data, then, one finding was clear: we have considerable work to do to increase FYW students' utilization of WC services.

For the five participants included in our study, we collected their rough and final drafts of the RPAs and used Google Docs' comparison feature to reveal all the changes they made across drafts. We gathered these tutees' WC utilization data and the post-session client report forms created by their tutors after their tutoring sessions. We each scored students' rough and final drafts using the course outcomes rubric, then met for norming sessions to resolve any discrepancies between our scores. Table 3 outlines the scores each of the five students earned on course outcome eight across their rough and final drafts. We then synthesized these scores with tutors' post-session client report feedback to determine how tutors' feedback aligned with or diverged from our direct assessments of students' RPA drafts.

Table 3: Excerpt from the norming spreadsheet for Outcome 8: Effectively follow an academic documentation style

Student	Rough Draft	Final Draft
1	Needs major improvement	Meets expectations
2	Needs minor improvement	Meets expectations

Student	Rough Draft	Final Draft
3	Needs minor improvement	Meets expectations
4	Needs minor improvement	Meets expectations
5	Needs major improvement	Needs major improvement

Aggregating scores in this way was particularly advantageous for checking our numbers. Our 2021 FYW assessment had already identified students' ability to make effective revisions as a target area for improvement, and the 2021 WC assessment had previously relied solely on indirect measures such as students' satisfaction and utilization rates to establish the effectiveness of its services. Combining both gave us a fuller picture of FYW students' writing process from the time they met with a tutor until the time they turned in their final drafts to their FYW instruction (see Appendix C for an example of our norming session notes).

What Aldohon (2021) found through observations, we found by qualitatively reviewing tutor session notes, looking for evidence that tutors coached FYW students on aspects of their writing that correspond with the course outcomes. We could also compare tutors' focus to the focus that the FYW students requested for their tutoring sessions, as each student selected lower-order and higher-order concerns they wanted to address in their session from the same checklist that tutors completed when they recapped the focus of their feedback after the session. Lower-order concerns included spelling, punctuation, grammar, formatting, and other sentence-level considerations. Higher-order concerns included the persuasiveness of the evidence, considerations of audience and purpose, and the overall organization of a piece. Putting in tutors' written accounts of how they advised their FYW students enabled us to see whether and how their formative assessments might help FYW students be more successful in their writing course. These written accounts also reflect a complicated rhetorical situation, as the tutors know that they are writing for many audiences: the student who benefits from the summary of their feedback, the FYW instructor who may receive a copy of the note (upon the student's request), and the WC director who will use their accounts for tutor training and the improvement of the WC's services.

To the labor questions raised in our literature review, substantial amounts of time were needed to assess the five rough drafts, five final drafts, and five draft comparisons and resolve the discrepancies between our observations. This kind of assessment labor, however, is common among faculty within a writing program. Reaching across writing programs may result in a different allocation of time without necessarily increasing the total time involved in the assessment process.

An Enhanced View of the Writing Center: Insights from Collaborative Assessment

One advantage of evaluating the students' WC drafts using the FYW rubric was that it enabled us to determine how well tutors' focus on higher and lower-order concerns aligned with our direct assessments of the drafts and the changes first-year writing students made for their final drafts. Tutors demonstrated success with identifying both the high and low-order concerns listed as the foci of their sessions with FYW tutees. Beginning first with lower-order concerns, every student in our corpus received feedback related to an academic documentation style. This feedback aligned with our rubric scores indicating that every student who participated in our study had needed either minor or major improvement in this area. Moreover, our FYW students not only realized that this was an area they needed to work on, but in four out of the five revisions (80 percent), students showed improvements in their ability to effectively follow that style (see Table 3). After their tutoring sessions, these FYW students were generally better at creating parenthetical citations and citing borrowed information in accordance with MLA or APA guidelines, with minimal errors in their works cited and bibliography pages.

Across this feedback, tutors helped FYW students improve citations and formatting by reminding them of the work they did in their tutoring sessions, offering examples that modeled correct formatting, and providing general guidelines for students to follow. For the FY writers that improved in this category on the course outcomes rubric, we saw evidence that tutor feedback assisted students' improvements in their drafts.

For the one first-year writer who did not improve in this category, there was still evidence that the tutor advised the student on how they might improve:

> In our session, we took a fine-tooth comb to your references and exactly where you needed to add in-text citations. I have added a link in this email to Purdue OWL's MLA style guide that I highly recommend utilizing whenever you are unsure of any specifics. I've also added a tutorial on how to create a hanging indent for your work cited page, as we had discussed.

The advice captured here seems helpful for the tutee, and the tutor also included a resource to support the student as they continued working with MLA format. However, our direct assessments revealed that this tutee did not revise as the tutor coached. Although our assessment method did not enable us to capture *why* this particular FYW student failed to address the tutor's feedback, we can speculate about possible causes that could inform our efforts toward continuous improvement in both spaces. Perhaps there was a gap between the strategies the tutor utilized in the session and this FY writer's learning needs, in which case we might enhance tutor training by practicing strategies for checking students' knowledge or brainstorming a variety of techniques that can be used to teach citation guidelines. An alternative conclusion is that the FY writer may struggle with revising on their own, even after receiving direct guidance. In this case, more direct instruction and support for revision in the FYW course may be warranted. While more robust qualitative data (like interviews with the FYW and the tutor) could certainly help to illuminate what happened in this instance, these speculations still give us useful insights, particularly when considered alongside other patterns that emerge from our collaborative approach to assessment.

While it would be unreasonable to expect students to perfectly implement the feedback they receive from a tutor, the fact that this tutee left egregious citation errors in the final draft of their essay—including failing to distinguish between information borrowed from sources and their own summary, synthesis, or analysis—suggests that instead of treating this issue like a lower-order concern, as the tutor seems to have done, it could have been addressed as a higher-order issue. In this case, the tutee added citations for some statistics, as the tutor advised, but failed to provide citations for other information that appeared to us to be taken from a source. Consequently, while tutors in general seem to be effectively supporting tutees on this lower-order concern, our collaborative approach to assessment enabled us to see that additional training focused on identifying when lower-order concerns become higher-order issues would be beneficial.

There was evidence of tutors providing feedback on high-order concerns as well. Two out of the five FYW students (40 percent) showed improvement incorporating evidence throughout the essay either through better use of summary, paraphrasing, or direct quotation. For the FY writers that improved in this category, we saw some evidence that tutors assisted with their improvements in their drafts. Below are some examples where tutors documented how they advised tutees to use evidence:

> Make sure to embed your quotes smoothly into your paper and to provide your own commentary [. . .] Some tutor recommendations include reviewing over the document that I have made comments on during our session.
>
> I suggest reading though [sic] your paragraphs to find areas where you can separate out the paragraphs to organize your terms/claims/evidence.

It is unclear exactly what comments tutors made on students' drafts. We may see that tutors have robust strategies for advising FYW students. Nevertheless, it appears that the tutor gave direct advice on how the student may support ideas with evidence. Notable is that for the one essay that did not improve, the tutor did describe a conversation about evidence in their session description:

> I think you could easily find studies that show how cyberbullying can increase rates of depression and suicide and how vaping/drinking underage can increase rates of certain physical illnesses.

Similar to lower-order concerns, there are multiple reasons why a tutee might have ignored this advice. And as Holly-Wells, Jamieson, and Sanyal have noted, tutors are sometimes too far removed from the classroom context to hope to reinforce whatever research strategies had been taught. Or, if they had given direct advice verbally, it may be that the advice given was not as thorough as the tutor believed at the time, as Aldohon has observed. Yet, we feel encouraged that the tutor did advise well despite the tutee failing to act on the advice in a way measurable by our direct assessment of this FYW student's writing. Again, this lack of revision suggests that tutees may struggle to use feedback to revise their writing, a pattern that indicates more direct instruction in the FYW course would be valuable.

In their tutoring sessions, tutees often indicated that their rubric would influence their revisions, writing things like, "My goal is to fall mostly into the exceeds expectations category on the rubric." Every tutor who supported our participants indicated "Assignment requirements" as a high-order concern addressed in their tutoring sessions. It is encouraging to see FYW students and tutors using the faculty-defined rubric to negotiate assignment expectations. Seeing this realized in our assessment data can help assure faculty that FYW students are getting constructive feedback that can help them be more successful in the course, and it may also assure faculty of the utility of the rubric in the stochastic environment of a SLAC. Faculty may see added benefit to using rubrics not only for evaluation of students' products, but as a tool that helps present FYW students with a unified support system for revision. We can use these insights as we work with FYW faculty to increase WC utilization by FYW students.

In addition, our findings suggest additional opportunities for improving tutor training and FYW instruction. In all but one instance, our rubric evaluations indicated that every FYW student's rough draft needed either minor or major revisions in developing their thesis statements. However, the tutors' session descriptions did not indicate that this need was addressed in the tutoring session. Furthermore, the final drafts of the RPA essay did not show substantial revision to students' thesis statements. This data clearly demonstrates that more instruction related to developing thesis statements would be beneficial in both the FYW course and in tutor training.

Further opportunities for improving tutor training involve paying careful attention to how tutoring strategies are executed to ensure they are effective. For instance, tutors in our WC are trained to pair praise with constructive advice for improvement. This strategy has been shown by Nancy Sommers (1983) to respect writers' work and agency. But sometimes, tutors using this strategy actually provided contradictory advice, such as the following quote from a post-session report form:

> I think overall you have a good argument with a lot of good evidence to back up your points. However, I do think you can add some more evidence about what exactly social media does.

In this case, the tutor tried to couple praise for well-evidenced points with encouragement to provide additional evidence for a specific aspect of the argument. By folding this important feedback in with praise, the tutee may not have recognized the importance of this comment. Our own direct assessment of this rough draft showed that the student did not meet expectations for providing evidence to support their thesis. In this case, providing blanket praise for a student's use of evidence when they have not sufficiently supported their argument makes this feedback less effective, not more effective. We acknowledge it can be difficult, even for writing teachers, to find ways to compliment student work when it is below expectations. But this example highlights how essential it is to be specific and concrete when offering praise, particularly when it's related to an issue a student is generally struggling with. Identifying a specific moment where the student was effectively using evidence could have set a helpful benchmark for them to strive to achieve without detracting from the significance of this issue. This is a strategy we can certainly work on developing through tutor training.

Since we did not directly observe tutor interactions as Aldohon (2021) has done, it is also possible that tutors may need coaching on how to more fully document their sessions with tutees. For instance, many tutors documented that they assisted tutees with grammar and mechanics, but there was little advice given in the session descriptions that indicated that tutors helped with these lower-order concerns. One tutor offered the OWL at Purdue as a short-hand resource for formatting the manuscript, and one tutor offered advice about "flow" and suggested reading essays aloud to hear for interruptions. We do not view these suggestions as bad advice or as fully absent of advice, but there was little in the way of direct help on how tutees could improve. Yet, we often see these aspects addressed when tutoring sessions are observed, and we did see improvement during our direct assessments of students' drafts. It is likely that tutors gave helpful advice on the drafts that, as we noted earlier, we cannot not see through the revision process and that was not captured in the session descriptions.

An Enhanced View of First-Year Writing: Insights from Collaborative Assessment

One substantial result of this study is that the pilot of our collaborative assessment clearly corroborated the results of our annual first-year writing assessment. Our FYW assessment aggregates faculty's direct and indirect assessments of students' RPA essay and identifies students' weakest areas. At the time of our pilot, the weakest area identified was FYW students' ability to make higher-order and lower-order revisions that improve the effectiveness of their writing. In the direct assessment completed for this pilot, three out of five final drafts were determined to need minor improvement in making revisions, and the remaining two final drafts needed major improvement. It was reassuring to see our annual assessment data corroborated by our pilot assessment of FYW students who sought help from WC tutors. This corroboration helps strengthen our assessments, indicating further validity of our findings, and provides insight into the struggles our FYW students are facing. Our FYW students are receiving feedback they are not acting on. By increasing support for revision in both the WC and the FYW course, we can create opportunities for continuous improvement greater than what the FYW coordinator or the WC director alone could accomplish.

The FYW coordinator has at times met resistance from adjunct faculty teaching FYW because they often teach at multiple institutions and have varying degrees of trust in WC support. Likewise, the WC director has encountered skepticism about how well tutors support students' writing processes, likely because faculty generally perceive that students "can't write." As Gray and Hoyt (2020, 1) have observed, faculty often refer "their worst performing students in hopes that a tutor can bring the students up to speed." Perhaps surprisingly in our pilot assessment, we saw both weak rough drafts and strong rough drafts, and both benefited from WC tutoring. Our indirect measures in the annual FYW assessment captured how faculty feel they give all students, not just struggling ones, extensive feedback on drafts to help students revise, but that the advice was generally not heeded. Our pilot assessment captures a similar trend and allows us to document exactly how beneficial a tutoring session can be even when tutees fall short on the necessary revisions.

One of the greatest advantages of this collaboration is that we can share the results of our assessments with faculty to help them better trust the WC and even begin to develop a sense of solidarity with this service. By doing this, we hope to instill greater confidence that FYW students are indeed empowered to revise. One of our key challenges in pursuing this effort will be to identify what additional barriers may be preventing FYW students' revisions. The FYW coordinator will seek the help of faculty and staff to revise the FYC curriculum to support more revision as identified in this study and the FYW assessment, with added insights about how the WC can support this effort. Doing so supports the WC because we do not want tutors' efforts to go to waste, and because we want FYW students to truly appreciate the benefits of their tutoring sessions.

Paths Toward Collaborative Assessment at SLACs

Our pilot assessment is still a work in progress. Yet, one of the advantages for administrators at SLACs is the ease with which we can collaborate across divides that might be more challenging to bridge at larger institutions. Were we to attempt this assessment with a student population of the size common at larger universities, we would need the help of an Information Technology department to create a more powerful system of data gathering and sorting to help us create, manage, and query our corpus.

While the size of our pilot data set prevents us from drawing firm conclusions about the state of writing at our institution, our point at this initial stage is to outline the process we used to align our assessment methods—which will streamline our efforts and produce larger data sets in the future—and highlight the kinds of insights that are made possible by a collaborative approach to assessment that utilizes data we were already collecting for separate assessments.

Gladstein and Ragaignon (2012) demonstrated how the leadership of WPAs supports writing at SLACs. Our institution had a FYW coordinator and a WC director completing separate assessments. Of SLACs with a similar structure, SLACs looking for data-driven measures of student success and writing center support may find strategies in our literature review and in our approach that will be useful. But while the majority of approaches rely on indirect measures such as surveys, interviews, and observations, our study utilizes the strength of direct measures of students' writing in ways that reveal students' processes in relation to their products. Moreover, our model study utilized direct measures and data each respective WPA was already gathering but examined in a new way with a specific focus on the needs of our FYW students. We see this pilot as an efficient use of WPAs' time. WPAs at other SLACs can similarly think about new ways to leverage the data they are already collecting to strengthen the insights offered for both their writing center and their writing program(s). It is our hope that these preliminary insights will encourage WPAs at other SLACs to begin looking across data sets and conducting collaborative assessments at their own institutions.

As Cheatle and Bullerjahn (2015) remind us, collaborating with faculty in support of continuous improvement efforts is crucial to the efforts of writing program administration. At the time of writing this chapter, we are sharing the results of our study with faculty and staff much as we have with our FYW assessment and inviting insights on how to further interpret these data and better align WC support with the pedagogy of our FYW faculty, and vice versa. We are sure this will be a fruitful conversation. Faculty and staff may have insights into the obstacles students encounter while revising their final drafts of the RPA. Faculty and staff may also want to collaborate with each other during brown-bag sessions brainstorming how to encourage revision in FYW. We imagine the results of our study can be used to build the reputation of our WC as a resource for FYW students (and all students). Our report shows that WC tutors can and do help tutees reach the outcomes of our FYW course, and the support will only grow in efficacy as we work toward continuous improvement of writing instruction and support at our SLAC. If we are successful in making our case to faculty and staff, they can become partners with, and advocates for the WC.

Anson (2021, 10–11) shows how sustainability requires that any initiative be scaled gradually, be sensitive to and expect change, and periodically or regularly revisit and revise efforts up to and including faculty and staff workloads, and our SLAC is no exception. Negotiations over workload have been continually required between English, the dean's office, and the provost to determine the most equitable workload possible between our two WPAs. What was once codified informally to create our positions later involved listing the responsibilities for each role and quantifying the time needed to complete the work. There were several attempts to quantify responsibilities of the WPA, but all attempts felt intrusive because other aspects of faculty productivity are measured by output (course evaluations, observations, publications) and not by hours spent.

Proceeding with caution, a minimum of one hour per week is allocated to meetings at our SLAC's department, school, college, and university levels. A spike in student support happens once each semester, as faculty and staff help advise students on courses for the following semester. Service commitments at the department, college, and university-level require two hours per week on average, with student-focused committees and efforts supporting diversity, inclusion, and equity, often requiring far more hours in a given week. Perhaps unique to our institution is that faculty and staff assist with recruiting efforts by meeting with prospective students who visit campus and writing welcome notes to students who have been successfully admitted to our programs. Generously, that would divide thirty-two remaining hours per week between two classes (sixteen hours) and administrative duties (sixteen hours). That is to say nothing of allocating time for professional development, travel, and scholarship—or simply clearing one's email inbox every morning, afternoon, and evening. Upper administration had to accept that our many duties would be slow because of the time reserved to do them. Job descriptions were crafted that clearly demarcated the where the WCD and FYWC's responsibilities begin and end. A list of responsibilities was codified and approved by all stakeholders, and assessments are included in our tenure and promotion plan. Later, the workload would be codified in a memo of understanding that is renewable every two years and kept in our dean's office (but that process came later than our study).

We present one model of how WPAs in a SLAC can use data to assess how WC tutors support students of our FYW program for the purpose of continuous improvement, but others are of course possible. We learned much from the process, and it is our hope that other WPAs at SLACs can consider leading collaborative assessments that utilize indirect measures and direct measures to invite discussion on how to improve both WC support and FYW curricula.

Bibliography

Anson, Chris M. 2021. "WEC and the Strength of the Commons." In *Writing-Enriched Curricula: Models of Faculty-Driven and Departmental Transformation*, edited by Chris M. Anson and Pamela Flash, 3–14. WAC Clearinghouse: University Press of Colorado. https://doi.org/10.37514/PER-B.2021.1299.1.3.

Aldohon, Hatem. 2021. "Writing Centre Conferences: Tutors' Perceptions and Practices." *Educational Studies* 47, no. 5: 554–73.

Cheatle, Joseph, and Margaret Bullerjahn. 2015. "Undergraduate Student Perceptions and the Writing Center." *WLN: A Journal of Writing Center Scholarship* 40, no. 1–2: 19–26.

Fodrey, Crystal N., and Chris Hassay. 2021. "Piloting WEC as a Context-Responsive Writing Research Initiative." In *Writing-Enriched Curricula: Models of Faculty-Driven and Departmental Transformation*, edited by Chris M. Anson and Pamela Flash, 167–80. WAC Clearinghouse: University Press of Colorado. https://doi.org/10.27514/PER-B.2021.1299.2.07.

Giaimo, Genie. 2017. "Focusing on the Blind Spots: RAD-Based Assessment of Students' Perceptions of Community College Writing Centers." *Praxis: A Writing Center Journal* 15, no. 1: 1–10.

Gladstein, Jill M., and Brandon Fralix. 2017. "Supporting Data-Driven Conversations about Institutional Cultures of Writing." *Peer Review* 19, no.1: 21–24.

Gladstein, Jill M., and Dara Rossman Regaignon. 2012. *Writing Program Administration at Small Liberal Arts Colleges*. Anderson: Parlor Press.

Holly-Wells, Jennifer, Sandra Jamieson, and Maya Sanyal. 2014. "From Silos to Synergies: Institutional Contexts for Writing Fellows." *Praxis: A Writing Center Journal* 12, no. 1: 54–89.

Okuma, Taryn. 2013. "Understanding Student Perceptions of the Writing Center—A Conversation Between a Student, a Writing Center Instructor, and a Director/Professor." *Another Word* (blog), Writing Center at the University of Wisconsin-Madison. April 29, 2013. https://dept.writing.wisc.edu/blog/understanding-student-perceptions-of-the-writing-center-a-conversation-between-a-student-a-writing-center-instructor-and-a-directorprofessor.

Olinger, Andrea R. 2021. "Self-Contradiction in Faculty's Talk about Writing: Making and Unmaking Autonomous Models of Literacy." *Literacy in Composition Studies* 8, no. 2:1–38. https://doi.org/10.21623/1.8.2.2.

Swaak, Taylor. 2022. *Using Student Data Responsibly : How to Protect, Analyze, and Act on the Information You Have.* Chronicle of Higher Education.

Appendix A.

Researched Persuasive Argument Collaborative Assessment Rubric

Outcome 1. Write about college-level texts critically and analytically.		
The essay successfully identifies the main ideas, arguments, values, and/or attitudes in cited sources.	Exceeds expectations	Comments:
	Meets expectations	
	Needs minor improvement	
	Needs major improvement	
The essay consistently offers explanations or evaluations of cited sources that offer an accurate reading of the source.	Exceeds expectations	Comments:
	Meets expectations	
	Needs minor improvement	
	Needs major improvement	
The connections between cited sources and the student's ideas are clear, though one of these aspects may receive more attention.	Exceeds expectations	Comments:
	Meets expectations	
	Needs minor improvement	
	Needs major improvement	
Outcome 2. Find, evaluate, and integrate research sources into your papers.		
The essay cites six sources, at least three of which are academic.	Exceeds expectations	Comments:
	Meets expectations	
	Needs minor improvement	
	Needs major improvement	

Each source is credible and appropriate, offering support for the essay's argument.	Exceeds expectations	Comments:
	Meets expectations	
	Needs minor improvement	
	Needs major improvement	
Signal phrases are often present, effectively integrating most citations into the essay.	Exceeds expectations	Comments:
	Meets expectations	
	Needs minor improvement	
	Needs major improvement	
Quotes are well chosen and fully represent the source's point, though at times some unnecessary information may also be included.	Exceeds expectations	Comments:
	Meets expectations	
	Needs minor improvement	
	Needs major improvement	
Outcome 3. Develop a clear thesis statement and organization for a college paper.		
The introduction effectively sets up the essay, drawing the reader into the essay's focus.	Exceeds expectations	Comments:
	Meets expectations	
	Needs minor improvement	
	Needs major improvement	
The thesis statement effectively introduces the persuasive argument that will be developed in the essay.	Exceeds expectations	Comments:
	Meets expectations	
	Needs minor improvement	
	Needs major improvement	
Topic sentences are generally present and fully introduce the main idea being developed in most body paragraphs.	Exceeds expectations	Comments:
	Meets expectations	
	Needs minor improvement	
	Needs major improvement	
The focus of each body paragraph is generally discrete, with most main ideas being presented only once in the essay.	Exceeds expectations	Comments:
	Meets expectations	
	Needs minor improvement	
	Needs major improvement	

The organizing principle for the essay's structure is generally effective. The focus of each paragraph logically builds on the preceding paragraph, resulting in a thorough development of the essay's argument.	Exceeds expectations	Comments:
	Meets expectations	
	Needs minor improvement	
	Needs major improvement	
Outcome 4. Support main ideas with evidence.		
Evidence is incorporated throughout the essay with thorough use of summary, paraphrase, and direct quotation.	Exceeds expectations	Comments:
	Meets expectations	
	Needs minor improvement	
	Needs major improvement	
Each main idea is supported with at least one piece of evidence, effectively developing all the essay's main ideas.	Exceeds expectations	Comments:
	Meets expectations	
	Needs minor improvement	
	Needs major improvement	
The evidence presented is generally relevant to the main idea being developed, though some of the evidence presented may not be necessary.	Exceeds expectations	Comments:
	Meets expectations	
	Needs minor improvement	
	Needs major improvement	
Outcome 5. Write clearly in an appropriate tone for your audience.		
The essay sustains a consistent tone, with variations that are appropriate for persuading an audience that disagrees with the essay's thesis.	Exceeds expectations	Comments:
	Meets expectations	
	Needs minor improvement	
	Needs major improvement	
The essay engages with the needs of readers, providing some background information and explaining unfamiliar experiences, terms, or concepts.	Exceeds expectations	Comments:
	Meets expectations	
	Needs minor improvement	
	Needs major improvement	

A Data-Driven Model of Collaborative Assessment

Outcome 6. Make global and sentence-level revisions that improve the overall effectiveness of your writing.		
Revisions have been made that address most of the global and sentence-level concerns that were present in the first draft.	Exceeds expectations	Comments:
	Meets expectations	
	Needs minor improvement	
	Needs major improvement	
The changes made improve the effectiveness of parts of the essay, though some revision may still be needed.	Exceeds expectations	Comments:
	Meets expectations	
	Needs minor improvement	
	Needs major improvement	
Outcome 7. Effectively follow an academic documentation style.		
Citations are consistently present and generally correct. Small errors or omissions that do not interfere with readers' ability to locate sources may occur.	Exceeds expectations	Comments:
	Meets expectations	
	Needs minor improvement	
	Needs major improvement	
The essay follows most aspects of the documentation style's manuscript format.	Exceeds expectations	Comments:
	Meets expectations	
	Needs minor improvement	
	Needs major improvement	

Appendix B: Example of Writing Center Post-Session Client Report Form

Data from Post-Session Client Report Form	
Length	40 mins
Tutor	[Tutor's Name]
Student requests	Making sure the information provided is detailed and that the ideas flow together. I also need help with the formatting of my works cited page.
Higher order concerns addressed	Assignment requirements | organization |
Lower order concerns addressed	Grammar/mechanics | manuscript format |
Session recap and suggested next steps	Hi [Student's Name], In today's session, we went over your persuasive essay. We re-formatted your works cited page and we learned how to make a hanging indentation. We worked on the format of your quotes that you used. If a quote is longer than four lines as you type it into your document, you would have to reformat it. We discussed about this reformatting by using Purdue OWL as our reference. Make sure to embed your quotes smoothly into your paper and to provide your own commentary. Your ideas connected easily throughout your paper and there was enough detail that had been provided. Some tutor recommendations include reviewing over the document that I have made comments on during our session. I'll have it attached to this report form and it will be emailed to you. During our session, we also talked about the Writing Lab. The Writing Lab is in the computer lab on the first floor of the library. It will be opened at 6pm-8pm from Sunday to Thursday. If you have any questions or concerns, feel free to email us at [writing center email address] or to stop by the writing center. It was a pleasure working with you and good luck on your assignment! Cordially, [Tutor's Name]

Appendix C: Example of Norming Notes from Collaborative Assessment

NAME: [Student's Name]		
Outcome	Rough Draft Norming Notes	Final Draft Norming Notes
1	Generally good and accurate.	
2	Only 2/3 academic sources. Some signal phrases present, but others are missing.	Still short one academic source. All quotes have a signal phrase or lead-in of some kind.
3	Thesis statement outlines the three main points covered in the essay (like a five-paragraph format). The persuasiveness was lost in not fully explaining the topic.	Added block quotes Thesis remains the same Some elaboration for the topic present
4	Points generally followed the forecast. Weak summary. Most quotes are relevant but might include excessive detail.	Added better summary Didn't remove excessive details
5	Appropriate	
6	X	Mostly LO revisions present. Some summary clarifies some HO concerns.
8	Needs page numbers, block quotes not incorporated correctly, misspelled citations, no page or paragraph numbers. No hanging indent.	Still no page numbers Reformatted long quotations as block quotes

5 "We've always done it this way, so why change it?" Navigating Change in a First-Year Writing Program

Nicole Weaver

Abstract: This chapter describes the process of navigating and implementing change to a long-standing proficiency exam assessment within a first-year writing program. Part of the process described is a qualitative interview research study that was conducted at the institution—a small suburban liberal arts college of approximately 2,700 undergraduate students, located in the northeast. Through discussion of the power of tradition and ritual, this chapter aims to be useful in providing a model of possible action steps administrators can take in initiating and enacting meaningful and ethical changes to assessment practices at their institutions.

In July 2019, I was in Baltimore, presenting at the annual conference of the Council of Writing Program Administrators (CWPA). I had been in my position as assistant director of a first-year writing program for two years. During those two years, I intentionally had been taking time to learn the program and its history. The history was, at that time, still the present: the program was rooted in a strong, firm sense of tradition and ritual. My conference presentation focused on how I had designed a research study to initiate change to our entire program, but most specifically and importantly, its end-of-semester assessment: a proficiency examination that had existed for decades. As soon as it became clear to audience members that I was presenting on a proficiency exam as something we still administered, I observed looks and sounds of disbelief. One audience member audibly gasped; another rolled his eyes and stared at the ceiling. During the discussion portion of the session, the questions came quickly: How is a proficiency exam still being given at your college despite all of the existing research? Why are you, as only an assistant director, initiating the change? While the comments and questions were, I think, well-intentioned, I felt rattled, nervous, and embarrassed. With one minute left in the session, an audience member sitting in the back corner of the room raised her hand. She said she wanted to thank me for being honest—instead of the typical presentation focusing on positive changes that have been made and exciting directions for the future, she said she appreciated my focus on the actual. She said there were many writing programs struggling with breaking away from deeply rooted rituals and traditions. Indeed, such struggles have been documented by scholars such as Josye Brookter (2012) and Dan Melzer (2013).

In aligning practices with research, however, these struggles are, for the most part, markers of the past. In the 1980s, Peter Elbow and Pat Belanoff shifted from using proficiency exams to using a portfolio system to determine student proficiency at the end of their university's first-year writing class. In writing of this change then, Elbow and Belanoff (1986, 336) stated, "We believe proficiency examinations undermine good teaching by sending the wrong message about the writing process: that proficient writing means having a serious topic sprung on you (with no chance for reading, reflection, or discussion) and writing one draft (with no chance for sharing or feedback or revising)." In 1991, Belanoff identified four myths of writing assessment, all of which served as foundational pillars of the proficiency exam assessment: we know what we are testing for; we know what we are testing; agreeing on criteria means agreeing on whether individual papers meet these criteria; and it is possible to have an absolute standard and apply it uniformly (55). In 1994, Russel Durst, Marjorie Roemer, and Lucille Schultz wrote of their work, "We, the program administrators, decided to adopt portfolios, replacing a long-established, sit-down exit exam at the end of the sequence" (219). In a 1999 article, Kathleen Blake Yancey divided the history of writing assessment into three overlapping waves, with objective tests occurring in the first wave (1950–1970), holistically scored essays occurring in the second wave (1970–1986), and portfolio and programmatic assessment occurring in the third wave (1986–present). With the foundation of this research, I designed my own research study and sought to thoroughly understand the past of the first-year writing program at my institution so that I could work to meaningfully shape its future.

Methods

I have since completed the study that was the focus of my 2019 conference presentation in Baltimore. The study, titled "Full-Time Faculty Histories and Perceptions of the First-Year Writing Program," began in June 2019 when I received Institutional Review Board (IRB) approval and institutional funding. As my first step, I contacted all full-time department faculty members to solicit their participation in my qualitative interview study. From that pool of fifteen possible respondents, I conducted in-person semi-structured interviews with thirteen full-time faculty members (see Appendix A). There is a tension here in that I interviewed the people who actually teach the least in our first-year writing program, which staffs the majority of its sections with adjunct faculty members. This, however, was a strategic decision on my part, as I knew a major programmatic change in assessment would need to be voted on and approved by full-time department members. Each interview lasted between thirty and seventy-five minutes; all interviews occurred between June and September 2019. In accordance with my study's IRB protocol, I do not provide any identifying information in this chapter when I provide respondents' direct quotations. Of the thirteen participants, nine are quoted throughout this chapter. In order to eliminate the possibility of revealing potentially identifying information through an analysis of all quotations by one participant, I also do not assign a number to these participants (e.g., "anonymous informant #1").

The goals of this study were to gather a history of the first-year writing program at my institution and also to gather faculty members' thoughts on the design and content of the program itself, including the proficiency exam assessment—a high-stakes student assessment that was not being used for programmatic assessment. Embedded within these goals was an underlying purpose: to determine whether change to our writing program and its assessment was palatable. As one respondent told me during an interview, "Over time, it's the practice that's done over and over again that acquires the value and the significance, and the reasons that went into it in the first place get lost sometimes." Through my interviews, I wanted to uncover those reasons that had, it seemed, become lost in the tradition of the assessment event itself.

I audio recorded each interview and had the files transcribed for data analysis purposes; I then analyzed all data according to the methods of grounded theory (Charmaz 1995; Corbin and Strauss 2008). Charmaz describes these methods as systematic but flexible guidelines for analysis that result in constructing ideas and theories that are "grounded" in the data.

This contrasts with research approaches that begin with a stated hypothesis or theory and then test that hypothesis or theory. Grounded theory methods allow for interpretative analyses that rely on "knowledge from the 'inside'" and that "attempt to describe, explain and understand the lived experiences of a group of people" (Charmaz 1995, 30). In order to define "what the data are all about," I first completed specific line-by-line coding of the interview transcripts, known as open coding (37). According to Charmaz, coding involves "naming segments of data with a label that simultaneously categorizes, summarizes, and accounts for each piece of data" (43). This open coding process led to focused coding, which involves utilizing the most frequent codes discovered through the open coding process. Through this focused coding, I created more conceptual categories for the data and began to see the relationships, patterns, and connections between and within these categories.

According to Blumer (1969, 26), the concepts or themes that emerge during the coding process "usually become the chief means for establishing relations between data; and they are usually the anchor points in interpretation of the findings." Accordingly, in this chapter, I present the results of my data analysis as themes that emerged from the grounded theory process. Each theme is a synthesis of all interview responses and thus does not focus on the participants as individuals, but rather on the commonalities found among all interview responses. This helps to ensure the confidentiality of the study's participants. The themes are presented to provide a chronological look at the what and the how of writing assessment within a first-year writing program at a small liberal arts college (SLAC). I discuss how writing assessment has been defined, how it has been changed, and how it has affected the students, the instructors, and the overall first-year writing program.

What Was: Tradition, Control, "Big Data," and Anxiety

> *Some of the organizational features of SLAC writing programs reveal long-standing practices based more in tradition than in function. (Rutz 2012, x)*

In this first section, I present data from my interview study that focuses on the proficiency examination, its perceived value, and its recognized problems. Throughout this chapter, I use the gender-neutral singular "they" to refer to all respondents. This is an intentional choice to protect the anonymity of respondents and to add a level of consistency to my writing. Through themes that focus on the powers of tradition, control, and data, as well as on the related emotional effects, I discuss how writing assessment was defined and how the assessment impacted the first-year writing program, its instructors, and its students.

The Power of Tradition, Ritual, and History

> *Best assessment practice relies on new developments to shape assessment methods that prioritize student learning. Best assessment practice evolves. Revisiting and revising assessment practices should be considered periodically, as research in the field develops and evolves, and/or as the assessment needs or circumstances change. (CCCC 2022)*

The aspect of tradition and ritual in a writing program is nothing new; as I was reminded at the end of my Baltimore presentation, the story I told wasn't unique. A three-part proficiency examination had, until recently, been a defining component of first-year writing at my institution since the 1990s. This length of time may, in some part, be attributed to frequent turnover in the directorship of the first-year writing program. Additionally, all department members' terminal degrees are in literature as opposed to rhetoric or another related field; apart from occasionally teaching first-year composition courses, then, it is neither the intellectual focus nor, given how infrequently they teach first-year writing, the felt need of these faculty members to be initiating changes to the first-year writing program.

Part one of the proficiency examination tested students' textual analysis skills; part two tested students on grammar, mechanics, and usage; part three tested students' ability to compose a timed and handwritten argumentative essay based on several provided readings—readings that students encountered for the first time during the exam itself. (In 2018, the department chair and I made a small improvement that provided students with the essay readings weeks in advance of the exam itself. All other conditions of the exam remained. I sometimes think of this change, the first that had occurred to the exam in decades, as the first small step of the changes that were to come.) While parts one and two were administered during a class period, part three was administered during a three-hour block on the Saturday before the last full week of classes for the semester. Students needed to pass part three in addition to passing either part one *or* part two to pass the overall exam and receive credit for their first-year writing course; failing the exam meant retaking the course. Each part three essay was evaluated by two scorers; however, scorers submitted a rubric only for those essays scored as deficient. As a result, the program has only ever collected data on a small number of the essays submitted, essays that were unrepresentative of typical performance. Furthermore, this data has provided information limited strictly to areas of weakness in student writing: the rubric required scorers to note only things that were "wrong" with students' essays. This focus on the negative is one of the long-established problems of standardized tests. The proficiency examination was delivered to students in the manner described above until the spring 2020 semester, when the COVID-19 pandemic prevented the exam's administration.

During my interview study, several respondents discussed the importance of history and tradition with regard to the proficiency exam. One instructor discussed liking the "emotional and cultural effect in terms of the culture of the college, of having one day where every first-year student is writing something." Another instructor noted liking "the sense of occasion," "the way in which it creates a milestone in students' experience," and the way it "gives the department a sense of identity." In one interview, the respondent talked about using this milestone aspect to their advantage in the classroom to create a sense of teacher and student vs. the test. Instead of aligning their positionality with the test itself, this respondent positioned the test as the obstacle to work together against. They reported saying to students, "I didn't invent the test; it's out there. Everybody has to pass it. It's been here for twenty years; it's not going anywhere. So let's you and me work together, and I'll coach you." Given that students' successful completion of the course was tied to passing the proficiency examination, it is easy to understand why students would want to feel as though they had their instructor "on their side" to "beat" the examination. This feeling was undoubtedly aided by the fact that instructors did not score their own students' part three examinations: "It's a fact that I'm not grading them. That's a big thing because I'm their coach then. I'm the person who's there to help them to get through this. We have a whole different relationship, right from day one almost. I'm kind of their buddy and the person to encourage them and say, 'Yes, you can pass that.' But if I were giving the grade, then it's a different story."

Although these instructors identified a "positive" way to work within the tradition of the proficiency exam, several other professors discussed the negative pressures associated with teaching to a high-stakes test. Five of the thirteen respondents talked about "teaching to the test," with one noting that this "took time away from preparing students to develop writing as part of their other coursework." This instructor seems to position the test as "other"—as not aligned with the writing students are otherwise completing in the course. As Brookter (2012, 42) pointed out in their dissertation study on moving away from a proficiency exam model, "Colleges and universities across the country have found the need to measure English proficiency by testing for precision and balance following in the tradition of Harvard University, and many institutions do this testing despite the fact that they also question whether the test is an accurate measurement of the instruction in college composition on their campuses." There is, then, historical precedent that proficiency testing often continued despite realizations of its misalignment with course instruction and best practices in the development of students' writing. This was particularly true at my institution, where instructors spent the semester teaching students the process of writing only to have the semester end with a consequential assessment of one writing product, another marker of the staying power of the "one-ding" writing assessment.

Controlling the Curriculum, Its Instructors, and Its Students

> *Admissions, placement, and proficiency-based assessment practices are high-stakes processes with a history of exclusion and academic gatekeeping. Educational institutions and programs should recognize the history of these types of measures in privileging some students and penalizing others as it relates to their distinctive institutional and programmatic missions. (CCCC 2022)*

It wasn't just tradition that kept the proficiency examination in place: deeply embedded beliefs in the exam's power to let students know "we were serious about writing here" also perpetuated the exam's existence. Several instructors talked about these effects as positives, saying that they valued keeping the exam because "it helps students take the course more seriously" and "it sets a threshold that says, 'All right, you're not going to get through the net.'" Tellingly, another instructor stated, "We're not just going to pass you on because you checked all the boxes. You have to actually learn something and show us that you've learned it." Implicit in this statement is the idea that students were learning how to write impromptu timed essays throughout the semester. In reality, this was not the case, and students were being asked to show something through the examination that they did not learn in the course. Despite this, still another instructor expressed, "I think all of that is great. I would hate to see us eliminate the proficiency exam. I think it's an important concrete way of showing that we're not just saying it." Additionally, the exam persisted because of its association with setting standards for the quality and content of instruction for first-year writing faculty, the majority of whom have been and continue to be adjuncts. One faculty member stated that the proficiency exam "has served a kind of administrative purpose in terms of setting standards with adjuncts because we rely so heavily on them." Another said they had "no objection to the proficiency test" because "that's the way to keep faculty honest" and to hold "the faculty accountable." Important (and perhaps obvious) to note here is the fact that an instrument—such as a proficiency examination—used for individual student assessment is essentially unsuitable as an instrument for individual faculty assessment—such as a teaching observation.

Despite one instructor saying that the "nice thing about the proficiency exam" is the way it worked "to control the curriculum and make sure that everybody was leading to that testing mechanism at the end," several others described the control as negative and constraining: "Just by nature, I don't like the idea of feeling like I'm teaching to a test, and ultimately that's what it always felt like to me. I think it affected how I felt the course went, this idea of this gatekeeping thing at the end. I've never felt that comfortable with it." Several other instructors experienced the exam as constraining. As one instructor described, "I will tell them, 'You just need to simplify for this task' because it makes them think in a box. If they're going to be successful in that exam, they can't take many risks." On the one hand, then, the exam addressed fears of potential "curriculum drift," while on the other hand, the exam contradicted instructors' teaching throughout the semester.

Respondents identified just such tensions resulting from teaching to the test, particularly when the test does not align with the course outcomes: "I have problems with the final exam. It can become so formulaic. Just that whole essay approach. But you want students to be able to be successful in the exam. So you begin to teach toward the exam. But is that really allowing them to be really good, critical, creative thinkers? I don't think so." Developing students' critical thinking skills is one of the course's main learning objectives, but this instructor concluded that the proficiency exam created teaching and learning circumstances directly in contrast to that objective. In their position statement on writing assessment, the CCCC (2022) states, "Writing tasks and assessment criteria should be informed and motivated by the goals of the institution, the program, the curriculum, and the student communities that the program serves." Without this alignment, the assessment is a flawed instrument. Throughout my interviews with instructors, it was apparent that many recognized this mismatch between what was taught and what was tested, but still, the proficiency examination remained. As one instructor stated, any steps toward more of the creative and critical thinking intended in the course learning objectives were met with the reality of the power of tradition: "I find that the main problem for that kind of creative initiative is just a kind of, what's the word I'm looking for? Not traditionalism, but there's this sort of entropy that sort of sets in where people say, 'We've always done it this way, so why change it?'" The instructors were living and experiencing the inadequacies and constraints of the exam throughout the semester, but the power of tradition and of a "this is just the way it is" mindset held those conditions firmly in place.

Not surprisingly, these constraints negatively affected students and their learning. One professor noted that although the exam gives the course a certain focus, it does not do anything to actually help students' writing. Another professor shared this sentiment: "I don't see it as a learning tool. And I think if it's not a learning tool, it doesn't really have a place." Another described it as an "artificial situation" that doesn't "tell us anything about what students have learned." The proficiency exam did not provide students with opportunities to reflect, discuss, or revise over time, and thus likely resulted in students developing inaccurate and inconsistent notions of what writing is. Several scholars have used the word "constrained" in their descriptions of impromptu tests: Roberta Camp (2009, 113) described how this type of test "draws on only the most constrained of the processes and strategies available to writers," and Edward White, Norbert Elliot, and Irvin Peckham (2015, 21) stated that "timed, impromptu tests send a harmful signal that someone's writing ability can be inferred from such a constrained measure." The conditions of the exam itself also raised concerns, with one aspect being that students wrote their exam essays by hand: "But the handwriting is another false element to the whole thing. Who does that anymore?" The various constraints surrounding the proficiency examination negated what and how instructors taught. To the students, the message was clear: the talk differed from the walk, and the walk was the consequential determiner of their successful course completion.

Several participants described the exam as not inspiring their best teaching and as standing in stark contrast to what they tell students about writing effectively: "The exam doesn't actually measure what we're teaching them in class directly, which is how to develop a paper through an iterative process over the course of several weeks about something that you're studying in a class." Another professor stated, "It too much diminishes the work during the fifteen weeks of the course, by suggesting that what you do in one three-hour block really can erase what you've done for fifteen weeks. That seems to me kind of an incoherent theory of what the class is." In 2009, scholars Peggy O'Neill, Cindy Moore, and Brian Huot stated, "When consequences are high stakes . . . we have an even greater responsibility to ensure that methods are appropriate and theoretically sound, and that the results are valid; that is, they improve teaching and learning" (94). Faculty came to conclude that the proficiency examination did not fulfill this responsibility; however, several instructors did identify a responsibility they believed the exam was fulfilling—providing data that was helpful to the department and the college.

The Perceived Power of "Big Data"

> *Best assessment practice generates data that is shared with faculty and administrators in the program so that assessment results may be used to make changes in practice. These practices make use of assessment data to provide opportunities for reflection, professional development, and for the exchange of information about student performance and institutional or programmatic expectations. (CCCC 2022)*

Another anchor in the proficiency exam's staying power was a sense of the importance of the data produced from the exam's scoring. Several professors discussed the value of the proficiency exam in producing "big data assessment numbers" for the institution and its accrediting body. One instructor suggested, "The department has looked like the physics department in terms of our ability to generate data around our students. I think it would be a huge mistake to lose that tool, mostly because of [our accrediting body] and the way the institution is going to respond to us." This impression was incorrect, however: the big data was not big. It reported only on the small percentage of students for whom a deficiency rubric was completed.

Accordingly, the perceived importance of this data may have been overestimated. As another instructor explained, "Because they're doing it as a deficiency rather than an actual scoring of student writing, I don't think it's that helpful. I wouldn't not overhaul the program and eliminate the proficiency exam because of assessment. If the program said, 'Let's come up with an alternative to the proficiency exam,' I would not say, 'No, you can't do that; we need that for assessment purposes.'" Here the instructor is talking about student assessment—using the exam to determine students' successful course completion—not programmatic assessment. As another instructor similarly noted, good data depends on a good instrument: "If that's really the culmination of our ability to evaluate how effectively they write, I think that's a flawed instrument at this particular point." One instructor also noted that good data is useful data that informs changes and improvements: "Are we doing anything differently in [the course] because we see that [data]? I don't think so. Have we really done anything with that information? I don't think so." As this instructor rightly points out, collecting data that is not used to inform meaningful changes to practice renders the assessment process useless at the level of the writing program itself.

Emotional Toll

> *Writing and writing assessment are labor-intensive practices. Labor conditions and outcomes must be designed and implemented in pursuit of both the short-term and long-term health and welfare of all participants. (CCCC 2022)*

In addition to the effects discussed in this section, the proficiency exam also took an emotional toll on students and instructors alike. One instructor identified the psychological hardships it induced for students: "It's so stressful for the students. It's a tremendous amount of anxiety." As another instructor explained, "Students with anxiety come across that exam [and] it absolutely tortures them." The anxiety was not limited to the students: "On the professor's part, what if my students fail?" One respondent noted that the exam "intimidates adjuncts" and went on to say, "It intimidates me [a full-time professor] when I teach writing." This instructor talked about the apprehension of being judged by your colleagues based on how many of your students did not pass the proficiency exam. Consistently, O'Neill, Moore, and Huot (2009, 99) wrote, "Compositionists recognize that privileging the score of a single essay test over the instructor's course grade not only undermines the composition curriculum but also calls into question the authority of composition instructors (not to mention contradicting what we know about effective assessment and writing development and competency)." Having myself experienced the exam's administration as both an adjunct faculty member and as a full-time faculty member (albeit a non-tenure-track one), I identified with these same feelings of apprehension, mistrust, and intimidation.

Moving from What Was to What Is: A Common Essay for Programmatic Assessment

> *Nevertheless, SLACs can adapt to changing expectations, often embracing a challenging new idea more easily than a larger institution. (Rutz 2012, x)*

In this second section, with the framework of the results I presented in the previous section, I discuss how I moved forward with my collected data. In the table below, I present a list of my action steps organized by academic year. As you will see, my interview study was only one component of the process of initiating change to our first-year writing program.

Table 1: Action Steps by Academic Year

Academic Years	Action Steps
2017–2019	1. Learn the first-year writing program and its history 2. Design qualitative interview research study and obtain IRB approval
2019–2020	1. Conduct thirteen interviews and complete coding of transcripts
2020–2021	1. Compile thematic analyses of coding results 2. Write proposal and design corresponding pilot study to be completed in the 2021–2022 academic year
2021–2022	1. Present proposal to department 2. Complete pilot study with faculty focus group 3. Present pilot study results to department 4. Department votes to retire proficiency examination

Context

As stated earlier in this chapter, the three-part proficiency examination was delivered to all first-year writing students (approximately 600 students per academic year) until the spring 2020 semester, when the COVID-19 pandemic prevented the exam's administration. To adjust to remote-learning circumstances and to align assessment more meaningfully with what we know about writing as a collaborative and recursive process, the first-year writing program implemented a common essay assessment for the 2020–2021 academic year. Preceding this academic year, I was promoted to director of writing, a move that undoubtedly was helpful as I navigated this common essay implementation and the forthcoming proposal and pilot stages. Strangely enough, the pandemic was also helpful: it made replicating the proficiency exam's format and testing conditions impossible. As part of this change to assessment practice, parts one and two of the proficiency examination were eliminated, and the essay portion of the exam (part three) was revised to a common essay model. Students across all sections responded to the same group of readings and the same related argumentative essay prompt to compose a four-page essay; the readings (three to five readings total) were integrated into each section's syllabus in the weeks before the common essay was due. Over three weeks, students and instructors discussed the readings and essay prompt, students submitted a first draft to which instructors provided ungraded feedback, and students revised their writing according to that feedback. In these ways, the common essay reflected the way writing has always been taught in the critical writing course—as a process that is recursive and responsive to instructor feedback.

In writing about managing change in writing programs, scholar Geoffrey Chase (1997, 47) stated, "Specifically we need to think about the *local conditions* at our institutions, evaluate the *internal coherence* of our programs, and consider the degree to which our programs are *externally relevant*." While the common essay model is not as externally relevant to existing research on writing assessment as a portfolio model, it does align with the current local conditions of the institution: it is a change that the writing program had the infrastructure to absorb, especially coming on the heels of a pandemic. The common essay model creates internal coherence through alignment with our program's learning objectives. Additionally, the common essay and corresponding rubric align with the CCCC (2022) position statement on writing assessment: they provide opportunities to look at what students are doing well in their writing and how strategies learned show in that writing, including those strategies that recognize writing for the essentially social activity that it is.

During the 2020–2021 and 2021–2022 academic years, however, the common essays were scored in the same way the proficiency exam's part three essays had been scored—with a deficiency rubric that produced data on only a small number of essays and that was a deciding factor in students' course completion. While the common essay model itself, then, was a step forward, particularly in aligning instruction with assessment, that step was still, unfortunately, rooted in the history and tradition of "one-ding" writing assessments. Based on several conversations I had with writing faculty, while this instructional alignment was appreciated, the high-stakes nature of the assessment was still daunting—a feeling that was intensified due to students' (and instructors') additional pandemic-related stressors and struggles. As an administrator of the first-year writing program, however, I did not feel a sense of pushback from first-year writing faculty members regarding the common essay; rather, I felt a renewed sense of energy to keep pushing forward, to keep making the changes that so many instructors had been hoping for but not expecting. To remove the final barrier to progress, I conducted a pilot study during the 2021–2022 academic year, alongside the traditional format, to show the value of using the common essays for programmatic assessment of our first-year writing program instead of for high-stakes student assessment. Although there was no way to replicate this during the pilot study, in the future, students will submit their final common essays both to their course instructors as a graded component of the first-year writing course and to a separate course within the college's learning management system (LMS) for programmatic assessment.

Proposal and Pilot Study

My first step in initiating this pilot study was writing and delivering an eighteen-page proposal to department members. This proposal had two primary purposes: first, to explain the rationale of replacing the proficiency examination with a common essay; second, to explain the rationale of using the common essay as a tool for programmatic assessment. Within the proposal, which was co-authored with another department member, we presented the details of the common essay process, including a timeline for the pilot project to be completed during the 2021–2022 academic year, and a new assessment rubric. We then presented supporting evidence for the adoption of this proposal in the form of research-based best practices, analysis from my qualitative interview study, and statements of support from relevant professionals within the academic community (see Appendix B). Here is a timeline of the proposal and the resulting pilot study:

Table 2: Timeline

Date	Action Steps
September 2021	1. Deliver proposal to department faculty members for review
October–November 2021	1. Form faculty group for pilot study
December 2021	1. All course sections complete the common essay assessment 2. All common essays are scored in the traditional format
January 2022	1. Sample of common essays uploaded to assessment software program for rubric scoring by faculty pilot group
March 2022	1. Pilot group meets to discuss data produced during scoring process
April 2022	1. Pilot results shared with department for review and discussion 2. Official department vote on implementation of common essay for programmatic assessment purposes

One goal of the pilot study, in addition to collecting data on student writing across the program according to program learning objectives, was modeling what the process would look like in future academic years by using a portion of the common essays submitted during the fall 2021 semester. My first step after delivering the proposal was to solicit five department members for the pilot study group. With the financial support of a student learning assessment group on campus, we were able to provide faculty participants with a stipend for their participation. In addition to scoring essays according to the developed rubric, participants attended three meetings: an introductory meeting, a meeting focused on grade-norming and reliability, and a concluding meeting to discuss the scoring process.

From the common essays that were submitted during the fall 2021 semester to a central learning management system course, a random sampling of one hundred essays was uploaded to a shared space assessment program. I determined this sample number in consultation with the institution's institutional research office. Using several practice essays, the faculty scorers participated in a reliability exercise and discussion prior to scoring on their own; this proved to be invaluable in ensuring a smooth, cohesive, and consistent scoring process. The faculty readers then used the provided rubric to score twenty essays each, with each essay being read one time. The rubric guided each scorer to consider what students were doing well in their writing in the areas of their thesis, use of evidence, development of counterargument, structure and organization, and demonstration of usage expectations of academic English. Although it is beyond the scope of this chapter to present the pilot results in detail, collecting criteria-based data on a large, representative sample of the common essays resulted in usable information on where our students are with their writing: what they are doing effectively and where they need to improve. As the CCCC (2022) position statement on writing assessment explains, "Assessment of writing programs, from first-year composition programs to Writing Across the Curriculum programs, is a critical component of an institution's culture of assessment. Assessment can focus on the operation of the program, its effectiveness to improve student writing, and how it best supports university goals." The information we collected is being used to make changes and improvements to our teaching practices, and we are tailoring professional development opportunities for instructors to the results of our data collection. I presented the pilot results to the department in April 2022, after which the department voted unanimously and officially to replace the proficiency exam with the common essay model.

Conclusion

If, as my experience in Baltimore suggested, the field clearly knows better than to use a proficiency examination model of assessment, then why does this study matter? The ethical problems of the proficiency exam model have, after all, been made abundantly clear. According to the CCCC (2022), "Assessments that involve timed tests, rely solely on machine scoring, or primarily judge writing based on prescriptive grammar and mechanics offer a very limited view of student writing ability and have a history of disproportionately penalizing students from marginalized populations." The proficiency exam as it existed at my institution also had consequences for the instructors, particularly contingent faculty members.

The ethical problems of other forms of assessment, however, may not be as clear. What, as writing program administrators at both small and large institutions, can we consider to make the ethics of assessment inclusive of students and faculty alike? Who is included in assessment work and decisions, and who is excluded? Part of my strategic approach to this study's design was informed by feelings of exclusion: how would a non-tenure-track writing program administrator gain a seat at the decision-making table? As an adjunct faculty member giving the proficiency examination before I was hired in my full-time capacity, I can remember feeling lucky that I had a job that allowed me to administer assessments to students. In other words, I was so grateful to have a job that it rendered me (temporarily) unable to reflect on the assessment process in which I was participating. What are the consequences of our assessment practices on ourselves, on each other, and on our students? More broadly, how do the conditions of our labor affect our ability, perceived or actual, to initiate change to any practice, assessment or otherwise? As noted by the CCCC (2022), "There is no perfect assessment measure, and best practices in all assessment contexts involve reflections by stakeholders on the effectiveness and ethics of all assessment practices." In my work now, post the study described in this chapter, I am focusing my reflections on how to advocate for our adjunct faculty members to participate in the programmatic assessment process in the future, how to create professional development opportunities for our instructors based on those programmatic assessment results, and how to ensure compensation for the work involved in both. The CCCC (2022) stated, "Ethical assessment practices involve asking difficult questions about the values and missions of an assignment, a course, or a program and whether or not assessments promote or possibly inhibit equity among participants." Regardless of whether we work at a SLAC, a mid-sized college, or a large university, the most important work we can do is to ask and to face the difficult questions, and to know where to turn for help brainstorming the answers. As Carol Rutz (2012, ix) wrote in her foreword to the first text in this series, Gladstein and Regaignon's *Writing Program Administration at Small Liberal Arts Colleges*, " . . . SLACs have much to learn from one another—and much to teach colleagues at other, larger institutions."

As noted by the CCCC (2022), "Ethical assessment is always an ongoing process of negotiating the historical impacts of writing assessment, the need for a clear portrait of what is happening in classrooms and programs, and the concern for the best interests of all assessment participants." The historical impacts of scholars studying proficiency exams were largely occurring before the time my institution was beginning its proficiency examination. We now, in 2023, have a clear plan in place for programmatic assessment, which Yancey (1999) placed in the third wave of writing assessment, beginning in 1986. At times, the process of navigating the much-needed and long-overdue changes to the first-year writing assessment at my institution was painfully slow and painstakingly deliberate. Reassurance comes, though, from Geoffrey Chase (1997, 53–54) who noted, "Composition programs need to change and develop over time . . . This is as it should be." What results is, perhaps, an imperfect description of an imperfect process. Both description and process, though, align with the spirit of what I heard three years ago from the back corner of a room in Baltimore—they are the real; they are the actual; they are the struggle. One of the most significant takeaways from this process, for me and hopefully for others, is the importance of knowing your audience, assessing their needs, and responding accordingly. In my case, I knew that to enact a change as big as removing the proficiency exam from its long-standing throne in our first-year writing program, I needed to respond to the needs of my audience members—in my case, the department members who would ultimately be voting for or against adopting the change. I needed to show what was wrong, why it was wrong, and what a better way forward was, and I needed to show these things with data from our department, from our first-year writing instructors, and from our first-year writing students. Slow and deliberate? Yes. Rewarding and worthy? Yes. Still work to be done? Always.

Bibliography

Belanoff, Pat. 1991. "The Myths of Assessment." *Journal of Basic Writing* 10, no. 1: 54–66.

Blumer, Herbert. 1969. *Symbolic Interactionism: Perspective and Method.* Oakland: University of California Press.

Brookter, Josye Marie. 2012. "What's in a Test? Constructions of Literacy and Its Implications for English Proficiency Test Design." PhD dissertation, University of Southern Mississippi.

Camp, Roberta. 2009. "Changing the Model for the Direct Assessment of Writing." In *Assessing Writing: A Critical Sourcebook*, edited by Brian Huot and Peggy O'Neill, 102–30. Boston: Bedford/St. Martin's.

CCCC (Conference on College Composition and Communication). 2022. "Writing Assessment: A Position Statement." https://cccc.ncte.org/cccc/resources/positions/writingassessment. Accessed July 2023.

Charmaz, Kathy. 1995. "Grounded Theory." In *Rethinking Methods in Psychology*, edited by Jonathan A. Smith, Rom Harre, and Luk Van Langenhove, 27–49. Thousand Oaks: Sage.

Chase, Geoffrey. 1997. "Redefining Composition, Managing Change, and the Role of the WPA." *WPA: Writing Program Administration* 21, no. 1: 46–54.

Corbin, Juliet, and Anselm Strauss. 2008. *Basics of Qualitative Research: Techniques and Procedures for Developing Grounded Theory.* Thousand Oaks: Sage.

Durst, Russel K., Marjorie Roemer, and Lucille M. Schultz. 1994. "Portfolio Negotiations: Acts in Speech." In *New Directions in Portfolio Assessment: Reflective Practice, Critical Theory and Large-Scale Scoring,* edited by Laurel Black, Donald A. Daiker, Jeffrey Sommers, and Gail Stygall, 286–302. Portsmouth: Boynton/Cook.

Elbow, Peter, and Pat Belanoff. 1986. "Portfolios as a Substitute for Proficiency Examinations." *College Composition and Communication* 37, no. 3: 336–39. https://doi.org/10.2307/358050.

Melzer, Dan. 2013. "Using System Thinking to Transform Writing Programs." *Writing Program Administration* 36, no. 2: 75–94.

O'Neill, Peggy, Cindy Moore, and Brian Huot. 2009. *Guide to College Writing Assessment.* WAC Clearinghouse: University Press of Colorado. https://doi.org/10.2307/j.ctt4cgrbz.

Rutz, Carol. 2012. "Foreword: Writing Programs at Liberal Arts Colleges: Treasures in Small Packages." In *Writing Program Administration at Small Liberal Arts Colleges,* by Jill M. Gladstein and Dara Rossman Regaignon, ix–xi. Anderson: Parlor Press.

White, Edward, Norbert Elliot, and Irvin Peckham. 2015. *Very Like a Whale: The Assessment of Writing Programs.* Logan: Utah State University Press.

Yancey, Kathleen Blake. 1999. "Looking Back as We Look Forward: Historicizing Writing Assessment." *College Composition and Communication* 50, no. 3: 483–503. https://doi.org/10.2307/358862.

Appendix A

"Full-Time Faculty Histories and Perceptions of the First-Year Writing Program": Semi-Structured Interview Questions

I asked the following questions to each study participant. Depending on answers and contextual differences, I utilized additional questions not noted here.

1. Tell me about the history of the first-year writing program as you have experienced it.

2. Have you ever taught in the first-year writing program? When? For how long?

3. What, in your opinion, has the first-year writing program done well? What has worked well in first-year writing courses?

4. What, in your opinion, has the first-year writing program perhaps fallen short of doing?

5. Would you currently recommend any changes be made to the first-year writing program? If so, what would those changes be?

6. How valuable do you feel the current student assessment (the proficiency exam) in the first-year writing program is? Is this type of assessment one that you think the first-year writing program should still have? Why or why not?

7. For those who have taught in the first-year writing program: When have you felt / did you feel the most rewarded and engaged in your teaching of this class? When, on the other hand, did you feel disengaged and unmotivated in your teaching of this class?

Appendix B

Replacing the Proficiency Examination with a Common Essay:

Proposal Table of Contents
Executive Summary
Proposal
       Pilot implementation
       Potential benefits
       Potential costs
Proposed common essay rubric
Timeline
Support for proposal: research
       On the need to replace the proficiency exam
       On the value of assessing the program, not the student
       On the value of the common essay

Support for proposal: Results of interview study
Support for proposal: Fall 2020 instructor feedback
Support for proposal: Statements of support
Works cited
Appendix: Potential objections to the proposal

6 Amplifying Student Voice in Writing Program Assessment through Mutual Mentoring and Students as Partners

Hannah Bellwoar and Abby Madar

Abstract: In this chapter, the authors—one of whom is a writing program administrator and professor and one of whom is a student and project coordinator for the writing program—argue that through, students-as-partners (SaP), and feminist qualitative research frameworks, pedagogical partnerships can be used to center students in assessment work and bring about institutional change. Using their partnership at Juniata College—a rural liberal arts college in central Pennsylvania with a student population of about 1300—as a case study, this chapter shows how amplifying student voice through their partnership benefits them personally as well as the college as a whole, particularly equity-seeking groups at the college. They provide a framework for collaborative analysis of qualitative data in assessment work to amplify student voice.

Our Stories of Mentoring Relationships

Hannah: When I was an undergraduate student studying literature at Temple University, I decided to take a class that would train me to be a writing tutor. Though I knew nothing about the field of writing studies, the course and opportunity sounded interesting to me. After I completed the course and became a writing associate and writing center tutor, I became so energized by writing studies that I decided to go to graduate school in the field. What energized and inspired me? A network of mentoring: the one-on-one meetings with my professor and writing program director Eli Goldblatt, the professional development and staff meetings with other writing center tutors and the writing program administrators, and the conversations with my peer writing center tutors. For the first time in my academic career, I felt like I had a voice, and that the ideas I contributed had value and were meaningful contributions, that I had value. I was hooked. It was not until 2019, twenty years later, that I realized I was involved in mutual mentoring.

Abby: My senior year at Juniata College was full of new opportunities for me, including how I was welcomed into faculty discussions and how I learned about academic research from a variety of sources. Hannah Bellwoar was a mentor for me in different ways, as she was not only the advisor for my senior capstone project, but also the supervisor for my work as a Juniata associate (JA), and the assessment and project coordinator for general education and writing. We met regularly throughout the year, so she always knew where I was at in my process of writing and learning. She provided guidance and instruction for me as the traditional idea of a mentor would, with her the expert and I the listener. What I did not expect was that I would become confident enough to feel as though my ideas were valued not only for my own project, but for projects that involved the college as an institution. As a JA, I attended meetings for the Office of Institutional Effectiveness, where I believed I would just listen to the faculty discuss ideas and learn from them. Instead, I realized that I could question things and offer my own perspective, and that participation would help me learn much more than being a silent observer.

Applying Our Experiences to Partner with Students in Writing Program Assessment

Though we acknowledge the value of having our voices be included and valued in our personal stories, we know that in writing program assessment, including student voice can be fraught and messy. Reports may represent one unified, homogenous student voice rather than multiple heterogenous and sometimes conflicting student voices. Student comments may be used to tokenize or misrepresent students with marginalized identities from equity-seeking groups (de Bie et al. 2021), which maintains hierarchical relationships rather than representing multiple student perspectives alongside other data to drive decision making. Though in writing program assessment both qualitative and quantitative data may be gathered, assessment is often focused on quantitative data and direct measures of student learning. We have found, however, that analysis of qualitative data undertaken by both faculty and students in collaborative partnerships can help with some of these traps.

We see broad connections between the work of assessment, particularly the use of qualitative data, and pedagogical partnerships. All of these can bring about institutional change. Assessment is designed to measure student learning and teaching effectiveness, designed to bring about institutional change. Qualitative data can be used to articulate harms and sense of belonging with more depth alongside quantitative data. Pedagogical partnerships can redress harms and work towards equity and justice. Taken together, these activities can be used to amplify student voice.

Furthermore, these activities are particularly well poised to bring about change in a small liberal arts college (SLAC) context. Gladstein and Regaignon, drawing on Raymond Williams' "structure of feeling," a common ethos among these types of institutions, articulate that SLACs typically take a collective approach to general education, have minimal leadership and bureaucratic structures, and support face-to-face and close work between students and faculty. They write, "Within the context of their particular structure of feeling, they can . . . adapt [best practices developed by the field] to the institution's goals" (Gladstein and Regaignon 2012, 194). Pedagogical partnerships are common and valued at SLACs, as we found at Juniata when we began working together in 2020. Indeed, Juniata has an elected general education committee where faculty regularly propose new courses and make changes to the curriculum, a flat administrative structure that reports to the associate provost, and student representatives on the committees and in the offices that govern general education. All of these components indicate that small and flat institutions like Juniata might be able to innovate and embrace the needs of new populations of students.

Juniata College is located in Huntingdon, Pennsylvania, a rural town of approximately 7,000 in central Pennsylvania, about three and a half hours from the major metropolitan areas of Pittsburgh or Philadelphia. It was founded in 1876 by members of the Church of the Brethren and maintains a strong connection with these roots, particularly through the Baker Institute for Peace and Conflict Studies. The current student body is 1,300 and the student-to-faculty ratio is twelve to one. Juniata is a predominantly white institution (70 percent white), and a majority of students are from Pennsylvania (60 percent). About one third of the student body are first-generation college students. Hannah Bellwoar is the director of general education and writing at the college, and she oversees the first-year writing sequence, writing across the curriculum, and the Connections course, which is an interdisciplinary course taken in the third or fourth year. As director of general education and writing, Hannah reports to the associate provost for institutional effectiveness and is part of the Office of Institutional Effectiveness along with the associate provost, director of institutional research, director of advising, and three student assistants. Abby was one of the student assistants, working directly with Hannah as the assessment and project coordinator for general education.

In this chapter, we argue that student-faculty partnerships can disrupt hierarchy and bring about institutional change. We use reflections on our process of analyzing qualitative data, writing assessment reports, and presenting our findings to explore how mutual mentoring and collaboration between faculty and students-as-partners in analyzing qualitative data can bring student voice into institutional assessment. We demonstrate how representing multiple perspectives alongside other data disrupts the hierarchy of admin/faculty/student, researcher/researched, and student/(multiply)-marginalized student and representing multiple and sometimes conflicting student voices works against one unified student voice, an oversimplification that overlooks how each participant is their own individual person. We see these partnerships changing the culture as a whole through grassroots efforts, shifting to mutuality from a hierarchical and power-based framework.

Welcoming students as partners (SaP) is key to contesting how power is used to maintain bias and hierarchy in educational institutions. Student voices should be valued in all aspects of their education, but they are often dismissed, particularly those of equity-seeking students. Gladstein and Regaignon call this "values in tension." They state "The focus on education as occurring through individual relationships (between faculty and students) leads to a notion that students can and must struggle with questions of direction and purpose in order to learn. This belief in autonomous individualism leads to a principled refusal at the institutional and the pedagogical levels to spell things out" (Gladstein and Regaignon 2012, 21). Therein lies the tension—as SLACs may value learning that happens in relationships, the relationships often remain hierarchical, excluding particular faculty and students as the institutions grow more diverse.

Pedagogical and Research Partnerships

We have observed that the small liberal arts college context at Juniata has allowed for partnerships between students and faculty in a couple of ways that had a big impact on our collaboration. According to Moore, the SaP framework "forefronts students and faculty working in collaboration to enhance teaching and learning," engages student voices, and pushes for shared ownership (Moore et al. 2020, 33). Shared ownership is particularly important in understanding these partnerships as collaborations—all collaborators regardless of rank are generating questions and following research trajectories in order to make observations and discoveries in the process.

Students-as-Partners in the Small Liberal Arts College context

As a collaboration in a student-faculty research team, through our partnership of one student and one faculty member, we were both able to contribute from our perspectives to represent the various student voices included in our assessment. By analyzing student voice in the qualitative research component of the assessment, the reports are not our voices alone but representative of multiple student voices. At its heart, we believe that these pedagogical partnerships between faculty and students can bring about institutional change; partnerships open up the possibilities and allow us to draw on more than our own experiences for change.

Furthermore, pedagogical partnerships such as the framework from de Bie et al. can redress harms and work towards equity and justice. Here are the three reasons they outline for how their framework can do this work:

1. Typical approaches to equity and justice focus on legislative changes and overlook affective harms or sense of belonging.

2. Those who have never experienced these harms may be less able to understand them.

3. Pedagogical partnerships emphasize respectful and reciprocal relationships that impact these harms and are well suited to bring about change.

They go on to say that pedagogical partnership "affirms students, especially those from equity-seeking groups, as knowers; recognizes students' knowledge gained from diverse backgrounds and experiences; and develops and shares students' knowledge, which can, in turn, facilitate broader change" (de Bie et al. 2021, 23). Certainly, this has been our experience with pedagogical partnerships, as our stories suggest. Abby was able to add a meaningful layer to her education through her work as a JA. She had always loved the college and its English department, but being a part of the work beyond being a student gave her a deeper understanding. It strengthened her relationships both with the college and faculty and also her relationship with her own education. Instead of simply doing whatever work she was told to do, as would be the case in a typical hierarchical supervisory relationship, she was able to be involved in decision-making and discussions considering the experiences of students and faculty. Feeling valued for her work was key for her growth in her varied roles at Juniata: student, learner, researcher, partner.

The SaP framework is reflective of the apprenticeship models valued at small colleges. According to Gladstein and Regaignon,

> Students at small colleges are apprentice scholars and leaders; they are all assumed to have an intellectual interest in their own educations. This approach to pedagogy and curricula then informs not just major curricula, which send high percentages of students to graduate school every year, but also general education. These institutions are premised upon a liberal arts commitment to the non-professionalizing education of the whole student. Their size makes this feasible. (Gladstein and Regaignon 2012, 15–16)

We believe SaP and apprenticeship models at Juniata are designed to give students voice—to allow them to be seen, acknowledged, and feel connected in the teaching and learning at the institution. For us, student perspectives and feelings about their learning are important to understand as part of the assessment process. Juniata has two programs for students that we feel fit this apprenticeship model— JA and writing associates. Abby became a writing associate in 2020 and a JA in 2021, serving in both of these roles before and during the assessment process.

The JA program follows an apprenticeship model, elevating students to collaborative experiences with faculty and administrative professionals. JA positions are meant to provide real-life experience to student employees, including research and other skills in academia, as well as management and leadership skills, depending on the position. JAs are senior students serving in "skilled roles in which they have had significant academic and/or experiential preparation." JAs have more responsibilities in their positions than other student employees, and they often work closely with faculty and staff who oversee the programs in which JAs work. In these ways, the JA program follows an apprenticeship model that "recognizes and rewards top performers and signals to students that they should start self-help early in their college careers. It will also generate résumé building experiences for students" (Juniata College 2022). Being a JA allows collaboration with their faculty or staff supervisors and can be an introduction to how a professional career may function. There are a limited number of JAs employed each year, and as a more competitive and coveted position, JAs can feel that their work is significant and unique to them.

The writing program at Juniata has three JAs: 1) The writing center JA works with the writing center director and manages writing center employees and events; 2) The writing associates JA similarly works with the writing associates director and manages writing associates; 3) The general education and writing program JA works with the director of general education and writing on assessment and other general education projects—Abby served in this position for the academic year 2021-2022.

As a JA, Abby worked with Hannah, who was her mentor on projects such as the assessment of first-year writing courses. JAs are often recruited by their supervisors because of prior relationships they have. Abby was recruited because of Hannah's observations of her skills in coursework—working on a student team with clients in the professional editing course and working as a qualitative researcher in the research methods and capstone courses. As a student partner, Abby was given freedom and responsibility to assess and analyze qualitative data from student surveys. The work we did together was collaborative, and both of our contributions to the project carried the same importance and respect.

Student partnership does not have to place students in the same role as a faculty member, they simply need the ability to provide equal contributions to a project. The trust and respect that students feel from being a valued partner can boost their confidence and prepare them for future endeavors. Working together on a task or project is a significant shift from traditional, more theoretical learning to more concrete, hands-on experience. Kuh includes mentored undergraduate research as a high-impact practice, noting that these educational practices benefit students from historically underserved groups in higher education, promoting equity and retention (Kuh 2008). Additionally, the SaP model promotes independence, motivation, and self-reflection from students (Felten, Bovill, and Cook-Sather 2014).

The writing associates program at Juniata demonstrates and is built on the model of SaP. It is a writing fellows and peer tutoring program for first-year writing, though there are considerations to expand it to other writing intensive components of general education. The instructor of each first-year composition and first-year seminar class has a writing associate assigned to that class who acts as the first-year students' college writing coach. Writing associates are modeled after SaP because they not only coach students on writing, but also act as the students' advocate to the professor should any challenges arise. First-year writing professors work closely with their writing associates, discussing assignments, student challenges, and support interventions. Writing associates provide a unique perspective from being "in between" the students and the professor. Their insight on how students are doing and how to help them succeed is valuable to the professor, and their knowledge on what constitutes a successful assignment is valuable to the students. In this way, SaP promotes shared ownership of the process and reciprocity in the work.

Mutual Mentoring: Networks of Partners

We think the framework of mutual mentoring makes a lot of sense for faculty, administrator, and student collaboration on assessment in a small liberal arts college context. According to Moore, "Whereas teaching and advising roles . . . often assume a hierarchical relationship, mentoring relationships are reciprocal and broadly encompassing of the whole person" (Moore et al. 2020, 31). They argue that although one-on-one mentoring is the norm in the field of writing studies, there is the potential to scale up access to undergraduate research through mutual mentoring.

Moore recommends that mutual mentoring be informed by research such as that on research teams and co-mentoring, which is "the collaborative, simultaneous mentoring of a student by two or more faculty members" (Ketcham et al. 2018, 155). The co-mentoring structure of the Office of Institutional Effectiveness at Juniata served this purpose. Mentees and mentors were able to mentor each other in a sustainable way, "broadening access to these meaningful relationships beyond the traditional one-to-one mentoring that is common in the humanities" (Moore et al. 2020, 32). We did this through group meetings where all members of the Office of Institutional Effectiveness shared ideas, asked questions, and provided feedback. Additionally, feedback was provided on Abby's work as a JA through the career readiness assessment form (See Appendix A).

Moore also recommends that mutual mentoring be informed by the salient practices of undergraduate research (Shanahan et al. 2015). These ten practices[1] support students' intellectual, personal, emotional, and professional growth as they engage in undergraduate research and can support structures of reciprocity within undergraduate research. We believe supporting reciprocity is central to making hierarchical change within the institution. It's not enough to invite students into assessment work; we must instead build structures that support students to freely and equally participate in all stages of the assessment research process.

We acknowledge that making structural changes such as these is challenging at institutions of higher education that are slow to change; SLACs can be more nimble and more readily do so, but building these structures can still be challenging for a variety of reasons. At Juniata, we often have one or a few people working on projects for institutional change; these projects are very dependent on the people in those positions supporting them rather than being a part of the structure of the institution. Since Hannah's research has been focused on collaborative mentoring and undergraduate research in writing studies, she was able to draw on co-mentoring models and habits of mind of mentors (Hall, Abbot, and Bellwoar 2019) to begin to build structures of support. For us, those structures were primarily meetings: weekly Office of Institutional Effectiveness meetings where Abby and other students provided input on projects including assessment and weekly one-on-one meetings where Hannah and Abby exchanged ideas and worked collaboratively on projects in real time. But meetings are time- and labor-intensive structures, and faculty will have various levels of motivation to sustain these structures (Morales, Grineski, and Collins 2017). While we agree with Moore that "mutual mentoring should extend from

---

1. The ten salient practices of mentoring are:
    1. Engage in strategic pre-planning.
    2. Set clear, and well-scaffolded expectations.
    3. Teach technical skills, methods, and techniques.
    4. Balance rigorous expectations with emotional support and appropriate personal interest in students.
    5. Build a community among members of the team.
    6. Dedicate time to one-on-one, hands-on mentoring.
    7. Increase student ownership over time.
    8. Support students' professional development through networking and explaining norms of the discipline.
    9. Create intentional opportunities for peers and near-peers to learn mentoring skills.
    10. Encourage and guide students through the dissemination of their findings. (Shanahan, et al., 362–70)

question-formation to shared writing, presenting, and publication, with an explicit assumption that all members are capable of contributing meaningfully" (Moore et al. 2020, 41) and saw that this extension was supported as well when members of the Office of Institutional Effectiveness wrote reports together and shared these reports with various college audiences, we understand the challenges for replicability and sustainability, especially when resources are scarce.

We drew on available resources to try to build sustainable structures to support our collaboration, which centered on mutual mentoring. Mutual mentoring draws on non-hierarchical collaborative networks, and each person in the network brings specific knowledge and experience, in this case, to the assessment work. There are other students, faculty, and administrators involved in the assessment work that also participated in mutual mentoring, for example, the associate provost of institutional effectiveness and his intern, another undergraduate student, the general education committee, and instructors of first-year composition who use the assessment data to make changes to the course to better support students. The network of relationships is formed to benefit all members of the network. In particular, we drew on preexisting Juniata structures to support our work: the English department's capstone course for mentored undergraduate research, which is included in Hannah's teaching load; the JA program that paid Abby for her work; the Lakso Center for the Scholarship of Teaching and Learning for professional development grants. By drawing on these, we were able to extend our collaboration in writing this book chapter.

Partnering with participants in qualitative research

We argue that because SLACs value relationships, qualitative research has the potential to support institutional change and amplify student voice. We use feminist qualitative research methods to support this argument. Wolf (1992), Kirsch and Ritchie (1995), and Ferganchick-Neufang (1999) have advocated for "reflexivity" in research, whereby researchers reflect on their own values and experiences in the research, knowing that "research is not and cannot be value-neutral or objective because the questions we ask, the methods we choose, the patterns we see, are all products of our subjectivity" (Ferganchick-Neufang 1999, 23). Ferganchick-Neufang argues that this is particularly important in writing program administration work because we must rely on the particular context we find ourselves in to drive decision making and support the faculty and students involved in the teaching and learning of writing at their institutions, faculty who are often contingent labor, and students who are often (multiply)-marginalized and equity-seeking.

While Wolf advocates for a shift away from seeing people being researched as "object," instead seeing people as "subject" of research, Kirsch and Ritchie propose a slightly different form of reflexivity for composition researchers, calling for them to "theorize their locations by examining their experiences as reflections of ideology and culture, by reinterpreting their own experiences through the eyes of others, and by recognizing their own split selves, their multiple and often unknowable identities" (**Kirsch and Ritchie 1995, 8**). Furthermore, they call for researchers to invite people to collaborate as "participant," participating not only in answering questions, but also in developing research questions, interpreting data, and shaping and guiding new lines of inquiry within the research project. Royster (2000) extended further the term "participants" by calling them "mentors/guides" of research.

As part of a self-reflective and inclusive approach to research in considering our own project, we see the ideas of critical participatory action research (CPAR) as essential in efforts to collect and analyze data, especially those that will be used to create or support equity initiatives. CPAR is designed to eliminate injustice in research. Fine and Torre explain, "Rooted in the activist call 'No research on us, without us,' CPAR projects reposition those who have traditionally been the objects of study . . . as co-researchers, sitting alongside traditionally trained researchers, crafting the questions, methods, analyses, and research products" (**Fine and Torre 2021, 3**). We think the concepts of mentor/guides and co-researchers align well with our understanding of pedagogical partnerships and the benefits of mutual mentoring.

Partnership in Assessment

Juniata revised its general education curriculum in 2019 and increased required first-year writing courses from one to two; students take first-year composition (FYC) in the fall and first-year seminar (FYS) in the spring. The revised curriculum also includes an e-Portfolio that students contribute to for each of the thirteen general education courses and experiences. Assessment is driven according to a five-year matrix (See Appendix B), where each component and learning outcome is assessed. For the first year's assessment, we gathered data on written communication, oral communication, and information literacy in the first-year courses.

The assessment had two main components—a rubric assessment of written communication and persuasive argument skills (See Appendix C) in a sample of eighty-three papers out of 370 from twenty-three sections of FYC taught in fall 2019, and a fall 2019 self-report data from 269 out of 422 first-year students and spring 2020 self-report data from 166 out of 422 first-year students on the process-oriented approach to writing instruction and oral communication they were taught. These surveys (See Appendix D) included quantitative and qualitative questions such as:

- If FYC helped them to learn how to construct arguments in college-level writing and use writing process strategies as outlined in the faculty handbook.
- How often they utilized the writing associates to develop a process-oriented approach to writing and meet the learning outcomes of the course.
- Open-ended questions about what students found most useful and what they would like to change about FYC.

As a student researcher, Abby wished to present as many student perspectives as possible, but her reflexivity put her in a position to only make evaluations on what to include based on her own bias of what she believed was important. She had to make decisions on what to include and what to exclude, which could allow her own thoughts and experiences to take over the data. Because she recognized this, she tried to identify a variety of feedback, even if it did not align with what she had personally experienced or believed. For student responses on how to improve the course, she pulled out quotes from students with concrete suggestions, even if she did not agree. As only one student, she did not want her own interpretation of the college to dictate what to share from the other students' feedback.

Identifying patterns was a way to get a consistent view of student perspectives. Abby went through each response and identified a category that it would fall under. Any student response that said they valued writing associates, conferences with their professors, or the writing center became a tally in one category—the "writing associates/conferences/writing center" category. After sharing her categories with Hannah, this category became "live feedback." Discussing the findings together was how we were able to analyze the data and flesh out what many students were saying. In this case, students said that a real-time dialogue with another person was helpful to improve their writing.

Student Voice in Qualitative Research

After gathering these data, we wrote up our analysis in reports (See Appendix E) and presented our assessment findings to the entire college faculty and to the FYC and FYS instructors specifically to make changes to the courses and close the loop on assessment. Here is a summary of our four key findings:

- Over 65 percent of the respondents agreed that FYC helped them to meet the learning outcomes of the course.
- Over 80 percent of the respondents agreed that FYC helped them use writing strategies embedded in the learning outcomes such as research, drafting, and editing papers.
- In scoring papers in the rubric assessment, scorers found the greatest weakness was discussion and identification of counterarguments.
- The qualitative questions on the survey showed that students found that live feedback was most useful to them in developing writing skills. This includes peer feedback, professor conferences, writing associates, and writing center meetings.

As we partnered to work with the qualitative data, we sought to invite participation in reciprocal and reflexive ways. The qualitative data we worked with were student responses to survey questions about the strengths and weaknesses of Juniata's first-year writing courses. Abby's position as a student collecting other student voices was an interesting one. Her goal was to identify patterns and themes, but she also did not want to ignore valuable feedback. At the same time, she was learning how to analyze data through the experience of doing so. She did not have a preconceived idea of what her findings might look like or how she would address them because she had little prior experience with qualitative research. As part of discovering things about qualitative research, she found that she could not elevate every student's voice. If only one person had a particular suggestion for how to improve their student experience in the writing program, they were not statistically significant, no matter how useful their suggestion may be. Qualitative research aims to amplify unique, individual voices, but the first step in approaching qualitative data is to identify patterns and themes. If an individual's response did not fit into a category, it was not part of a pattern and could easily be overlooked. We observed this limitation of assessment as it enabled dismissing one student voice as not relevant in order to generalize the findings so they could be useful to faculty.

Discussion with FYC faculty, a presentation to the general college faculty, and review by the general education committee further developed the assessment findings in the report. We met with FYC faculty twice during the fall semester—once right before the semester to discuss the preliminary survey and rubric assessment findings, and once in October to discuss changes to the class based on the findings, closing the loop. In the October meeting, FYC faculty gravitated towards the qualitative analysis, finding it very helpful to hear feedback from students about what was useful to them in the course and what they would change. The rubric indicated that the weakest category for students was presenting counterarguments, so instructors shared resources with each other to help students further develop those skills. The December presentation to the general faculty was well attended by instructors in the first-year experience, and the discussion focused around programming and initiatives to address student concerns. The general education committee read the final report in May and noted how important it was to them to see student voice amplified in the report.

Disrupting Hierarchy

We have seen the framework of mutual mentoring disrupt hierarchy between faculty, administration, and students. For example, in our collaboration analyzing qualitative data for writing program assessment, Abby brings her knowledge and experience of being an undergraduate student at Juniata, an experience that Hannah has never had, and reciprocally Hannah brings her knowledge and experience of being a faculty member and writing program administrator at Juniata, an experience that Abby has never had. Hannah and Abby both bring knowledge of qualitative research methods and the kinds of information it can provide, which is not a strength of any other members of the team and is typically left out of assessment work at Juniata. Just like the salient practices, reciprocal benefits extended into our intellectual, personal, emotional, and professional lives.

In our weekly meetings, we experienced many benefits working together on qualitative research. Abby consistently provided a different perspective on the data and a different voice than that of a faculty member or administrator. When we first started working with the qualitative data, Abby reviewed both of the qualitative questions on the student survey about what was most useful to students and what they would change about FYC, and she began to categorize the answers. While a preliminary report on the survey written by the associate provost found similar themes, Abby used quotes from students to bring further depth to those observations. Both analyses observed that students felt they learned how to write in FYC, but Abby's analysis of student quotes in the assessment report demonstrated that "Students perceived improvement, gained confidence over time, and pointed out how understanding the 'why' of writing is important for development." Traditionally in education students have had no power in their education. It disrupts hierarchy when we assert instead that what students have to say is important.

For Hannah, working with Abby was a positive reflective practice and an opportunity to distill down what she knows about qualitative research. After Abby first categorized the student quotes, she found ten discrete categories that students found most useful in FYC. When Hannah looked at those categories, she began to identify overlaps and teach Abby to look at the data in a different way. Together, we observed that students valued live feedback most about FYC, whether that be feedback from instructors in one-on-one conferences, peer feedback in class, feedback from the writing associate, or feedback from a writing center tutor. This collaboration led to our significant finding that students felt they benefited most from live feedback as part of their learning process.

We both saw benefits in collaborating on assessment to our own individual scholarly pursuits. For example, Abby was able to use what she learned about qualitative research in her JA position to complete a capstone project that also utilized qualitative research. The experience prepared her for organizing information gathered from conducting interviews. She was able to recognize themes in her participants' responses that became different points of focus in her analysis. In her writing, she started out with confidence in how she would approach elevating her participants' voices to be as essential as her own. Hannah's recent scholarship has centered around undergraduate student and faculty collaborations and publications, and assessment work with Abby provided an opportunity for her to see these collaborations in relationship to institutional work.

Significantly, our collaboration provided a different perspective on equity and a different way to work for equity at the college. In our weekly meetings with the Office of Institutional Effectiveness, faculty and administrator team members generated equity initiatives at the college to implement in FYC and beyond. Often, the student team members would listen as faculty administrators discussed implementation of these initiatives because there was a lot of background knowledge about the institution that the students didn't know. Abby and Hannah had their one-on-one meetings after these meetings and would debrief or plan to implement these initiatives.

In our one-on-one meetings, Abby would express confusion and ask questions about the way the institution worked and why they were doing things a particular way or not doing other things. Hannah would try to explain, though the answer is often that the institution has always done it this way. For example, one meeting we discussed Juniata's revisions to their academic amnesty policy. Abby questioned how it would work and pointed out its pitfalls from a student perspective. She believed that more student input would avoid creating ineffective or potentially harmful policies regarding students. The opportunity for reflection about the institution and planning for equity initiatives carved out important space for driving forward equity work at the college.

This learning and fresh perspective on institutional work aligns well with the goals of assessment, which is intended to make changes after gathering data and reflecting. Our collaboration allowed us to see what changes could be made or explain why we chose not to make a change. In these ways, we believe mutual mentoring can bring about institutional change.

We acknowledge the importance of receiving feedback from various faculty and administrative groups in making change at Juniata. Yet we realize that only select students were invited or took up the call to participate in the feedback process—students working in the Office of Institutional Effectiveness, students working as writing associates, and a student government representative serving on the general education committee. If students, our research participants, are to become mentors/guides, we acknowledge there is more work to do to include their feedback in the findings stage of the process.

Moving forward, including more students is another place to engage pedagogical partnership that promotes equity and justice, because if we value student voices we must recognize the historical barriers to all kinds of student voices, that some student voices are included or excluded more than others. De Bie et al. outline what it would look like to consider equity and justice throughout all aspects of partnership, including enhancing equity in recruiting students and ensuring every student feels invited to participate, attending carefully to the differences that each partner brings, rethinking the language used in equity work to understand it, considering how partnerships contribute to equity and justice when that is not their explicit purpose, and ensuring that we are addressing root causes of harm in the partnerships rather than tacking on equity and justice to initiatives as an afterthought. Because assessment is structured in a way that data is gathered and faculty and administrators then make decisions of what to change, it is still hierarchical to a certain extent despite the pedagogical partnerships, mutual mentoring, and student voice through qualitative research that we outline here. While we celebrate the accomplishments of our partnership, we acknowledge there is still a lot of work to do to make widespread institutional change.

Bibliography

de Bie, Alise, Elizabeth Marquis, Alison Cook-Sather, and Leslie Patricia Luqueño. 2021 *Promoting Equity and Justice Through Pedagogical Partnership*. Sterling: Stylus.

Felten, Peter, Catherine Bovill, and Alison Cook-Sather. 2014. "Engaging Students as Partners in Learning and Teaching (1): Benefits and Challenges—What Do We Know?" Paper presented at the International Consortium on Educational Development, Stockholm, June 2014.

Ferganchick-Neufang, Julia. 1999. "Research (Im)Possibilities: Feminist Methods and WPA Inquiry." In *The Writing Program Administrator as Researcher: Inquiry in Action and Reflection*, edited by Shirley K. Rose and Irwin Weiser, 18–27. Portsmouth: Boynton/Cook.

Fine, Michelle, and María Elena Torre. 2021. *Essentials of Critical Participatory Action Research*. Washington, DC: American Psychological Association.

Gladstein, Jill M., and Dara Rossman Regaignon. 2012. *Writing Program Administration at Small Liberal Arts Colleges*. Anderson: Parlor Press.

Hall, Eric, Sophia Abbot, and Hannah Bellwoar. 2019. "Developing Attitudes and Habits of Mind for Mentorship." *Center for Engaged Learning* (blog). September 10, 2019. https://www.centerforengagedlearning.org/developing-attiitudes-and-habits-of-mind-for-mentorship.

Juniata College. 2017. "Juniata Associates Guidelines." Office of Human Resources. Last modified 2017. Accessed July 4, 2022. https://www.juniata.edu/offices/human-resources/hiring-process/JuniataAssociates-Guideline2017.pdf.

Ketcham, Caroline J., Eric E. Hall, Heather Fitz Gibbon, and Helen Walkington. 2018. "Co-Mentoring in Undergraduate Research: A Faculty Development Perspective." In *Excellence in Mentoring Undergraduate Research*, edited by Maureen Vandermaas-Peeler, Paul Miller, and Jessie L. Moore, 155–79. Washington, DC: Council on Undergraduate Research.

Kirsch, Gesa, and Joy Ritchie. 1995. "Beyond the Personal: Theorizing a Politics of Location in Composition Research." *College Composition and Communication* 46, no. 1: 7–29.

Kuh, George. 2008. *High-Impact Educational Practices: What They Are, Who Has Access to Them, and Why They Matter.* Washington, DC: American Association of Colleges and Universities.

Moore, Jessie. With Sophia Abbot, Hannah Bellwoar, and Field Watts. 2020. "Mentoring: Partnering with All Undergraduate Researchers in Writing." In *The Naylor Report on Undergraduate Research in Writing Studies*, edited by Dominic DelliCarpini, Jenn Fishman, and Jane Greer, 29–44. Anderson: Parlor Press.

Morales, Danielle, Sara Grineski, and Timothy Collins. 2017. "Faculty Motivation to Mentor Students through Undergraduate Research Programs: A Study of Enabling and Constraining Factors." *Research in Higher Education* 58: 520–44. https://doi.org/10.1007/s11162-016-9435-x.

Royster, Jacqueline Jones. 2000. *Traces of a Stream: Literacy and Social Change Among African American Women.* Pittsburgh: University of Pittsburgh Press.

Shanahan, Jenny Olin, Elizabeth Ackley-Holbrook, Eric Hall, Kearsley Stewart, and Helen Walkington. 2015. "Ten Salient Practices of Undergraduate Research Mentors: A Review of the Literature." *Mentoring and Tutoring: Partnership in Learning* 23, no. 5: 359–76. https://doi.org/10.1080/13611267.2015.1126162.

Wolf, Margery. 1992. *A Thrice Told Tale: Feminism, Postmodernism, and Ethnographic Responsibility.* Stanford: Stanford University Press.

Appendix A: Juniata Associate Career Readiness Skills Performance Review – 2021-2022

Instructions

PRE-ASSESSMENT
Review the JA's job duties. Identify three most relevant Career Readiness Competencies (see below).
Ask JA to complete pre-self-evaluation 1-5 scale and comment on current skill level and plans for enhancement.
Return signed original to Human Resources by November 4, 2021. Please keep a copy for yourself.

POST-ASSESSMENT
Review the pre-assessment copy

Review all pertinent information to evaluate performance.

Meet with the JA to discuss the performance review. Together complete post-evaluation scale with comments, and suggestions for development. Also, complete #4 (Overall Evaluation).

Return signed original to Human Resources by May 12, 2022.

PRE-ASSESSMENT Form: Return signed original to Human Resources by November 4, 2022
Name of Juniata Associate _____

Juniata Associate's Position _____

Supervisor's Name _____

General Responsibilities of Juniata Associate _____
_____

Pick THREE of the CAREER READINESS COMPETENCIES most critical to success in the specific Juniata Associate position.

1. Critical thinking/problem solving
2. Oral/written communications
3. Teamwork/collaboration
4. Digital technology

5. Leadership
6. Professionalism/work ethic
7. Career management
8. Global/intercultural fluency

You may add comments, as you like, but <u>required comments for post evaluation on scores that are below 3</u>. Provide your rating in the space provided using the 1-5 scale:

5 = Outstanding
4 = Very Good
3 = Average
2 = Needs Improvement
1 = Poor

1. Juniata Associate Pre-Self-Evaluation: 1-5 scale _____

Student Comments: _____
_____

Juniata Associate and Supervisor's Post-Evaluation: 1-5 scale _____

Supervisor and Student Comments: _____
_____
_____

2. Juniata Associate Pre-Self-Evaluation: 1-5 scale _____

Student Comments: I think there is always room for me to communicate better and I think that I could be a lot more concise in both written and oral communication so that I can say less words but have a more significant effect.

Juniata Associate and Supervisor's Post-Evaluation: 1-5 scale _____

Supervisor and Student Comments: _____
_____

3. Juniata Associate Pre-Self-Evaluation: 1-5 scale _____

Student Comments: I think I am a good team member and I always try to think about the ideas of the group because my thoughts are not the only ones that matter and other people have other strengths that I do not bring to the table.

Juniata Associate and Supervisor's Post-Evaluation: 1-5 scale _____

Supervisor and Student Comments: _____
_____

4. Overall Evaluation (Post Assessment only). 1-5 scale _____
Supervisor and Student Comments: _____
_____
_____

_____
Signature of Evaluator – Pre-Assessment

_____
Signature of Juniata Associate – Pre-Assessment

_____
Signature of Evaluator – Post-Assessment

_____
Signature of Juniata Associate – Post-Assessment

Appendix B: General Education (GE) Assessment Plan (2019-2025)

Below is the GE assessment plan adopted by the general education committee and revised on March 31, 2020. The first column represents the assessment focus, labeled *GE Themes*. These GE themes connect our institutional learning outcomes with our stated GE student learning outcomes. This mapping is explicit in the Excel document called "GE Assessment Map," which includes the GE themes in the first column, our institutional learning outcomes, GE course learning outcomes, and accreditation requirements. The schedule shown below is a simplified version that only lists the GE themes for each year of a five-year schedule.

For each GE theme, we will spend one year planning and collecting data and one year implementing changes based on what we learn. The summer between these academic years will include a workshop where, among other things, we will discuss the results of the GE theme assessment and plan curricular/pedagogical changes based on our conclusions.

	Year 1 2019-20	Year 2 2020-21	Year 3 2021-22	Year 4 2022-23	Year 5 2023-24	Year 6 2024-25	Year 1 2025-26
GE Themes Below...							
First Year Experience	Planning and Collection	Planning and Collection	Closing the Loop		Planning and Collection	Closing the Loop	TBD
Oral and written communication	Planning and Collection	Planning and Collection	Closing the Loop				TBD
Scientific and quantitative reasoning			Planning and Collection	Closing the Loop			TBD
Analytical, creative and critical thinking. Quantitative literacy.			Planning and Collection	Closing the Loop			TBD
Information literacy	Planning and Collection	Planning and Collection	Closing the Loop				TBD
Values and ethics					Planning and Collection	Closing the Loop	TBD
Diverse perspectives						Planning and Collection	Closing the Loop
Interdisciplinarity				Planning and Collection	Closing the Loop		TBD
Civic Engagement						Planning and Collection	Closing the Loop

	COMMON OUTCOMES		
	OWC	ACT	ITL
Connections			
communicate effectively through written and oral expression			
address a challenging problem or question			
integrate knowledge and skills from different disciplinary approaches and ways of knowing			

First Year Seminar			
communicate effectively through written and oral expression			
demonstrate analytical thinking, critical questioning, and examination of evidence			
use a variety of credible primary and secondary sources as evidence			
First Year Composition			
write a persuasive argument using writing process strategies including invention, research, drafting, sharing with others, revising in response to reviews, and editing			
use a variety of credible secondary sources as evidence			

KEY FOR COMMON OUTCOMES

OWC	Oral and Written Communication
ACT	Analytic and critical thinking
ITL	Information and Technological Literacy

Appendix D Fall 2019 First Year Experience Student Survey

NOTE from the authors: We distributed this survey to first-year students in fall 2019, the first semester of offering the revised first-year composition class, as part of our assessment process. In addition to the questions using a Likert scale and some open-ended questions you see below, we also asked students for demographic information so we could disaggregate the data by marginalized identities such as race and gender.

Five-point Likert Scale: Strongly disagree to strongly agree

My first-year composition course helped me to . . .

- Write a persuasive argument paper
- Use credible secondary sources as evidence
- Think about perspectives of people different than my own
- Establish my Juniata portfolio
- Develop critical reading skills
- Develop analytical thinking skills

My first-year composition course helped me to use writing process strategies such as . . .

- Invention and brainstorming ideas
- Research
- Drafting papers
- Sharing writing with others
- Revising in response to reviews
- Editing

The library sessions within first-year composition helped me to . . .

- Find and evaluate sources
- Recognize the importance of archival materials
- Gain awareness of the library's resources and services

Multiple Choice Questions

How many times did you meet with your writing associate?

0,   1   2   3   4   5 or more

Why didn't you meet with your writing associate?

- I was too busy
- I wasn't required to
- I didn't think it would be helpful

Other (please specify) _____

Open-Ended Questions

1. What part (or parts) of your first-year composition course was most useful to you?

2. If you could make one change to your first-year composition to make it more useful for future students, what would it be?

3. What part (or parts) of your library sessions within first-year composition was most useful to you?

4. If you could make one change to your library sessions within first-year composition to make it more useful for future students, what would it be?

5. If you met with your writing associate, what part (or parts) of working with your writing associate was most useful to you?

Appendix E Assessment Summary for Written Communication 2019-2021

General Education Goal Assessed
Written communication

Course(s)
FYC 101 First Year Composition (FYC), all sections taught in fall 2019.

Course Objective/Learning Outcome related to General Education Goal
Written communication is an explicit goal of FYC. Here is an excerpt from the Faculty Manual describing FYC . . .

The goals of the course are to introduce students to different types of reading and writing using varied models, genres, and forms (such as popular, scholarly, digital, and print). These courses build students' information literacy skills, rhetorical knowledge, critical thinking, and knowledge of appropriate genre and style conventions. FYC courses will focus on developing these skills to prepare students for future academic work. FYC courses are capped at eighteen students per section.

Students will demonstrate their ability to meet the following learning outcomes:

- *Write a persuasive argument using writing process strategies including invention, research, drafting, sharing with others, revising in response to reviews, and editing*
- *Use a variety of credible secondary sources as evidence*

As evidenced above, FYC focuses on developing critical reading, writing, and analytical skills. FYC courses follow a process-oriented approach to college work and include peer review, individual conferences with the instructor, and revision cycles.

Focus of the Assessment
This assessment served as an assessment of written communication as outlined by Juniata's General Education assessment cycle. We conducted a survey of FYC students in fall 2019 to gather self-report data on the process-oriented approach to writing instruction in this course. We assessed written communication and persuasive argument skills in a sample of sev-

enty-four student papers (out of 370 uploaded to Portfolium) from sections of FYC taught in fall 2019.

Since this assessment coincided with the introduction of our new general education curriculum, the committee decided to focus the written communication assessment on the first-year experience. Getting early feedback about the skills being taught in the revised curriculum was considered a priority.

How did you collect your data (method and tools)?
We developed a survey and distributed it by email to all first-year students in fall 2019. We asked students if they felt that FYC helped them to learn how to construct arguments in college-level writing and use writing process strategies as outlined in the faculty handbook. We also asked students how often they utilized the writing associates to develop a process-oriented approach to writing and meet the learning outcomes of the course. We asked two open-ended questions about what students found most useful and what they would like to change about FYC, and we asked for demographic information. The survey instrument is attached.

To assess papers written in FYC, we developed a rubric that evaluated five categories: Construction/articulation of arguable thesis, appropriate use of sources and evidence, identification/discussion of counterarguments, formulation/articulation of logical conclusions, application of writing conventions/mechanics. The rubric guided the evaluation of how well students could reach the target writing standard for beginning college students in creating a persuasive argument and following writing conventions. We focused on these criteria to assess writing and persuasive argument skills, which are the learning outcomes for FYC.

Type of Data (qualitative, quantitative, both and indicate if direct or indirect methods)

Indirect Measures: We conducted a survey of FYC students. This survey gathered quantitative data from multiple choice questions about the course goals, and it gathered qualitative data from open-ended questions about what students found helpful and what students would change about the course. The survey also collected quantitative data about student demographics.

Direct Measures: We assessed argument papers based on a rubric that measured how well students fared with basic writing structure and conventions. This rubric measured quantitative data about the number of students who reached the target writing level.

Outline the Results of the Assessment: Student survey responses were consistently in agreement that FYC helped them develop learning course goals and writing strategies. There were no categories on the survey with the average of the numerical response below the threshold for agreement. To find out how students felt about their progress with FYC's learning outcomes, the survey had the students specify to what level they agreed with those goals completing the sentence, "My first-year composition course helped me to . . . ," with the responses being strongly disagree, somewhat disagree, neither agree nor disagree, somewhat agree, and strongly agree. Over 50 percent selected "strongly agree" that FYC helped them to "write a persuasive argument paper" (54.69 percent) and "use credible secondary sources as evidence" (52.24 percent). Forty to 50 percent selected "strongly agree" that FYC helped them to "think about perspectives of people different than my own" (47.95 percent) and "develop analytical thinking skills" (44.49 percent). Finally, 30 to 40 percent selected "strongly agree" that FYC helped them to "develop critical reading skills" (36.48 percent) and "establish my Juniata Portfolio" (33.47 percent). The range, then, for the strongly agree responses was 33.47 to 54.69 percent. After "strongly agree," the percentage for each category generally decreases as it approaches "strongly disagree." The percentages of "somewhat agree" for every category were in the range of 30.74 to 35.10 percent. "Neither agree nor disagree," had percentages with a range of 6.12 to 18.85 percent. Either "strongly disagree" or "somewhat disagree" had the lowest percentage of responses for every category. "Somewhat disagree" had a range of 2.86 to 6.97 percent, and "strongly disagree" had a range of 3.67 to 7.76 percent. The survey also investigated how students felt about using key writing strategies. Another question asked students to specify to what level they agreed to statements completing the sentence "My first-year composition course helped me to use writing strategies such as . . . ," with the responses the same as the previous survey question. Over 50 percent (specifically 50.21 to 55.74 percent) of students selected "strongly agree" for the statements that FYC helped them use the following writing strategies: Drafting papers (55.74 percent), research (51.64 percent), sharing writing with others (50.82 percent), revising in response to reviews (50.61 percent), and editing (50.21 percent). The writing strategy "Invention and brainstorming ideas" had the lowest percentage of "strongly agree" answers (42.86 percent). As with the previous question, the percentages generally decreased as they approached "strongly disagree," with the only exception being that "somewhat disagree" often had a lower percentage than "strongly disagree." The ranges of percentages were as follows: "Strongly agree" was

42.86 to 55.74 percent, "somewhat agree" was 29.51 to 38.37 percent, "neither agree nor disagree" was 7.38 to 13.06 percent, "somewhat disagree" was 1.63 to 3.69 percent, and "strongly disagree" was 3.27 to 3.69 percent.

The survey also asked a few open-ended questions that related to FYC. The first was "What part of your first-year composition course was most useful to you?" There were some significant common themes in the student responses. Ninety-eight out of 243 students (40 percent) said the most useful part of FYC was learning to write or how to improve their writing. This included learning about the writing process, learning college writing expectations, and working on essay drafts. Eighty-eight out of 243 students (36 percent) identified various kinds of live feedback as the most meaningful part of FYC. Out of these, thirty-four mentioned peer feedback or revision in general, twenty-nine claimed that conferences with their professors were most helpful, and twenty-five talked about the school resources, such as the writing center and writing associates. As for other common answers, twenty-two students left the question blank, eighteen felt that learning about research and identifying sources was important, and fifteen talked about their particular professor being the best part of their FYC experience. Ten students mentioned specifically that learning about argument was useful to them, but only one response mentioned counterargument.

The second open-ended question was "If you could make one change to your first-year composition course to make it more useful for future students, what would it be? Eighty students out of 243 (33 percent) either said they would not change anything about FYC, they could not think of any changes to make, or left a blank response. The most common theme for what students would change in FYC was related to the course load. Twenty-eight students out of 243 (11 percent) said they found the amount of work to be overwhelming. Four students pointed out that the amount of work and subsequent grading varies between FYC sections. There were twenty-four responses out of 243 (10 percent) related to students wanting the course to be more relevant to them and their writing education. Some of these were about wanting more focus on the class theme, and others were about desiring more explicit writing instruction. Other responses about changes students would make to FYC were less statistically significant, but there were some commonalities. Ten students were opposed to early morning classes, citing that it was hard to focus and that students would often skip the early classes. There were also eight students who wanted more live feedback, either from peers, writing associates and writing tutors, or their professors.

Direct Evidence: In assessing the student writing samples, 74 percent (fifty-three out of seventy-four) were deemed acceptable according to the rubric. The rubric had four sections: Capstone (superior), Milestone 2 (advanced), Milestone 1 (target), and Benchmark (developing). Acceptable work was based on meeting or exceeding Milestone 1 for writing. In the papers we assessed, we defined acceptable work as reaching the Milestone 1 (target) category. We would like first-year students to be on a path of improvement, but we do not expect advanced work yet. There were five assessment criteria on the rubric: Construction/articulation of arguable thesis, appropriate use of sources and evidence, identification/discussion of counterarguments, formulation/articulation of logical conclusions, and application of writing conventions/mechanics.

We found that counterarguments had the lowest percentage of acceptability (50 percent). "Identification/discussion of counterarguments" was at the target-level when the paper identified other arguments, but only addressed them minimally, as opposed to benchmark papers, which were aware of opposing positions, but did not address them.

Writing conventions/mechanics had the highest percentage (88 percent). "Application of writing conventions/mechanics" achieved the target level when the paper used language that was generally clear for readers, even if there were some mistakes. Benchmark papers used language that hindered the reader's ability to understand the writer's meaning.

Thesis, sources/evidence, and logical conclusions all had similar percentages (74, 76, and 73 percent, respectively). The first criterium, "construction/articulation of arguable thesis," was said to be target-level, and not benchmark, when the arguable topic was stated and described, but not clearly defined. There could be missing elements and the paper could lack elaboration. The work would be benchmark instead if the topic was only stated but not described at all, and if most elements of the task are missing. The next criterium, "appropriate use of sources and evidence," was at the target when the paper used credible and relevant sources, but not consistently. Benchmark papers would have sources that were not credible or relevant. "Formulation/articulation of logical conclusions" reached the target level when conclusions were clear based on the information present in the paper and some consequences and implications were clear. Benchmark papers had inconsistent conclusions to some information and oversimplified outcomes.

Discuss How the Results Tie to Other Information and/or Data (e.g., indirect institutional data, etc.)

We administered the National Survey of Student Engagement during the 2019-2020 academic year. The following questions were related to written communication and show how our students' self-reports compare to those at other institutions.

Question During the current school year, for how many writing assignments have you done the following?	Scale	JC Avg.	Peers Avg.	Aspirants Avg.	Mideast Privates Avg.
Summarized material you read such as articles, books, or online publications (1d)	1-Never 2-Sometimes 3-Often 4-Very Often	3.5	3.3**		
Analyzed or evaluated something you read, researched, or observed (1e)	1-Never 2-Sometimes 3-Often 4-Very Often	3.8	3.6**		
Argued a position using evidence and reasoning (1g)	1-Never 2-Sometimes 3-Often 4-Very Often	3.5	3.3**		
Addressed a real or imagined audience such as your classmates, a politician, non-experts, etc. (1j)	1-Never 2-Sometimes 3-Often 4-Very Often	3.2	2.9**		

Note: * = 0.05, ** = 0.01, *** = 0.001

Compared to first year students at other institutions, our students had statistically significantly higher scores in summarizing material, analyzing and evaluating research, arguing a position, and addressing an audience.

Analysis: How Do You Interpret the Results? What Does It Mean?

Based on the survey responses, we can see that the majority of students felt that FYC achieved its learning goals. Most students agreed with all of the statements that indicated the course taught them what it was designed to teach. The survey demonstrates that students feel they developed argument as a skill, since "writing a persuasive argument paper" was the most agreed upon learning outcome. It also shows that students are recognizing aspects of the writing process as important skills they have developed through FYC.

Students overall identified in their open-ended responses to the question "What did you find most helpful in FYC?" that through learning about writing as a process, FYC was helpful in teaching students how to improve their writing. One student wrote that what they found most helpful in FYC was "Doing the various writing processes over and over and becoming better at them with each paper that we wrote." Students perceived improvement, gained confidence over time, and pointed out how understanding the "why" of writing is important for development.

Students also particularly valued live feedback about their writing from others. For example, one student wrote, "I really enjoyed being able to have conferences with both my professor and my writing [associate]. It allowed me to get a lot of constructive feedback for my papers and allowed me to view prompts in different ways." It appears that students enjoyed feedback from multiple sources. Some talked about how much they enjoyed "group workshop days" in their classes. One person shared, "I have never enjoyed sharing my work with others for fear of criticism, but these workshops were very enlightening and fun, and I will be more likely to go to the writing center in the future." It seems apparent from these answers that the most important takeaways from FYC were writing skills and an openness for feedback and revision.

There was much less consensus among students for changes they would make to FYC compared to what they found useful in FYC. Some students had ideas for improvements, but many seemed to be happy with the course as it is. The most common issue that students pointed out was that some of them thought the course was too difficult or required too much work. Some of the solutions they offered included spacing assignments out more; for example, one student suggested that we "adjust the pacing of the course so that students have more time to write essays and get feedback." They also pointed out that the variation between FYC classes could make the workload and grading unequal across sections. One student said, "I would either make sure all professors grade similarly or I would make it a pass/fail class. Some professors rarely give out As, but I think that that is unfair for an FYC course because each student should have the same opportunity to get a good grade in the class." As for making the class more relevant to students, some of them felt that their FYC class was not explicit enough in teaching how to write for college. A student wrote that they would "have [FYC] be more focused on how to write a proper paper as opposed to just 'here's a prompt, now write.'"

Based on the analysis of the data and synthesis of information, what are next steps? Be sure to include an explicit timeline for next steps.

Beginning in August 2021, assessment and survey results were made visible to the FYC faculty learning community. FYC faculty discussed the results and particularly focused on intentional ways to bring counterarguments into the course work and explain how counterargument is a critical part of persuasion. In November 2021, they shared materials for teaching counterargument. Some of the methods discussed were looking at teaching different perspectives, such as identifying the different "They Say, I Say" perspectives. There was also the idea to look at writing to identify the arguments and counterarguments present. The consensus was to more explicitly label counterargument when teaching so that students will be able to recognize counterargument as an essential part of argument moving forward. The next steps were to make shared materials on teaching counterargument available on Moodle, which happened in December 2021.

Section III: Equity/Justice in SLAC Writing Programs

7 Assessing an Honor Code: What "Authorized Aid" Signals to Learners and Educators About the Writing-Collaboration Process

Genie Giaimo

Abstract: This chapter interrogates the impact of honor codes on the learning/writing process for college students in the 2020s with a particular focus on how we can create more inclusive honor codes. Using Middlebury College—a rural elite liberal arts school in New England with a student population of ~2,600—as a case study, this chapter analyzes the college's honor code language, challenging its vagueness and prescriptivism around student help-seeking behaviors, and specifically what counts as "authorized aid" for writing. Providing heuristics and an appendix to assess and enact meaningful changes in honor codes, this chapter ends with guidance on how to start campus-wide conversations about developing an inclusive twenty-first century honor code.

Introduction

When I applied to college—mostly small liberal arts colleges (SLACs)—there were applications that asked me to write about the school's honor code in the context of my own intellectual goals for growth and development. At the time, I could only focus on integrity and the fear that I might plagiarize the words of others and subsequently be forced out of the school. I was unable to think about the other elements of the honor code that, at least at one particular school, encouraged "collaboration over competition" (Haverford College, n.d.), intellectual curiosity, and freedom of thought. Back then, my working-class first-generation sixteen-year-old brain was only concerned with the discipline and punishment aspects of the honor code. I could see little beyond the veiled threats around the consequences precipitated by failure to uphold academic integrity.

I also didn't really understand academic integrity beyond a hazy grasp on citation standards. Back then, I was largely a solo writer. I outlined (if ever) alone, I revised (if ever) alone, and I rarely did peer review or other kinds of collaborative writing work. When I think about the rather lonely and partial writing process that I came into college with, I cannot help but wonder what my young adult self really felt about the honor code; perhaps it didn't apply to me, or I was already prepared to write with "integrity" because I knew MLA citation rules. Or maybe it was a mere formality required for college applications. In truth, students coming into college have so much on their plates that the honor code is just a drop in the proverbial bucket, particularly if they come from historically marginalized backgrounds and must navigate college without the support of family.

As a professor at a school with an honor code, I share the hope that students come in with intellectual curiosity, a willingness to engage with a variety of ideas, and a fundamental understanding not only of academic integrity but of academic responsibility. This communal element of an honor code is one that is at the center of writing center work, and, hopefully, writing education work more broadly. We raise each other up through collaborative and ethical engagement with intellectual work. However, as I prepare to teach a first-year seminar at a school that requires faculty to indoctrinate students to its honor code, I return, once again, to this peculiar artifact and scrutinize it. The impact of honor codes on a culture of writing in higher education is under-explored in the field, especially in research on liberal arts colleges. In this chapter, I rely on Middlebury as a case study and conduct rhetorical analysis of institutional documents and informal assessment of honor code compliance to explore how such policies might encourage punishment over pedagogy, particularly for historically marginalized students (Jamieson and Howard 2019, 69). I will also offer guidance to administrators and faculty on how to assess and revise (or perhaps remove entirely) honor codes, should they have the opportunity and authority to do so.

To understand this project, however, means we need to return to the history of why honor codes were instituted in the first place. Honor codes are common in colleges and universities around the country. Established over a century ago (McCabe and Trevino 1993), they appear in specific institutional types (typically small and more homogenous) at specific historical junctures like the turn of the twentieth century, the mid-1960s, and the turn of the twenty-first century. In fact, the mid-1990s saw a resurgence of interest in and establishment of honor codes in higher education (McCabe and Trevino 1993). While some studies have reported positive outcome from an honor code, such as student engagement in reporting cheating (McCabe, Trevino, and Butterfield 2001), and reduced levels of cheating (McCabe and Trevino 1993), there is still stark unevenness in whether and how faculty engage with honor code violations, with many reporting non-engagement (McCabe, Butterfield, and Trevino 2003). There are also widespread issues with cheating in higher education more broadly (Hauptman 2002; McCabe and Trevino 2002).

McCabe and Trevino (1993, 533) argue that adopting an honor code "is ill conceived if it is undertaken as the sole solution to the academic dishonesty problem." Because "academic dishonesty is a complex behavior influenced by multiple variables beyond the mere existence of an honor code" (533), student and faculty perception of the honor code, as well as educational awareness, is critical to engagement. In one of their earliest studies, McCabe and Trevino found that some schools with honor codes reported a lot of unethical behavior while a non-honor code school had one of the lowest rates of cheating (534).

Similarly, a more recent study (O'Neill and Pfeiffer 2008, 5) found that "the more severe a student perceives an academic cheating behavior to be, the less cheating behavior will be undertaken . . . regardless of whether the college has an honor code or not." The code, then, seems less important than a culture of academic integrity that is created through widespread awareness campaigns and student-faculty buy-in. O'Neill and Pfeiffer (2008, 5) argue that schools need to "elevate" honor codes to the point that community members "revere" them. I, on the other hand, suggest we assess and revise these codes to move away from prescriptive and flawed figurations of academic integrity, especially in writing and idea development.

A lot of the research on honor codes focuses on academic integrity and test-taking, rather than writing. Some scholars (McCabe and Trevino 2002; McCabe and Pavela 2004) believe that honor codes are a powerful tool to combat widespread cheating because they engage in student-led and community-focused conversations about academic integrity policies. There are, however, issues with community members' knowledge and perception of honor codes that impact positive engagement. One study found little difference in pre-and-post attitudes towards cheating after the creation of an honor code (Roig and Marks 2006). Additionally, because most studies focus on cheating and proctored exams, rather than writing, we know little about how these codes impact student writers and writing. In fact, beyond brief mention of plagiarism (and paper mills, in one case) most of these studies say little else about how honor codes do or should conceive of the writing process. One study endorses attending a writing center and allowing students extra time with such writing resources (McCabe and Pavela 2004). Yet the complex and often collaborative nature of writing—and the myriad ways in which students develop networks of writing/learning support—are understudied.

It is difficult, however, to assess community engagement with honor codes, because of its relationship to academic misconduct and, more broadly, cheating. As a WPA at a liberal arts college, I recently designed a research study on the use of writing-assisted AI like ChatGPT. While these tools are not yet officially banned in our honor code, my student researchers and I found that many students who are happy to talk off the record about their use of AI-assisted writing tools refused to be interviewed for our study. The fear of breaking the honor code—whether there was clear misconduct or not—compelled many students to drop out of our study. So, while this chapter offers detailed guidance on how to assess and revise honor codes through community-wide conversations, it is likely that WPAs and others will run into roadblocks when focusing on student practices that might impact grades, honor code compliance, and other institutional policies. At the end of the chapter, I provide a long-form assessment model that brings in multiple stakeholders and provides different assessment methods. Below, I share data from a student-led organization on honor code compliance as an example of a model for indirect assessment of such policies.

Middlebury's honor code and student compliance has been assessed by a student organization for several years through the campus newspaper, which is cheekily titled *The Campus*. The annual "Zeitgeist" student survey regularly draws responses from about 50 percent (n = ~1,250) of the student population (Sjodin 2023). Students answer questions about romantic relationships, academic foci, study abroad plans, financial aid status, social life, partying, and upholding the honor code. The raw data is not shared externally, and faculty and staff are not included in the data collection process. These informal "sense of the student body" surveys have found that many of the hallmarks of a successful honor code have eroded at Middlebury over the past decade. For example, student-led engagement in upholding the honor code is very low. Recently, students at Middlebury (among students at other schools) reported being reluctant to engage in the monitoring elements of the honor code (Greenberg 2015). Cheating issues at the college have also eroded another cornerstone of honor codes, such as un-proctored exams, so that certain departments are exempt from this element of the code (Grasgreen 2014). And, pertinent to this chapter, 64 percent recently reported breaking the honor code through using "unauthorized aid" such as peer support and learning aids (such as SparkNotes and translators) to write their papers. The number of students who report use of unauthorized writing aid has nearly doubled from 35 percent in 2019 to the current year (Keohane 2023). Newly reported this year, the survey tracked students' use of ChatGPT, which, while not necessarily banned outright (the honor code is very vague), was included as part of the academic integrity portion of the survey under "unauthorized aid."

The honor code pledge is very short—"I have neither given nor received unauthorized aid on this assignment" (Middlebury College 2017). Therefore, the weight of compliance turns on the concept of unauthorized aid, which is defined as any non-college learning support, or everything except the writing center, faculty, and in-class peers (i.e., peer review). Roommates, friends, teammates, family, and private tutors are all excluded from the code's articulation of acceptable aid. And while it might make sense to interrogate the kinds of writing support students are getting, this unilateral model of writing support creates a culture of uncertainty and fear, rather than one of collaborative and nuanced writing. This culture harms historically marginalized students and others who navigate their education through community-building and mutual aid. From a rhetorical standpoint, the code's framing of writing (and learning writ large) is individualist and institutional, neither of which characterize the wide array of writing situations and experiences students will have in college and throughout their lives. Given findings that "cheating" is rampant and that most of the other strictures of the honor code are no longer upheld by the student body, I suggest we start by rhetorically analyzing our honor codes—as I do below—and move from there to community-wide review of these documents and attendant policies.

Analyzing the Honor Code and Academic Integrity at Middlebury

Structurally and rhetorically, the honor code is presented as part of academic integrity in student and faculty handbooks. The location of the code within student and faculty handbooks signals to readers that this is a rules-focused policy. The actual honor code is a preamble to a rather lengthy student-handbook statement on academic integrity. On the faculty side, the rules of the policy are shared, but not the reasoning. Even in rhetorically analyzing the structure of the document, there is confusion over what element of the policy is the actual code versus what is academic integrity policy or if these two things are one and the same. Because of this, the honor code is frequently equated with academic integrity and, more specifically, avoiding plagiarism, and little else—though, arguably, this was not the intention of the code when it was created.

Written by undergraduate students in 1965, the Middlebury College honor code places primacy on student engagement in several core tenets of honor codes including monitoring cheating, self-governance of academic integrity, un-proctored exams, and upholding the honor code pledge. The preamble to the code in the student handbook foregrounds student engagement in all elements of the code:

> The students of Middlebury College believe that individual undergraduates must assume responsibility for their own integrity on all assigned academic work. This constitution has been written and implemented by students in a community of individuals that values academic integrity as a way of life. The Middlebury student body, then, declares its commitment to an honor system that fosters moral growth and to a code that will not tolerate academic dishonesty in the college community. (Middlebury College 2017)

Since then, the code has been reaffirmed by the student body on several occasions. However, several changes have also been made to the honor code over the last decade. For example, exams can now be proctored by faculty because of issues with cheating (Cheung 2014). Additionally, an academic integrity committee comprised of students, faculty and staff—rather than students, as the code put forth—was formed to evaluate and administer academic integrity at the school. Students' attitudes towards reporting cheating (another cornerstone of the honor code) have also shifted towards non-involvement and neutrality (Greenberg 2015). Cheating rates have also risen.

In 2019, one third of students surveyed by the student newspaper reported violating the honor code (Hodkin 2019) while nearly two thirds now report cheating in 2023 (Keohane 2023).

According to the faculty handbook, the honor code is a serious element of introduction to the Middlebury community. Students are required to sign a document stating that they, "have read the code and understand it," and they are given a multi-step orientation to the honor code upon their arrival. As the faculty handbook further states, the honor code—and adherence to it—is a shared responsibility among students and faculty (staff and student workers are not mentioned explicitly in this section of the guidelines). Faculty are expected to instruct students on citation practices and expectations for each assignment regarding independent or collaborative work, and access to sources, while students are expected "to seek clarification from their professors if they are unclear on any of these elements" (Middlebury College 2022). Resources such as the writing center, and the broader center for teaching, learning, and research (CTLR), are sanctioned as authorized aid under subsection b:

> Cheating is defined as giving, receiving, or attempting to give or receive any aid unauthorized by the instructor for any assigned work. On assignments other than exams, academic assistance from the staff of the Center for Teaching, Learning and Research (CTLR) and from Middlebury's professional librarians is considered authorized aid unless an assignment or course clearly indicates otherwise. (Middlebury College 2017)

Oddly, the honor code pledge—"I have neither given nor received unauthorized aid on this assignment" (Middlebury College 2017)—is listed well after the discussion of cheating and authorized aid. While this element of the honor code is under the "student responsibilities" subsection, there is far more focus on the elements *around* the actual pledge rather than on the pledge itself, which remains vaguely defined.

The language of the honor code—not just the pledge—centers around aid, what is authorized aid, and what is not. Students are expected to sign and later reproduce their honor code "pledge" or "oath" in projects, papers, and other kinds of assignments, as the professor and school see fit. As the handbook notes, "it is the responsibility of the student to write out in full, adhere to, and sign the honor code pledge on all examinations, research papers, and laboratory reports. Faculty members reserve the right to require the signed honor code pledge on other kinds of academic work" (Middlebury College 2017). Students include this statement in their writing, even when they are not prompted by the professor. A kind of signaling or formality that indicates that they are following the official rules governing the production of writing and idea development, the pledge assures that any support in writing and ideal development is limited and approved by the college.

Over the past ten years, however, as student and faculty adherence to the honor code has shifted, there have been several conversations about whether it makes sense in this current educational landscape to have an honor code. At the same time, many of the qualities of the honor code—student-led judiciary, monitoring, and code maintenance—have eroded. Yet most of the discussion around the honor code has been on compliance rather than how honor codes affect student learning outcomes. From the confusion and frustration that I observe in the writing classroom and in the writing center, creative and collaborative writing acts do not fit into the narrow bounds of the honor code. The code, at times, stifles ethical collaboration and help-seeking behaviors. My students (and peer tutors) report difficulty with group work, peer review, and other kinds of idea exchanges because they report worrying—among other things—that these activities are in violation of the honor code. And, as student-led research has found, most students report violating the honor code anyway, particularly around seeking unauthorized aid to complete writing and reading work.

Pushing Back Against "Authorized Aid" in and Through Writing Centers

The honor code's binary breakdown of aid as authorized and un-authorized muddies the ethical waters and likely contributes to the blasé attitudes of students around cheating and, importantly, reporting students who cheat. The code also doesn't capture how aid realistically flows or extends throughout a college network. For those with more secure attachments—and parents or guardians who have the time and resources to do so—aid such as private tutoring, AI and other programs, or family feedback is common. For those with less secure attachments—and parents or guardians who have little time and resources—however, any kind of aid such as feedback from friends, roommates, and teammates is an academic lifeline. The honor code at Middlebury assumes everyone is on an equal footing and fails to address inequity in terms of access to support networks or academic confidence and self-efficacy. Furthermore, it assumes that all students are willing to follow the rules, yet, as the "Zeitgeist" survey notes, some students seek support from highly educated parents or paid private tutors, which seems far less honorable than a first-generation student asking their roommate to read over their draft the night before it is due. Support exists on a spectrum that is not well defined by the honor code. For example, authorized aid can be unhelpful and not actually ethical (e.g., tutors who feed students answers), while unauthorized aid from a friend can be a lifeline for under-represented students navigating college. So, as we start parsing out networks of aid, the classed and raced elements of support come into sharp relief and we may conclude that marginalized students rely on informal networks for far different reasons (safety, care, empathy, mutual aid) than other students.

The values of the honor code, which require students to report on other students as well as carefully parse the kinds of academic support they seek, provides a tension when placed into context with a twenty-first century student population, which is far more economically and racially diverse. In this context, the honor code takes on negative and assimilationist valences where students surveil one another and themselves. Of course, the honor code predates our writing center by nearly forty years. It is from a different educational era in which academic support was limited—if it existed at all—and the student population was far more homogenous, white, and wealthy. Furthermore, the heavy emphasis on institutional services as authorized aid assumes a kind of institutional trust that might no longer be as widespread among the student population. In other words, students may distrust institutionally sanctioned aid by virtue of its association with the policies and punishments of the college. After all, as we found in our study of student use of AI-assisted writing, students are concerned that their use of writing and reading aids might admit wrongdoing or academic dishonesty and students (including peer tutors) are required under the honor code to report anyone suspected of cheating. The ramifications of these actions are, of course, significant as they could lead to loss of scholarship, sanction, and expulsion.

The honor code also signals a tacit boosterism that focuses not on help-seeking behaviors but on individual accomplishment. As a writing center director who does WPA work, I have worked with students and faculty who struggle with the purpose of the honor code and its pledge—"I have neither given nor received unauthorized aid on this assignment." Students struggle to ask for help and report not feeling deserving of academic support. At the same time, many access unauthorized support that is based on their means and access. The writing center sits at the crossroads of the institution and struggles with a dual mission of being an inclusive and anti-racist space at the same time as it is the authorized aid for writing on campus. Without specific attention, training, and recruitment, the writing center can become a space that polices honor code compliance and promotes and encourages prescriptivist ways of writing. This might include advice that focuses mainly on adopting standard white English to conform to institutional (not individual) expectations of what "good" writing and communication looks like. Or it might be a kind of narrowly focused "banking concept" of writing education (Freire 1970) that leaves little room for growth or self-driven exploration. Furthermore, the code's focus on the **individual over the collective impacts how students learn and overshadows larger conversations about what ethical peer-to-peer learning looks like. This primacy of the individual—and the belief in "ownership" of ideas—is also classist, Western, and white supremacist** (Okun 2021; Green 2016; Baker-Bell 2020; Inoue 2021). Of course, many writing centers and first year writing programs, including ours, actively push back against this kind of remedial and white-washing model of writing instruction in favor of linguistic justice and honoring multiple interpretations of English, but it becomes more challenging when the writing center is institutionally marked as the only legitimate space to seek writing support.

The vagaries and inequities of the honor code also produce uncertainty in the face of technological advancement and what constitutes violations, especially for students with disabilities. Sudden technological shifts have created concern for both faculty and student since the introduction of Web 2.0 (and likely before). Campus-wide discussions about Wikipedia and, currently, AI-assisted technologies have swept through the college, yet the honor code fails to encompass what kind of aid is sanctioned and what kind of aid violates the code. More concerning, the emergence of new technologies has prompted conversations of technology bans in the classroom, which can have detrimental effects on students with disabilities, multilanguage learners, and students who use technological assistance in their learning and writing processes. In this way, student behaviors aren't measured against their need but against the code's narrow definitions of aid. In both the use of unofficial networks of support and in the use of technology, not all practices are unethical, yet there is no room for nuance when interpreting the current honor code. In short, we know that "violations" are happening, but the blanket rules of the code make it difficult to parse intent. If student networks of aid and access were assessed, we might recognize that not all authorized aid is necessarily "good" and that not all unauthorized aid is necessarily "bad," or academically dishonest. For example, it is commonplace to use assistive writing technology, like Grammarly or Chegg, for workplace correspondence and ChatGPT is now replacing workers in fields like marketing. An honor code, then, could more explicitly parse different forms of writing-specific aid through identifying need, rhetorical context, and developmental stage.

The code doesn't engage modern composition pedagogy or best practices, like student empowerment and engagement (Carello and Butler 2015); instead, we are given hazy and ominous policies that lead us to believe that an academic violation is lurking around every corner. In reality, writing outside of college passes hands quite often. And the development of ideas and writing is socially and rhetorically complex (Clark 1988; Lunsford 1991; Harris 1992; Severino 1992). Instead of clarity around *why* we might seek specific kinds of aid, we are merely told that "Cheating is defined as giving, receiving, or attempting to give or receive any aid unauthorized by the instructor for any assigned work." In the hyper-competitive environment of an elite liberal arts college, honor codes reify competition over collaboration, the individual over the collective, the product over the process. The reasons for seeking out—or giving—unauthorized aid do not seem to matter, even though anti-racist work teaches us that unofficial grassroots (rather than institutional) structures like mutual aid and community-centered uplift can have profound positive effects. To re-think how honor codes are structured and enacted to be more inclusive as well as informed by writing pedagogy, I offer a roadmap (Appendix A) to assessing and revising (or removing) honor codes for those who have the power to do so.

Alternatives to the Honor Code

Honor code research is poised for yet another turn. The bulk of the research that this chapter cites occurred at the end of the twentieth century and the beginning of the twenty-first century, which coincides with the interactive elements of websites and social media networks that characterize Web 2.0. Even the valence of *how* honor codes can be successful in different circumstances and with new student populations is dated. In an *Inside Higher Ed* piece from 2005, McCabe and Pavela argue that a new honor code movement is currently under way. And, of course, millennials are at the center of that movement. The authors argue that this new group of students have received "intense parental attention (shuttled relentlessly from day care to music lessons to soccer games)-with results that appear to justify the effort."

They also argue that their rates of suicide and risky behavior is far lower than previous generations. Finally, they say that this new generation is "more optimistic" and "less depressed." In hindsight, of course, we can look at this brief prelude—for some millennial communities, namely wealthy white ones—before the financial collapse as perhaps part of a less disrupted generation. Yet, in looking at the long arc of history, with Columbine, 9/11, the opioid epidemic, the endless Iraq and Afghanistan wars, and all the surveillance, imprisonment, and threats that the Patriot Act and other local policies like New York's stop-and-frisk enabled, and all of a sudden we see this assessment as the deep breath before the plunge into a far more disruptive twenty-first century than many of us could have imagined. Our codes should reflect the precarity and nuance of the knowledge economy. They should include communal and inclusive structures for meaning making.

When honor codes encourage individualization and discourage collaboration and help-seeking within one's community, they are classist as well as white supremist. They also flatten the complex and nuanced nature of written (and other) forms of communication. Yet even more inclusive and well-developed honor codes ought to be interrogated as they are often gatekeepers of the school's knowledge economy and support nexus created in response to a broadening and diversification of college-going students and technological innovations. So, while these models might work in homogenous populations at relatively wealthy institutions—though my case study here shows that even in such elite institutions the code is not working all that well—they are a gatekeeping force that punishes specific student (and faculty/staff) populations who rely on more communal and non-punitive ways of learning and who experience real stakes should they run afoul of the honor code. My hope is that we can revisit honor codes within the landscape of politics, access, and education in the 2020s, and redefine what honor looks like in an academic setting to be a more inclusive and communal model.

I end this piece with some heuristics and a roadmap to communal revision and rethinking of honor codes (Appendix A) that I think can help to clarify the place of writing support in academic integrity:

1. Collaborative writing with peers should be encouraged and assigned. Work plans and time set aside for negotiating labor, however, needs to be included in such pedagogical models.

2. Students should create a "care map" where they identify the different kinds of spaces in which they can and do (or are likely to) reach out for help. This can include support from peer writing tutors but,

also, roommates, family members, friends etc. The care map can include academic support but, also, social and mental support.

3. We need to have more explicit conversations with our students about learning versus schooling (Blum 2016) and work to encourage academic joy and pleasure in our students—not just policies and penalties.

4. We need to introduce students to different forms of aid, including mutual aid where people exchange resources to uplift and support one another. Peer review is a great place to start this conversation around mutual aid for writers, but it is not the only way to do this work.

5. We need to explain why citation conventions are the way they are—it is not enough to just tell students how to cite but, also, to steep them in the academic language in which they are citing. Writing looks different when you rely on MLA citation versus APA, for example. Foreground this for students so they understand citation is more than page numbers and authors; it is stylistic and content-driven.

6. As a broader community, we need to discuss what values honor codes uphold and what expectations they leave unsaid. Implicit expectations are harmful to first-generation students and students who otherwise struggle to navigate the hidden curriculum of the American education system.

7. We need to talk to faculty about their expectations around academic integrity and how they cope with cheating in their classes. In a bureaucracy-heavy work environment, faculty might only engage with academic integrity perfunctorily.

8. We need to talk to students about what they value in learning and infuse that into our policies.

9. We need to account for a diversity of expression, voices, languages, and learning styles in our policies, especially about writing.

10. We need to do more assessment (Appendix A). Beyond assessing honor codes and their value, we can also assess, as some have done, perceptions, attitudes, and alternative models.

While this list is not exhaustive, I hope that it (and Appendix A) can kick off a conversation that interrogates the values and outcomes of our honor codes and academic integrity policies and how writing and its processes fit into these policies. The more unclear, vague, and ominous a policy, the more fractured engagement will be. We can have open dialogues about these topics and wade into the murky waters of class, race, and all that privilege and precarity bestows upon our academic behavior. Academic integrity—and plagiarism—is not value-neutral (Watson 2017), and neither is the teaching of writing. We need to do more to unpack how institutional policies, such as honor codes, impact the teaching and production of writing because this has downstream effects on our pedagogy, our inclusiveness, our writing programs and centers, and, of course, our students.

Bibliography

Baker-Bell, April. 2020. *Linguistic Justice: Black Language, Literacy, Identity, and Pedagogy.* New York: Routledge.

Blum, Susan D. 2016. *I Love Learning; I Hate School.* New York: Cornell University Press.

Carello, Janice, and Lisa D. Butler. 2015. "Practicing What We Teach: Trauma-informed Educational Practice." *Journal of Teaching in Social Work* 35, no. 3: 262–78.

Cheung, Jessica. 2014. "The Fading Honor Code." *New York Times.* https://www.nytimes.com/2014/04/13/education/edlife/the-fading-honor-code.html.

Clark, Irene Lurkis. 1988. "Collaboration and Ethics in Writing Center Pedagogy." *Writing Center Journal* 9, no. 1: 3–12.

Freire, Paolo. 1970. "The Banking Concept of Education." In *Thinking about Schools: A Foundations of Education Reader*, 117–27. New York: Routledge.

Grasgreen, Allie. 2014. "The Proctor Is In." *Inside Higher Education* (blog). February 24, 2014. https://www.insidehighered.com/news/2014/02/25/economics-department-proctor-exams-adherence-honor-code-wanes.

Green, Neisha-Anne S. 2016. "The Re-education of Neisha-Anne S Green: A Close Look at the Damaging Effect of 'A Standard Approach,' the Benefits of Code-meshing, and the Role Allies Play in This Work." *Praxis: A Writing Center Journal* 14, no. 1. http://www.praxisuwc.com/green-141.

Greenberg, Susan H. 2015. "Why Colleges Should Ditch Honor Codes. *Washington Post.* https://www.washingtonpost.com/posteverything/wp/2015/05/28/why-colleges-should-ditch-honor-codes.

Hauptman, Robert. 2002. "Dishonesty in the Academy." *Academe* 88, no. 6: 39.

Harris, Muriel. 1992. "Collaboration Is Not Collaboration Is Not Collaboration: Writing Center Tutorials vs. Peer-Response Groups." *College Composition and Communication* 43, no. 3: 369–83.

Haverford College. n.d. "Supplement." Office of Admissions. Accessed July 2, 2021. https://www.haverford.edu/admission/supplement.

Hodkin, Zeke. 2019. "One Third of Respondents Broke the Honor Code." *Middlebury Campus*. https://www.middleburycampus.com/article/2019/05/academics.

Inoue, Asao B. 2021. *Above the Well: An Antiracist Literacy Argument from a Boy of Color*. WAC Clearinghouse: University Press of Colorado.

Jamieson, Sandra, and Rebecca Moore Howard. 2019. "Rethinking the Relationship Between Plagiarism and Academic Integrity." *International Journal of Technologies in Higher Education* 16, no. 2: 69–85. https://www.ritpu.ca/en/articles/view/359

Keohane, Charlie. 2023. "Academics." *Middlebury Campus: Zeitgeist 4.0*. https://www.middleburycampus.com/article/2022/05/zeitgeist-4-0-2022.

Lunsford, Andrea. 1991. "Collaboration, Control, and the Idea of a Writing Center." *Writing Center Journal* 12, no. 1: 3–10. https://www.jstor.org/stable/43441887.

McCabe, Donald L., and Linda Klebe Trevino. 1993. "Academic Dishonesty: Honor Codes and Other Contextual Influences." *Journal of Higher Education* 64, no. 5: 522–38.

McCabe, Donald. L., Linda Klebe Trevino, and Kenneth D. Butterfield. 2001. "Dishonesty in Academic Environments: The Influence of Peer Reporting Requirements." *Journal of Higher Education* 72, no. 1: 29–45.

McCabe, Donald L., and Linda Klebe Trevino. 2002. "Honesty and Honor Codes." *Academe* 88, no. 1: 37.

McCabe, Donald L., Kenneth D. Butterfield, and Linda Klebe Trevino. 2003. "Faculty and Academic Integrity: The Influence of Current Honor Codes and Past Honor Code Experiences." *Research in Higher Education* 44, no. 3: 367–85.

McCabe, Donald L., and Gary Pavela. 2004. "Ten (Updated) Principles of Academic Integrity: How Faculty Can Foster Student Honesty." *Change: The Magazine of Higher Learning* 36, no. 3: 10–15.

McCabe, Donald L., and Gary Pavela. 2005. "New Honor Codes for a New Generation." *Inside Higher Ed*. https://www.insidehighered.com/views/2005/03/11/new-honor-codes-new-generation.

Middlebury College. 2017. "Academic Honesty, the Honor Code, and Related Disciplinary Policies." Middlebury Handbook. Last modified August 22, 2017. https://www.middlebury.edu/handbook/pages/ii-ug-college-policies/ug-policies/academics/acad-honesty.

Middlebury College. 2022. "Honor Code." New Faculty Handbook. https://www.middlebury.edu/academics/administration/newfaculty/handbook/honorcode.

Okun, Tema. 2021. "White Supremacy Culture." *Collective Liberation*. https://collectiveliberation.org/wp-content/uploads/2013/01/White_Supremacy_Culture_Okun.pdf.

O'Neill, Heather M., and Christian A. Pfeiffer. 2008. "The Impact of Honor Codes on Academic Cheating Within Liberal Arts Colleges." *Business and Economics Faculty Publications* 2. https://digitalcommons.ursinus.edu/bus_econ_fac/2.

Roig, Miguel, and Amanda Marks. 2006. "Attitudes Toward Cheating Before and After the Implementation of a Modified Honor Code: A Case Study." *Ethics and Behavior* 16, no. 2:163–71.

Severino, Carol. 1992. "Rhetorically Analyzing Collaboration(s)." *Writing Center Journal* 13, no. 1: 53–64.

Sjodin, Tony. 2023. "Introduction: The Spirit of the Times, in Transition." *Middlebury Campus: Zeitgeist 4.0*. https://www.middleburycampus.com/article/2022/05/zeitgeist-4-0-2022.

Watson, Missy. 2017. "Reworking the Policing of Plagiarism: Borrowings from Basic Writing, Authorship Studies, and the Citation Project." *Journal of Basic Writing* 36, no. 2: 78–108.

Appendix A: Roadmap to Revising and Rethinking Honor Codes at Liberal Arts Colleges

1. Assess student and faculty engagement in the honor code:
    i. Is there an understanding of the code?
    ii. Is there widespread buy-in for the code?
    iii. Where and when are students and faculty exposed to the code?
    iv. What is the level of code compliance?
    v. What are some "grey areas" of the code?
    vi. What ways do students and faculty work around the code?
    vii. What are some issues with the code?
    viii. What are some opportunities with the code?
    ix. Is the code current?
    x. Does the code still reflect the values and goals of the institution's learning culture?
    xi. Is the code inclusive for first-generation, BIPOC and other historically marginalized students?
2. Hold listening sessions, conduct anonymous surveys and/or deidentified interviews.
3. Compile data.
4. Present data to stakeholders.
5. Hold workshop days (or digital comment forums) for faculty and students to annotate and revise the honor code.
6. Workshop the annotated and revised code in smaller and mixed working groups of students, staff, and faculty.
7. Preview the revised honor code to student government and faculty/staff council for additional feedback.
8. Revise again in small mixed working groups.
9. Secure community-wide approval of honor code.
10. Institute revised honor code and promote it widely.

11. Continue to assess faculty and student engagement in the honor code.

12. Revise regularly on agreed-upon timescale (perhaps every 4 – 5 years with new cohorts of enrolled students).

A Key to Assessing and Revising a School Honor Code

Stakeholders: students, faculty, staff, alumni, administrators, etc.

Assessment Methods: surveys, interviews, focus groups, observations, artifact collection, listening sessions; townhalls; workshops; symposia; online/digital feedback, etc.

Assessment Group Structures: small mixed working groups (students, staff, faculty); large groups (faculty, staff, student council); student organizations; college-wide committee, etc.

Potential Assessors: student organizations (school newspaper), writing and rhetoric faculty, students in specialized courses (writing center practicum, writing studies course, data science course, etc.), faculty, administrators, faculty council, writing advisory committee, external reviewers, alumni, etc.

Analysis methods: narrative write-up, infographics, interactive data visualization (taAleau, RStudio Shiny app, Flourish, etc.), static data visualization (Excel, RStudio, SPSS, STATA, etc.), oral presentations, flyers, social media posts, etc.

Share-Out Models: internal publication (school newspaper), governance meetings (faculty council, student government, staff council), Board of Trustee meetings, chair and director meetings, department meetings, athletics meetings, college social media and marketing, faculty-focused workshops, student-focused workshops, mixed community-wide workshops, first year seminar courses, external conference presentations (IRB approval required), publications (IRB approval required), etc.

Honor Code Assessment Timeframes: annual, bi-annual, quinquennial, decennial etc.

8 Subverting Elitism with Equitable Assessment at a New England SLAC

N. Claire Jackson, Gabriel Morrison, and Hayley C. Stefan

Abstract: This chapter offers a snapshot of assessment practices from three contingent faculty members at the College of the Holy Cross, a Jesuit small liberal arts college in Worcester, Massachusetts. Constrained by institutional discourses on rigor and grade inflation, authors describe and reflect on developing equitable assessment models across various sites of writing. Because Holy Cross lacks a formal writing program, focused efforts at programmatic assessment and institutional change remain difficult. Thus, this chapter argues for ongoing faculty reflection around individual assessment practices as an approach towards incrementally changing institutional cultures of writing.

As a prerequisite for renewing a one-year contract at the College of the Holy Cross, a Jesuit liberal arts college in Worcester, Massachusetts, visiting faculty meet with their department chairs to review their teaching. To the surprise of Hayley, who was hired a year before Claire and Gabe, this review included an analysis of her grade distribution, alongside a breakdown of total students awarded each letter grade. Hayley was asked to reflect on the disparity between the average grades her students received and the averages of the department, a difference of about 0.1. The chair explained that English department faculty were encouraged to try to keep their average course grade in line with college averages, which were a further 0.1 lower than the average department grade. While the chair recommended asking other faculty about their assignments and assessment practices, she also noted that Hayley was not required to and that it was okay if she disagreed with the model, saying that many faculty disapproved. Despite that casual honesty, visiting faculty in the English department still receive this "Instructor Grade Analysis" report following each semester at Holy Cross, accompanied by a memo from one of the deans explaining that the document "provide[s] an opportunity to review your grades in relationship to departmental and college-wide averages." A letter shared with new faculty in the English department notes that "To keep grade inflation in check, we are encouraged to aim for course averages that more closely approximate the college average."

What this opening anecdote reveals is that our college is steeped in concerns about rigor, which likely stem from our status as an "elite" and highly selective institution. While administrators (and some faculty and students) seem to cherish the school's reputation as "rigorous," we are also being pressured to be more empathetic during COVID-19 in our teaching and assessment; therefore, meaningful assessment is reduced to buzzwords that deflate the potential for student and faculty learning. This contradiction, where grade analysis bumps up against sincere curricular intervention, is indicative of the challenges to implementing equitable assessment practices at our small liberal arts institution. That is, "we say we want students to be successful, but not really too successful. If too many are successful, our current models of valuation mean something is dangerously wrong in the system" (West-Puckett, Caswell, and Banks 2023, 35). While a growing contingent of faculty have expressed interest in more equitable modes of assessment, these larger discourses of rigor and selectiveness constrain efforts to enact such assessment models. However, we argue that this discourse of rigor, which is so deeply embedded into our campus culture, makes our commitment to equitable assessment measures even more urgent, as students on our campus frequently have traumatic experiences with rigor, often suffering from high levels of stress and an increasing need for mental health services.

Moreover, as a Jesuit institution, a commitment to social justice is a central part of Holy Cross's mission. Our mission statement makes these commitments clear, noting that "Holy Cross seeks to exemplify the longstanding dedication of the Society of Jesus to the . . . promotion of justice" and that all members of the college should work "to seek justice within and beyond the Holy Cross community" (College of the Holy Cross, n.d.). Thus, we see our work to develop and promote equitable assessment practices as part and parcel of our college's expressed commitment to social justice. Readers would be right, however, to question how a commitment to social justice can be fulfilled at an institution like ours, because of its selective admissions and shockingly high cost of tuition. This is a common critique of Jesuit institutions. However, as Patricia Bizzell (2016, 45) notes, Jesuits never intended to "become the schoolmasters of the rich and powerful." In fact, the original Jesuit schools were meant to be free and open to all in order to provide a "general benefit to the public good" (45). Therefore, while we recognize the ways in which our college is not accessible, we would like to position our assessment efforts in line with Jesuit tradition to provide an education that is accessible to all.

While our chapter, unlike many others in this collection, is primarily focused on classroom assessment, the close attention to instructors' grading practices we describe reflects some of the intersections between classroom assessment and large-scale programmatic assessment. As Jennifer Grouling explains, when a student artifact moves out of the classroom genre system to that of a large-scale programmatic assessment, it "no longer belongs to the classroom or any particular student. Rather it is an exemplar text—a representation not of *a* student, but of *the* student, a subject position within the institution of the university" (2022, 124). A similar move is happening with the grades we assign our students. In the grade analyses described above, which compare the average grades we assigned in each class to those of our department and the college as a whole, grades no longer represent the learning of the individual students we assigned them to. While we may have assigned a particular grade based on our assessment of a student's writing, learning, labor, or engagement, the college uses that distribution to assess our teaching ability. Too many "A" grades no longer represent the success of students but rather the failures of instructors to maintain high standards. Yet, as West-Puckett, Caswell, and Banks note, "grading occurs after a period of learning and thus isn't randomized" (2023, 150). Therefore, enforcing predetermined grade distribution requirements makes little sense, especially in small classes without enough data points for statistical relevance. Because enacting large-scale programmatic assessment is difficult on our campus, due in part to the lack of a formal writing program and our institution's deeply entrenched beliefs about instructor autonomy, we have each sought ways in which our individual classroom assessment practices, and Gabe's faculty development work, might "use our individual power to shape the institution" (Grouling 2022, 155) and disrupt the institutional discourses that constrain efforts for more equitable assessment practices.

All three of us find the discourse around grade inflation to be antithetical to our grading philosophies and the expressed aspirations of our institution. We reject the notion that rigor must be equated with difficulty or exclusiveness. We believe that more students earning high grades means more students were provided with the conditions they needed in order to succeed, which contributes to, rather than detracts from, academic excellence. As contingent and newly-hired faculty, however, our efforts are constrained by the precarity of our positions and institutional emphasis on rigor. Assessment methods that subvert this emphasis on rigor may be riskier and, in some ways, more controversial at an elite institution than at perhaps a more socioeconomically or ethnically diverse institution. At the same time, the extensive instructor autonomy afforded by our SLAC context allows us to undertake this subversive work in spite of institutional pushback. In the remainder of this chapter, we reflect on our own approaches to equitable assessment to show how such tactics can resist the narrative of rigor constructed by selective educational institutions.

Some Developing Critiques of Grading Contracts

All three of us have been informed by current literature on labor-based grading contracts. However, while labor-based grading contracts have frequently been touted as an anti-racist assessment measure, more recent scholarship has begun to critique their ability to automatically provide equity within writing classrooms. For example, in her recent short essay "Your Contract Grading Ain't It," Sherri Craig (2021, 145) argues that "contract grading expresses anti-Black racism in unforeseen and deeply felt ways" as it ignores the systemic anti-Black racism that undergirds English departments and writing programs more broadly. She argues that viewing contract grading as an inherently anti-racist practice ignores the structural white supremacy that informs both our individual classrooms and our larger institutions.

This approach, Craig claims, "does the most injustice to our Black students . . . because it attempts to convince them that the university cares for their lives and their experiences" (2021, 146) when more traditional grading approaches still exist in most other classes at the institution, or when even the teachers who implement contract grading do little to interrogate "practices with deep white supremacist origins in other areas of their courses" (146). Therefore, while Craig is clear she is not arguing against the use of grading contracts, she asserts that it "ain't the answer to anti-racist practices in writing programs" (146). Craig's article reminds us that institutional context determines the disruptive potential of any assessment technology. It is for this reason that the three of us feel the need to consider our efforts at equitable assessment practices across the various contexts in which we work at our small college.

Drawing on disability studies, Mathew Gomes, Bree Bellati, Mia Hope, and Alissa LaFerriere (2020) reflect on how using a labor-based grading contract has worked to "standardiz[e] participation labor" and, as such, "was misaligned with [Gomes's] purposes for using grading contracts" as they "privileged able-bodied and neurotypical students who sustained a steady level of physical health throughout the duration of a term and contributed in normative ways." Ultimately, Gomes, Bellati, Hope, and LaFerriere draw a parallel between the way having a single language standard within a writing classroom reifies racist outcomes and the way a single participation standard reifies ableist outcomes. That is, measuring labor through factors such as attendance, speaking in class, or amount of time spent on a single task privileges able-bodied and neurotypical students and ignores the many ways disabled and/or neurodivergent students may meaningfully engage in the course. Thus, while labor-based grading contracts may decrease overt linguistic racism within the classroom, they do little to undercut, and may even strengthen, the ableist paradigms through which we conceive of labor and participation (see also Kryger and Zimmerman 2020).

Ellen Carillo's (2021, 18) recent work echoes these claims, as she argues that labor-based grading contracts "obscure the problematic normative body and conception of labor at their center." She critiques a few specific aspects of Asao Inoue's (2019) oft-cited labor-based grading contract model, such as the requirement for students to spend a certain amount of time laboring on specific assignments and how this "single standard" is "indebted to able-bodied labor practices" (Carillo 2021, 21). Moreover, in thinking about the recent rise in diagnoses of depression and anxiety among college students, instructors should anticipate this when constructing their grading approaches, rather than employing what she describes as Inoue's "wait-and-see then be-compassionate-and-let-go" model of accommodations for mental health issues (29). As such, Carillo advocates for an engagement-based, rather than labor-based, approach to assessment, which provides opportunities for students to "choose the form of engagement that is suitable and possible for them at a particular moment in time, that can help bridge willingness and ability" (58–59). While the three of us have each been informed by and found uses in such scholarship on labor-based grading contracts, these recent critiques, as well as our backgrounds in queer, trans, and disability studies, animate our attempts to enact equitable assessment practices.

Overview of Writing Instruction at Holy Cross

Like many SLACs, our institution has little in the way of a formal writing program, making concentrated attempts at improving assessment measures difficult. The most wide-reaching attempt at writing instruction is the required year-long, interdisciplinary Montserrat course for first-year students. Faculty across all disciplines teach for Montserrat, which is defined as "an innovative first-year program that provides students with a dynamic introduction to the liberal arts" (College of the Holy Cross, n.d.). Because Montserrat includes "strong writing and effective communication" as one of its seven program goals, the course represents what Jill M. Gladstein and Dara Rossman Regaignon (2012) deem an embedded writing requirement. That is, while not explicitly listed as a writing requirement, Montserrat is an example of "curricular requirements—including first-year seminars and capstone exercises—that articulate writing as one of their goals" (Gladstein and Regaignon 2012, 96).

While Gladstein and Regaignon do note that "embedded writing requirements may indicate that an institution is more saturated with writing and sites of writing instruction than it first seems" (2012, 96), they did find that because writing is *a* goal, and not *the* goal of these types of courses, this "can mean there is an institutional mandate to *assign* writing, but little faculty development on how to *teach* or evaluate it" (105). While former Holy Cross faculty member Patricia Bizzell notes that "faculty concern about students' writing ability provided one motive for the creation of Montserrat" classes, which "are supposed to be 'rhetoric-intensive'" (2016, 51), she echoes Gladstein and Regaignon's concerns about such first-year seminars by acknowledging that it's unclear whether Montserrat "consistently deliver[s] the full-bodied rhetoric instruction that was envisioned" given the program's many diverse outcomes (2012, 52).

In addition to Montserrat, Holy Cross *does* have a first-year writing (FYW) course situated within the English department. However, the course is currently an elective, taught only by the English department's two rhetoric and composition faculty, which satisfies no common requirements. Interestingly, these twelve seats are *limited* to first-year students, so a student who decides they want more explicit writing instruction in their sophomore year would not be able to take the course. In the last few years, only three sections of this course have been offered per year (two in the fall and one in the spring), so only about thirty-six first-year students are receiving the explicit writing instruction FYW provides each year. The English department also offers one section per year of a by-permission 200-level intermediate academic writing course, open to students beyond the first year and capped at twelve students. However, because our rhetoric and composition minor, housed in the Center for Interdisciplinary Studies, requires students to take either FYW or our intermediate academic writing course, the twelve seats in this course are usually filled by students pursuing the minor. This course thus does little to provide formalized writing instruction to students outside of the minor who have not taken FYW in their first year. The rhetoric and composition minor also offers other elective writing courses, such as "Writing about Data and Policy" or "Digital Literacy." Finally, the college also offers a "Passport" program "designed to assist promising first-year students achieve their full potential during their transition to the educational experience at Holy Cross" (College of the Holy Cross, n.d.). As part of this program, students participate in a four-week residential component before their first year, which includes a course on the elements of writing argument. Many of these students go on to take our elective FYW course as well, suggesting that it acts in some ways as a basic writing course.

Holy Cross has an independent center for writing, established in 2015, with both a director and assistant director who hold professional staff positions. In addition to overseeing a peer tutoring center called the writer's workshop with professional staff writing tutors, the center for writing sponsors a variety of campus and faculty outreach programs aimed at improving the way writing is incorporated throughout the curriculum. The center for writing, however, does not have any administrative authority to issue requirements or supervise the way that writing is taught or assessed at the college, so encouraging widespread faculty uptake of evidence-based practices can be challenging.

In the remainder of this chapter, we detail our attempts at integrating equitable assessment practices across some of the sites described above. First, Claire will discuss her work with engagement-based grading agreements in the elective FYW course. Hayley will then discuss her grading practices in her sections of Montserrat. After Claire and Hayley's narratives provide snapshots of their work in specific courses, Gabe will zoom out to the institution at large to discuss his faculty development efforts around equitable assessment as assistant cirector of the center for writing.

Claire's Grading Agreements in FYW

I began using labor-based grading contracts in 2016 because focusing on a student's labor in the course, rather than making a judgment about the quality of their writing and language, seemed to naturally gel with the translingual, holistic approach to writing assessment that informed my teaching. Modeled after Inoue's (2019) contract, my initial contracts measured how often students attended class, their contributions to class discussion, their timely completion of assignments, and the labor they put into revising their written assignments after receiving feedback. While I continued to use versions of this contract for several semesters and mostly found them to be a useful approach to assessment that did not require students to conform to white linguistic norms, I was always uneasy with the measurement of class participation as a form of labor, as there are myriad ways students may participate in a course that aren't always visible to us as instructors. Moreover, several instances in recent years caused me to consider the ways in which such an approach reifies ableist paradigms, leading me to settle on my current assessment approach in FYW, which I call an "engagement-based grading agreement." Appendix A includes a version of the grading agreement I used as of the writing of this chapter.

During the spring of 2018, almost my entire FYW class came down with severe cases of the flu. Thus, many students had to miss more classes than the number of absences allowed in our contract. Similarly, a student in my business writing course in the spring of 2019 often missed deadlines for assignments because she was a single mother attending to a newborn. I did renegotiate grading contracts with students midway through the semester, as Inoue suggests. Therefore these particular circumstances could have simply led us to renegotiate how many absences or late assignments we thought were reasonable or led me to grant exceptions to students like the single mother. However, these events had me questioning the reasonableness of setting any type of attendance requirement to earn a particular grade, as we can never predict everything that will happen to a student during a given semester, nor should we expect them to disclose their trauma or medical histories to us in order to receive an exception. Therefore, I felt I could no longer justify the rigidity of many labor-based grading contracts. This concern became even more pressing when COVID swept the US in spring 2020 and students' lives were seriously disrupted. Many had difficulty completing any work—as did I. It was at this point that I knew I needed to rethink my approach to assessment in order to build in significant flexibility to account for the diverse needs, experiences, and abilities of all students.

As I worked to redesign my approach to grading, I was heavily influenced by Gomes, Bellati, Hope, and LaFerriere's (2020) "Enabling Meaningful Labor." As they explain, "participation is not always well-defined or understood by instructors and students" (Gomes, Bellati, Hope, and LaFerriere 2020, 1). The article offers a narrative from an instructor of a writing-intensive English course and three narratives from undergraduates in that course, as they explore what types of participation emerged as "meaningful" and the implications these have for assessing participation. What these narratives make clear is that the large amount of choice students had in *how* they participated in the course significantly influenced their perceptions of whether the assessment was "fair," with one student even noting that this was "one of the few classes [she had] taken where in-class attendance and speaking in class are not the only way to show participation" (7).

The appendices to Gomes, Bellati, Hope, and LaFerriere's article make this focus on choice clear. In the final version of their contract, students are told that in addition to all graded assignments, they must "complete eight of the following fifteen engagement opportunities" (2020, 12). These range from activities like attending class, contributing to class discussions, emailing the instructor discussion questions before class, completing additional writing responses, attending office hours, etc. What is especially useful is the additive approach to similar opportunities, so that attending ten of twenty-five class sessions, then twenty of twenty-five class sessions, and finally all twenty-five class sessions counts as the completion of three engagement opportunities.

In redesigning my grading contract, I drew heavily on this model offered by Gomes, Bellati, Hope, and LaFerriere (2020), requiring students who want to earn an "A" to complete each of the major assignments, as well as eleven of twenty-two possible class engagement activities. These ranged from attending class and participating in class discussion to posting a reflection on the day's discussion to our discussion board in the LMS (something my quieter students do frequently, with very interesting contributions!) or attending the writer's workshop (our writing center) or office hours. Moreover, to center student choice and agency, I included a stipulation that if students have any ideas for how they might demonstrate class engagement that are not currently listed, they should run it by me, and each semester students have offered different meaningful ways they might demonstrate class engagement. Following Carillo's (2021) concerns that a focus on labor just replaces one standard with another, I started calling this approach to assessment "engagement-based" rather than "labor-based." While engagement as a concept may also be used in ways that prioritize some learners over others, I felt it important to use a term besides "labor" to highlight the flexibility of this approach, rather than using measures like time spent laboring on an assignment embedded into Inoue's (2019) labor-based approach. I also felt the legalese language of "contract" reinforced the power dynamics between teacher and student I was trying to avoid. Thus, I shifted to calling this a grading agreement rather than a grading contract.

As I hope is obvious, this grading agreement remains a living document. Not only have I made changes each semester based on what I noticed worked or didn't work for students the previous semester, I also often make small changes throughout the semester as students ask questions about the document or note certain things about it. Perhaps most radically, since first drafting this chapter, I have since removed attendance completely from the grading agreement. In previous versions of my grading agreement, attending class was a way students could show engagement, with multiple attendance benchmarks for students to potentially meet. However, I found this occasionally encouraged students to come to class when they were sick, which is a practice I do not want to encourage during an ongoing pandemic (and I question why it was something we stressed even before a pandemic). Now, I simply tell students that while I believe attending class whenever they are able will improve their learning, and that I try to make every class feel useful and relevant, I trust them if they decide they need to miss class. This approach also avoids the extra labor for an instructor when a student needs to make up something they missed. For example, I do peer review activities during class, and students can meet engagement benchmarks by participating in the peer review process. If a student is absent for a peer review class, I no longer need to find a way for them to make up that work and instead suggest they consider engagement opportunities that emphasize similar skills, such as making an appointment at the writer's workshop and writing a reflection on how the appointment contributed to their revisions.

Students have responded overwhelmingly positively to this grading agreement. Students have emailed me early in the semester, explaining that they appreciate a system that rewards them for working hard, even if their efforts are less successful by other measures. Similarly, students have thanked me profusely at the end of the semester, stating that this flexible approach to grading, which recognized the complexities of their lives outside of our class, felt especially conducive to learning, as they could engage in ways that felt meaningful to them and allowed space for them to attend to their own lives as difficult and unpredictable events happened throughout the semester. Moreover, I have found that taking this approach has prompted more sophisticated writing from my students, as they are able to take risks and try new things, without worrying about this harming their final grades. And, importantly, the vast majority of these students have earned strong final grades.

Hayley's Grading Practices in Montserrat

I came to the use of equitable grading practices from the fields of disability and mad studies. Within these fields, writers often couch equitable assessment models within the broader conversation of accessible teaching and the more well-known Universal Design for Learning (Hamraie 2020; Womack, Blanchard, Wang, and Jessee 2015). Discussions of the former increased during the early stages of the COVID-19 pandemic, as a focus on empathy in teaching (and the broad ways that can be interpreted) flourished across public and academic discourse on social media, public journalism, and scholarship. In these conversations, assessment became a balancing act between intellectual rigor and survival, as we navigated heightened experiences of precarity for our students and ourselves. Though certainly not new conversations, empathy in teaching during a pandemic translated often into flexibility in assessment, through which instructors are asked to more overtly perform care work in the classroom.

By design, Holy Cross's Montserrat program seems a natural place to implement an empathy-based assessment model. The program fosters community-building through the development of the first-year experience in clusters, organized around shared events, dormitories, and educational concepts. Despite an emphasis on common themes and shared spaces, experiences in the classroom vary widely for students and faculty. As we note above, writing skills make up one of the program's foundational skills that students should strengthen and develop over the year-long course, alongside reading, analysis, and oral communication. Other program goals range from building awareness about campus resources to encouraging habits of reflection—outcomes that are not wholly divorced from the way we hope our students practice writing, but which are not embedded within an emphasis on writing as learning.

New faculty like me receive little guidance on teaching and grading in Montserrat. Materials like the Montserrat program goals are discussed at an annual planning workshop and are accessible to instructors through a shared cloud folder, though newer faculty like me are unlikely to encounter them unless searching for them. Faculty learning and development primarily operate within this day-long workshop or in optional workshops or events coordinated by other offices, including the center for writing. Thus, while faculty might find a supplemental document titled "Montserrat First-Year

Writing Goals" within the same shared folder, its existence cannot be said to truly shape how faculty teach or assess writing in the Montserrat classroom. And indeed, the goals reflect only what "all Holy Cross students should develop the ability to" do, not how faculty should help students accomplish these goals or measure students' progress. Therefore, I modeled my fall 2021 Montserrat class around what, to my mind, seemed the central strengths of the Montserrat program—its emphasis on community-building and acclimation to college and introducing students to the types of critical thinking and academic writing they would be asked to do. Students and I spoke frequently about how we each come to the classroom with different histories and, often, different terms for overlapping writing moves. These conversations about not knowing or knowing differently were integral to positioning our classroom as a space of learning the conventions of academic writing as one variation of a larger genre.

I used this emphasis on learning rather than evaluating when discussing my grading model with students. Drawing from discussions with Gabe on contract grading, faculty workshops on specifications grading, and conference and social media conversations about accessible pedagogy, I shaped assessment in my Montserrat courses to favor completion, reflection, revision, and collaboration. Inoue's labor-based grading contracts functioned as starting points, from whence I made changes to address my personal concerns around "labor" and embodiment to more clearly align with principles of disability justice (Sins Invalid 2019) and the UDL. I presented students with a graphic representation and screen-reader ready version of what work needed to be completed to earn each letter grade, included here in Appendix C. I later supplemented these with a document explaining the grading system, offering a sample breakdown of how final grades were calculated, alongside resources for learning more about our and other forms of equitable assessment, included in Appendix B. On individual projects, students receive no letter grades, but instead written feedback from me identifying their arguments, celebrating their successes, and identifying areas we can continue to focus on in their future work.

In practice, this model of assessment extends beyond calculating grades. Like Claire, I offer multiple means of earning participation or engagement credit. Eschewing discourse of labor for how it often presumes able-bodiedness and a particular relation to timeliness, I also give no penalties for late submissions. These choices come directly from my work in disability and mad studies, following scholars including Moya Bailey (2021) and Margaret Price (2021). Bailey calls for an "ethics of pace," encouraging herself and others to rethink productivity and instead "demand a different orientation to work" (2021, 287). Both Bailey and Price remind their readers that timeliness and productivity affect multiply-marginalized students and faculty the greatest. Conceptualizations of time and labor reinforce an experience of higher education, then, that is predominantly white and able-bodied, since, as Price says, "most disabilities don't run on chronological time—they run on crip time" (2021, 270). I tell my students that I will accept late work; if they foresee handing in work beyond two days late, I request that they either meet with me or send me a note about their plan to complete the work. In doing so, I am meeting my students' stress with grace and highlighting alternate timeframes for my students, making it clear that I want the students to benefit from practicing the skills of our assignment, rather than suffer from overwork.

Although this is a relatively new practice, feedback from students has been largely positive. Students in spring 2022 reported feeling comfortable taking chances in their writing without fearing that their grades would suffer. Another student shared that ours was perhaps the first class for which she wrote what she wanted to write, rather than what she imagined the professor wanted to hear. While anecdotal and certainly limited by the imbalance of the student-professor relationship, this feedback encourages me to continue working toward increased student agency in my classroom and, with my own limited capacity as a contingent faculty member, across the institution overall.

In the parameters set by the college and department, however, this form of assessment might be more of a failure, as my grade distribution has fluctuated much more, approximating 0.17 more than department averages and 0.29 higher than the overall college average. Nor has the difference between my grading and my peers' gone unnoticed. During a review process before teaching the Montserrat course for 2022, the college curriculum committee used a request for more information on the previous year's syllabus to question the relationship between my course's intellectual value and grading structure, writing in a private email: "This lack of specificity raises concerns for me about the course's intellectual rigor. The course is probably plenty challenging; students rate her courses highly—but then, she also gives high grades."

Gabe's Faculty Development Efforts

While rethinking and revising the assessment structures I use has been critical to the social justice aims of my instructional philosophy and praxis, the changes I enact only impact the limited number of students enrolled in my courses. In my role as assistant director of the center for writing, however, I have the opportunity to encourage stakeholders across campus to revise their assessment philosophies through faculty development and outreach. I believe this work is critical. As important as it is for the discipline of composition studies to continue to develop and research more equitable assessment strategies, the reality is that the vast majority of writing instruction that happens across the curriculum is carried out by teachers who do not have a background in writing studies or composition pedagogy. This is particularly true in places like Holy Cross, where there is no formal writing program or FYW course. Since Holy Cross lacks an institutionalized writing in the disciplines apparatus to incentivize ongoing faculty development, this work is challenging. The center for writing has essentially had to rely on a "customer service" model for writing across the curriculum, providing support when faculty seek it out but unable to create any consistent application of writing pedagogies in the curriculum. In spite of this, some of the strategies we have adopted to encourage the uptake of more equitable writing assessment practices seem promising.

Encouraging Continuing Conversations

For years now, the center for writing has offered workshops and curated materials on contract grading and inclusive approaches to writing instruction. During spring 2021, these efforts intensified, with Asao Inoue speaking to the Holy Cross community in a series of virtual events. Inoue's workshops generated strong interest across campus. Afterward, the center for writing sponsored a series of one-to-one consultations as well as small faculty working groups that continued meeting to explore more equitable alternatives to traditional assessment practices. When I entered the role of assistant director in fall 2021, there was still considerable momentum behind these conversations, and we have built on this momentum by hosting several follow-up discussions. These discussions about ungrading and grading contracts continue to be the most well-attended of any events we organize. There are a number of possible reasons for this, including the way the COVID-19 pandemic realigned faculty attitudes toward their own labor and students' wellbeing, but our college's culture of rigor and elitism also seems to be an especially important factor—the significance placed on grades weighs on, and troubles, many faculty. Despite this interest, we have noticed a trend that is difficult to counteract: Many faculty who have enthusiastically attended several of our workshops are still hesitant to consult further about developing their own nontraditional grading systems or to experiment with actual changes to the assessment ecologies (Inoue 2015, 77) of their courses. Although we have not yet been able to formally assess the impact on classroom norms of workshops and events we have held, we hope that intentionally cultivating opportunities for faculty to learn more about equitable assessment practices will keep the issue in campus discourse and prompt faculty to keep learning and keep questioning their assessment methods. Ultimately, widespread and lasting change will depend on more extended dialogues, peer-to-peer sharing, and incentives for faculty to devote time to revising their courses.

Inviting Multiple Approaches

Though Asao Inoue's workshop on labor-based contracts kicked off a continuing series of discussions inviting faculty to reimagine assessment practices, the center for writing has maintained throughout that there is no one "best" way to assess writing equitably, and we have solicited concerns and critiques of the methods we have introduced alongside interest and questions. Cognizant of the problems labor-based contracts may pose for some students and faculty, we advocate a pluralistic approach to assessment and have intentionally invited faculty in diverse disciplines to take on leadership roles as group facilitators to explore (un)grading models with peers. Some faculty have opted to use labor-based grading contracts (Inoue 2019); others have taken up specifications grading (Nilson 2015); a group of mathematics faculty have explored mastery-based learning techniques that reduce the consequences of failure for students.

Most faculty have adapted and iterated existing models to better suit their own specific contexts. Because different disciplines have distinct epistemologies, teaching traditions, and writing conventions, instructors across the curriculum face assessment exigencies and pressures that differ from those familiar to composition teachers, and there is no one-size-fits-all model for what equitable assessment should look like in all contexts. What I try to remind faculty is that no assessment system by itself eliminates inequity, but trying a system that contrasts with the status quo presents an opportunity to reflect, to make values embedded in grades more visible. Thinking critically and regularly about our expectations and classroom policies is our best tool against replicating what Inoue (2019, 8) refers to as the "standard operating procedures" (Sue 2015, 90) we have been conditioned to see as natural.

Making It Easy

Often, the biggest barrier to meaningful change is how daunting the *logistics* of implementing those changes appear. One of the most frequent reservations I hear about contract grading, for example, is that instructors are not sure how they will be able to track or account for the work that students are doing using gradebooks or the LMS. While I try to point out that the difficulty of accounting for labor, engagement, or other metrics might reveal the difficulty of accurately accounting for quality that is often elided by conventionalized grading habits, logistics can indeed pose legitimate constraints. The reality is that educational structures at all levels work to position contract grading and other ungrading (Blum 2020) practices as outside the mainstream. For example, Holy Cross's LMS (Canvas) provides very few options for inputting grades that are not letters or numbers, a problem that has been documented by other authors (Laflen and Sims 2021, 123). To ameliorate this issue, the center for writing partnered with an instructional designer to create grading schemes and course templates that more easily accommodate several different versions of contract grading. We have also curated materials on equitable assessment into a digital archive, shared broadly with faculty. While I find it is usually productive for faculty to grapple with the conceptual, ethical, and pedagogical dimensions of ungrading as they determine the right ways to incorporate these practices into their teaching, providing models and smoothing areas of potential logistical overwhelm allows teachers to focus on the assessment problems that matter most.

With no formalized writing programs or instruction, assessing writing becomes a productive common ground to foster interdisciplinary conversations about writing and teaching. With decentralized writing infrastructure, faculty development in writing becomes all the more important as a means of intervention for not just improving the assessment of writing, but also making *teaching* more socially just.

Conclusion

While the dispersed and unformalized nature of writing instruction at our small college makes it difficult to present a unified picture of how we think equitable assessment might work, these three narratives show the importance of engaging in this work. In short, our students struggle to perform in the ways many traditional grading systems ask them to. Students frequently tell Hayley and Claire that they not only learned a lot from their classes, but felt valued and seen as a whole person. However, as shown throughout this chapter, enacting equitable assessment practices does not come without struggle. Following Craig's (2021) assertion that grading contracts are not by themselves anti-racist, we acknowledge that the assessment practices we discuss are not inherently anti-racist or anti-ableist solutions. Claire's narrative makes this explicit, as she demonstrates the ways her approach to grading agreements has shifted throughout her teaching career as she encountered ways in which particular students might be disadvantaged by particular models of grading. Therefore, we propose that meaningful institutional change happens through frequent reflection and collaboration across faculty and staff. Rather than recommending so-called best practices for equitable approaches to assessment, we propose that we instead view such practices as an interactive process that we constantly need to revise and evaluate due to the needs of our students. As reflective practitioners, we should always be asking ourselves: Who is harmed by my assessment practices? And what can I do to mitigate this harm? (See also Inoue and Poe 2020; West Puckett, Caswell, and Banks 2023, 43). Yet the answers to these questions are shifting terrain—different institutions, student populations, and circumstances may necessitate different approaches.

In our context, which is marked by a culture of elitism and exclusionary conceptions of academic rigor, working to subvert the primacy of grades and arbitrary or unjust notions of excellence seems especially urgent. While we have been motivated by finding ways to pursue greater equity for marginalized student populations, we have also been motivated out of concern for all students' physical and mental wellbeing, which has been threatened both by the pandemic and the intense pressures (and sometimes trauma) that our institution's academic elitism can create. As a consequence, we are less concerned with promoting a specific method of assessment than advocating for developing practices that resist tendencies toward rigor and exclusion at liberal arts colleges like ours. Ultimately, we believe the uncritical valuation of rigor can have profoundly damaging effects on instructors as well as students. Any approach that seeks to prevent some of this harm is a step in the right direction.

Subverting the exclusionary legacies of elitism in our curriculum has the potential to cultivate radical and positive institutional change that extends beyond the bounds of a single classroom. We have recently been encouraged, for instance, that the deans at our college are forwarding an agenda of "inclusive excellence" and the provost is adopting contract grading in her own teaching. While we cannot take credit for these developments, we agree with Porter et al. (2000) that it is the collective and practical actions of many stakeholders combined with intentional and strategic reflection on those efforts that has the potential to create meaningful institutional change.

While the focus of this chapter has been on how classroom ("small a") assessment practices respond to and influence larger institutional assessment logics, the equity-minded reflection on grading we advocate for may hold promise for institutional ("large A") assessments as well. What would it look like to do an assessment of instructors' grading practices across an institution? How might an assessment of instructors' grading philosophies complement or complicate the insights gleaned from a large-scale assessment of students' work and/or grades? How do programmatic assessments account for an institution's or unit's culture regarding rigor and what grades symbolize? And how might faculty reflection on grading and equity become an explicit goal of programmatic or institutional assessment? Although our institutional roles and the absence of traditional writing programs at our college pose barriers to pursuing many of these questions, we hope they prove generative for WPAs and individual instructors planning assessments at other SLACs.

We are lucky to be situated at a college that affords the pedagogical autonomy and labor conditions needed to undertake such thoughtful and strategic reflection on assessment practices. Still, work that counters the status quo carries risks, especially for untenured faculty like us, as the opening to this chapter illustrates. Our experiences have reaffirmed the value of community and solidarity in such efforts. We hope that by sharing our experiences both within our institution and beyond it in spaces like this collection, we can incrementally erode the toxic elitism we have critiqued in this chapter and also develop coalitions that are capable of carrying forward this critique across other sites and levels of SLAC education.

Bibliography

Bailey, Moya. 2021. "The Ethics of Pace." *South Atlantic Quarterly* 120, no. 2 (April): 285–99. https://doi.org/10.1215/00382876-8916032.

Bizzell, Patricia. 2016. "Historical Notes on Rhetoric in Jesuit Education." In *Traditions of Eloquence: The Jesuits and Modern Rhetorical Studies*, edited by Cinthia Gannett and John C. Brereton, 39–59. New York: Fordham University Press.

Blum, Susan Debra, ed. 2020. *Ungrading: Why Rating Students Undermines Learning (and What to Do Instead)*. 2nd ed. Morgantown: West Virginia University Press.

Carillo, Ellen C. 2021.*The Hidden Inequities in Labor-Based Contract Grading*. Louisville: University Press of Colorado.

College of the Holy Cross. n.d. "Mission Statement." Last modified 2022. https://www.holycross.edu/about-us/mission-statement.

College of the Holy Cross. n.d. "Montserrat." Last modified 2022. https://www.holycross.edu/holy-cross-approach/montserrat.

College of the Holy Cross. n.d. "Passport." Last modified 2022. https://www.holycross.edu/support-and-resources/academic-services-and-learning-resources/passport.

Craig, Sherri. 2021. "Your Contract Grading Ain't It." *Writing Program Administration* 44, no. 3: 145–46.

Gladstein, Jill M., and Dara Rossman Regaignon. 2012. *Writing Program Administration at Small Liberal Arts Colleges*. Anderson: Parlor Press.

Gomes, Mathew, Bree Bellati, Mia Hope, and Alissa LaFerriere. 2020."Enabling Meaningful Labor: Narratives of Participation in a Grading Contract." *Journal of Writing Assessment* 13, no. 2. https://escholarship.org/uc/item/1p60j218.

Grouling, Jennifer. 2022. *Adapting VALUEs: Tracing the Life of a Rubric through Institutional Ethnography*. Fort Collins: WAC Clearinghouse.

Hamraie, Aimi. 2020. "Accessible Teaching in the Time of COVID-19." *Critical Design Lab* (blog). March 10, 2020. https://www.mapping-access.com/blog-1/2020/3/10/accessible-teaching-in-the-time-of-covid-19.

Inoue, Asao B. 2015. *Antiracist Writing Assessment Ecologies: Teaching and Assessing Writing for a Socially Just Future*. Fort Collins: WAC Clearinghouse.

Inoue, Asao B. 2019. *Labor-Based Grading Contracts: Building Equity and Inclusion in the Compassionate Writing Classroom*. Fort Collins: WAC Clearinghouse.

Inoue, Asao B., and Mya Poe. 2020. "How to Stop Harming Students: An Ecological Guide to Antiracist Writing Assessment." *Composition Studies* 48, no. 3 (Fall). https://compositionstudiesjournal.files.wordpress.com/2021/02/poeinoue_full-3.pdf.

Kryger, Kathleen, and Griffin X. Zimmerman. 2020. "Neurodivergence and Intersectionality in Labor-Based Grading Contracts." *Journal of Writing Assessment* 13, no. 2. https://escholarship.org/uc/item/0934x4rm.

Laflen, Angela, and Mikenna Sims. 2021. "Designing a More Equitable Scorecard: Grading Contracts and Online Writing Instruction." In *PARS in Practice: More Resources and Strategies for Online Writing Instructors*, edited by Jessie Borgman and Casey McArdle, 119–39. Fort Collins: WAC Clearinghouse.

Nilson, Linda Burzotta. 2015. *Specifications Grading: Restoring Rigor, Motivating Students, and Saving Faculty Time.* Sterling: Stylus Publishing.

Porter, James E., Patricia Sullivan, Stuart Blythe, Jeffrey T. Grable, and Libby Miles. 2000. "Institutional Critique: A Rhetorical Methodology for Change." *College Composition and Communication* 51, no. 4 (June): 610–42.

Price, Margaret. 2021. "Time Harms: Disabled Faculty Navigating the Accommodations Loop." *South Atlantic Quarterly* 120, no. 2 (April): 257–77.

Sins Invalid. 2019. *Skin, Tooth, and Bone: The Basis of Movement Is Our People.* 2nd ed. Berkeley: Sins Invalid.

Sue, Derald Wing. 2015. *Race Talk and the Conspiracy of Silence: Understanding and Facilitating Difficult Dialogues on Race.* New York: Wiley.

West-Puckett, Stephanie, Nicole I. Caswell, and William P. Banks. 2023. *Failing Sideways: Queer Possibilities for Writing Assessment.* Logan: Utah State University Press.

Womack, Anne-Marie, Annelise Blanchard, Cassie Wang, and Mary Catherine Jessee. 2015. *Accessible Syllabus.* Last modified 2022. https://www.accessiblesyllabus.com/.

Appendix A: Claire's FYW Grading Agreement

Grading Agreement for ENGL 110: Introduction to Academic Writing

For this class, we will be using an engagement-based approach to grading. An engagement-based grading approach relies primarily on the level to which you engage in the course. That means that your final course letter grade will be the result of your completion of our major assignments and your completion of what I am calling "class engagement activities" (as detailed explicitly below).

Overall Grading Criteria

If you complete all the major assignments and the amount of class engagement activities that I ask of you, you will receive a grade of "A" for this course. **To receive an A grade**, you must complete the following criteria:

1. All four major assignments (fulfilling all criteria)
2. Satisfy the "class engagement" criteria by completing eleven (11) of the listed class engagement activities.

To earn a grade of B, you must still complete item 1 above but have completed no more than nine (9) of the class engagement activities.

To earn a grade of C, you must still complete item 1 above but have completed no more than seven (7) class engagement activities.

I hope not to assign any grades lower than a "C"; however, students who only fully complete three (3) major assignments, or fewer than seven (7) class engagement activities **will earn a grade of D.**

Students who only fully complete two (2) major assignments (or one or none of the major assignments), or fewer than five (5) class engagement activities **will earn a grade of F in the course.**

For each student, I will keep a chart that records your completion of assignments and your class engagement activities. Your individual chart will be shared with you so you can access it at any time. I am willing to discuss your chart at any time if you have questions, concerns, observations, etc.

Class Engagement Criteria

There are many legitimate reasons for which a student may need to miss class, or for which they may not be able to conform to typical notions of "participation" that measure how often students speak in class. Therefore, I have created a singular class engagement grade that offers multiple pathways in which you can demonstrate your engagement in the class and the materials, dependent on your skills, abilities, personality, or personal circumstances of this semester.

To satisfy the class engagement criteria and earn an A in the course, you must complete eleven of the twenty-two class engagement activities listed below. It is possible more engagement activities will arise as the semester progresses (in fact, if you have an idea for one, let me know!). Similar activities are cumulative, so, for example, if you submit three discussion questions on twelve occasions, you will have completed three class engagement activities (6 through 8 under "Class Participation").

Writing Responses

1. Complete three of the regular writing responses on time (by end of the day before the intended class period).

2. Complete six of the regular writing responses on time (by end of the day before the intended class period).

3. Complete nine of the regular writing responses on time (by end of the day before the intended class period).

4. Complete twelve of the regular writing responses on time (by end of the day before the intended class period).

5. Read a threshold concept not assigned in class and write a 1-2 page response in which you discuss how this concept relates to our assigned course readings and your own experiences with writing (one additional participation milestone for each threshold concept response submitted).

Class Participation

1. Arrive prepared to one of two individual conferences.

2. Arrive prepared to two of two individual conferences.

3. Contribute to class discussions occasionally (in at least ten class sessions).

4. Contribute to class discussions regularly (in at least twenty class sessions).

5. Contribute to class discussions frequently (in at least thirty class sessions).

6. Email me three (3) discussion questions on four (4) occasions in preparation for class. Questions are due by end of the day on the Sunday, Tuesday, or Thursday immediately prior to class meeting.

7. Email me three (3) discussion questions on eight (8) occasions in preparation for class. Questions are due by end of the day on the Sunday, Tuesday, or Thursday immediately prior to class meeting.

8. Email three (3) discussion questions on twelve (12) occasions in preparation for class. Questions are due by end of the day on the Sunday, Tuesday, or Thursday immediately prior to class meeting.

9. Post a reflection on the class discussion with some follow-up thoughts/questions to our discussion board three (3) times (due before the first class period after which you are reflecting upon).

10. Post a reflection on the class discussion with some follow-up thoughts/questions to our discussion board six (6) times (due before the first class period after which you are reflecting upon).

11. Post a reflection on the class discussion with some follow-up thoughts/questions to our discussion board nine (9) times (due before the first class period after which you are reflecting upon)

Peer Feedback and Revision

1. Offer peers substantial feedback during one of two peer feedback sessions.

2. Offer peers substantial feedback during two of two peer feedback sessions.

3. Revise one (1) major assignment an additional time after receiving feedback from me.

4. Revise two (2) major assignments an additional time after receiving feedback from me.

Out of Class Engagement
1. Attend appointments during my office hours on at least two occasions.
2. Attend a writer's workshop appointment for one of our major assignments and submit a follow-up memo about the appointment's contribution to your assignment.

Criteria for Completing Major Assignments
For each of the major assignments to be considered complete, there are a few expectations for the level to which you engage with the assignment. These criteria are:

- You must complete the entire assignment (that is, complete all requested requirements) in the manner asked and turn it in in the appropriate manner (i.e. bringing a draft to class, uploading to Canvas, etc.).
- You must complete every required draft.
- When the job is to revise your writing, you are expected to not just copy-edit or "touch up" your work but to reshape, extend, complicate, and/or relate those ideas to new things. Revisions must somehow respond to or consider seriously feedback you received (from me or your colleagues) or the new ideas you were exposed to before being asked to revise.

If you turn in essays that do not fully meet the criteria, you will be asked to revise them until they do. However, once you have made those revisions, the assignment will be considered complete and, per our agreement, you will not lose any points or suffer a decrease in grade.

Appendix B: Hayley's Montserrat "Explanation of Course Grades" Handout

Explanation of Course Grades

Our course uses a form of engagement-based assessment. This means that I prioritize your involvement in class, completion of assignments, and revision of work. To help make grading more transparent, I have provided you with a grade menu for each component of our course, which outlines ways that you might achieve a F, D, C, B, or A grade in this course. Because each of the components of our class leaves room for you to do different levels of work, this is only one potential model for each grade. You can move your final grade up or down based on the work you complete for each component.

Why Are We Using This Grading Style?

The grading styles that most of us are used to involve students submitting assignments to faculty, who evaluate the work through values like merit (i.e., how "good" the work is), effort (how hard a student worked or how much time is perceived to have gone into the work), and eloquence (how much a student's writing style conforms to formal conventions of academic writing). While we each may have ideas about these qualities, our understanding of them likely varies widely. Growing research by students, teachers, and scholars tells us that the values we use to evaluate student work often depend upon the assumptions built into our society, including those of class, disability, gender, language, and race. In efforts to make evaluation more equitable, many faculty implement alternative grading practices, such as contract grading or specifications grading. These practices try to reduce the subjectiveness of "good" work by clearly outlining the steps a student must take to achieve each grade. Our particular grading style assesses students based on ways of evaluating your engagement in the course. You earn credit for the work you complete, rather than losing credit for work not completed. The goal here is to encourage students to practice the skills baked into each assignment, rather than submit rushed work to meet a deadline.

What This Looks like in Practice

Rather than grades on individual assignments, you will receive a grade for each component of our course. That is, you will practice skills and complete work toward an overall course engagement grade, a compositions grade, a presentation grade, a community and campus involvement grade, and a creative project grade. Those component grades each make up a different perspective of your final course grade. For each major assignment, I will send you a detailed note with my feedback on your work. This feedback will include my overall understanding of your argument or project ideas, what I perceived as your strengths and project highlights, what skills or ideas we might work on together to develop further, and suggestions on how you might do so. I've drawn up a sample of random grades below to demonstrate this. Holy Cross grades are marked by letters, but I've translated them to number grades here to show you the math behind this.

Course Component	Component Grade	Percent of Final Grade	Calculated Grade
Course engagement	89	20	17.8
Compositions	92	25	23
Presentation	89	15	13.35
Community/campus involvement	86	25	21.5
Creative project	92	15	13.8
			89.45

A (96), A- (92), B+ (89), B (86), B- (82), C+ (79), C (76), C- (72), D+ (69)

How to Check on Your Course Progress

You can evaluate your progress in our course on your own by keeping track of the work you complete and submit and checking these against the grade menus on Canvas. I will distribute periodic progress reports of the work I observe or review, too. At any point in our course, you can also email or meet with me to get a sense of what you have achieved in our class.

Want to Learn More?

Check out these resources to learn more about alternative grading styles.

Blum, Susan D., ed. 2020. *Ungrading: Why Rating Students Undermines Learning (and What to Do Instead)*. Morgantown: West Virginia University Press.

Carillo, Ellen C. 2021. *The Hidden Inequities in Labor-Based Contract Grading*. Louisville: University Press of Colorado.

Inoue, Isao B. 2019. *Labor Based Grading Contracts: Building Equity and Inclusion in the Compassionate Writing Classroom*. WAC Clearinghouse: University Press of Colorado.

Klotz, Sarah, and Carl Whithaus. 2021. "Contract Grading as Anti-Racist Praxis in the Community College Context." *Empowering the Community College First-Year Composition Teacher: Pedagogies and Policies*, edited by Meryl Siegal and Betsy Gilliland, 62–80. Ann Arbor: University of Michigan Press.

Konrad, Annika. 2021. "Access Fatigue: The Rhetorical Work of Disability in Everyday Life." *College English* 83, no. 2: 180–99.

Stommel, Jesse. 2020. "Ungrading: An FAQ." Jesse Stommel. Last modified February 6, 2020. https://www.jessestommel.com/ungrading-an-faq/.

Appendix C: Hayley's Fall 2021 Grade Menu and Course Engagement Activities

Grade Menu
Your Agency as a Student

	A	B	C
Course Engagement	Two or more activities per week	Two activities per week	One or more activities per week on average
Compositions	Two major composition assignments Revisions of composition I Reflection of composition II More than six composition activities	Two major composition assignments Revisions of one major composition More than five composition activities	Two major composition assignments More than four composition activities
Presentation	Script Handout Close reading of activist art	Script Close reading of activist art	Script Close reading of activist art
Community/campus involvement	Community-based learning (CBL) journal Attendance at five events (including Divine cluster event) Brief Instagram posts for each	CBL journal Attendance at four events (including Divine cluster event) Brief Instagram posts for each	CBL journal Attendance at three events (including Divine cluster event) Brief Instagram posts for each
Creative project	Creative project Artist statement	Creative project Artist statement	Creative project

This grade menu outlines ways that you might achieve a C, B, or A grade in this course. Because each of the five components of our class leaves room for you to do different levels of work, this is only one potential model for each grade. That means you can move your final grade up or down based on the work you complete for each component. A C grade is based on completion; if you complete all of the assignments in the C column, then you will achieve a C in the class. To achieve an A or B grade, I'll ask you to more deeply engage with each assignment. This might include revising a composition project or critically reflecting on a creative project. I will explain the processes for each assignment and its grading scale on assignment prompts on Canvas.

Course Engagement Activities

Participating in our class can take many shapes. I've outlined some options for getting credit for participating in our class on the syllabus. Each week, I ask that you submit a participation self-checkout form. This asks you to report back on how you engaged in and were a part of our class community this week. I'll keep track of this, too, but reflecting on the week and how you thought about our course content is also a great way to process information and strengthen your understanding of it.

Daily Options
- Contributing to class conversation
- Creating discussion questions
- Taking notes for the class
- Monitoring the backchannel during class

Weekly Options
- Recording/writing a weekly wrap-up
- Meeting with Prof. Stefan
- Sharing a relevant resource
- Visiting the writer's workshop
- Reporting on a campus resource

9 Developing Anti-Racist Assessment of First-Semester Writing Seminars to Support Students from Historically Underrepresented Groups

Diane LeBlanc and Bridget Draxler

Abstract: This chapter presents a model for assessing student learning using anti-racist assessment practices. We developed this model to evaluate first-semester writing seminars that enroll primarily first-generation, Pell-eligible, multilingual, and international students at St. Olaf College, a selective, residential liberal arts college in rural Minnesota with approximately 3,000 undergraduate students. Our model is designed to assess student learning while addressing larger questions of how to measure characteristics of process engagement, language development, confidence, affect, and use of support resources. Drawing on results from a multi-year assessment project, this chapter explains how we combined institutional data, focus groups, artifact scoring, and scoring participant reflections to design and implement anti-racist pedagogy and assessment.

Introduction

We teach at a small liberal arts college[1] with a seventeen-credit general education curriculum, which includes themed first-year seminars and first-year writing courses taught by faculty across

---

1. St. Olaf College is a private, residential liberal arts college that enrolls approximately 3,000 undergraduate students, 95 percent of whom live on campus. A

the curriculum.[2] While first-year writing existed prior to implementation of this updated general education in 2021, St. Olaf did not require or offer a first-year seminar. To close preparation gaps, approximately seventy students each year took a full-credit developmental writing seminar during fall semester to boost their transition experience and prepare for a spring-semester first-year writing course. We offered two fall courses in this sequence, one for students who had graduated from a US high school (we both taught this course) and one for students who identified as international students. These first-semester writing seminars, required of students who placed into them, typically enrolled twelve or fewer students, included embedded writing tutors and emphasized faculty/student interaction.[3] But for twenty years, unlike first-year writing, first-semester writing seminars did not carry general education credit or count toward any majors, which meant institutional protocols for cyclical assessment did not prompt or require assessment of student learning in these courses. Individual instructors assessed student learning with graded assignments, student reflections within assignments, and course evaluations. To understand and measure student learning with

---

historically predominantly white institution founded by Norwegian Lutheran immigrants, St. Olaf enrolled 22 percent domestic BIPOC students and 10 percent international students in the first-year class of fall 2022. First-generation students made up 20 percent of that class, and 23 percent identified as legacy students, with a family member previously attending the college. While many students complete a STEM major, 33 percent of students participate in the college's well-known music programs. Enrollment numbers have remained strong in recent years as retention and graduation rates declined slightly: 90 percent of students retain from the first to second year, and 80 percent graduate in four years. The college meets the demonstrated financial need of every student, including the cost of studying abroad/away.

2. We are grateful to Dr. Rebecca Richards, our colleague and co-researcher who helped design and implement this assessment plan during her time at St. Olaf. Special thanks to Victoria Gutierrez, Kelsey Halverson, Mickey TerLouw, and especially Meiyi Chen, our student research team.

3. In fall 2021, we transitioned these courses to writing-intensive first-year seminars to integrate them into a new general education curriculum. Five distinct first-year seminars are designated as writing intensive to replace previous first-semester developmental writing courses, and students now earn general education credit for these seminars. These first-semester writing seminars retained their learning outcomes (Appendix A), size, and embedded writing support. They continue to prepare students for first-year writing courses, which enroll nineteen students and emphasize thesis-driven arguments, researched writing, and writing as a process.

greater equity in these courses, we proposed an assessment project as part of a four-year, $800,000 Mellon Foundation grant[4] that funded college-wide projects to enhance curricular equity and inclusion.

We began our project with intentions to gather data to answer a question we heard frequently from first-year writing faculty: *Didn't this student take that writing course with you last fall? Why can't this student . . . in my first-year writing class?* Fill in the blank with anything from "use a comma after an introductory clause" to "cite a work in an anthology," and you'll understand our impulse to want a quantifiable measure of student learning. We saw transformational learning in these courses, but our justifications were largely anecdotal. We hoped quantitative data might demonstrate the effectiveness of these courses and shift our colleagues' attention from student performance to student progress toward learning outcomes (Appendix A). That impulse, however, gave way to more authentic questions as we developed our assessment model and learned from students the significance of experiences and learning that aren't easily quantified.

This chapter presents a model for assessing student learning in first-semester writing seminars that enroll primarily first-generation, Pell-eligible, multilingual, and international students. Our model, drawing primarily from current work by Linda Suskie (2018), Edward White (2015, 2016), Asao Inoue (2015, 2019), and Asao Inoue and Mya Poe (2020), is designed to assess student learning while addressing larger questions of how to measure characteristics of process engagement, language development, confidence, affect, and use of support resources. Drawing on results from a multi-year assessment project at St. Olaf College, this chapter explains the following elements of project design in context of anti-racist pedagogy and assessment:

- General institutional research board approval
- Institutional data selection and analysis
- Focus group design and data coding
- Artifact scoring and participant reflection opportunities
- Conclusions and caveats

---

4. The Mellon Foundation grant proposal, *To Include Is To Excel*, was a collaborative effort among the college Office of Government, Foundation, and Corporate Relations, the Office of Institutional Effectiveness and Assessment, and senior leadership. During 2017- 2021, the grant supported sixty-four projects for curriculum and assessment transformation. Draxler and LeBlanc were members of the advisory group, and LeBlanc served as a liaison between the grant administrators and the college Center for Innovation in the Liberal Arts.

Snapshots of our data offer sample measures and illustrate how our assessment model evolved. Our larger focus, however, is the model itself: its goals, its design and development, and its potential applicability to other writing programs.

The featured assessment project began with a broad objective to measure how well first-semester writing seminars equipped students to succeed in the required first-year writing course. Our objective narrowed predictably as we developed our assessment model. We centered anti-racist practices at the core of assessment design in three ways: 1) we integrated multiple measures, including institutional data, focus groups with former students and tutors, and faculty/staff workshops that evolved from reading and scoring student artifacts to reflecting more broadly on evaluation standards and practices; 2) we revised a scoring rubric to replace deficit-based language with terms to affirm "emerging" writers, only to discover that old tropes clung to the alternate language; and 3) we engaged undergraduate student researchers, including some who were previously students in the first-semester writing seminars.

Results confirmed that students who succeeded in first-semester writing seminars developed help-seeking habits, responded to feedback with greater agency, and transferred habits and skills that enabled them to succeed in first-year writing. But despite these affirming results, we discovered areas in which our assessment practices reinforced systemic biases. Most significantly, we initially asked faculty and staff readers to assess decontextualized writing samples with a benchmarking rubric. The activity ultimately reinforced scorers' implicit bias, recognized students' preparation and prior knowledge, and prevented equitable assessment of student learning. It also corroborated research conclusions that scoring guides, as assessment tools, are best situated in context of course curriculum and student process (White 2007), and that empowering assessment sees beyond a written artifact to consider the material conditions in which students live and write (Inoue 2015, 88). The scoring activity, ultimately, was most valuable as a professional development opportunity through which readers reflected on their expectations and reading biases before and after the scoring. The workshops enabled us to reflect critically on and challenge the use of rubrics within this project and for general education writing assessment more broadly.

This assessment project further revealed the role of affective experiences in students' development as writers. In focus groups, students consistently acknowledged that these courses prepared them to ask for help, to understand and respond to feedback, to develop a process for writing, and to be confident in their identities as writers. These results affirmed essential development through desirable learning outcomes (Appendix A). At the same time, our findings reinforced the need for equity-based efforts to adopt standards of proficiency that recognize world Englishes and to redefine critical ability in ways that decenter white, upper-middle class educational and social experiences.

In addition to elements of project design, this chapter includes the following resources to enable readers to replicate or adapt this assessment model to their own institutional contexts:

- First-semester writing seminar and first-year writing learning outcomes (Appendix A)
- Focus group questions (Appendix B)
- Codes for focus group transcriptions (Appendix C)
- Pre- and post-workshop reflection prompts for faculty/staff scoring workshops (Appendix D)

Project Description, Goals, and Objectives

Our study's primary purpose was to measure the effectiveness of first-semester writing seminars. These courses, taken during fall semester of the first year, served students from underrepresented groups, including recent immigrants, refugees, first-generation and Pell-eligible students, and students from racial and/or linguistic minoritized communities. From 2012 to 2016, the course for multilingual international students enrolled 96 percent nonresident international students and 27 percent first-generation college students. The course for students who had graduated from a US high school enrolled 83 percent domestic multicultural students and 82 percent first-generation college students; in addition, 75 percent of the students met federal low-income designation, and 67 percent met both federal low-income and first-generation college student designation.

Two specific research questions drove our assessment project:

1. Do these first-semester writing seminars fulfill the intended learning outcomes (Appendix A), offering students underrepresented at St. Olaf the skills and habits of mind to succeed as college students and writers?

2. Are these learning outcomes appropriate for the course sequence, or should we revise them to create a more effective curriculum and supportive, equitable environment for student learning?

To answer these questions, we pursued three project goals:
1. To analyze institutional data
2. To conduct focus groups with former students and embedded tutors in these courses
3. To facilitate faculty/staff reading and scoring of student artifacts.

Methods

Assessment Design Origins

We devoted the first year of our project to reading assessment literature, creating instrument prototypes, and identifying means to measure both student learning and program equity and effectiveness. We drew first from two familiar sources: Suskie's *Assessing Student Learning: A Common Sense Guide* (2018) and White, Elliot, and Peckham's *Very Like a Whale: The Assessment of Writing Programs* (2015). The intentionally anti-racist model we imagined, however, required framing with theory and practice specific to anti-racist assessment. Inoue's *Antiracist Writing Assessment Ecologies* (2015) provided anti-racist theory and sample rubrics based on labor and student-generated criteria instead of conventions and language standards defined by a dominant group. Meanwhile, relevant assessment literature cited Poe's research on writing assessment, particularly bias in holistic scoring, and development of anti-racist teaching practices. We blended best practices and theory from these sources, highlighted below, as our assessment model and understanding of early results evolved through trial and error.

Suskie's *Assessing Student Learning* presents a variety of assessment models and contexts, guides users through learning outcome and rubric design, and suggests strategies for analyzing, responding to, and acting in response to data. We were assessing learning in courses with long-standing outcomes based on the WPA *Outcomes Statement* and informed by skills, habits of mind, and experiences described in the "Framework for Success in Postsecondary Writing" (2011), so early chapters confirmed assessment elements already in place. Suskie's book was most helpful as we designed and recruited for student surveys and focus groups (Chapter 21) and faculty/staff scoring sessions of student essays (Chapter 12). *Assessing Student Learning* was our repeated reminder to design a model that was cost-effective in terms of both time and money.

White et al. look at and beyond individual student learning to focus on writing program assessment. Viewing writing as a construct, they assert that writing (the construct) must be assessed in context of the learning environment or ecology (where instructors model constructs for writers). This theoretical position rejects the common practice of engaging non-course faculty in holistic scoring of anonymized artifacts because, regardless of training and norming, readers who lack understanding of the learning and assessment ecology in which writers write will rely on a myth of universal standards and score with implicit bias. White et al.'s model aligned with our goal to move beyond the pretense of objectivity and interrater reliability based on dominant norms. Their research bolstered our theoretical framework even as the scale and costs of assessment in their case studies, particularly a first-year assessment of gains measured by a placement sample and an end-of-semester sample, were beyond our project scope.

In *Antiracist Writing Assessment Ecologies* (2015), Inoue takes White et al.'s emphasis on construct and ecology further to define "white racial habitus" and its impact on writers of color. We drew heavily from Chapter 2, "Antiracist Writing Assessment Ecologies," to theorize the impact of ecology on writers at our predominantly white institution. Inoue's attention to roles of dialogue, language negotiation, and power politics in anti-racist classroom assessment ultimately would confirm that we could not facilitate anti-racist holistic scoring of essays by non-course faculty with a common rubric outside of the classes (ecologies) in which students wrote. Regardless of the descriptive rubric we aimed to create, scoring without the context of student process and labor would reflect reader bias.

Shortly after we completed our assessment project, Inoue and Poe (2020) published their infographic, "How to Stop Harming Students: An Ecological Guide to Antiracist Writing Assessment." By then, we were developing professional development workshops and gathering teaching resources to support remote teaching during a global pandemic and to adopt or deepen anti-racist teaching in response to police brutality and racial injustice. "How to Stop Harming Students" became an essential tool for framing our assessment project in both hindsight and forward action.

Summary of Activities

We applied for IRB approval to work with vulnerable populations, a common category for students in our study. Our project design and ethics plan emphasized student safety and well-being in several ways. To meet the criteria of a no-risk project with intended dissemination beyond the college, our intended IRB approval level, we

- gathered disidentified writing samples from faculty with student permission;
- limited participants' time commitment and compensated them for their time;
- waited to conduct focus groups until after we posted semester grades;
- trained student researchers (vs. faculty) to lead focus groups; and
- integrated opportunities for meaningful reflection into the students' optional participation.

We analyzed institutional data in two areas to examine patterns among students who enrolled in first-semester writing seminars in fall 2012 and fall 2013[5]: course grades and demographic representation in published instrument results. The grade analysis was a simple comparison of course grades in first-semester writing seminars and subsequent first-year writing. To understand existing data about student critical thinking and writing, and to determine who that data represented, we also reviewed recent college assessment reports. We focused on data from published instruments (e.g., National Survey of Student Engagement, CIRP Freshman Survey, Collegiate Learning Assessment Plus [CLA+]) that our institution administered regularly. Our goal was to determine the kinds of information that might predict or reflect student performance in these courses. To that end, we focused on results of the CLA+, which St. Olaf administered every three years until discontinuing it in 2019. CLA+ is a value-added measure of student learning. In 2012, it used an institution's average SAT score to predict student performance and to compare student performance among comparator institutions. If student scores aligned with or exceeded predicted scores, institutions were "adding value." Scores lower than predicted performance defined areas for institutional response. CLA+ is a direct assessment that requires participants to complete two tasks: 1) respond to a scenario using data and documents as evidence to construct an argument, and 2) answer document-based questions accurately.

To complement direct assessment provided by institutional data, we gathered indirect measures of student development and engagement through student focus groups. Interview responses enabled us to assess be-

---

5. We began our project in 2017. To allow for longitudinal data analysis in all general education writing courses, we identified students in the class of 2016 who had taken the first-semester writing seminars as first-year students 2012. Our initial plan to analyze longitudinal data wasn't manageable, but we studied select institutional data about the cohort that we originally identified. Focus groups involved more recent classes.

havioral learning outcomes that we could not measure directly. These focus groups centered student agency within our assessment model, both as research partners and focus group participants. Working closely with us, a student researcher who was formerly a student and an embedded tutor for a first-semester writing seminar interviewed thirty-four students in fourteen focus groups (two to three students per group) to document their experience in first-semester writing seminars. The same student researcher interviewed eleven embedded tutors in six focus groups (two to three tutors per group). The interviewer asked students questions about their processes, habits, and mindsets as writers, along with advice that they would give future students in these writing seminars (Appendix B). A transcription service transcribed the interviews, we pre-coded categories, student researchers sorted responses into pre-coded categories, and we then clustered responses according to five areas aligned with course learning outcomes: writing, reading, library research, affect, and transfer (Appendix C). Grant funding enabled us to compensate both the researcher and student participants, which was important for us to communicate that we valued their time and knowledge. We measured student learning through focus groups that embedded learning in the assessment process itself.[6] Invited to reflect in community on their learning experiences, focus group participants both reported and reinforced the writing habits and beliefs they developed in the courses.[7]

To reach our third goal of gathering quantitative measures of student learning in the first-semester writing seminars, we developed a holistic scoring rubric and facilitated two day-long writing assessment workshops, in fall 2018 and spring 2019, involving thirty-two faculty and staff.

We worked our way into several dead ends as we created the rubric. We imagined a tool that would measure student achievement of course learning outcomes but not further disadvantage students with standards defined by dominant discourse conventions and language. As we reviewed our course

---

6. Focus group results also were useful to us in practical ways. Several students noted that they enjoyed and learned a lot from the seminar but were disappointed that they didn't earn general education credit; students now earn general education credit for the current first-semester writing seminar.

7. For another assessment tool that draws on students' self-efficacy, see Schmidt, Katherine M. and Joel E. Alexander. 2012. "The Empirical Development of an Instrument to Measure Writerly Self-Efficacy in Writing Centers." *Journal of Writing Assessment*, 5(1). Retrieved from https://escholarship.org/uc/item/5dp4m86t. While we often conduct self-efficacy surveys based on Schmidt and Alexander's model within first-semester writing seminars, we chose focus groups for our assessment project to avoid contributing to student survey fatigue.

rubrics, AAC&U value rubrics for critical thinking and written communication, and sample rubrics by Suskie and by John Bean (2011), we found standards defined by dominant discourses. To design an equitable assessment instrument, we aimed to reframe participants' perceptions of rhetorical variations and language differences in two ways. First, we developed rubric categories according to course learning outcomes to focus scoring primarily on what we were teaching about audience awareness and use of sources, with lesser attention to writing conventions. We likewise framed writing conventions in terms of clarity instead of correctness. (The learning outcomes related to habits, mindset, and process were conspicuously absent from the rubric because we cannot capture those process skills in measurable criteria from a single artifact.) Second, we used asset-based language to label the benchmarks "underdeveloped," "emerging," "proficient," and "beyond expectations." We avoided numbers and common deficit-based labels such as "does not meet expectations" or "needs improvement."

At each workshop, participants completed pre- and post-workshop reflections to document how they responded to student writing that challenges the norms of standardized academic writing. The pre-workshop prompt asked readers to select among three stances, and the post-workshop prompt asked participants to reflect on attitude changes due to workshop activities. The stances, adapted from Matsuda and Cox (2011), were assimilationist, accommodationist, and separatist (Appendix D). Both workshops included a guided norming activity (reading, scoring, and discussing scores) to define rubric terminology and to establish interrater reliability within teams of two readers. During the fall workshop only, participants scored a total of forty-nine essays and briefly discussed their scores and use of the rubric. In our results section below, we explain why our second workshop eliminated direct artifact assessment and focused on professional development.

Results and Discussion

Institutional Data

Institutional and assessment data are the building blocks of narratives about student learning. We knew that students in our first-semester writing seminars were oversampled through institutional data gathering about "underrepresented students." But were their experiences part of the college's larger learning narrative based on institutional assessment data? The original goal was to identify information that might predict or reflect performance in these courses, but the data revealed much more about both our students and our institutional culture. Our assessment model challenges the use of published instruments whose results create learning narratives without intentional efforts to represent minoritized students in proportion to the overall student population.

Because we were assessing the first of a two-course sequence, we began with the most accessible and direct measure of learning: course grades. Multiple-measure assessment goes beyond correlative measures such as comparing first-semester writing seminar grades to subsequent first-year writing grades, but grade comparison offered a baseline for knowing if students in first-semester writing seminars then successfully completed first-year writing. Instead of comparing actual grades, which reflect instructor values and bias, we plotted grade gains and losses in the progression from the fall to spring writing courses. In fall 2012 and fall 2013, 107 students completed first-semester writing seminars and advanced to first-year writing in the subsequent semesters.[8] Among those students, twenty-one students earned the same final grades in the fall and spring courses, thirty students' final grades decreased up to two-thirds of a letter grade (e.g., dropping from B+ to B-) and fifty-six students' final grades increased up to two-thirds of a letter grade (Figure 1).

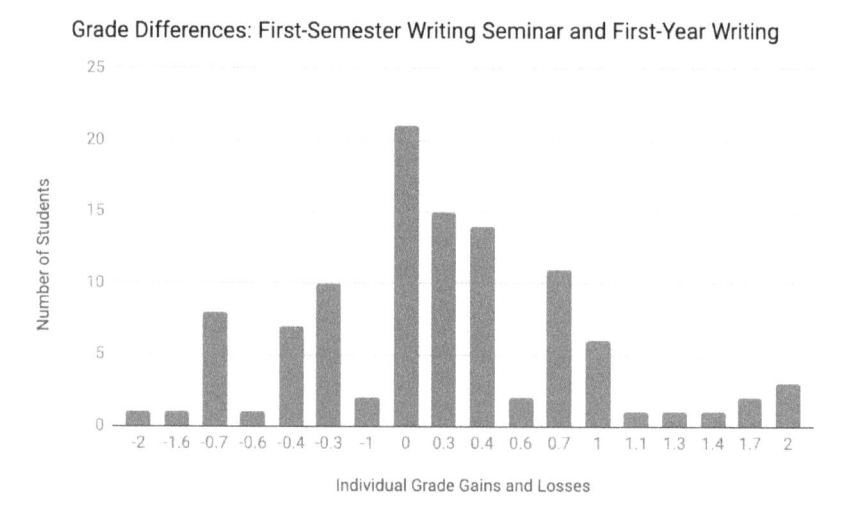

Figure 1: First and Second Course Grade Comparisons. Bar graph created by the authors.

---

8. An additional five students did not advance to first-year writing, and an additional six students completed first-year writing through alternate coursework.

The largest decreases and increases in the spring course grades were within one third of a grade from those earned in the first-semester courses. In other words, grade analysis revealed that most students earned similar grades between their fall and spring writing courses, often improving their grades slightly from fall to spring.

To some extent, then, grades in the first-semester writing seminars were reliable predictors of student academic performance and overall engagement in first-year writing. Students who succeeded in a first-semester writing seminar subsequently succeeded in first-year writing, but the correlational data alone don't explain why or how students succeed. Our assessment model included multiple measures of writing knowledge, skills, and learning behaviors to determine the ways in which the first-semester writing seminar contributed to students' successful completion of first-year writing.

Similarly to course grades, national survey data provided an incomplete perspective on student performance. The cohorts we assessed had two opportunities to complete the CLA+: fall 2012 and spring 2016. In fall 2012, 185 first-year students (class of 2016) completed the CLA+ and scored in the 92nd percentile, slightly higher than performance predicted by one CLA+ indicator, the class of 2016 average SAT scores. The college used this overall ranking of "proficient mastery" to norm the general critical thinking and writing ability of first-year students in its assessment narrative.

This proficiency narrative contributed to standardized expectations for writing and critical thinking at our institution. Ideally, a proficiency measure reflects the preparation of all students to enable curriculum and academic support to respond appropriately. To understand whose preparation and learning among the entire student population was reflected in CLA+ data, we burrowed into CLA+ reports for demographic information. This information was essential to frame and respond to the proficiency narrative, create transparent learning benchmarks, and support all student writers.

The fall 2012 St. Olaf CLA+ sample, though less diverse than the CLA+ schools sample, generally represented the class of 2016 in terms of race, ethnicity, and first-generation status. The reports did not, however, include Pell eligibility or low-income designation information for the class of 2016. That information correlates with performance on standardized tests and informs a cohort's average scores. For example, Mattern, Radunzel, and Harmston's research on ACT composite scores and family income documents an achievement gap between test-takers from families with incomes higher and lower than $80,000. Because 75 percent of first-semester writing seminar students who graduated from a US high school between 2012 and

2017 met federal low-income designation, we wanted to know the degree to which they were or were not represented in the CLA+ data and in the subsequent proficiency narrative. Knowing their degree of representation was essential to building an inclusive narrative of student critical thinking and writing at our institution.

Our conclusion came down to rough comparisons. On average, 75 percent of participants in our study met Pell eligibility/federal low-income designation, whereas the reported sample of students from CLA+ schools who met similar income criteria was 32 percent. Because CLA+ used SAT/ACT scores to determine and compare entering academic ability among first-year students at CLA+ schools, and research correlates family income with standardized test scores, the resulting performance standard was an inaccurate representation of entering academic ability. It was, in fact, a myth of ability. Students with below average SAT/ACT scores, who comprised the majority in our study, were disadvantaged by a performance narrative defined by privilege more than ability. Because our goal was to understand and define ability in context of students' fully intersectional identities, CLA+ ultimately proved unhelpful in providing meaningful direct assessment data to represent students in our study.

We turned next to institutional data from the National Survey of Student Engagement (NSSE) for insights into first-year student behavior and engagement. NSSE provided an overview of student ability that was indirect, measuring self-reported habits and behavior such as hours per week spent studying. In addition to general student information, our institution also collected specific information through NSSE about writing. These questions asked students the number of writing assignments for which they gave or received peer feedback on a draft, summarized or analyzed texts, argued a position using evidence, or addressed a real or imagined audience. One compelling result indicated that audience awareness was among the lowest writing-related scores on the NSSE survey across the board, but especially at St. Olaf (2.9 at writing selective institutions and 2.7 at St. Olaf); our students were statistically significantly lower than our peer institutions in audience awareness.

We paired this NSSE data with self-efficacy surveys that first-semester writing seminar students completed during embedded tutor meetings (a pre/post survey intended for goal-setting purposes). These surveys revealed that while 50 percent of students started the course able to identify the intended audience for their writing, 80 percent were able to do so by the end of the course. This comparison has important limitations: they were different cohorts of students, the language varied slightly between NSSE and self-efficacy surveys, NSSE was a scale whereas our survey required yes/no, and our sample size was small. However, pairing macro- and micro-level data enabled us to see measurable gains in an area of student learning that was a weakness for our institution broadly, but a strength within first-semester writing seminars. Despite its limitations, this pairing of data points gave some weight to observations that we had made previously only anecdotally.

Although data gathered through published instruments such as CLA + and NSSE often expand locally designed assessments and enable comparison of cohorts across institutions, they rarely answer program- and course-specific questions. In fact, big institutional data sets and smaller programmatic data samples tell different stories of critical-skills ability. These divergent narratives highlight our concerns about equity, particularly the myth of ability: a performance standard that emerges from data and privileges standardized tests as predictors of ability while representing only a homogenous subset of majority students. This myth of ability sets an institutional benchmark that excludes capacity for and makes invisible the tremendous learning and growth that first-year seminar students experience.

Focus Groups

The focus groups posed a research challenge common to small liberal arts colleges: the number of participating students and tutors resulted in a sample size too small for significant analysis. Without aspirations of statistically significant data, however, our process could be intentionally iterative and flexible. While we initially imagined groups of five to six students, scheduling challenges resulted in conversation groups of two to three students. We believe the smaller groups contributed to conversations with frequent exchange among participants, instead of individuals simply reporting to the facilitator in a wheel-and-spoke model. In addition, the timing enabled us to collect some students' perspectives within two to three months of course completion and others a year after course completion, providing us (and students) with various layers of hindsight. These focus group responses provide a snapshot of student learning that has subsequently informed curriculum development.

Student focus group responses revealed that the first-semester writing seminars were fulfilling their learning outcomes and that students perceived these outcomes as valuable and transferable. We coded interview responses into five dominant categories: reading, writing, library research, affect, and transfer (Appendix C). Across these categories, students consistently described their experiences in these first-semester writing seminars as preparing them to ask for help, respond to feedback, and develop a process for writing as they gained confidence in their identities as writers. Students also emphasized growth in intrinsic motivation, agency, and confidence, particularly as a result of their shared identities with class peers and embedded tutors. Students described learning as to annotate and read slowly, to question and evaluate texts in the research process, to value feedback as not shaming but as an essential part of the writing process, and to visit office hours, research librarians, and the writing center. Institutional data and one-time artifact scoring cannot tell us about students' writing processes and habit development, their help-seeking behaviors, and response to feedback: student achievement of these elements of our learning outcomes can be measured and communicated only by the students themselves.

Faculty/Staff Reading and Scoring

We initially included scoring workshops in our assessment model with hopes of gathering a quantitative measure of student development in the course. But from the outset, our prior training in assessment made us uneasy about holistic scoring of anonymized artifacts. We negotiated our goals for the scoring workshops to settle on a twofold purpose: to involve faculty and instructional staff in assessing the degree to which student writing in first-semester writing seminars demonstrated the criteria defining an emergent writer, and to engage participants in inclusive strategies for reading and responding to student writing.

Within the asset-based framework of the rubric we had created, scoring revealed overwhelming participant consensus, with almost every artifact scored as "emerging" in every category, such that the data reflected inter-rater reliability but, in its uniformity, simultaneously caused us to question its validity and usefulness. More troubling, though, was finding that our rubric had reinforced the very biases we had hoped to curb. While our first response was to fault the scorers' use and application of the rubric, we soon had an experience that led us to question the rubric itself. After this workshop and prior to the second workshop, we attended the 2019 CCCC annual convention, where Inoue delivered the chair's address, "How do we language so people stop killing each other, or what do we do about white language supremacy?" Inoue's address posed a direct challenge to holistic scoring of artifacts and the data we had gathered in the first scoring workshop. At our CCCC roundtable, we shared our assessment work-in-progress and invited feedback about the rubric and the workshop scoring results.

Inoue's key points about white language supremacy framed the discussion, and feedback confirmed that our rubric privileged standardized edited American English (SEAE) and conventions such as focus and organization, which may reward simplistic arguments with rote structures. Despite our efforts, our inclusion of data from artifacts scored by readers with a rubric enforced racist practices of applying a standard metric to disembodied writing divorced from the ecology in which writers wrote.

Our scoring workshop model also failed to anticipate that most faculty and staff could not readily flip the deeply embedded paradigm that "emerging" reflects a deficit, not an asset. As researchers, we had devoted months to grappling with and articulating that shift. So while readers consistently scored the artifacts as emerging, they expressed concerns that students were not performing at the level of "proficient" or higher, even when we explicitly stated that proficiency was the benchmark outcome of the second course in the sequence. Any rubric, we determined, when applied to decontextualized student writing, is likely to reinforce the assumptions of white language supremacy. The distinction between learning outcomes and rubric categories is crucial to understanding the limits of direct assessment, which may evaluate decontextualized artifacts of learning but not measure students' dynamic learning.

For the second workshop, then, we eliminated data gathering to focus exclusively on faculty and staff professional development. We discussed strategies for equitably evaluating student writing and made space to include excerpts from Sommers' *Responding to Student Writers* (2012) and Inoue's 2019 CCCC chair's address. We devoted extensive workshop time to norming activities that invited them to rethink how they read and respond to culturally and linguistically diverse student writing.

The pre- and post-workshop reflection surveys provided a snapshot of participant perspectives and growth. Pre-workshop reflections described disciplinary training and conventions that informed participants' expectations when reading and evaluating student writing. They generally expressed hesitation, frustration, and lack of strategies for responding to non-standardized academic writing. Participants seemed aware of inequity issues involving language and writing but were unsure of how their individual assessment practices contributed to or had potential to change larger systemic problems.

In post-workshop reflections, some participants expressed optimism that a change to grading practices could increase equity, but they also remained determined to enable students to meet dominant norms. We concluded that many were stuck between their commitments to equity and their perceived disciplinary, departmental, or institutional pressures to ensure that students achieve a particular, though problematic, standard of proficiency. Others problematized assessment with more complexity, expressed through their reticence to name or adopt a separatist stance even when their reflections named concrete steps for increasing attention to and decreasing penalties for writing that evidences linguistic and cultural difference.

The pre- and post-workshop reflection surveys became artifacts of study in their own right. Whereas we had hoped they would measure shifts resulting from workshop activities, they collectively indicated degrees to which readers beyond first-semester writing seminars valued or devalued writing by students in these courses. Our efforts to assess student learning through holistic scoring yielded instead a sample of institutional bias that favored standardized English and essay conventions. No matter how much students developed as writers, their writing would not be valued until the institutional narrative of "proficient" or "effective" writing changed.

Emphasizing professional development instead of data gathering at the second workshop, then, removed our attempts to quantify the degree to which students were meeting learning outcomes. But the workshop was an opportunity to equip participants more intentionally with anti-racist strategies with which to respond to future student writing. Similar to the focus groups, the assessment *process*, more than the results, became an opportunity for our institution (alongside our students) to learn, reflect, and grow.

Conclusions

Our assessment project prompted three actions. We have 1) shared results with assessment colleagues and further explored equitable data gathering and reporting; 2) disseminated results of our study to increase institutional understanding of how race and ethnicity, class, family education, and linguistic background influence students' preparation and agency as writers in our particular institutional context; and 3) revised course assessment tools to serve learning outcomes with more equitable standards.

Our findings reinforce the need for equity-based efforts to adopt standards of proficiency that recognize world Englishes and to redefine critical ability in ways that decenter white, upper-middle class educational and social experiences. Now that these first-semester writing seminars belong formally to the general education curriculum and are subject to assessment, we are contributing to the formation of new assessment models that will validate students and their development as writers in the first-semester writing seminars. We anticipate that these changes will provide students more explicitly with the affective experiences they need in the first year to develop the habits and mindsets to grow as writers. We also continue to offer professional development focused on inclusive writing instruction, feedback, and evaluation.

As instructors of first-semester writing seminars, we also have substantively changed our teaching practices, particularly how we evaluate student writing. We are continually developing ways to improve and engage students with feedback based on our assessment results. In our course redesign for the new general education, we have retained the emphasis on help-seeking behavior, active reading, and learning to respond to feedback, and we now have data to justify that emphasis. We also have gained increased appreciation for student insights about their learning. Integrated reflective activities promote metacognition while giving us insights to improve as teachers. Our model has changed the way we assess student writing, but it has also changed the way we teach it.

Bibliography

Bean, John C. 2011. *Engaging Ideas: The Professor's Guide to Integrating Writing, Critical Thinking, and Active Learning in the Classroom*. 2nd ed. Jossey-Bass Higher and Adult Education Series. San Francisco: Jossey-Bass.

Council of Writing Program Administrators. 2011. "Framework for Success in Postsecondary Writing." Accessed December 4, 2022. https://wpacouncil.org/aws/cwpa/pt/sd/news_article/242845/_parent/layout_details/false.

Inoue, Asao B. 2015. *Antiracist Writing Assessment Ecologies: Teaching and Assessing Writing for a Socially Just Future*. WAC Clearinghouse; Anderson: Parlor Press. https://doi.org/10.37514/PER-B.2015.0698.

Inoue, Asao B. 2019. "How Do We Language So People Stop Killing Each Other, or What Do We Do about White Language Supremacy?" Chair's address at CCCC Annual Convention, Pittsburgh, March 2019. https://www.youtube.com/watch?v=brPGTewcDYYURL.

Inoue, Asao B, and Mya Poe. 2020. "How to Stop Harming Students: An Ecological Guide to Antiracist Writing Assessment." *Composition Studies* 48, no. 3 (Fall): https://compositionstudiesjournal.files.wordpress.com/2021/02/poeinoue_full-3.pdf.

Matsuda, Paul Kei, and Michelle Cox. 2011. "Reading an ESL Writer's Text." *Studies in Self-Access Learning Journal* 2, no 1: 4–14.

Mattern, Krista, Justine Radunzel, and Matt Harmston. n.d. "ACT Composite Score by Family Income." ACT Research and Policy. Accessed July 2023. https://www.act.org/content/dam/act/unsecured/documents/R1604-ACT-Composite-Score-by-Family-Income.pdf.

Sommers, Nancy. 2012. *Responding to Student Writers*. 1st ed. Boston: Bedford/St. Martin's.

Suskie, Linda A. 2018. *Assessing Student Learning: A Common Sense Guide*. 3rd ed. San Francisco: Jossey-Bass.

White, Edward M., Norbert Elliot, and Irvin Peckham. 2015. *Very like a Whale: The Assessment of Writing Programs*. Logan: Utah State University Press.

White, Edward M., and Cassie A. Wright. 2016. *Assigning, Responding, Evaluating*. Boston: Bedford/St. Martin's.

Appendix A

Learning Outcomes for First-Semester Writing Seminar

Learning outcomes for the first-semester writing seminars we assessed state that students who complete the course successfully will demonstrate the following:

1. Engaged reading, writing, speaking, and listening as part of an academic conversation

2. The ability to identify intended audience when reading and writing and/or construct an argument for a specific audience

3. A developing ability to locate, to read, to evaluate, to use, and to document sources to support opinion

4. The ability to engage in writing as a systematic process, using flexible strategies for generating drafts, responding to feedback, revising, editing, and proofreading.

Learning Outcomes for First-Year Writing

Learning outcomes for first-year writing state that students who complete the course successfully will demonstrate the following:

1. The ability to write effectively in a variety of forms for the generally-educated reader.
2. The ability to engage in writing as a systematic, interactive process, using flexible strategies for generating drafts, responding to feedback, revising, editing, and proofreading.
3. Proficiency in using research to support critical inquiry, including the ability to identify, evaluate, analyze, synthesize, and document appropriate sources.

Appendix B

Focus Group Questions
Student Questions
Reading Process and Habits
1. Describe your reading process in this course.
2. How much time, on average, did you spend reading each week for this course? Did your reading process change during this course? If so, how? Why?

Writing Process and Habits
1. Describe your writing process in this course.
2. How did you respond to and incorporate feedback in your writing process?
3. How much time, on average, did you spend completing each formal essay for this course, from the time you got the assignment to the time you submitted it?
4. Did your writing process change during this course? If so, how? Why?

Discussion and Discourse
1. Can you give any examples of any activities or assignments that invited you to participate in an academic discussion?
2. What are the most important things you learned in this course? What two or three things that you learned have you applied in another course?

3. What elements of writing were most difficult to learn?

Broader Impact

1. Did you learn any new habits for being a college student in this course?

2. What advice would you give a student who is about to start this course?

Embedded Tutor Questions

1. What kinds of writing skills did you most often focus on in your sessions?

2. What kinds of questions did your students have? How did you answer those questions?

3. What were some of the improvements you saw over the course of the semester in the students' writing or writing habits?

4. What area(s) might the course expand to address student questions or challenges?

Appendix C

Codes for focus group transcriptions
Student focus groups—coding pre-set terms

1. Reading process (RP)
2. Writing process (WP)
3. Library research process (LRP)
4. Time on task (TOT)
    a. Reading
    b. Pre-writing
    c. Researching
    d. Drafting
    e. Revising
    f. Editing

5. Response to feedback (RF)
    a. Fixing/corrections
    b. Synonym for minor changes
    c. Synonym for deep feedback
    d. Ideas/questions
6. Academic discussion (D)
    a. Scholarly conversation/engagement with sources
    b. Class discussion
7. Transfer (T)
    a. Knowledge/Information
    b. Writing
    c. Reading
    d. Content
    e. Research
8. Habits for being a college student
    a. Writing
    b. Reading
    c. Research
    d. College Life Skills
9. Challenges (Chal)
10. Advice (A)
11. Confidence (Con)

Tutor focus groups—coding pre-set terms

1. Session focus (SF)
    a. Tutor led
    b. Student led
2. Student questions (Q)

3. Improvements (I)
    a. Reading skills
    b. Reading habits
    c. Writing skills
    d. Writing habits
    e. Research skills
    f. Research habits
4. Curriculum changes (CC)
5. Confidence (Con)
6. Learning experience/value for tutor's own education (V)

Appendix D

Pre- and Post-Workshop Reflection Prompts for Scoring Workshops

Pre-Reading Reflective Prompt for Scoring Workshop

Before we begin reading student essays, please write a brief reflection in response to the following prompt. In the space below, write for approximately seven minutes, then you and your reading partner will share responses with each other.

Readers often take one of three stances when responding to L2 (second language) texts or texts that challenge the norms of academic writing. Which do you feel most aptly describes your stance when you read an essay by a writer whose primary language is not English? How did you develop this stance?

    a. Assimilationist: I tend to respond with the goal of helping the writer write a thesis-driven, linear, error-free essay as soon as possible.

    b. Accommodationist: I tend to respond with the goal of helping the writer develop academic style while maintaining the personal, cultural, and linguistic identities that constitute the differences I observe in their writing.

c. Separatist: I tend to respond with the goal of helping the writer maintain personal, cultural, and linguistic identities in writing while advocating for readers to read with understanding of and appreciation for variations and differences in writing.

Source: Matsuda, Paul Kei, and Michelle Cox. 2011. "Reading an ESL Writer's Text." *Studies in Self-Access Learning Journal* 2, no. 1: 4–14.

Post-Reading Reflective Prompt for Scoring Workshop

Reread the reflection you wrote before you read and assessed essays today. Has this workshop confirmed, shifted, confused, or otherwise altered your stance? How will you apply today's experience to your work with students? In the space below, please write a brief reflection (ten minutes) to share during our closing conversation.

Section IV: Complicated/Complicating Assessment

10 This Will Never Be 20/20: What Reflection Teaches Us about Assessment

George Cusack, Julie Christoph, Kara Wittman, and Bridget Fullerton

Abstract: In this chapter, the authors discuss a joint project, launched in fall 2020, to scaffold and assess metacognitive writing in the first-year seminars at their institutions, Bates College, Carleton College, Pomona College, and the University of Puget Sound. The institutional cultures at these four liberal arts colleges prioritize faculty autonomy in teaching, and the faculty teaching the theme-based first-year seminars across the curriculum implemented metacognitive writing for this project in diverse ways. Partly because of this diversity and partly because of the nature of metacognitive writing itself, the authors' attempt to assess students' metacognitive development using a quantitative, rubric-based model ultimately failed to produce usable data. The authors discuss what went wrong with this process and introduce an alternative model for assessing metacognitive writing, a more qualitative method that embraces the idiosyncratic nature of students' development and the tremendous insight that this kind of writing can provide into students' individual struggles, experiences, and concerns. Appendices include both assignment and assessment materials developed through this project.

Introduction

Assessment can be one of the most important, and challenging, parts of writing program administration (WPA) work at small liberal arts colleges (SLACs) because of the special role that long-serving faculty members have on our campuses. As Jill M. Gladstein and Dara Rossman Regaignon (2012, 21) note, SLAC faculty "prefer collaborative rather than executive models of decision-making." They tend to value personal autonomy as professionals, while also embracing a governance culture that relies heavily on faculty engagement in shaping the policies and practices of the institution in the classroom context and beyond. Even at institutions with fairly centralized administrative cultures, on-the-ground teaching is a highly individualized practice. Thus, a curricular initiative with broad support from the administration or the faculty as a whole will still require buy-in from the individual faculty who will implement it in order to succeed. This tension between autonomy and shared governance offers a context in which SLAC WPAs are more likely to be effective through influence and interpersonal connection than through policy-making and executive fiat. Though this influence work can be slow, the small size and relatively thin hierarchy of SLACs can facilitate nimble change when there is political will. In addition, though Gladstein and Regaignon's research indicates that most campuses participate in writing assessment work for the purpose of re-accreditation, they also note that when assessment projects connect with faculty values and evince a spirit of shared governance and collaboration, change can happen relatively quickly.

While there are examples of assessment work at SLACs (several of which Gladstein and Regaignon highlight), most of the existing models are built around the assessment of formal writing, such as multi-year portfolios, standardized essay assignments from first-year seminars, or capstone projects. Given the increasing awareness of the importance of reflective writing in student development, however, it seems timely to ask, what might a successful model for assessing reflective and metacognitive writing look like at SLACs? How can assessment help in encouraging faculty to engage students meaningfully in metacognitive practice? Assessment models designed to assess the end products of writing may not be as effective when applied to the recursive, iterative, loopy and meandering processes involved in metacognition. This may be especially true at SLAC institutions, where the curricula often emphasize personal growth, experimentation, and learning from one's mistakes as integral to the learning process. Can the blunt instrument of writing assessment-at-scale possibly capture the uneven movement of real reflection and metacognition?

Our cross-institutional research project revealed some pitfalls with traditional assessment strategies designed for different kinds of institutions than SLACs, as well as opportunities for implementing new approaches to student reflection in and beyond this liminal moment of the COVID-19 pandemic. Through our work together on this process, we have moved toward thinking about the educational disruptions of 2020 as an opportunity for what Shawna Shapiro (2011) calls "institutional mediation." Building from our own collaborative experience, we have suggestions for assessment strategies that are suited to the purposes that reflective writing serves in our courses and that can promote change in the ways SLAC faculty think about their students' metacognitive development. We also offer a few specific assignments that might support this work. We have some of our own reflections to share as well, as we learned a great deal about the messy rooms of intellectual reflection and self-perception over the course of this project, and our work taught us something about the salutary limits of assessment.

Methodology: Reflecting on Entering College in Fall 2020

In spring of 2020, the WPAs at our four SLAC institutions—Bates College, Carleton College, Pomona College, and the University of Puget Sound—began a multi-site study of metacognitive writing in our institutions' first-year seminar (FYS) courses. Our hope was that we would be able to document the ways that metacognitive training at the beginning of students' college careers, especially during a pandemic, could help them identify their strengths and weaknesses, navigate challenges, and develop a stronger sense of belonging in college. All of our colleges were in variously incipient stages of a conversation about the potential of reflective, metacognitive writing, and we could see already in April 2020 that the pandemic was a disruptive event that would likely change how our campuses approach students' transition to college.[1] Our plan in the study was to

---

1. Our collaborative efforts initially stemmed from a shared interest in, and ability to, design and deliver a faculty development program focused on reflective writing and metacognition. Similarities in the size, scope, and focus of our FYS programs helped our cause: we each have around thirty to forty sections of FYSs capped at fifteen to twenty students and taught by faculty across disciplines, and all of our first-year students take an FYS in partial fulfilment of a writing requirement at our institutions. Further, George, Kara, Julie, and Bridget all had a personal interest in connecting with other SLAC WPAs due to our heightened sense of isolation in the face of the COVID-19 pandemic. Indeed, one added and unexpected bonus of our two-year project was the much-needed collegial connection and sustained—and sustaining—emotional and intellectual support we received from each other in our many virtual meetings, email exchanges, and one conference presentation despite

1. create a shared set of metacognitive learning outcomes;
2. recruit FYS faculty to collectively develop and teach writing assignments based on those goals;
3. collect and assess the student artifacts produced by those assignments, looking for whatever insight we could find into the students' experiences, challenges, and, in particular, their metacognitive growth; and
4. interview study and control faculty and students about how their experiences of fall 2020 affected their work in their FYS.

The curriculum we created hinged on two "bookend" assignments: paired essays students would complete at the beginning and end of their FYS classes. The bookend prompts, which were standardized across all schools and sections involved in the study, asked students to consider and articulate their expectations for college, the personal strengths they expected would help them, and the challenges they anticipated ahead of them (see Appendix A). These assignments had their roots in the "Teaching for Transfer" curriculum developed by Kathleen Blake Yancey, Liane Robertson, and Kara Taczak (2014), aiming to lead students to articulate their cognitive progress so that they could apply and build on it in subsequent terms. Between the bookends, students would also complete a series of reflective writing assignments, ranging from simple time-management exercises to deeper examinations of their personal backgrounds in the vein of Northwestern's "Difference Education" model (Stephens, Hamedani, and Destin 2014). To allow for differences in instructional style and institutional culture, each WPA worked with their own faculty to design these in-term assignments. For the standardized bookend assignments, we developed a shared set of student learning outcomes (SLO) (see Appendix B); together, the bookends and SLOs were meant to serve as a basis to assess our curriculum after the FYS courses had concluded.

By synchronizing, collecting, and assessing the students' reflective writing systematically, we hoped to gain insights that would help us improve FYS curricula on an institutional level, refining it to be more responsive and sensitive to the individual needs of students at moments of acute crisis. We also hoped to learn something about facilitating a sense of belonging when the possibility of community was attenuated in the short term by the

---

our differing time zones, institutional positionalities, and geographic locations. This connection ultimately inspired our turn away from quantitative assessment of reflective writing towards the discussion-based model we advocate for below.

pandemic and, in the long term, by the marginalizing and exclusionary structures of higher education.

We had little doubt that repeated, iterative, metacognitive writing would help the students individually—the literature on that, which we review in more detail below, is substantial and compelling. However, we also knew that our students would come to college with varying levels of training and academic preparation and a wide range of social and cultural frameworks through which they would come to understand and navigate their college experiences. By getting a broad snapshot of students' transition to college, particularly in the heavily disrupted moment of fall 2020, we hoped to understand not only what was exceptional about that moment, but also how our understandings of disruption, challenge, and inequity can inform our pedagogical work with students entering college at any moment. In essence, the pandemic heightened several known shortcomings in the way our institutions welcomed, oriented, and matriculated our students, and we hoped to learn both what that meant for students immediately and what that could teach us about stress, distress, community, and care in the long term.

To that end, over the summer of 2020, we collectively recruited twenty-three faculty participants, representing twenty-two FYS sections across the four SLACs. Of those sections, more than half were entirely remote, a dramatic departure from the norm. Participating instructors worked with their WPAs to develop reflective writing prompts that were standardized across the FYS sections within each institution, supplementing the bookend assignments that were standardized across the four institutions. This allowed the WPAs to collect a rich archive of reflective writing at the end of the fall 2020 academic term, documenting the ways that 173 students from locations around the world confronted the transition to college in the midst of a global pandemic and an unprecedented upheaval in the culture of higher education.

The diversity and depth of material at hand was moving, and it provided a welcome insight into students' experiences that would otherwise have been impossible. Fall 2020 was a challenging semester for faculty accustomed to teaching in person and getting to know students well, as both faculty and students were missing the coordinates—social, spatial, intellectual, physical, and interpersonal—that would help them connect and understand each other. One faculty member reflected in a post-term interview: "I make the distinction between metacognition versus metacognition during a pandemic because, much like Zoom conversations, the way in which we gather information about our students and the way in which their lives are boxed are so radically different."[2] The sheer depth and volume of material we collected presented a new challenge: how to read and assess this material in a systematic way while still being sensitive to the vast differences in individual students' experiences and between this cohort of students and every previous cohort. Confronting this challenge would lead us to rethink our approach both to metacognitive writing and to assessment.

Results: Confronting the Limits of Quantitative Assessment

At the heart of our assessment plan was a quantitative assessment of the bookend essays, based on our shared learning outcomes. Though we planned to supplement these quantitative results with student and faculty follow-up interviews, we hoped that the bookend assessment results would provide a concrete overarching set of results for our project. To that end, we developed a rubric based on the AAC&U's VALUE rubrics for Integrative Learning and Lifelong Learning (see Appendix C). In summer 2021, we recruited a team of faculty readers from two of the campuses (Carleton and Puget Sound) to read and score the bookend essays using our rubric. Some of these readers had taught sections included in the study, but most were unfamiliar with the project prior to the assessment.

Participating faculty were trained to use the rubric through a single, mandatory norming session, in which one of the WPAs explained the nature of the project, discussed how to apply the rubric, and took the faculty through multiple sample readings.[3] The faculty then read roughly twenty-three bookend essays each, which allowed each essay to be read by two different readers. These readings were administered asynchronously using the Moodle CMS platform. Reading assignments were largely random, though the WPAs did manually prevent any of the readers from reviewing the work of their own students or from reading both the opening and closing bookend from any given student. The bookend essays were anonymized

---

2. Anonymous, interview with author, January 2021.

3. Specifically, faculty readers were required to attend one of two Zoom sessions covering the same material. A handful of participants were unable to attend either session live, but watched a recording of the second session before they began reading.

to the extent possible, though the coding did indicate whether a given essay was an opening or closing bookend.[4]

But despite our best efforts to create a clear and consistent assessment framework, the quantitative results were disappointing, in more ways than one. When we averaged the scores across all four schools, students seemed to go slightly *backward* between the opening and closing bookend essays on two of our three metacognitive indicators (self-assessment and predictive thinking). The third indicator (adaptive metacognition) showed slight forward progress, but the inter-rater reliability was so poor on all three indicators that none of these numbers were reliable, let alone statistically significant, and contradicted the conclusion expressed consistently in follow-up interviews that students and faculty alike had benefited from the reflective assignments. These results were perplexing, and they required us to rethink the way we might use reflective writing to understand and improve our teaching.

Analysis: The Trouble with Assessment by the Numbers

Though we have ideas about how our quantitative assessment model might have been improved, we also believe that quantitative assessment as a methodology might simply be the wrong way to achieve the kinds of pedagogical insight we were seeking—especially given the structure of feeling on our SLAC campuses. Metacognitive writing is, by its nature, heavily informed and inflected by the context in which it's written and the particular alchemy of the environment in which it's assigned. This makes systematic attempts to assess and quantify artifacts of metacognitive writing as products problematic at best.

In retrospect, even if our VALUE-based assessment project had produced clear results, they could only have shown us broad trends in student growth, entirely removed from the contextual factors that produced or inhibited it. As most writing instructors know, we gain the most benefit from reading students' metacognitive writing when we engage the contextual messiness of students' experiences, rather than filtering it out. This is particularly true at SLAC institutions, which generally prioritize the de-

---

4. To elaborate: student aides working under a confidentiality agreement read through the individual essays and removed students' names and the names of the institutions they attended. Given the nature of the prompts, though, many essays still included biographical information about the students and references that made it possible to identify their institutions.

velopment of student-teacher and student-student connections, and which tend to give their faculty more autonomy (and greater responsibility) to define and adjust their teaching methods. What SLAC instructors need most, then, from an assessment of reflective writing is a framework to help them process the experiences that their students share with them in ways that can directly inform their teaching.

In the sections below, we'll examine the limitations of rubric-based assessments of student metacognition in more detail, based on both our own experiences and the relevant scholarship. We'll then discuss our proposed alternatives in more detail, recommending ways that SLAC WPAs in particular might train faculty to design metacognitive assignments, teach and respond to students' writing, and assess the resulting artifacts in ways that are consistent and systematic but also attentive to pressing institutional (and global) contexts and responsive to the needs of the instructor and their students. On that front, we'll consider three "valances" of writing assessment—individual students, whole classes, and institution-wide practices—and consider the ways that metacognitive writing assessment might operate in each of these valances.

Eliciting and Identifying Metacognition: What We Know. Existing research on metacognitive training in general and metacognitive writing in particular consistently affirms their importance to student development. A lack of metacognitive training in secondary education makes it more difficult for students to learn and navigate the "hidden curriculum" of academic practices that college instructors expect, but do not explicitly teach or mandate (Smith 2013). Conversely, curricula and pedagogical techniques designed to develop students' metacognitive skills have been shown to promote academic success (Wardle 2009; Lobato 2012; Cummings 2015; Finer 2017), increase feelings of self-efficacy (Bergey et al. 2019), and reduce the "achievement gap" between privileged and underprivileged students (Stephens et al. 2015). Metacognitive training is particularly important for students transitioning to college because it enables students to transfer knowledge across curricular contexts. D. N. Perkins and Gavriel Salomon (1989) note that transfer "does not take care of itself"; students must consciously make connections between current and prior learning, and they must be deliberately taught how to do so. Metacognitive training facilitates this in part because it raises student awareness about their educational experiences, their habits of mind, and the relationship between the two. This allows students to both apply existing knowledge creatively to new situations and to recognize and think critically about challenges to their success.

However, the literature on the *assessment* of metacognitive writing is significantly more conflicted and fraught. Scholars generally agree that, beyond the direct benefit students receive from completing them, well-designed and integrated metacognitive assignments can be incredibly valuable tools for instructors. To give just two examples: Robert Grossman (2009) provides a schema for varying levels of reflection, which he suggests faculty can use to identify, among other things, gaps in students' understanding, prejudices or preconceptions that instructors might address productively in class, and areas for improvement in students work or writing processes. On the institutional level, Elizabeth G. Allan and Dana Lynn Driscoll (2014) illustrate the ways student reflective writing can be used to improve instructional design and faculty development. In both of these cases, though, the authors indicate that gleaning pedagogically useful insights requires a fairly labor-intensive analysis of the details of students' work. Allan and Driscoll in particular began their assessment project with a rubric-based approach similar to our own, which revealed some potentially interesting patterns in students' understanding of the writing process and ability to transfer knowledge. To make sense of their data, though, they had to perform a more qualitative analysis of a small subset of their collected artifacts.

In some very specific applications, metacognitive assignments can produce more quantifiable outcomes in student achievement. For example, Nicole M. Stephens, MarYam G. Hamedani, and Mesmin Destin (2014) designed a controlled intervention in which a group of incoming first-year students at Northwestern read and responded to recollections from senior students about their transition to college. This intervention produced a measurable reduction in the "achievement gap" for low-income students, as well as a significant improvement in the students' self-reported mental health (Stephens et al. 2015). The actual assessment data for this project, however, did not come from the students' writing, but rather post-intervention measures including surveys, video testimony, and the students' GPA. Thus, the students' writing provides some insight into *why* their academic performance improved, but the authors required external sources of data to document the improvement itself.

It's also important to note that Stephens, Hamedani, and Destin's (2014) intervention was an extracurricular one, conducted prior to the start of fall classes. When integrated into an FYS course, the instructional contexts in which students write become more variable, and the ways in which instructors introduce reflective assignments, teach the skills necessary to complete them successfully, and integrate these elements into the overall discourse of their course can vary wildly. This was particularly true at our SLAC institutions, where instructors have tremendous autonomy over the design and content of their courses. This variation can affect the level of metacognition students display in ways that don't accurately demonstrate the students' abilities. As David Denton (2011, 847) notes, instructors who emphasize process and reflection throughout their instructional methods encourage students to emulate this in their writing, whereas instructors who "emphasize content coverage while employing didactic and expositive methods" can actively discourage reflective thought in their students, even when their writing assignments explicitly call for it. Similarly, Susan Callahan (2000) illustrates that variations in either the instructors' or the students' understanding of what reflection is and how one can recognize it can pose challenges to both the students' ability to complete reflective writing tasks and instructors' ability to assess their writing effectively.

The logistics of large-scale writing assessment also become more complicated in the context of a first-year seminar: recruiting faculty to assign specific writing prompts, securing permission from individual students to study their writing in response to those prompts, working with faculty to collect the student artifacts, and then finding and training readers to assess them are all difficult tasks, and accomplishing all of them in a way that provides a robust sample often strains possibility. In the initial study of their teaching for transfer curriculum, for example, Yancey, Robertson, and Taczak (2014) had to rely on a pool of just seven students to assess and compare three separate pedagogical approaches to first-year composition.

Beyond the logistical issues, though, lies the deeper problem that metacognitive development, and by extension reflective writing, resists the kinds of objective narratives of progress that product-based quantitative assessment seeks to produce. This makes the application of an assessment agenda to student metacognitive writing difficult at best and counterproductive at worst. Phyllis Creme's (2008, 50) study of grading of student learning journals argues that while students want reassurance that reflective writing "counts" in a meaningful way toward their grade, students tend to engage most readily with reflective assignments that allow "a space for the free exploration of their own and others' thinking, and for the unfolding process between the inkling of an idea and its fruition," experimenting with different configurations of, conclusions about, and perspectives on their experiences. Creme (2005, 294) notes that this form of writing requires "an empathetic, not a judgmental reader" and that rubric-based grading models create an atmosphere of judgment that undermines the students' ability to create their own understanding of themselves. Similarly, Tony Scott (2005, 3) argues that when students are given a reflective writing task with the explicit understanding that it will be used for assessment purposes, they tend to minimize self-reflection in favor of "stylized narratives of progress" that might support the assessment agenda but obfuscate students' individual experiences.

Why Assessment of Metacognitive Writing at SLACs Requires Reflective Work. Certainly, there are ways in which our work with the VALUE rubric could have been more effective. The basic design of our study, the nature of our subject matter, and the particularities of our institutional contexts all posed challenges that would inevitably complicate our quantitative assessment. Even though our sample size seemed almost ambitiously large, including nearly a third of the FYS instructors at our institutions and resulting in bookend essays from 173 students (319 individual artifacts in total) that strained our time and resources to anonymize, format, and upload to the online scoring platform, it was a notable achievement for a voluntary project that asked faculty to engage in significant collaborative work over the summer.

And yet, unwieldy as the sample corpus was logistically, it was still too small to compensate for the substantial variations in the ways the bookend assignments were administered. Since each instructor was responsible for introducing, assigning, and collecting the metacognitive assignments created for the study (and faculty at all of the participating institutions are accustomed to exercising significant autonomy in their courses), students received and composed their bookends in very different contexts. In some courses, the bookends and the metacognitive assignments completed between them formed a substantial part of the course dialogue: instructors discussed the assignments beforehand, commented on the individual responses, and discussed the responses collectively in class. On the opposite extreme, though, some students received the bookend assignments as *digressions* from the course material and dialogue, being asked to complete them with no little to no explanation or follow-up.

Instructors' methods for responding to the bookends in class also varied significantly. Some, as noted above, did not comment on the students' metacognitive writing at all, while some wrote thoughtful and thorough comments that guided students to reconsider their responses or apply their reasoning to future assignments. Some instructors awarded students points for completing the assignments, while some offered no grade-based incentives.[5] Some had students complete the bookends outside of class, some made them in-class writing assignments, and some administered the opening bookend out of class and the closing in the final class session of the term. It's difficult to imagine that these factors could fail to affect the effort and understanding students brought to their writing, and that's in addition to particular temporal and spatial disjunctions created by the pandemic.

The norming and scoring process created additional complications. Recruiting faculty readers posed new logistical challenges. Scrounging money for stipends, exhausting personal contacts, and no small amount of begging yielded a reader pool that was just a bit smaller than we needed to have each artifact read and scored by three separate readers, as we'd originally planned; we thus settled for just two readers for each artifact, which made conflicting scores on the same artifact more difficult to resolve. As the results came in, it also became clear that several readers did not follow the guidelines discussed in the norming session. Most notably, readers were directed to assign scores of zero (out of a possible three) only if the writer made *no attempt whatsoever* to display a given metacognitive process. Since the bookend prompts were designed to elicit all three of the metacognitive processes our study sought to measure (self-assessment, predictive thinking, and adaptive metacognition), this means that a given essay should only receive a zero if the writer essentially ignored part of the prompt, and this is how readers were explicitly told to apply the score.[6] However, the scoring results indicated that a certain percentage of the faculty interpreted the zero score differently, awarding it to essays that followed the prompt, but did not do so (in the readers' assessment) in a way that displayed significant

---

5. To our knowledge (and relief), none of the instructors graded the actual *content* of students' reflective writing; instead, they either did not grade the writing at all or used some form of completion-based grading. At Carleton, the instructors and the WPA developed a shared set of grading criteria (see Appendix D), which the instructors were encouraged to share with their students, that laid out a basic set of expectations but stressed that, "in order to receive full credit for these assignments, you'll need to make a good-faith effort to respond to the prompts with clarity and detail."

6. These guidelines for the zero score were included in the slide deck that accompanied the norming session (which was made available to readers after the session as well), explained orally by the WPA leading the session, and reiterated several times during the review of sample essays.

metacognition. In other words, some readers used the zero as a subjective measure of content of the essays, while others (following our design) used it as an objective measure of the students' engagement with the prompt. This means that two readers could agree in all substantive ways about the content of a given essay, but still assign it different scores because they applied the rubric differently.

Some of these issues could be addressed in another iteration of this study. As is always the case with this kind of assessment, the readers' response to the rubric revealed several points that could be refined, clarified, and expanded, and these changes might produce more consistent results. Similarly, knowing the points in the rubric design that sparked confusion or resistance could help us to norm the readers more effectively. A larger study population would also make it more resilient to contextual variations in the individual student artifacts. On the norming front, different readers or better norming might help.

Any of these alterations, however, would be difficult for these authors to accomplish given the resources of our programs and the natures of our institutions. Our actual sample size required a tremendous amount of work and collaboration to assemble. And, given the nature of the writing assignments—students reflecting on their transition to college—faculty at the study institutions are the most qualified readers, since they have the best understanding of the contexts that students are transitioning into and the academic and institutional challenges they're navigating. And yet, the faculty's expertise also made them resistant to standardization. Comments from readers in the norming session indicate that some variations in scores, particularly for low-scoring essays, reflected entrenched opinions about how one evaluates and responds to student writing. For example, faculty explaining why they thought a given essay displayed "no attempt" at metacognition, despite following the prompt, indicates that faculty accustomed to autonomy in the ways they evaluate writing can only with difficulty let this go.

And, in some ways, the product-based VALUE assessment work we did mirrored the product/process challenge that crème (2008) and Scott (2005) identify, and in so doing undermined our larger goals of encouraging faculty on our campuses to engage in metacognitive writing assignments. Asking faculty to assess the products of student work as evidence of metacognition invited "a judgmental reader" rather than an "empathetic" one (Creme 2008, 294). Given that the metacognitive bookends were assigned as formative writing, we now have concerns about the validity of using our rubric to assess the resulting artifacts in that way.

If our VALUE assessment scheme *had* worked as planned and reliably revealed that students tended to improve their metacognitive abilities when they were presented with these two very specific assignments in certain very specific ways, such a finding would almost certainly have found its way into some institutional reports on teaching effectiveness; perhaps it would even get a line-item in a reaccreditation document or two. But how much would it actually help instructors to integrate thoughtful, context-sensitive metacognitive exercises into their FYS courses? How would it help instructors understand and connect with their students, particularly the students most likely to feel displaced, alienated, and marginalized by their transition to traditionally white institutions? How much would it reveal about the actual struggles that individual students go through in their transition to college, or the on-the-ground work that the most effective SLAC faculty do to connect with their students, or the ways we can understand and improve these experiences? And, finally, how might an assessment template engineered to produce reliable results according to a VALUE-based quantitative scale actually flatten out the complex topography of the first-year college experience, rendering smooth and invisible the bumps and crevasses of imposter syndrome, exhaustion, mental health struggles, and our students' struggle with the twin specters of capitalism and colonialism (productivity, normativity, and subjection, for example) that haunt our pedagogy and their learning? How, put bluntly, might assessment short-circuit empathy?

Toward a More Reflective Approach. Inspired by the qualitative feedback on our project that we received from our interviews with student and faculty participants in the fall 2020 FYS classes, we decided in spring 2022 to fundamentally change our approach to assessing the reflective writing artifacts we collected through our study. Two of the project leads solicited faculty from their institutions to participate in what we called "popup workshops" to look again at student writing from the fall 2020 data collection. At these workshops, we asked participants to read dossiers that included the bookend essays and other submissions from individual students. Faculty were then asked to make marginal comments on the writing and to reflect on these through the lens of a three-part prompt:

1. What strikes you about these students' reflections? If you were these students' instructor, how might these reflections help you to connect with the students individually?

2. If you were these students' instructor, what connections, if any, might you see between their experiences and patterns in students of struggle, recognition, experience, or anxiety that you have seen in other students you have taught—in the past two years, or more generally?

3. How might these reflections inform your teaching more broadly? What concerns do you have about using this kind of writing (workload in responding, how to respond, how to not be overwhelmed with student experiences)? What assignments might be relevant to your future teaching? What benefits might you anticipate for students' participation in this kind of reflective writing?[7]

The conversation shifted considerably when we asked faculty to think about the texts as offering formative material that might be helpful to them in their work as teachers, rather than as an opportunity to judge an individual student's achievement. Being asked to think about the content of students' metacognitive writing in this way shifted something in ways that surprised even the faculty members. One faculty participant—who had, the previous week, attended a faculty workshop in which demographic information about her campus's students' increasing mental health challenges was provided—said, upon reading the student writing,

> As a reader . . . , I was thinking to myself, life really is hard for everybody. They come from very different backgrounds and then they all have some problems that are severe enough to cause mental stress and anxiety, depression. I was surprised by that. I shouldn't be, but I was.[8]

Even though several faculty members who taught sections in our fall 2020 FYS study found it useful to know what was going on in the lives of their students, many also expressed discomfort with students divulging what they felt was too much of their own lives in the metacognitive writing they had been assigned to do. We should note that this discomfort cuts two ways: on the one hand, faculty members felt concerned that students were sharing, and thus revisiting, difficult and potentially traumatic experiences

---

7. The precise wording of these questions varied a bit between the popup workshops, but the essence of the prompt was the same in all of the workshops: leading faculty to consider how the students' reflective writing might inform their interactions with the students individually, how it might inform their approach to that particular class, and how it might inform their teaching overall going forward.

8. Anonymous, in group workshop with author, June 2022.

at the behest of people in power; on the other hand, the same faculty members were suddenly brought to the threshold of care work and emotional labor they might never have imagined doing—and had not been trained to do. These concerns largely manifested when instructors imagined reading the reflections in the context of their own classes, though. In the context of the assessment workshop, being able to discuss *anonymous* students' experiences was useful in ways that seemed to be different than in writing assigned in their own classes *or* in compiled demographic data from their own campuses.

In the popup faculty workshop, conversations shifted to how assignments might guide students to grow in desired ways, rather than whether students had achieved certain benchmarks. The focus shifted from product to process. An important part of that shift was toward considering the role of faculty in shaping student work. Looking at the diversity of student responses and faculty assignments, one faculty member noted, "I noticed that the way the students answered depended heavily on how the assignments were structured."[9] As with the faculty member who was surprised about student mental health challenges, this faculty member knew intellectually that assignment design matters. But it's rare that individual faculty members have the opportunity to look at each other's assignments—especially assignments from faculty at other SLACs, whom they don't know but who are aiming at the same learning objectives. Another faculty member underlined this insight further, noting "it never occurred to me that we could even *ask* students these kinds of questions."[10] In the context of this reflective assessment, the diversity of assignments was an asset that offered faculty an opportunity to benefit from the kind of assignment tinkering that usually takes multiple semesters to achieve in one's own classes.

Another part of the shift was in thinking about the value of peer review. One of the metacognitive assignments that some faculty used was a "learning assist" assignment that asked students to reflect each week on something they had learned from a peer. Student responses ranged from comments about course content (e.g., "___ identified a problem of anthropological study in African society, which is that African people were probably tired of being studied by westerners. This is a perspective I have not considered before. This made me think of the importance of building relationships with African people or whomever you want to study as opposed to treating them as just 'subjects' for your paper") to comments about process (e.g., "___ was

---

9. Anonymous, in group workshop with author, June 2022.

10. Anonymous, in group workshop with author, June 2022.

a great assist in class this week. He's amazingly insightful and I found myself copying down many of his remarks. He's astutely self-aware and willing to backtrack on topics for the sake of achieving a more civil discourse. His annotations on Hypothesis are always thought-provoking and allow me to delve deeper into the writing through another's perspective").[11] Some faculty who had been skeptical of using peer review in class took to it in a new way after being asked to reflect on how the process of peer review affected individual students' metacognitive growth. This window, via assessment, made them interested in thinking about models of peer review in ways that had not seemed attractive in past experiences with professional development workshops encouraging the use of peer review as a tool. Assessment here truly functioned as an opportunity for non-hierarchical and pedagogical *self-assessment*, emerging not from a directive given by a WPA, but from faculty's collaborative reflection on students' reflective writing.

Yet another part of the conversation was about the interrelationships between student reflection, faculty workload, and the helpful and harmful effects of individual privacy/secrecy. While faculty valued the insights into student experiences, they wondered whether it is useful to know about their own students' metacognition—and some raised the same issue Scott (2005) raises about the performativity of metacognitive growth when students sense that there are correct answers to be conveyed to the grading professor. Many of our campuses are thinking about revising advising structures, and there were fruitful conversations about possibilities for inviting students to do the reflective writing in advising contexts where it is not graded but where a faculty member has the opportunity to make the writing "count" without being graded. There were also conversations about possibilities for sharing anonymized reflections like the ones faculty in the popups read, but with students (to normalize working through discomfort) and with other faculty (to remind them that "life really is hard for everybody"). It is worth noting that we might see empathy as a common, if nearly invisible thread running through these "popup" conversations in which a shared sense of difficulty, stress, and uncertainty stitched faculty members together with each other, and with faculty from other institutions, while also connecting students to faculty, and most importantly, faculty to students.

---

11. Anonymous, student responses to reflection assignment in fall 2020 study sample.

Conclusion: Reflecting on Reflection in Assessment

The conversations sparked by the popup workshops were generative in ways that the VALUE assessment the previous summer, which had been frustrating for everyone, had not been. We are now in the process of thinking about how to use these reflections on reflection in our assessment of individual students, whole classes, and institution-wide practices. In many ways, the more reflective approach fulfilled the potential that exists at SLACs for assessment loops that feed into teaching and learning. Faculty at SLACs generally have strong motivation to be good teachers and to meet student needs. And yet, SLAC faculty are often resistant to being told "best practices" or subjected to assessments that seem pro forma or beneficial only to external auditors.

When asked whether the VALUE rubric assessment was worthwhile, faculty did say they believed it might be persuasive for some faculty to know that, say, metacognitive assignments moved students two points on a VALUE rubric. But, given how challenging we found it to administer a study that could garner a statistically significant "two point" account of student metacognition, we think that doing such work at SLACs may not be practical. And, for this kind of work, that might be fine, because our project taught us other things about attempting to account for putative improvements in self-awareness, intellectual preparedness (as if such a thing were monolithic), and the ability to think about one's own thinking and learning using the conceptual rigidity of the quantitative rubric. For one, *backward* is perhaps where we all want to go when we ask for reflection, and backward is messy. Perhaps some of our students went backward because we had succeeded in getting them to disrupt the careful story they had learned to tell about their own progress as thinkers (often the same story an admissions essay demands). We know that literacy narratives, for example, risk encouraging a one-way "out of the darkness, into the light" story that elides the complexity of individual development and the eddies of knowledge and awareness (Inayatulla 2013). Moving backward in a reflection on arriving to college and learning to navigate academic discourse communities as an undergraduate can mean finding more complex, less unilineal narrative structures to account for who we are and how we learn, and the small-to-big integers of a quantitative rubric cannot reflect such narrative complexity. Moving backward can also mean returning to a place of safety, which isn't a rhetorical move we should discount or even, perhaps, always discourage, particularly in the throes of a global pandemic or any other shared traumatic event.

Perhaps even the controversial "zero" score showed us that in some of our thinking we don't understand zero as an absence, but as the presence of something we can document as failure (not good enough, versus just not there)—and if that inflects how we respond to our students' efforts to reflect on their own process, are we in turn just encouraging progress narratives? Quantitative assessments have an arithmetic logic, we'd suggest, that works counter to the errant nature of self-discovery. A zero (an absence) adds nothing to a score, whereas the absence in reflective writing might simply be silence—a true instrument of reflection, a moment of not-knowing or not-being-able-to that is crucial to the process.

The quantitative rubric also cannot capture what one of history's paragons of reflection, the essayist Michel de Montaigne (1958) calls the "becoming" self, the "drunken, staggering" self that cannot be kept still. Teaching our students to inhabit a state of becoming means we work against them if we use the summative nature of a number to evaluate their progress; that math suggests we only *become* from smaller to greater. But why would that be necessarily true, especially in written reflections, where we ask our students to *write* through the messy fragments of their own histories, intellectual and otherwise, putting these incomplete puzzles in front of their professors in *print*? Perhaps here another essayist is even more useful: Sor Juana Inés de la Cruz (1997), arguing, just one hundred years after Montaigne, from her cloister in New Spain (present-day Mexico City) for the right to compose her written reflections in ways that flouted the sacred progress narratives of the Catholic church: "If I knew all I should," she says simply, "I would not write."

It takes a great deal of learning to know what one does not know, and when we ask our students to reflect on their own thinking and learning in the form of writing, it stands to reason that one index of progress might register as negation, as zero. Thus instead of arranging our students' gains along a number line, perhaps we might use the dialogic potential of small groups of faculty at small liberal arts colleges to recognize and work with the ebb and flow of thinking in our students. And something like this, finally, is what we'd like to offer as the takeaway from our own assessment, and from this piece. In trying to assess reflective writing, reflection taught us something about assessment: reflection shows us what the relentless forward-looking gaze of assessment misses, which is that sometimes moving forward has everything to do with looking in the mirror, looking at each other, and looking back.

Bibliography

Allan, Elizabeth G., and Dana Lynn Driscoll. 2014. "The Three-Fold Benefit of Reflective Writing: Improving Program Assessment, Student Learning, and Faculty Professional Development." *Assessing Writing* 21 (July): 37–55. https://doi.org/10.1016/j.asw.2014.03.001.

Bergey, Bradley W., Rauno K. Parrila, Annie Laroche, and S. Hélène Deacon. 2019. "Effects of Peer-Led Training on Academic Self-Efficacy, Study Strategies, and Academic Performance for First-Year University Students with and without Reading Difficulties." *Contemporary Educational Psychology* 56 (January): 25–39. https://doi.org/10.1016/j.cedpsych.2018.11.001.

Callahan, Susan. 2000. "Responding to the Invisible Student." *Assessing Writing* 7, no. 1 (February): 57–77. https://doi.org/10.1016/S1075-2935(00)00016-7.

Creme, Phyllis. 2005. "Should Student Learning Journals be Assessed?" *Assessment and Evaluation in Higher Education* 30, no. 3 (June): 287–96. https://doi.org/10.1080/02602930500063850.

—. 2008. "A Space for Academic Play: Student Learning Journals as Transitional Writing." *Arts and Humanities in Higher Education* 7, no. 1 (February): 49–64. https://doi.org/10.1177/1474022207084882.

Cummings, Chris. 2015. "Engaging New College Students in Metacognition for Critical Thinking: A Developmental Education Perspective." *Research and Teaching in Developmental Education* 32, no. 1 (Fall): 68–71. https://www.jstor.org/stable/44290289.

Denton, David. 2011. "Reflection and Learning: Characteristics, Obstacles, and Implications." *Educational Philosophy and Theory* 43, no. 8: 838–52. https://doi.org/10.1111/j.1469-5812.2009.00600.x.

Finer, Bryna Siegel. 2017. "The Genre Transfer Game: A Reflective Activity to Facilitate Transfer of Learning." *Teaching English in the Two-Year College* 44, no. 3 (March): 315–28.

Gladstein, Jill M., and Dara Rossman Regaignon. 2012. *Writing Program Administration at Small Liberal Arts Colleges*. Anderson: Parlor Press.

Grossman, Robert. 2009. "Structures for Facilitating Student Reflection." *College Teaching* 57, no. 1 (Winter): 15–22. https://doi.org/10.3200/CTCH.57.1.15-22.

Inayatulla, Shereen. 2013. "Beyond the Dark Closet: Reconsidering Literacy Narratives as Performative Artifacts." *Journal of Basic Writing* 32, no. 2 (Fall): 5–27. https://www.jstor.org/stable/43744165.

Juana Inés de la Cruz. 1997. "Response to the Most Illustrious Poetess Sor Filotea de la Cruz." In *Poems, Protest, and A Dream: Selected Writings*, translated by Margaret Sayers Peden, 1–76. New York: Penguin Books.

Lobato, Joanne. 2012. "The Actor-Oriented Transfer Perspective and Its Contributions to Educational Research and Practice." *Educational Psychologist* 47, no. 3: 232–47. https://doi.org/10.1080/00461520.2012.693 353.

Montaigne, Michel de. 1958. "Of Repentance." In *The Complete Essays of Montaigne*, edited by Donald Murdoch Frame, 610–20. Stanford: Stanford University Press.

Perkins, D. N., and Salomon, Gavriel. 1989. "Are Cognitive Skills Context Bound?" *Educational Researcher* 18, no. 1 (January–February): 16–25. https://doi.org/10.2307/1176006.

Scott, Tony. 2005. "Creating the Subject of Portfolios: Reflective Writing and the Conveyance of Institutional Prerogatives." *Written Communication* 22, no. 1 (January): 3–35. https://doi.org/10.1177/0741088304271831.

Shapiro, Shawna. 2011. "Stuck in the Remedial Rut: Confronting Resistance to ESL Curriculum Reform." *Journal of Basic Writing* 30, no. 2 (Fall): 24–52. https://www.jstor.org/stable/43443916.

Smith, Buffy. 2013. *Mentoring At-Risk Students through the Hidden Curriculum of Higher Education*. Lanham: Lexington Books.

Stephens, Nicole M., MarYam G. Hamedani, and Mesmin Destin. 2014. "Closing the Social-Class Achievement Gap: A Difference-Education Intervention Improves First-Generation Students' Academic Performance and All Students' College Transition." *Psychological Science* 25, no. 4 (April): 943–53. https://doi.org/10.1177/0956797613518349.

Stephens, Nicole M., Sarah S. M. Townsend, MarYam G. Hamedani, Mesmin Destin, and Vida Manzo. 2015. "A Difference-Education Intervention Equips First-Generation College Students to Thrive in the Face of Stressful College Situations." *Psychological Science* 26, no. 10 (October): 1556–66. https://doi.org/10.1177/0956797615593501.

Wardle, Elizabeth. 2009. "'Mutt Genres' and the Goal of FYC: Can We Help Students Write the Genres of the University?" *College Composition and Communication* 60, no. 4 (June), 765–89. https://www.jstor.org/stable/40593429.

Yancey, Kathleen Blake, Liane Robertson, and Kara Taczak. 2014. *Writing across Contexts: Transfer, Composition, and Sites of Writing*. Logan and Boulder: Utah State University Press and University of Colorado Press.

Appendix A: Bookend Assignments

Opening Bookend

In roughly 500-750 words (about 1.5-2 double-spaced pages of type) describe what you anticipate for yourself in the coming year:

- What personal skills, experiences, and strengths do you bring to college with you? Given the expectations you have for what college will be like, how do you imagine your particular skills and experiences might emerge as assets for you in college?
- What do you imagine written and oral communication (writing and speaking, reading and listening) will be like at the college level? How do you imagine you'll learn to navigate and learn more about those things?
- Do you anticipate any challenges? If so, what are some of those? How do you expect you might deal with them?

Keep in mind that this is not an admissions essay! You've been accepted, and we're so glad you're here! This is more of a time capsule, an honest index of who you are and where you are now at the beginning of your college career. You'll write this assignment again at the end of the semester, so imagine you're writing with your future self as your audience.

Closing Bookend

In roughly 500-750 words (about 1.5-2 double-spaced pages of type) please revisit the following questions:

- What personal skills, experiences, and strengths did you bring to college with you and how do you think about them now? Given the expectations you had for what college will be like, what particular skills and experiences emerged as assets for you in college and which ones surprised you?
- How do you now think about written and oral communication (writing and speaking, reading and listening) will be like at the college level? How have you learned to navigate and learn more about those things, and what strategies and skills will you take into your other work in college?
- What were some of the challenges? Which ones were unpredictable or surprised you? How did you navigate them?

Appendix B: Student Learning Outcomes (SLOs) for the Metacognitive Curriculum

Upon successful completion of this course, students should be able to:

1. Employ strategic and adaptive decision-making in their academic work, including effective time management, planning for multiple commitments and multi-step projects, effective use of college resources and support services.

2. Critically examine their experiences to identify how these can be assets in their academic work and to realistically assess their personal strengths and areas for improvement

3. Consider their role as active and engaged members of scholarly communities, including how they contribute to these communities, and how participating in these communities affects their education.

Appendix C: Rubric for Assessing Student Metacognitive Development

	Absent (0)	Nascent (1)	Emerging (2)	Developing (3)
1) Self-Assessment: the ability to examine past experience and generalize personal qualities that might be an asset or create challenges in college ("Here's where I've been and who I am.")	Does not provide any assessment of personal strengths, weaknesses, or areas for growth.	Identifies strengths, weaknesses, or areas for growth in general or abstract terms while suppling few, if any, supporting details or examples. Personal experiences or details described in the essay are not clearly connected to student's self-assessment.	Assesses personal strengths, weaknesses, and areas for growth and provides either concrete supporting details or personal experiences that put these qualities in context (but not both).	Assesses personal strengths, weaknesses, and areas for growth using concrete supporting details and discusses personal experiences that put these qualities in context.
2) Predictive Thinking: the ability to consider future situations, especially challenges or difficulties, based on past experiences and information at hand ("Based on what's happened and what I've learned, here's what's ahead.")	Does not imagine potential situations or challenges ahead.	Describes potential situations or challenges ahead in vague or general terms that do not indicate significant critical thought.	Describes potential situations or challenges ahead in ways that indicate some critical thought and/or detailed thinking, but still operates in very vague or broad terms. Engages to a limited extent with information available to them about their institution or classes.	Describes potential situations or challenges ahead in specific terms that indicate student has considered them thoroughly. Supports conclusions with specific information about their institution or classes.
3) Adaptive Metacognition: the ability to apply skills and knowledge creatively and effectively to new situations. Essay may convey this by describing student's response to past circumstances or by predicting their response to anticipated challenges. (?When x happened, I responded with y." or "If x happens, I'll do y.")	Does not address responses, reactions, or adaptations that the student made to challenges in the past or possible adaptations the student might make to the experiences or challenges they anticipate in the future.	Describes responses, reactions, or adaptations in vague terms, making few, if any, significant connections between their behavior and their perceived personal strengths and weaknesses.	Describes responses, reactions, or adaptations in some detail, but does not connect these to their perceived personal strengths and weaknesses. Or, describes responses, reactions, or adaptations in vague detail but with significant connections to perceived personal strengths and weaknesses.	Describes responses, reactions, or adaptations with significant detail. Connects these adaptations and reactions in specific and detailed ways to the personal strengths and weaknesses they have identified.

Notes

- Please apply the same standards to opening and closing bookend essays.
- Be careful not to over credit essays that nod at significant and/or sympathetic experiences, but don't explore or engage them in depth.
- The "Absent" category means just that—the essay contains no language that even gestures towards the quality in question.
- Try to be cognizant of perceived gender identity; occasionally ask yourself if you would give an essay the same scores if the author identified as male or female.

The following factors should NOT affect an essay's assessment score:

- Quality of writing
- Consistency of reflection/metacognition (i.e. if an essay reaches a certain level at any point, it should be scored on that level)
- Perceived sincerity or truthfulness of the author's conclusions
- Perceived wisdom or naivete of the author's conclusions

Appendix D: Grading Criteria for Reflective Assignments (used by Carleton instructors)

The reflective assignments you complete this term (i.e. the bookend assignments, the bi-weekly reflective assignments, and the learning assists) are *informal* writing assignments. This means that I will not expect to see a thesis, evidence from our readings or outside sources, or a fully developed argumentative structure in your reflective assignments.

This does, not, however, mean you can simply write *anything* on the reflective assignments. In order to receive full credit for these assignments, you'll need to make a good-faith effort to respond to the prompts with clarity and detail.

So, while reflective writing is "informal" in this course, the best reflective writing will:

- Be organized (NOT just stream of consciousness)
- Follow the length guidelines for each assignment
- Offer concrete details about experiences, thought processes, and/or practices

- Connect those experiences, thought processes, and/or practices to course-related material and discussion, whenever possible and appropriate
- Be accessible to an outside reader—that is, include enough information that someone who doesn't know you well (like your instructor) can fully understand them

11 Percentages, Averages, and Exclamation Points: Parsing Assessment, Evaluation, and Research in the Writing Center

Kristina Reardon

Abstract: This chapter reviews the differences among research, evaluation, and assessment—words that are often mistakenly used as synonyms in day-to-day conversation, but which may have distinct processes for approval, even as writing program administrators (WPAs) pursue two or all three through a given protocol or study. This chapter uses a project involving all three modes as a case study, exploring the importance of framing evaluation and assessment as research for institutional review boards (IRBs) and assessment committees if one hopes to share results beyond their own campus. The study was conducted at the College of the Holy Cross—a Jesuit liberal arts school in the city of Worcester, Massachusetts with a population of ~3,000, and then ported over to Amherst College—an elite liberal arts college in the town of Amherst, Massachusetts, with ~1,900 students, when the researcher changed institutions mid-study. It offers insights and questions that aim to support WPAs in planning research at small liberal arts colleges and presenting it to required boards or committees for approval.

Data, data, data. Any good writing center collects it. If we are fully staffed and intentional with our labor, we even have systems to organize it. But when it comes time to write end-of-year reports—often conveniently required right after final grades have been submitted and students and nine-month coordinators have left for the summer—all that data can be difficult to parse. At the end of the 2020-2021 academic year, I served as director of the writer's workshop (the peer tutoring center) at the College of the Holy Cross, a small liberal arts college in Worcester, MA, with a student population of approximately 3,000. The writer's workshop—one arm of the larger center for writing—has a staff of two part-time professional tutors and around two dozen peer consultants, some of whom did double duty as writing fellows in classes that requested embedded writing support. The workshop saw around 2,000 appointments annually, and in 2020-2021, I reported a moderate uptick in usage statistics in the first paragraph of the annual report with great enthusiasm, **bolding** and <u>underlining</u> our total number of appointments, determining the rate at which usage had increased that year, and then logging that in italics. **Bold**! *Italics*! Use of a percentage increase calculator! The summary had all the hallmarks of a hook to a report written explicitly to justify our existence and budget and to say: *Look how very hard we have been working this year!*

I trotted out the usual statistics in the rest of the report: More than x percent of survey respondents found their meeting helpful! About y percent found session notes useful, too! I add the exclamation points here for emphasis and to reflect my general mood as I remember it when I wrote my part of the report. But I know that even after I edited out any exclamation points, a few things remained to be clarified: how, in a stressful pandemic year, our traffic increased; the type and quality of those many appointments; and why these numbers mattered to begin with. As a writing center director, I felt a sense of pride in those usage statistics. I knew they meant something. Yet I also knew, now and then, that I felt a sentiment that Gregory S. Blimling argues that many researchers do: pressure to produce significant results, usually defined as "something big, surprising, catastrophic, or awful" (2004, 8). In my case, as far as I knew, nothing catastrophic or awful had happened. (Cue a sense of relief.) But it felt like something big had happened that year, and I reached toward what I felt were impressive numbers to try to convey that.

The mode of thinking and doing that I employed as I worked on this report might be classified as a form of fast thinking, even if it felt like this work of tallying, sorting, and making sense of usage numbers occupied valuable time. Building on Daniel Kahneman's *Thinking, Fast and Slow* (2011), higher education scholar Rishi Sriram (2017) links Kahneman's fast thinking and slow thinking to the work of academic administrators called to perform research, evaluation, and assessment. In brief, Kahneman describes fast thinking as automatic and quick and slow thinking as requiring deep, effortful attention to complex problems that cannot be solved quickly (2011, 20–21). Rather than posing one mode of thinking as bad and the other as good, Kahneman explains how fast thinking productively takes the front seat, quickly producing impressions and feelings, while slow thinking kicks in when difficulties arise that fast thinking mode cannot address. He describes it at one point as "a surge of conscious attention whenever you are surprised" (Kahneman 2011, 24). Looking back at the 2020-2021 academic year, I was surprised that during an online year, appointments increased overall. I had expected the opposite, having so profoundly valued in-person interactions and having read on higher education social media groups that many tutoring and student success centers perceived a decrease in appointments during that year. Fast thinking helped me see a broad pattern, but slow thinking would be necessary to understand it. To do this, I would not only need to pause but to do the work of research, not just evaluation or assessment.

It is worth noting that an annual report tells a story, and I chose the summary of the rhetorical moves from the report for dramatic effect here. My summary represents just part of a longer document co-authored with center for writing director Laurie Ann Britt-Smith that detailed the full range of activities of the center, from peer tutoring to teaching to faculty development and more. Yet numbers—especially big ones (in **bold** and <u>underlined</u>!)—are part of our rhetorical toolkit in describing and explaining the nature of our work. I do not want to diminish reporting raw usage statistics. It can be rhetorically savvy to report such statistics (especially when they are rosy) to those in the university community who may evaluate the worth of a center or make funding decisions that impact it. But looking more deeply at the story of the writer's workshop requires more than the simple recitation of numbers. Sriram (2017) makes an analogous call to student affairs professionals in his guide to quantitative research, writing that we must move beyond averages if we are to interrogate our dutifully collected data with any sense of sophistication.

Deep analysis, a form of slow thinking, takes time—much more time than the few weeks we had at the end of the semester to crunch data and make sense of the year's events. The quick writing that must occur to close out the academic year resembles research in some ways and works not at all like research in others. Annual reports are, of course, not research articles, but they can serve as valuable moments of reflection, and as necessary, albeit brief, pauses in our work. They can even serve as part of, or inspiration for, research projects with appropriate planning. What follows is a narrative of moving beyond percentages, averages, and exclamation points—and questioning the very nature of research and assessment, and their relationship to writing center work.

Collecting Data for the Sake of Collecting It

As I wrote the annual report narrative, I studied the data I had on hand, working to analyze and reflect on what it meant as I attempted to preliminarily make sense of the numbers and the experience of the year. I had a lot of data by that point. WC Online collected appointment statistics for the short- and long-term fellows; demographics of student users; and session notes logged for any out-of-class sessions. I had become accustomed to collecting information for the sake of collecting it, in fast thinking mode: knowing it would be useful someday, somehow, and that it was vital for efforts in evaluation, assessment, and possibly research (with proper IRB approval, of course)—but struggling to analyze it in a way that communicated meaning beyond percentages and averages. I had a sense I was not the only writing center director ever to feel this way; casual conversations with colleagues and in online forums over the years had revealed to me that appointment-booking systems like WC Online collect rich datasets that would allow for a range of analytical approaches that not everyone had time to dive into. I needed to figure out what questions I wanted to ask of all that data, data, data from 2020-2021. I needed to slow down.

To pause for a moment: it is worth noting that fast thinking and slow thinking are not opposites, just as assessment/evaluation and research are not diametrically opposed. Sriram emphasizes that "the two systems need to be partners, dancing together to the rhythm of your mind" (2017, 12):

> Thinking fast generates hypotheses and hunches about cause-and-effect relationships. Thinking slow provides more objective feedback on how variables influence one another. Then, thinking fast decides how to make sense of that feedback and, more importantly, what actions to take. (Sriram 2017, 13)

It helped to think of my annual accounting of center data in the annual report as *necessary* fast thinking, the type that might yield more robust slow thinking, both necessary parts of an iterative cycle that blurred the distinctions between assessment, evaluation, and research. Yet in writing center work, it can be easy to fall into a fast thinking-only mode. Sometimes it is expedient, even beneficial, to do so. We need usage data to illustrate our reach, augment our arguments about our worth, and justify funding. On top of that, sometimes things are busy, and stressful, and move quickly; in centers with frequent turnover or without adequate support (in terms of protected time or research funds), fast thinking work might be the expectation, the norm, and may feel like the only reasonable option. But if we take Sriram's careful delineation to heart—that fast thinking can help us hypothesize about cause-and-effect relationships—the next logical step is to dive into slow thinking, where we isolate variables and study their impact. In a world of fast and slow thinking, where the terms evaluation, assessment, and research can feel like synonyms, how do we distinguish among them—and does this distinction matter?

Assessment, Evaluation, and Research

Distinguishing among assessment, evaluation, and research is not quite as simple as slotting one into the fast thinking and one into the slow thinking binary, to be sure. Effectively engaging in all three does involve a shift from making something of data that was uncritically collected to intentionally collecting particular types of data for well-defined reasons. While we can always find ways to analyze information that WC Online generates, to truly engage in slow thinking, we have to consider what we are collecting, and how and why, more carefully. When we do so, we can start to see how assessment, evaluation, and research overlap in many ways—but serve different functions and, as such, often require different planning, design, and application. The distinctions and overlaps among research, evaluation, and assessment were driven home to me when I submitted an IRB application as I sifted through end-of-year data in 2021.

In addition to offering semester-long writing fellows for the few 100-level introduction to academic writing classes that the college offers each fall (Holy Cross does not have a writing requirement), in 2020-2021, I piloted what I came to call "Rent-A-Fellow"—a short-term fellows program meant to meet students where they were and to keep traffic steady in the writer's workshop during an uncharacteristic (for Holy Cross) shift to the online during the COVID-19 pandemic. The first part of the pilot ran in the summer and fall of 2020. Even though these semesters took place during difficult moments for students, fellows, and faculty alike, I received positive feedback. I felt encouraged to study the program more fully after blogging about it for *WLN: A Writing Center Journal* (Reardon 2020). I drafted three surveys: one each for faculty, students, and fellows. I wrote interview questions to follow up on the surveys. I understood that by distributing surveys and conducting interviews I was involving human subjects in my work. Since I hoped to publish parts of what I learned and not just use my analysis for internal purposes, I waited to collect survey and interview data. I wrote an IRB application—nine pages single-spaced—and entitled the project "Assessing the Efficacy of Writing Fellows' Work at Holy Cross." I diligently submitted this application to my campus IRB.

But, ah. I had used the dreaded "a" word: assessment. My study was approved as exempt—but the first approval letter noted that "if you intend to publish from the data, the Office of Assessment and Research will need to see an amended version of your IRB application." At first, I was confused. I had submitted IRB applications successfully many times before for both surveys and interviews without a hitch. Wasn't I supposed to able to run a program assessment without IRB approval if the results were only for internal use, for program-specific improvement? I had submitted the application with express hopes of publishing . . . I wouldn't have needed to submit one at all, I thought, if I didn't want to publish. Or did I? What did it mean to receive an approval with this kind of limitation noted? Was I wrong about my assumptions about being able to run basic surveys for internal use without IRB approval?

IRB, Permissions, and Sharing Work

My initial instruments included a mixture of questions on impressions of the goals of the program, satisfaction with the program, and what each group learned about writing. No red flags there, necessarily, but it became clear to me through emails and a conversation with members of the IRB team that critical questions remained, including: What was I assessing? What was I evaluating? And what was I researching? Building on the momentum of annual report writing featuring all that data, data, data that was automatically collected, I summarized in broad strokes what I hoped to learn from it. On further review, though, I could see how my application lacked a clear rationale for collecting the specific type of data I proposed, as well as detailed questions about what I hoped to learn from it, beyond usage statistics.

Sorting out the answers to these questions took slow thinking—*before* data collection (unlike when I analyzed the myriad of data WC Online stored each year for annual reports). In *Research in the College Context*,

Frances Stage and Kathleen Manning offer a concise distinction among the three activities with which I was trying to engage:

> Assessment and evaluation usually involve making a judgment about the future direction, performance, or ultimate usefulness of an educational enterprise. Research is typically associated with knowledge and theory generation. (Stage and Manning 2003, 5)

They further distinguish assessment from evaluation by writing that assessment can be described as an effort to collect data that *describes* an institution, while evaluation involves an effort to *improve* an institution. They also, in the course of their book, use the word "research" to reference all three, as "referring to the three activities separately by name . . . would be cumbersome" (2003, 5). Unwittingly, I also used the word "assessment" as a catch-all phrase in my IRB write-up—albeit with less intentionality, and without the qualifiers that Stage and Manning offer.

Ernest Boyer's model of the scholarship of application is a useful way to understand how assessment, evaluation, and research are often productively blurred. Boyer describes the scholarship of application as the range of generative insights that can come from on-the-ground service to the institution, when service is tied to "one's special field of knowledge" and new insights and knowledge are "relate[d] to, and flow directly out of, this professional activity" (Boyer 1990, 22). The work of managing a writing center or coordinating a writing program easily fits this model of service. Boyer notes that universities often do not see service as scholarship. I highlight his observations because they help explain why it can be hard for IRBs, assessment committees, and those of us involved in writing programming to distinguish where our day-to-day professional duties (like writing a report or sending out a post-program survey) end, and where our scholarship begins. Often, they are one and the same. Critically, however, institutional policies that govern each are often different.

I came to understand later, after reading more fully the information that the Holy Cross Office of Assessment and Research offers in its policies and procedures, that if I was collecting assessment data to share outside the college context—in writing or a presentation, it "also require[s] the review and approval of the campus-wide sub-committee on assessment and planning" (2020, 3). Unknowingly, by combining my assessment and evaluation with my research, I had created a situation where there were additional hurdles to clear. These were not impossible hurdles. They were not even unreasonable ones. But they were hurdles that required I propose doing more than collecting information to tally and sort to produce percentages. In addition to specifying where data would be stored, for how long, and exactly what kind of data I would be collecting, I needed to specify what questions I was planning to ask of this data, even broadly speaking. I needed to better define my research project, not just collect information for internal assessment or evaluation.

As I reflect on this rather complicated (for me) IRB approval, I find that returning to Stage and Manning's suggestions about framing research questions provide a helpful exercise in slow thinking. They suggest writing a statement of the problem under consideration, then composing a general question that fits the mode "I want to find out who/how/why . . . ," followed by sub-questions, and the rationale for the research (Stage and Manning 2003, 12). In my haste to file my IRB protocol, I found myself working on sub-questions and rationales, never quite landing on a clear and concise "I want to find out . . . " It was through conversations with both the representative of the IRB who spoke with me, and colleagues in composition (I was luckily enrolled in the Dartmouth writing research seminar at the time) that I clarified what I was *assessing and evaluating* and what I was *researching* (see Table 1).

Table 1. Shifting research questions

Original framing of research problem and questions in IRB proposal	Revised framing of research problem and questions in IRB proposal
This study aims to determine how three main constituencies (professors, students, and writing fellows) understand the role of the writing fellow in the classroom and how the relationship among all three groups is mediated by session notes produced at the end of tutorials. The goal of the study is to ask all three groups via survey and focus group questions to describe and rate their experiences, with a broader goal of understanding how writing fellows impact students' writing processes as they learn to write at Holy Cross . . .	My initial IRB application detailed a plan for assessing the short-term writing fellows program. This included some questions in the interviews and surveys that were evaluative and were meant to provide feedback to the center for writing for ongoing efforts to improve the program. Within this larger framework for assessment is a research question that corresponds to larger questions in the field of writing studies: What do faculty, students, and fellows learn from each other through their collaborative efforts on writing assignments? Any publication submissions that would result from this project would be in direct response to this question.

As part of my written documentation to the IRB to eventually obtain permission to publish my work, I clarified that some questions in the interviews and surveys were meant to provide feedback to the center for writing for ongoing efforts to improve the writing fellows program (assessment and evaluation). Within this larger framework for assessment, I wrote a research question about what students, faculty, and fellows learned about writing by engaging in the writing fellows program.

Moving forward at Amherst College, where I moved in 2021 to assume the role of director of intensive writing, I have been more intentional in distinguishing among assessment, evaluation, and research. I have come to use the following questions to orient my work:

1. Is my goal to gather information to *understand* a program or project better? (assessment)

2. Is my goal to gather information to *improve* a program or project? (evaluation)

3. Is my goal to gather information to analyze it so I can *build and share knowledge*? (research)

It is probably clear by now that it is possible to pursue just one of these three options, but it is far more likely we often pursue two or even all three at the same time. We need explicit IRB approval for human subjects research, but I have also learned that unless I am completing a very basic or quick survey that I know for sure I will never want to share with anyone outside my office or institution, it is often beneficial to first pursue IRB approval—and any related assessment committee approvals since, as we know, there can be no retroactive IRB approval. Pursuing IRB approval before every survey can be a time-consuming process, however. IRBs at small liberal arts colleges are often powered by a single faculty advisor or a small committee of staff and faculty more accustomed to reviewing work in the sciences and social sciences than in the humanities. For my part, I was accustomed to a very dedicated and helpful faculty member in the social sciences at Holy Cross reviewing my IRB proposals quickly and making only small suggestions before approving them as exempt. I learned that when designing a research project involving assessment or evaluation, I needed to allot more than triple the usual time to the planning process and IRB review, even if the expected result was an exempt ruling. Combining assessment and evaluation with research, then, requires slow thinking. It simply cannot be done quickly.

"It is not uncommon for researchers to want to make changes after they begin a study."

All of this reflection on IRB may seem a minor point. Sometimes modifications to protocols need to be made before full approval is obtained. Getting approval to publish assessment data is complicated. Often this involves emails or conversations. Mine were with kind and helpful colleagues. Usually, IRB merits a single sentence in a research article: "The [college name] human subjects committee approved this study . . . " Yet working in fast thinking mode—the mode that saw me happily compile averages and percentages in my annual reports that could be gleaned from data we already held in our appointment booking software—I had quickly drafted surveys and interview questions that would gather information to improve my program (evaluation) and to understand it better (assessment). I was accustomed, like the good writing center professional I was, to collecting data, data, data as part of normal operating procedures. Writing an IRB application forced me to be more intentional with my process, to engage slow thinking, to frame my research questions so I could move beyond understanding and improving to knowledge building.

I don't necessarily want to wax poetic about IRB—or become dismissive of the fast thinking labor that often goes into annual reports or post-program assessments. In truth, I think that some slow thinking happens in annual reports each year, especially as they require cohesion and some semblance of narrative; a list of statistics does not constitute a report. But I was reminded through the process of IRB submission that even slower thinking is required for deliberate, ethical, specific, and useful assessment/evaluation and research. Part of that slow thinking involves distinguishing, even for one's self, among the three. Further, research is always slow work. Evaluation and assessment can be fast or slow work, but neither can usually be shared beyond campus without IRB approval . . . which often requires reframing them as a form of research, with clear research questions and goals that may go beyond improving or describing.

A final note on IRB: as I worked with data and realized I needed more information than I initially anticipated, I submitted several further modifications. Some were to accommodate new sub-questions that emerged. I added personnel to my study. I changed institutions, which meant where I stored files changed—and that I had to resubmit IRB paperwork to my new institution as well. If I was done collecting data, this was all that was needed—but if I had been mid-data collection, I may have needed to reapply to the IRB at my original institution as an outside scholar to continue to interview or survey students. I learned to resubmit my protocol to change my method of transcription. Such modifications are expected and natural over the course of a long or complicated study, such as one that blends assessment, evaluation, and research over several months or years. I was reassured by the guidance on submitting modifications on the Holy Cross website, quoted in one of my subheadings, that it is not uncommon for researchers to want to make changes after they begin a study. Further reassurance came from conversations with the faculty IRB representatives at both Holy Cross and Amherst as they helped me chart a course forward, even when I made unwitting mistakes along the way.

Questions to ask before starting your evaluation, assessment, or research project

- Will I want to share the results of this project with anyone outside my office, or outside my institution? If so, it is best to submit your plan to the IRB before you begin data collection because there is no retroactive IRB approval.
- Does my study involve human subjects—through surveys, interviews, or data collection about human subjects from pre-existing sources (ex: WC Online)? If so, you should consult with the IRB first—even if you think your study may be exempt.
- Is there a campus research or assessment committee that I need to consult in addition to IRB? If so, you should consult with the related groups before or during your IRB review process to ensure that you have permission to share data.
- Is my aim assessment, evaluation, or research—or some combination? Can I articulate my specific aims in terms that clearly communicate to IRBs and research/assessment committees how and why I am collecting such data—and how assessment and/or evaluation constitutes research? If not, then it might be time to engage in slow thinking and redefine aims.
- Have I accurately described protocols that are specific enough that the IRB and/or research/assessment committees understand my process—but loose enough to allow for me to (ethically) pivot as needed? If you are too specific—say, you note that you will always begin an interview with the same sentence, you may find it difficult to form a reasonable conversation with a participant, or you may find yourself inadvertently violating your protocol. It is usually better to use specific but flexible terms such as "I will greet the participant

and explain the goal of the study . . . " rather than inserting a direct quote you will use. Of course, you can always file a modification to your protocol if you feel you need to change things.

Elements of the IRB process can seem extremely formal and even legalistic, and they can feel more directed at scholars working in science and the social sciences rather than in writing studies specifically. Trainings (like the CITI program course most IRBs require) and documents that govern IRB stress the seriousness of behaving ethically and not making mistakes in research studies that involve animals, medical trials, etc. Yet it has been my experience that many evaluation and assessment projects on writing are often deemed exempt, and once exempt, there is often little guidance at small liberal arts colleges on what to do if things change, or if something goes wrong during the course of the study. It is helpful to remember that behind the legalese of IRB policies, there are colleagues reviewing our work—a form of peer review. At small liberal arts colleges, such colleagues, at least in my experience, are often ready to help you figure out how to best proceed, especially at places where IRB is new or where you might be one of only a few scholars submitting proposals outside the sciences and social sciences. If I had worried less about timing and bothering the IRB and had asked more questions earlier in the process, I might have saved myself some stress and possibly the need to submit so many modifications.

The Work of Assessing and Researching Rent-A-Fellow

Of course, designing a research question, thinking fast and slow, and then receiving permission to collect data is really only the beginning. After data collection, analysis begins. This, too, can vacillate between fast and slow. To draw out this distinction, I will work through approaches to the revised research questions that my study, broadly speaking, proposed to all three constituencies (faculty, staff, and students):

1. What is the purpose of the fellows program?
2. What did each constituency learn about writing from the other?

One way of addressing these questions involves analyzing responses to questions on class attendance. This data was collected as part of a survey on Google Forms, which separates responses in an Excel sheet but also creates graphs and calculates percentages for easy, quick reporting. I asked faculty: "Do you see value in having the writing fellows attend class?" I provided responses options on a five-point Likert scale, where a 1 was the lowest ranking and a 5 was the highest ranking (so, for the first question, a 1 would be no value, and a 5 would be a great deal of value).

The fast thinking way of understanding the professor's approach to class attendance would be to affirm that all constituencies found fellows' class attendance valuable (see Figure 1).

Percentage of groups that found fellows' class attendance valuable

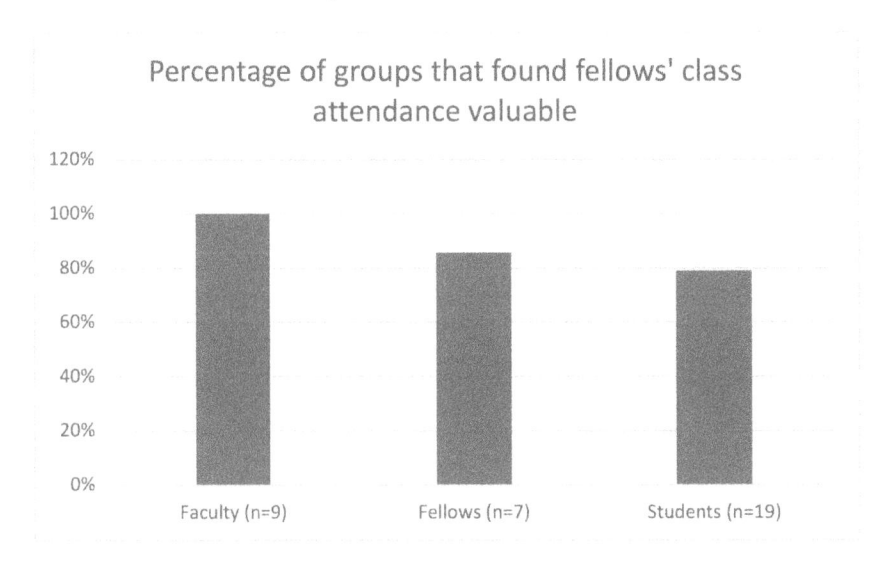

[Bar graph showing: Faculty (n=9) at 100%, Fellows (n=7) at approximately 87.5%, Students (n=19) at approximately 79%]

Figure 1. Percentage of groups that found fellows' class attendance valuable. Bar graph created by the author.

To elaborate on what the figure shows: all groups found class attendance valuable, though there were slight differences among groups. Diving deeper: 100 percent of faculty surveyed (n=9) gave writing fellows attending class a ranking of a 5—extremely valuable. This is significant, given that 75 percent of faculty who had fellows responded to the survey (there were twelve total, some for multiple classes or sections). Meanwhile, in fast thinking mode, I could report the fellows' responses: with an 87.5 percent response rate (n=7, out of a possible eight), the results were similarly compelling. All but one fellow saw value in attending. Moving quickly, I could tally student responses. With nineteen participants, the total response rate was significantly lower (closer to 11 percent), but it did give me a sense that students viewed things similarly: the majority (79 percent) offered a 4 or 5 rating (meaning the class attendance was useful). All of these numbers seem to add up to one thing: that for the majority of survey respondents across all three constituencies (faculty, fellows, and students), class attendance had

268 Kristina Reardon

some value. These numbers paint a rosy picture in general of the value of class attendance.

However, I do not want to fall into the false dichotomy that survey work involves *only* fast thinking. Above, I used fast thinking to blur rankings and categories together to simplify results intentionally. This approach can be useful to gain an initial snapshot of the data—or, simply, to work quickly under a deadline to produce a reasonably accurate statistic. But I will pull apart one statistic to show how slow thinking can yield more complex results: the 79 percent statistic that said students saw value in class attendance blends those who gave it a 4 or 5 ranking on the Likert scale. This makes the text I wrote easier to digest, and for certain purposes, it is not necessary or useful to parse the distinction between a 4 or 5. To engage in slow thinking about this survey result, I would want to tease that distinction apart and acknowledge the 15.8 percent (n=3) who reported feeling neutral and the 5.3 percent (n=1) who said it was *not* useful. A more detailed, accurate reporting of all three constituencies' responses follows in Figure 2.

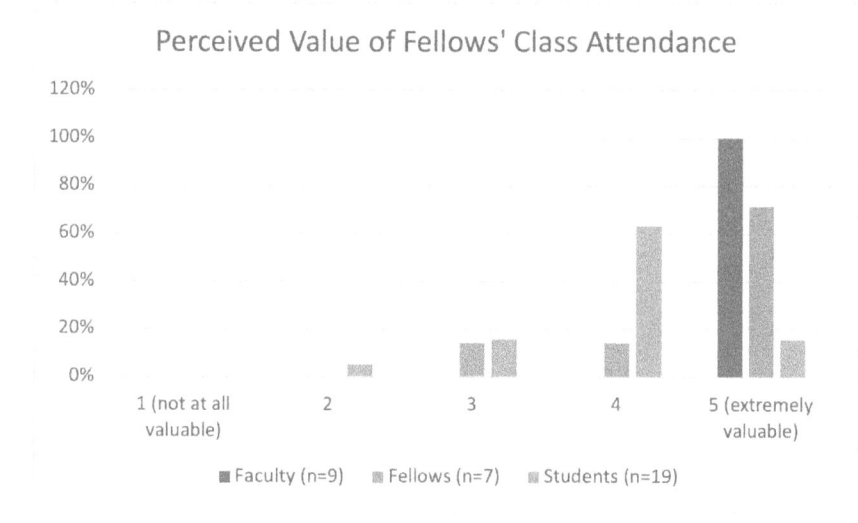

Figure 2. Perceived value of fellows' class attendance. Bar graph created by the author.

Looking at these deeper results, it is still true that faculty seemed to value class attendance most, with fellows seeing slightly lesser value and students seeing slightly lesser value, though the majority of each group saw some value in it (Figure 2). What becomes starker is that students' responses varied much more than faculty response. There were no outliers in the faculty data, and the faculty response rate for the survey was strong (75 percent). It may or may not be worth hypothesizing about the one student who did not find value in class attendance or the small number of students and fellows who felt neutral. However, a smaller percentage of students (11 percent) were surveyed. For basic program evaluation, I might be able to generally draw the conclusion: all constituencies felt class time was valuable, so it should be continued. For research purposes, I would want to survey students again and, perhaps more slowly, try to recruit a higher percentage of students. After all, respondents who replied quickly in the few weeks the study was open may be the students who liked the fellows and may be predisposed to ranking their work, including class attendance, positively. Yet even within the same limited dataset, these thoughts lead me from a basic evaluation question about usefulness to a sharpened research question: in what ways do faculty and students (including fellows, who are also students) understand the value of the fellows program *differently*?

The open response comments here begin to shed some light: two out of five student comments pointed to the fellow explaining their availability and/or how to book appointments as the main value of class attendance (rather than anything to do with assignments or class content), while one student wrote: "not much attendance in class, but her help outside of class was very helpful." Meanwhile, faculty saw things slightly differently. One wrote:

> I would definitely like for a fellow to attend a few classes as long as it wouldn't be too burdensome—so that they can get a feel for the course as a whole and how a particular assignment fits in. And so that the class members can get to know them and increase the comfort level with making an appointment.

In this comment, we can see an overlapping value with student responses; one of the key benefits of class attendance, it seems, is creating space for students to understand how to make appointments and to connect to the fellow. But the faculty member framed the fellow's attendance in terms of their pedagogy and relationship building, something the students and fellows did not comment on in this part of the survey.

Meanwhile, I also asked the fellows an additional question, beyond the usefulness of class attendance: "You held thirty-minute sessions with students. Overall, how much did class attendance impact your sessions?" 71.5 percent (n=5) reported that class attendance in some impacted sessions.

Contrast that to the 87.5 percent (n=7) who found class sessions useful. There is something interesting in the fellows' own assessment of their work. What did the two who found class attendance useful find it useful for, if not sessions? In interviews, more than one fellow mentioned class attendance gave them a basic context for the course, but at least one was lukewarm about attending—noting that it really only felt useful if the specific writing assignment was being discussed. Another fellow said that attending class would allow her to speak up and communicate concerns students had in sessions to the professor directly, allowing her to act as a translator or intermediary. Another fellow, whom we will call Emily, cited familiarity as an important element of class attendance:

> Students] were more comfortable, definitely, because they knew me. I wasn't just some person they're meeting for an hour who's coming to judge their writing. They knew, "Oh, that's Emily. She's been in our classes and all that. She's here to help."

Further review of all the fellows' transcripts might illuminate further what the fellows found useful, exactly, about class attendance—and why class attendance mostly, but not entirely, seemed to impact the sessions they held. A deeper review would involve coding these interview transcripts to understand more detail and the broader patterns these details fit into, but survey data, when parsed thoroughly, provides an overview of the sorts of nuance interviews might provide.

Three key ideas about the value of class attendance, and of the fellows in general, seemed to emerge here:

1. Explaining program mechanics (including booking appointments)
2. Understanding the assignment and course context
3. Relationship building

I did not have enough open response data to code methodically, but this deeper—slower—dive into the intricacies of one question's responses provided a first draft of the ideas or values I could trace in coding my interviews later. Indeed, each of the three categories became a parent code when I analyzed data that asked students, faculty, and fellows to describe what they understood as the main role of writing fellows.

Conclusions

To consider the question about what faculty, fellows, and students learned about writing from one another requires a deeper, slower dive into the dataset, as I did when I added one of the professors who taught with writing fellows to my protocol so we could together analyze students' and fellows' work after her class was over (Klotz and Reardon, 2022). But by understanding if each constituency valued certain parts of the program that are critical to it (class attendance, for example), we can begin to isolate and understand one element of the learning process. By understanding how at least one triad of faculty-fellow-students answered the same question reflecting on the same experience from different vantage points, we can see how the experience of the fellows program was, at the very least, slightly different for each. As I begin to reflect on the more extensive data set, I wonder if the way each constituency experienced the other impacted how they learned from one another. The professors mostly interacted with fellows in class; it would therefore make sense that they found class attendance valuable. Meanwhile, students and fellows interacted most closely in one-on-one sessions; it would likewise make sense that class attendance—where fellows might or might not participate in class—would feel less impactful than a thirty-minute conversation.

Fast thinking pushed (quickly drafting questions) me to slow thinking (analyzing responses), while that slow thinking pushed me back to fast thinking (hypothesizing about what the responses meant). This push and pull is part of assessment, evaluation, and research. I am reminded of the distinction between assessment, evaluation and research that I derived from Stage and Manning. Research involves generating knowledge, while assessment and evaluation provide information that can help shape future educational practices. The evaluations and assessments that comprise applied research often shape educational practices, even as they build knowledge for publication. The distinction among assessment, evaluation, and research is perhaps less one of methodology and more one of framing questions and securing permission to share outside one's program or campus.

Bibliography

Blimling, Gregory S. 2004. "White Blankets May Make You Smarter and Other Questionable Social Science Findings." *About Campus* 9, no. 3: 2–9.

Boyer, Ernest. 1990. *Scholarship Reconsidered: Priorities of the Professoriate.* New York: Carnegie Foundation for the Advancement of Teaching.

College of the Holy Cross. 2020. "Assessment, Evaluation and Survey Data Collection, Use and Dissemination Policy for Institutional Assessment and Research." Accessed July 25, 2022. https://www.holycross.edu/sites/default/files/files/policyprocedure/data_policies_final_-_2020_02_20.docx.pdf.

College of the Holy Cross. n.d. "IRB FAQ's." Accessed July 25, 2022. https://www.holycross.edu/office-sponsored-research/office-sponsored-research/office-sponsored-research/research-responsibilitycompliance/human-subjects-research/irb-faqs.

Kahneman, Daniel. 2011. *Thinking, Fast and Slow.* New York: Farrar, Straus, and Giroux.

Klotz, Sarah, and Kristina Reardon. 2022. "Crafting a Writing Response Community through Contract Grading." *Journal of Response to Writing* 8, no. 2: 106–26.

Reardon, Kristina. 2020. "Rent-A-Fellow, or How We Engaged Students at the Moments They Needed Writing Support Most." *Connecting Writing Centers across Borders* (blog), *WLN: A Journal of Writing Center Scholarship.* August 10, 2020. https://www.wlnconnect.org/blog/2020/08/rent-a-fellow-or-how-we-engaged-students-at-the-moments-they-needed-writing-support-most/.

Sriram, Rishi. 2017. *Student Affairs by the Numbers: Quantitative Research and Statistics for Professionals.* Sterling: Stylus.

Stage, Frances K., and Kathleen Manning. 2003. *Research in the College Context: Approaches and Methods.* New York: Routledge.

12 Layered Conversations: Methodologizing Lore as a Scholarly Assessment Practice

Sarah Kosel Agnihotri, Holly Blakely, Matthew Fledderjohann, and Kim Fahle Peck

> *Two words that haunt writing center professionals are "research" and "assessment."*
>
> —Neal Lerner

Abstract: This chapter applies a methodological approach to the process of developing, sharing, and using lore as a means of academic inquiry and assessment. By detailing the way four writing center administrators at four different institutions engaged with Lori Salem's call to understand who isn't visiting writing centers, this chapter argues that disciplinary knowledge about assessment can be gained by intentionally putting small inquiry projects in conversation with each other. Specifically, methodologizing lore in this way highlights the value of simultaneity and partnerships. This work suggests that, especially for writing center administrators at smaller institutions, assessment initiatives are increasingly feasible and productive when they merge an administrator's every day and scholarly labor and when they build upon partnerships with other offices, departments, staff members, and students.

It started with informal meet-ups. The four of us—all non-tenure-track writing center administrators (WCAs) at small liberal arts colleges (SLACs)–and Roger Powell, our assigned IWCA Mentor Match Program[1] mentor, gathered regularly via Zoom. Through the tumultuous

---

1. For an overview and analysis of IWCA's Mentor Match Program, see McBride and Rentscher (2020).

months of 2020 and 2021, we swapped resources, discussed articles, and talked about what was and wasn't working. These meet-ups helped us investigate and build upon our individual centers' lore and assess our centers' alignment with the mission of helping students grow as writers and thinkers.

One of the topics we returned to through these lore-building conversations was inspired by recent scholarly interest in who doesn't visit the writing center (Salem 2016; Cheatle 2017; Giaimo 2017). We realized we had each been considering non-visitors through our assessment efforts. Even though our individual reflections and speculations were more engagement with lore than with empirical study, we found our merged conversations useful—both for what they suggest about inquiry of non-writing center visitors and for how our resulting conversations functioned as a form of scholarly engagement that connected our disciplinary and everyday labor. As NTT administrators laboring through the pandemic, we were not in positions to conduct large-scale quantitative assessment projects or RAD research on non-visitors like that completed by Salem, Cheatle, or Giaimo. However, we agreed that our informal conversations about what was and wasn't working were valuable and could be productively extended beyond our small circle. Rather than be deterred by our inability to engage in RAD research at this time, we explored ways to contribute to the conversation about non-visitors by leveraging the unique advantages of working at SLACs.

In what follows, we use our engagements with the issue of "non-visitors" as a case study to suggest a way of "methodologizing lore"—applying intentional inquiry to the practices of lore building as a scholarly assessment practice useful for the SLAC context. Such a methodology begins with discussing what is and isn't working. Then, we use those conversations to reflect on our individual experiences and clarify what has happened, before returning to that discursive space to continue sharing our thoughts. Conclusions emerge through the layered conversations—the accumulation of lore intentionally juxtaposed against others' experiences. This collaboration expands on Gillespie's (2001) work—a deliberate lamination of others' conversations about writing center strategies on top of each other to locate meaning from the accumulated experiences as part of a contextualized assessment practice. One person's anecdote might not provide enough evidence to understand an issue, but four WCAs' varied and stratified assessment experiences can reveal possibilities.

We begin this chapter by positioning methodologized lore in relation to the existing conversation about lore, assessment, and labor. Then each author details our stories—our local, focused, situationally specific engagement with the question of who doesn't visit our centers. In doing so, we showcase how small-scale assessments, blended with everyday labor and merged in conversation, can reveal useful insights. Holly considers usage patterns, student populations, and perceptions about writing centers at SLACs compared to other institutions. Kim relates the difficulty she had in getting non-writing center visitors to respond to surveys about why they weren't visiting. Matthew shares experiences supporting and learning from an undergraduate researcher assessing who doesn't visit the writing center. Sarah draws from conversations she's had with academic advisors to consider how outreach approaches from other student services could inform WCAs. Our conclusion considers what is gained when we bring these experiences—this lore—together: how the throughlines and tensions between them point to future strategies and methods for outreach, assessment, or research for WCAs who, like us, have big questions they want to explore and are interested in using what time and resources they can to extend the key conversations in our field while attending to the responsibilities and realities of their institutional contexts.

Methodologizing Lore

Lore has had a contested place within the annals of writing center practice. North (1987, 24) defined "lore" as being "concerned with what has worked, is working, or might work in teaching, doing or learning writing." Horner (2000, 378) has said lore is "that knowledge practitioners produce and draw upon in responding to the daily exigencies of their teaching." Yet many have critiqued the lack of systemization in the use of lore for guiding local and disciplinary knowledge. Babcock (2015, 39) has linked lore with anecdote and asserted that both "are based on remembering events with no documentation or guiding questions up front." This characterization would seem antithetical to the formal, evaluative work of assessment. Additionally, writing center scholarship has purposely moved away from a reliance on lore as disciplinary knowledge, instead placing value on RAD research—inquiry that follows Haswell's standards of being replicable, aggregable, and data-supported.

Despite the increased attention RAD research has received, Driscoll and Perdue (2014) acknowledge that WCAs face an array of challenges as they engage with RAD methodologies. One of which is "the uniqueness of each writing center and context, the uniqueness of each individual student served, and the lack of generalizability of said contexts" (Driscoll and

Perdue 2014, 118). The importance of employing research methodologies that acknowledge uniquenesses across contexts has prompted scholars to develop alternatives to RAD research—for example counterstories (Faison and Condon 2022) and qual-RAD method(ologies) (Martini 2022). Faison and Condon's (2022) counterstories draw from critical race theory to situate individuals' experiences with racism. This focus on race positions counterstories as a methodology that is doing a different kind of work than what we propose in this chapter; however, we see alignment between what we call "methodologizing lore" and Faison and Condon's championing of scholarship that "embraces narrative not as distinct from theorization but integral to the knowledge-making endeavor" (2022, 9). We see even more direct parallels between methodologized lore and the "method(ology)" that Martini utilizes. Her research acknowledges "the value of rich, site-specific research, participant voices, and the subjectivity-bound perspectives that individuals offer, leading them to tell stories that are simultaneously representing and misrepresenting the realities of a situation" (Martin 2022, 18). As Martini develops her ideas about her writing center's strategic partnerships, she draws inspiration from Lockett's (2018, 33) admission that "the language of RAD tends to strip the human experience of its nuance and may risk diminishing the various ways we might interpret experience as data."

As NTT administrators, we see our engagement in these kinds of experience-specific, alternative research methodologies as ways for us to participate in scholarly inquiry even though this work extends beyond our official job responsibilities and is uncompensated. Ours is not a unique position. Geller and Denny's (2013) study of writing center professionals found that interview participants in staff or administrative positions did not feel like they had the time to engage in scholarship as much as they wanted to. As Hall (2017, 9) acknowledges, "[e]ven among writing center practitioners who do value making scholarly contributions to the field, exigency, time, and resources to carry out research are often lacking, confounding the growth and development of knowledge making in writing center studies." An additional layer of complexity comes from the IRB process. One of us, like a participant from Geller and Denny's (2014) study, struggled to receive IRB approval as a staff member because their institution's IRB review process is restricted to faculty researchers. Others had not sought IRB approval since the work was part of internal assessment or student research, which limited their ability to share data more broadly.[2]

Our contexts at SLACs also inform how we engage with scholarly inquiry. This environment offers certain advantages, such as creativity and flexibility, yet it also brings challenges (Stay 2010, 147). The small size and close community typical of institutions like ours offer advantages in easily developing relationships and making connections across campus. That same structure can also lead to difficulty in having enough time and resources for the many responsibilities encompassed in WCA positions. Towle (2019, 43) notes that "if we want to have conversations about labor or pedagogy or assessment, we have to include institutionality . . . as one of the pillars of context for understanding larger shifts in writing center and program work." This also applies to research, scholarship, and assessment, particularly as NTT administrators like us work at the intersection of what Casswell, Grutsch McKinney, and Jackson (2016) call "disciplinary" and "everyday labor." Assessment is an obvious avenue for this intersection; Thompson (2006, 36) highlights the interconnection between assessment and research, suggesting it is often difficult to distinguish research from assessment. Yet, for WCAs at SLACs, whose assessment might be on a smaller scale, the opportunity to share our assessment as research beyond our institutions might be limited. While institutional constraints have resulted in limited scholarship that models assessment research at SLACs, those without the imperative or support to engage in empirical research nevertheless have options for using, sharing, and merging our assessments to benefit the writing center community. What follows are stories of our individual assessment efforts juxtaposed to help administrators consider approaches to assessment, in this case, focused on the exploration of who does not visit the writing center and why.

Who We are According to Those We Don't See: Holly's Story

This year Cedarville University (CU), a SLAC in west central Ohio, welcomed a record-high 1,200 freshmen. For the last few years, Cedarville's

---

2. Institutional review boards can vary widely, both in how they interpret federal policy related to ethical research (Anderson 1996) and internal processes that govern how often proposals are reviewed or the timeframe researchers can expect approval or feedback. We highlight this because it connects to assessment-as-research challenges that WCAs at SLACs may face.

enrollment numbers have been record- breaking; as such, our writing center (CUWC) has seen increased numbers of visitors. Despite our usage increasing, non-users are still an important part of our considerations. As working in a SLAC is a relatively new context for me, a significant part of my ability to identify and serve non-users requires understanding my center's institutional context.

Over the years, I have worked with many diverse populations of student writers—including writers at a state university, at a private Catholic college, and in an inner-city community college. At all these institutions, some students struggled with foundational elements of writing, including syntax and sentence boundaries. Many of these writers were ill-prepared for college. Even so, they often spoke of how getting a college education was their one great dream.

Cedarville University is a private Christian, liberal arts university located in the rural town of Cedarville, Ohio. Many of our students were either homeschooled or attended private Christian schools, and their parents have frequently been involved in life-long ministry, either as pastors or missionaries. Cedarville students can choose from a number of STEM majors (ranging from various branches of healthcare to engineering and accelerated MBA programs) or liberal arts majors (such as theater, history, and literature). With a long history of being a competitive school, the university had a 62 percent acceptance rate in 2022. Thus, the student body at CU has presented me with a different dynamic. There are still struggling writers at CU, particularly given how COVID disrupted many undergrads' junior and senior years of high school; however, that percentage is much smaller than I experienced previously, and they are rarely as ill-prepared for college writing as my other students were.

Part of this is due to the positionality of CU's struggling writers versus my previous students—many CU students were homeschooled or attended private schools, come from financially-solvent families, and are second or third-generation college students. As a result, many CU students consider a college degree a minimum qualification for a good life rather than a dream. However, as the number of writers has increased at CU, so has the number of struggling writers. Many of these students feel the need to apologize for not being prepared for college writing. Imposter syndrome is a real issue for these students, and many fear they are not "Cedarville material."

Before COVID, many of CU's struggling writers did not make repeat visits beyond what their composition professors required. Now, we are seeing more repeat visits but still not enough given the current context, as I know from experience how valid Denny, Nordlof, and Salem's (2018, 81–82) argument is that writing centers are especially helpful in supporting students who struggle with imposter syndrome. However, many of CU's struggling writers still ask a roommate or family member to proofread their work rather than come to us. One reason for this is the historical reputation the CUWC had as a bastion for "the best writers." In contrast, weaker writers felt uncomfortable coming to us for help with lower-order concerns, perhaps due to overemphasis of the "we don't proofread" mantra, which never explicitly defined what was meant by "proofreading." Thus, students whose goals were to perform better on assignments rather than flex their writerly muscles felt out of place. If we are honest, most student writers want a better grade and have little desire to romanticize writing. This is not to say that writing was unimportant to them, but it meant that we needed to meet these students realistically, not in the absence of their priorities. Otherwise, once they completed composition, many of these students never returned to the center unless it was required.

Instead of writers voluntarily using our center, we have seen the following trends: 60-70 percent of our appointments consistently come from dual-credit-earning high school composition students, traditional composition students, and English majors. Of course, these are the classes where a lot of writing is assigned, but professors for these classes also typically require students to attend at least two to three writing center appointments during the semester, hoping that the students will realize its benefits and return on their own. Unfortunately, our usage records through the 2021-2022 school year did not indicate the fulfillment of that expectation. Instead, the vast majority of our appointments continued to come from English-related courses, which means that most of our non-users are those not taking English courses.

Another issue was the common belief that the CUWC was only helpful for those writing English papers. This perception has revealed itself in many contexts, including the usage data for yearly assessment reports, but it has primarily been manifested in the research compiled by various tutors in training. Every spring, I teach English 3550: Writing Center Theory and Training to the incoming tutors who will begin work the following fall. Each time I have taught this class, students have written their final papers about the campus's perceptions of the CUWC. Those papers have frequently raised the question of the CUWC's relevance to non-English majors.

One criticism has re-emerged through these projects: that the CUWC is primarily helpful with English papers because writers believe most of our tutors are English majors. While English majors apply to be tutors at higher rates, English majors make up only 30 percent of our staff. The other 70 percent comes from fields such as professional writing, health sciences, the arts, and the humanities. Our center has been making concerted efforts to attract tutors from a variety of majors for a few years.

However, this is not a concern I have commonly found at other writing centers. It caused me to question if the difference is related to the CUWC's situation within a SLAC. Of the writing centers I have previously worked with, the CUWC is the most closely linked to an English department. Perhaps this relationship leads to what Waldo (1990, 73) observed when he said that writing centers are often seen as subservient to English departments. However, this does not explain why this connection is a problem. Instead, I suspect that the belief that English departments have what Fitzgerald and Ianetta (2016) describe as romantic views of writing, meaning that their texts are more internally focused and expressive, could be to blame. This leads some students to believe that tutors from English majors will direct them to take a romantic slant with their papers. This view of writing within the field of English was also noted by Bumstead's (2018) recognition that few English majors visited his center, but students from other majors made regular use of tutoring. He argued that the English department's romantic notion of writing made English majors less likely to use the center because they thought writing was a self-expressive, individual pursuit. In my situation, the belief that the CUWC's close association with the English department prioritizes a romantic notion of writing may be resulting in a fair amount of our non-use. For our writing center to seem relevant to struggling writers, who are primarily not English majors, we need to further emphasize the diversity among our tutors, our recruitment across the majors, and our training in writing across the disciplines.

Even with increased usage, our non-users are important to us, and as our numbers of non-users diminish, we must renew our awareness of our changing context. To not do so may render us ineffective to those who currently depend on us and irrelevant to those who are newly discovering us. As we continue to answer Salem's call to consider our non-users, we must continually reassess ourselves with the goal of strategically serving students.

The Challenge of Hearing from "Non-Visitors": Kim's Story

I direct the writing center at York College of Pennsylvania (YCP), a private college with approximately 4,000 students with a focus on professional programs including business, nursing, and engineering in addition to traditional liberal arts majors. With an acceptance rate of 78 percent, YCP tends to attract students from the mid-Atlantic region who might otherwise go to local state colleges but are looking for a smaller college experience.

Like Holly, I've noticed patterns related to who does and does not use the writing center, but I had less of a sense of what was behind these patterns. Thus, I sought to discover *why* some students do not use the writing center. This has been on my mind for several years, especially regarding warning grade outreach. Warning grades (WGs) are the mechanism my institution uses to communicate with students who at the halfway mark of the semester do not have a passing grade in a course. In the last few years, I, along with colleagues from our academic support center, have been charged with outreach and intervention based on warning grades. I was tasked with reaching out to all students who receive WGs in our general education writing program courses and sharing information about how the writing center can support their success. I also compared the list of students who receive WGs with their usage of writing center services. Table 1 shows the total number of students who received WGs in writing program courses over three semesters and shows that more students do *not* take up the invitation to use the writing center to support their success than those who do. Additionally, many students who received a WG and opted not to use the writing center earned a final grade in the course below a 2.0—the required minimum grade to pass the course.

Table 1. Warning Grade Writing Center Usage and Course Success

	WGs in writing program courses	# with WC appts.	# with no WC appts.	% students used WC after outreach	# with no WC appts., grade < 2.0	% students with WGs, no WC appts., grade < 2.0
Fall 2019	29	8	21	27	8	28
Spring 2020	33	5	28	15	8	24
Fall 2021	20	2	18	10	12	60

I wanted to know more about why students might not use the writing center, particularly ones who had received specific encouragement to meet with a tutor to address challenges they were facing in a writing course. To understand what may make these students not seek writing center help, I sent an electronic survey to the sixty-seven individuals who had received outreach but had chosen not to visit our center. This was an internal assessment survey, and one for which I did not apply for IRB approval, so I will not share the specific results. Instead I am focusing on completion of the survey in general. Despite offering a $10 gift card to complete the survey and sending reminders, I only received six responses. The challenge of hearing from "non-visitors" suggests that traditional ways of gathering data, such as surveys, might not be effective with this cohort.

Salem (2016, 161) claims, "some students arrive at the university primed by a complicated interaction between academic standing and identity to seek tutoring help." Yet the reverse also seems to be true—some students are primed by a complex ecology to be less likely to seek help. In her thesis exploring why developmental writing students did not visit the writing center at John Carroll University (another SLAC), Tomusko (2018) suggests that unlike students who may not visit the writing center because they are already confident in their writing skills, developmental writers avoid the writing center because of academic anxiety and fixed mindset. According to Tomusko, these students "saw their writing as something that would never improve no matter how much work and effort they put into it" (1). I wondered if the population I was interested in, those whose instructors identified as struggling in writing-intensive courses, might avoid the writing center for similar reasons.

I had decided to send students surveys because it's cheap, quick, and accessible (Grutsch McKinney 2015, 72). Surveys seemed like a straightforward methodological approach to get answers to my question of why these students who received warning grades and were invited to use the writing center did not. Previous research of non-visitors' perceptions of the writing center has used surveys successfully to reach both visitors and non-visitors (Colton 2020). Yet Grutsch McKinney (2015, 82) warns, "Whether you are randomly selecting or hand-picking people from your population to respond to your survey, you will have to put some effort into encouraging response. Some researchers plead, some describe the benefits to participants, and some offer prizes or money." The low response rate to my survey shows just how difficult it can be to encourage response, even with modest monetary inducement.

One issue that perhaps challenged my attempts to use surveys to ascertain these student perspectives could be related to survey fatigue (Adams and Umbach 2012, 579). College students are bombarded with emails and survey requests from their institutions, the stores they visit, the services they use, etc. Students are less interested in answering one more survey if they do not perceive its relevance (Porter, Whitcomb, and Weitzer 2004). This seems like common sense but becomes important when considering the issue of non-visitors in writing centers. Students who do not visit a writing center may not think it is relevant or useful for them to respond, thus a survey about writing centers will not seem salient either.

Additionally, as I researched survey response in general, I realized that factors that influence students' use, or lack of use, of academic resources like the writing center might similarly impact their likelihood to participate in surveys soliciting their perspectives on these services. Research on student evaluation surveys in higher education have considered the issue of student nonresponse. Summarizing past research on why student response rates to course evaluation surveys differed across institutions, Adams and Umbach (2012, 579) note that response was more likely from students with high performance and achievement (as measured by grade, cumulative GPA, and SAT score) and "that students with lower SAT scores, male students, and students of color were less likely to respond." Additionally, they found that "[g]rades were also influential factors of participation [in student evaluations]. Even with interactions, low grades (Ds and Fs) correlated with . . . nonresponse when compared with grades of A, B, C, and [satisfactory] at a statistically significant level" (583). Essentially, research has shown that students with academic risk factors or lower academic achievement are less likely to complete academic surveys. Thus, specific kinds of research might have a response bias and therefore challenge representation and inclusivity.

Ultimately, this is a narrative of research failure. In my attempts to connect my everyday and disciplinary labor using the common method of surveys to answer a question about why a cohort of students did not use the writing center, I stumbled upon the truth that this method is likely not well suited to understanding non-visitors, at least not in my institutional context. Whether it is due to survey fatigue, perceived salience, or trends relating to academic achievement and survey response, several factors work against researchers using surveys to target non-visitors, especially those currently experiencing academic difficulties.

INVITING THE STUDENTS TO DO ALL THE WORK: MATTHEW'S STORY

I am the writing center director at Le Moyne College—a regional Jesuit institution in central New York that enrolls about 3,000 undergraduate and graduate students. As a way to help my center's tutors best serve these students, I've developed our tutor training course around the practices of original research. Last year when one student—Kanaan—focused his inquiry on who does and doesn't visit the writing center, I was given a chance to support a project that aligned with my personal interests. As such, Kanaan's project re-envisioned our classroom into a research lab—a space where a student's learning expanded my own questions—and allowed me to engage simultaneously in disciplinary and everyday labor while opening new perspectives into the question of what motivates writing center visits.

Kanaan's interest in this topic sprang from his (in)experience with the writing center. He explained he'd never visited the writing center because, "I'm already really comfortable with writing and editing my own work. So that made me wonder, is that one of the primary factors that keep people from coming in?" To explore if others' writing confidence similarly kept them away from our center, Kanaan developed a survey that he distributed to Le Moyne students who had and hadn't visited the writing center. Kanaan invited one hundred students to respond—eighty randomly selected writers who had visited the writing center in the past two semesters and twenty Le Moyne students Kanaan connected with via Snapchat who hadn't visited the writing center. He gathered sixteen responses from writing center users and thirteen from non-users. Survey participants identified their gender and major and answered questions about their confidence and anxiety related to academic writing, sharing their writing, and how many times they visited the center. Students who visited more than twice, only once, and never were guided to different questions about their experiences with and/or perceptions of the center.

In analyzing the data, Kanaan was struck by the limited connection between writing confidence, anxiety, and writing center visits. He gauged confidence by asking, "On a scale of 1-10, how confident are you in your academic writing?" The average score for all the participants (6.9) struck him as high.[3] But Kanaan was surprised that the thirteen individuals who hadn't visited the writing center generated a lower confidence average (6.3) than the sixteen who had (7.5). These writers' confidence—while high across the board—was higher for writing center frequenters. Kanaan's hypothesis that people don't visit the writing center because they feel more confident about their writing was disrupted by this sample.

---

3. My reporting on the details of Kanaan's survey was the result of generalized information he provided and direct conversations we had. I received IRB approval to communicate with Kanaan about his study and his findings with the expectation that we would not explore details of individual responses.

However, as Pajares and Johnson (1994, 323) establish, writing confidence is multifaceted. A writer can become more confident in their ability to accomplish specific writing tasks without gaining confidence in their overall writing ability. Similarly, Kanaan wondered if a writer could be confident in their writing while also being hesitant about sharing that writing with others. As he explained, "I'm pretty confident in my writing. But regardless, I still don't really want to put it out there all the time." This had inspired Kanaan to ask participants: "Do you experience any anxiety when it comes to sharing your academic writing with others?" Two of the sixteen (13 percent) writing center visitors and four of the thirteen (31 percent) non-writing center visitors answered "yes." It's possible that this kind of anxiety keeps students away from the writing center. As a tutor says in Rafoth's (2010, 152) "Why Visit Your Campus Writing Center?", "The ability to share something as personal as a piece of writing can be a daunting task for some students." But the possibility that students generally don't visit the writing center as a result of this anxiety is complicated by Kanaan's findings that five of the thirteen (38 percent) non-writing center visitors he surveyed said they experience no anxiety when sharing their academic writing. Again, Kanaan's survey results conflicted with his expectations.

Kanaan's final question asked non-visiting respondents, "Are there any reasons why you haven't visited the writing center?" Five respondents provided no reason. Five others said they had never thought they needed to. However, eleven of the thirteen were amenable to making a future appointment. They seemed okay with the idea of the writing center; they just didn't believe it provided them with anything they needed. They have not adopted the compositional truism that all writers benefit from talking to other, smart writers about their writing. This echoes Leahy's (1990, 44) assertion that writing centers "want to work with all writers," but that doesn't mean all writers want to work with writing tutors. This also reaffirms Salem's (2016, 162) questions about students' perceptions of writing centers. How many students don't visit our centers because they don't believe they have anything to gain from our services? When do writers feel they "need" to talk with a tutor? What does this suggest about students' perceptions of writing and the purpose of writing centers?

When I asked Kanaan what he took away from his research, he mentioned how positively the students who had visited the writing center viewed the center. He explained, "[Doing the survey] increased my view of how valuable the writing center is, because I remember reading through some of the reviews and hearing how students genuinely felt as though their writing would probably take a significant toll without visiting the writing center." Before becoming a tutor, Kanaan hadn't thought much about our center. The other non-writing center users he surveyed may not have had his combination of confidence and reticence to share their writing, but most of them agreed that the writing center simply wasn't something they needed. After conducting this research and encountering the responses from writing center users, Kanaan's opinion shifted. As a tutor-in-training engaged in this research project, he saw that "[p]eople who experienced the writing center believe it works."

For me, this experience has underscored the value of inviting undergraduate tutors to engage directly in this scholarly question. Kanaan's work suggests that tutors can serve as direct conduits to the experiences of students who aren't visiting our writing centers. Whether it's through their position as students, their external perspectives on composition, their varied personal networks, or their insider knowledge of what's happening across campus, undergraduate tutors can provide additional insight and questions regarding their peers' writing center usage.

Of course, the value of welcoming undergraduates to explore real issues through original research projects transcends the insight they can provide on this particular issue. When we facilitate tutors' participation in research by making our centers places where tutors "perform experiments, test hypotheses, and contribute to the pool of knowledge in our discipline," we merge the everyday labor of training and professionalizing tutors with the disciplinary labor of critically exploring the questions informing our field (DelliCarpini and Crimmins 2010, 206). This becomes a productive way for NTT WCAs to engage with the issues of our discipline while managing our workloads. We can become something like facilitators of research labs—advisors learning with and from tutors while we guide their development as writing center professionals.

Collaborating Across Campus: Sarah's Story

When our group began exploring who doesn't visit writing centers, I was a WCA at Madonna University in Michigan. This private, Catholic university serves approximately 3,000 students studying in varied undergraduate majors as well as in graduate programs for nursing, education, and business. Many of the students commute to campus and balance their classes with part- or full-time jobs.

Having previously worked in academic advising, I recognized an opportunity to explore our research question through my everyday labor since

I had maintained my relationship with the advising department and was actively collaborating with them to promote our center. Three former colleagues agreed to share their perspectives: Nicole, a former director of advising; Laura, an advisor with experience in SLAC and community college settings; and Shannon, an advisor who has held advising roles in SLAC and R1 institutions.[4] As we talked, themes arose related to how the challenge of student engagement cuts across departments and how interdepartmental collaborations could flourish; those are outlined in the Table 2 series.

Table 2 Series. Academic Advisor Suggestions
(1 = Shannon, 2 = Laura, 3 = Nicole)

Help Each Other Understand Non-Visitors: Advisors' Insights into Why Students Might Not Engage
Negative stigma connected to wrap-around services in high school (1)
Misunderstanding of services available (1,2)
Lack of time to use services (1,2)
Feeling intimidated about asking for help (1,2)

Collaborate and Share Perspectives When Analyzing Student Data
Examine entry- and upper-level courses with large enrollments to determine how many of those students utilize the WC (3)
Ask advisors which classes students are more likely to struggle in and explore if those students use the WC (2)
Ask for advisors' perspectives on WC data, since they assess student data through a retention and persistence lens (3)

Gather and Share Anecdotal Evidence
Share trends in students' comments about the WC during advising appointments (1,2,3)
Share trends in how students react to warning grade and registration reach-outs that include discussions about the WC (1,2,3)
Train new advising team members on how to glean information from students (3)
Realize advisors might not have time for an in-depth student conversations about the WC and/or students may feel uncomfortable sharing why they don't visit (1,2,3)

---

4. My university's IRB considered that these conversations did not meet the definition of Human Participant Research subject to IRB oversight.

Decide on specific writing center-focused questions for advisors to ask, then share responses with the WC (3)
Build Strong Relationships between Advisors and WCAs
Engage in collaborative brainstorming sessions (3)
Advertise each other's events (1)
Co-host events when possible (1)
Annually invite each other to staff meetings (2,3)
Send emails from the WC at the beginning of each semester to remind advisors of WC services, hours, and upcoming events (2,3)
Track which new ideas were tried, what worked, and what didn't (3)
Help Advisors Make Effective Referrals
Share trends in how students respond to WC referrals (1,2,3)
Educate advisors on the writing center's philosophy and approach (1,2,3)
Educate advisors on how students make appointments (1,2,3)
Maintain an informative writing center website that advisors and faculty can use when making referrals (2,3)
Prepare for Collaboration Barriers
Encourage inter-departmental appreciation (2,3)
Understand that lack of time and/or resources might be a challenge (2,3)
Ensure both departments have champions who understand the value of collaborating and are excited about making it happen (2,3)

The more writing centers and advising departments collaborate and experiment, the more they can strengthen their relationship and better understand who the non-visitors are and what interventions succeed in reaching them. These collaborations could go beyond data collection into outreach and partnerships, with advisors actively promoting the writing center to students disinclined to visit. This would require that advisors receive in-depth information about the writing center so that they can customize their student referrals. Laura elaborated, "[I]f I can speak more confidently, clearly, about that, it's all going to help my interaction with the student and help encourage them to go to the writing center—and when they get there hopefully have a more effective appointment."

For this to happen, building a good relationship between the two departments is foundational. There needs to be mutual understanding and appreciation, along with the belief that collaboration would be mutually beneficial. That is an advantage SLACs have because departments can get to know each other more easily than at larger institutions, making it simpler to collaborate and holistically and proactively address student needs. Yet it is also important to recognize what barriers might exist. Nicole addressed the reality that "at a small school, everyone is strapped for resources, everyone is doing five different jobs. . . . " In those situations, no matter how excited both groups might be about a collaboration, it is unlikely they will have the attention and resources to make it happen. Keeping these potential barriers in mind could help WCAs and advisors who are eager to collaborate to strategize how they can succeed within the constraints of their other responsibilities.

Relationship-building might be a key component of figuring out the question of writing center non-visitors in the context of SLACs and specifically relationships between advising departments and writing centers. Shannon summed it up well when she explained, "[advisors] are not necessarily the ones that fix the problem; we're the ones that are referring and connecting students to those resources. So having a relationship with your writing center . . . is so key." As Martini (2022, 7) suggests, writing centers can build relationships across departments, and that is a savvy approach in SLAC environments where it is beneficial to maximize resources. Collaborating with advisors could provide writing centers with another way of learning about and reaching non-visitors.

What We Learn by Layering Conversations

Our narratives provide snapshots of independent assessment initiatives that explore who does and does not use the writing center, why, and what strategies can encourage usage. The snapshots' limited, informal nature means they function as simple reflections on what worked and didn't work—as lore. The level of each of the assessment projects discussed was appropriate for institutional assessment and might provide helpful insight based on our contexts; however, each project is not systematic or large enough in scale to create wider disciplinary knowledge. Yet, taken together, these studies provide insight into assessment itself. They indicate ways that WCAs at SLACs might approach their individual centers' assessment questions and the questions more broadly asked within the field.

This work is undoubtedly familiar to any WCA who has read list-serv threads, chatted with presenters after a conference panel, or talked shop with other WCAs over lunch. We're advocating for an embrace of these conversations as productive ways to guide our assessment practices. Learning what has and hasn't worked at other centers, particularly those in similar institutional contexts, reflecting on what these layered experiences suggest, and intentionally applying these conversations to our WCA work affords us opportunities to connect our everyday and scholarly labor, strengthen partnerships across our institutions, and—in this case—understand how we might continue identifying what may and may not motivate students to visit our centers. Additionally, when considered collectively, these narratives point to a few conclusions about assessment work generally, namely, the importance of embracing simultaneity in our assessment practices and utilizing partnerships, including with students, to help us connect with writers and advance our disciplinary knowledge. Martini (2022) notes that writing centers are uniquely positioned to engage in partnerships across campus that will benefit everyone involved, and we observed how those opportunities can intersect with assessment work.

Regarding simultaneity, these narratives and the approach we took of putting our initiatives into conversation with each other highlight the value of making assessments part of both our everyday and disciplinary labor. As Schendel (2012, 115) claims, assessment must be multipurposed since "[t]here simply isn't time for a writing center director . . . to fit a completely new and ongoing activity into the daily work of the center. For that reason, assessment can only really work for writing centers when it's integrated into the other work of the center." For example, assessment findings can exist to both report to other administrative stakeholders and to inform a director's own priorities. But this value of simultaneity transcends just developing projects and reports for multiple audiences. Holly asked who isn't visiting the writing center while considering students' perceptions, merging her exploration of usage patterns and perceptions of the writing center with her analysis of appointment data and teaching of the tutor training course. Matthew simultaneously trained a tutor in research methodologies while leveraging that tutor's connections to learn about people who weren't visiting the center. Along the way, the tutor learned to more deeply appreciate what the writing center does.

These simultaneous efforts are driven in part through the partnerships we have developed with others on our campuses—partnerships that have aided our efforts to explore disciplinary questions and emerged as a central element of these assessment initiatives. Holly, Matthew, and Sarah had success starting to understand who does and doesn't use the writing center and why through working with partners (students and academic advisors) who shared the workload, provided new insight, and pointed the investigation in unexpected but productive directions. As Lerner (2003, 73) notes, "Collaborating with colleagues across our institutions can serve the dual purpose of capitalizing on local expertise and sending the message that the writing center is serious about assessment." Such partnerships can have benefits for writing centers, other stakeholders, and students.

When thinking about non-visitors, we are trying to figure out not just who they are but why they are not pursuing a relationship with the writing center and how we can address that. Perhaps part of the answer lies in building relationships, with colleagues in other departments, peer tutors, students, and beyond— layering our conversations and methodologizing our lore. Opportunities exist "to start thinking more strategically and creatively about how we can work *with* departments across campus" (Martini 2022, 7). Methodologizing lore allows us to examine multiple narratives and include the conversation itself as part of the assessment. This gives us the opportunity to push against the inherently anecdotal and unstructured aspects of lore while still being able to engage with scholarly questions without relying on the resources or capacity necessary for undertaking large-scale RAD research.

These layered conversations do not provide us with generalizable insight into who isn't visiting writing centers, nor are the experiences of one director completely transferable to another's context. SLAC WCAs advancing their assessment practices by prioritizing simultaneity and partnerships does not reveal what is keeping writers away from their centers. Rather, methodologizing lore presents opportunities to learn about assessment practices, methods, successes, and failures through an intentional amassment of experiences. Our individual assessment efforts may not function as disciplinary knowledge on their own, but, when insight is the goal, small can be especially useful when small assessments are amassed.

Bibliography

Adams, Meredith J. D., and Paul D. Umbach. 2012. "Nonresponse and Online Student Evaluations of Teaching: Understanding the Influence of Salience, Fatigue, and Academic Environments." *Research in Higher Education* 53, no. 5: 576–91.

Anderson, Paul V. 1996. "Ethics, Institutional Review Boards, and the Involvement of Human Participants in Composition Research." In *Ethics and Representation in Qualitative Studies of Literacy*, edited by Peter Mortensen and Gesa E. Kirsch, 260–85. Urbana: National Council of Teachers of English.

Babcock, Rebecca Day. 2015. "Disabilities in the Writing Center." *Praxis: A Writing Center Journal* 13, no. 1: 39–50. http://www.praxisuwc.com/babcock-131.

Bumstead, Andrew. 2018. "English Major Representation in the College Writing Center." *Peer Review* 2, no. 2 (Fall). https://thepeerreview-iwca.org/issues/issue-2/english-major-representation-in-the-college-writing-center/.

Caswell, Nicole, Jackie Grutsch McKinney, and Rebecca Jackson. 2016. *The Working Lives of New Writing Center Directors*. Logan: Utah State University Press.

Cheatle, Joseph. 2017. "Challenging Perceptions: Exploring the Relationship Between ELL Students and Writing Centers." *Praxis: A Writing Center Journal* 14, no. 3. http://www.praxisuwc.com/joseph-cheatle-143.

Colton, Aaron. 2020. "Who (according to Students) Uses the Writing Center?: Acknowledging Impressions and Misimpressions of Writing Center Services and User Demographics." *Praxis: A Writing Center Journal* 17, no. 3. http://www.praxisuwc.com/173-colton.

DelliCarpini, Dominic, and Cynthia Crimmins. 2010. "The Writing Center as a Space for Undergraduate Research." In *Undergraduate Research in English Studies*, edited by Laurie Grobman and Joyce Kinkead, 191–211. Urbana: National Council of Teachers of English.

Denny, Harry, John Nordloff, and Lori Salem. 2018. "'Tell Me Exactly What It Was That I Was Doing So Bad': Understanding the Needs and Expectations of Working-Class Students in Writing Centers." *Writing Center Journal* 37, no. 1: 67–100.

Driscoll, Dana Lynn, and Sherry Wynn Perdue. 2014. "RAD Research as a Framework for Writing Center Inquiry: Survey and Interview Data on Writing Center Administrators' Beliefs about Research and Research Practices." *Writing Center Journal* 34, no. 1: 105–33.

Faison, Wonderful, and Frankie Condon, eds. 2022. *CounterStories from the Writing Center*. Logan: Utah State University Press; Louisville: University Press of Colorado.

Fitzgerald, Lauren, and Melissa Ianetta. 2016. *The Oxford Guide for Writing Tutors: Practice and Research*. New York: Oxford University Press.

Geller, Anne Ellen, and Harry Denny. 2013. "Of Ladybugs, Low Status, and Loving the Job: Writing Center Professionals Navigating Their Careers." *Writing Center Journal* 33, no. 1: 96–129.

Giaimo, Genie. 2017. "Focusing on the Blind Spots: RAD-Based Assessment of Students' Perceptions of Community College Writing Centers." *Praxis: A Writing Center Journal* 15, no. 1. http://www.praxisuwc.com/giaimo-151.

Gillespie, Paula. 2001. "Beyond the House of Lore: WCenter as Research Site." In *Writing Center Research: Extending the Conversation*, edited by Paula Gillespie, Alice Gillam, Lady Falls Brown, and Byron Stay, 39–51. New York: Routledge.

Grutsch McKinney, Jackie. 2015. *Strategies for Writing Center Research*. Anderson: Parlor Press.

Hall, R. Mark. 2017. *Around the Text of Writing Center Work: An Inquiry-Based Approach to Tutor Education*. Logan: Utah State University Press.

Haswell, Richard H. 2005. "NCTE/CCCC's Recent War on Scholarship." *Written Communication* 22, no. 2: 198–223.

Horner, Bruce. 2000. "Traditions and Professionalization: Reconceiving Work in Composition." *College Composition and Communication* 51, no. 3: 366–98.

Leahy, Richard. 1990. "What the College Writing Center Is—and Isn't." *College Teaching* 38, no. 2: 43–48.

Lerner, Neal. 2003. "Writing Center Assessment." In *The Center Will Hold: Critical Perspectives on Writing Center Scholarship*, edited by Michael A. Pemberton and Joyce Kinkead, 58–73. Logan: Utah State University Press.

Lockett, Alexandria. 2018. "A Touching Place: Womanist Approaches to the Center." In *Out in the Center: Public Controversies and Private Struggles*, edited by Harry Denny, Robert Mundy, Liliana M. Naydan, Richard Sévère, and Anna Sicari, 28–42. Louisville: University Press of Colorado.

Martini, Rebecca Hallman. 2022. *Disrupting the Center: A Partnership Approach to Writing across the University*. Louisville: University Press of Colorado.

McBride, Maureen, and Molly Rentscher. 2020. "The Importance of Intention: A Review of Mentoring for Writing Center Professionals." *Praxis: A Writing Center Journal* 17, no. 3: 74–85. http://www.praxisuwc.com/173-mcbride-and-rant.

North, Stephen M. 1987. *The Making of Knowledge in Composition: Portrait of an Emerging Field*. Portsmouth: Boynton/Cook.

Pajares, Frank, and Margaret J. Johnson. 1994. "Confidence and Competence in Writing: The Role of Self-Efficacy, Outcome Expectancy, and Apprehension." *Research in the Teaching of English* 28, no. 3: 313–31.

Porter, Stephen R., Michael E. Whitcomb, and William H. Weitzer. 2004. "Multiple Surveys of Students and Survey Fatigue." *New Directions for Institutional Research* 121: 63–73.

Rafoth, Ben. 2010. "Why Visit Your Campus Writing Center?" In *Writing Spaces: Reading on Writing 1*, edited by Charles Lowe and Pavel Zemliansky, 146–55. Anderson: Parlor Press.

Salem, Lori. 2016. "Decisions... Decisions: Who Chooses to Use the Writing Center?" *Writing Center Journal* 35, no. 2: 147–71.

Schendel, Ellen. 2012. "Integrating Assessment into Your Center's Other Work: Not Your Typical Methods Chapter." In *Building Writing Center Assessments That Matter*, edited by Ellen Schendel and William J. Macauley, 115–36. Louisville: University Press of Colorado.

Stay, Byron. 2010. "Writing Centers in the Small College." In *The Writing Center Director's Resource Book*, edited by Christina Murphy and Byron Stay, 147–52. New York: Routledge.

Thompson, Isabelle. 2006. "Writing Center Assessment: Why and a Little How." *Writing Center Journal* 26, no. 1: 33–62.

Tomusko, Emily. 2018. "Anxiety at John Carroll: Why Developmental Writers Avoid the Writing Center." Master's essay, John Carroll University. https://collected.jcu.edu/mastersessays/95.

Towle, Beth. 2019. "'It Depends on Who You Talk To': Mapping Writing Center-Writing Program Relationships at Small Liberal Arts Colleges." PhD diss., Purdue University Graduate School.

Waldo, Mark. 1990. "What Should the Relationship Between the Writing Center and the Writing Program Be?" *Writing Center Journal* 11, no. 1: 73–80.

Coda: What Comes Next? The Future of SLAC Research and Assessment

Genie Giaimo and Megan O'Neill

We started this collection wanting to build out from the landmark work of Gladstein and Regaignon (2012). As we dove deeper into the questions that arose, we found deeper and deeper questions arising alongside them. What we have collected is a valuable set of methodologies, data, experiences, and perspectives on the work we do, and now we face the next steps in the field: what comes next?

As WPAs and WCDs ourselves, we see these chapters doing the hard work of surfacing what is, as mentioned in the introduction, often hidden labor: the workload that is not countable in hours but in tasks and initiatives. A WPA's accountability to assessment may look from the outside as just another task on their long list of responsibilities, but as these chapters ably demonstrate, the emotional, intellectual, ethical, and psychological toll is substantial, and made worse when we cannot reliably show our institutions the value of assessment work.

It seems clear, reading these chapters, that the field is growing and moving into new shapes. An overdue and welcome development is the increasing focus on social justice, whether it is focused on diversity, equity and inclusion, or linguistic justice, or students' rights to their own languages. Questions about who has access to academic literacy, who controls that access, and what they do with that access will continue to drive the field in new directions.

At the same time, there are also very real challenges articulated in this collection, including the issues of doing assessment work as a non-tenure track faculty member, or trying to train people into doing assessment, which may or may not work. These chapters show us the pitfalls but also the opportunities of bringing many different stakeholders into writing research and assessment. Because of the small size of SLACs, it is possible to impact every single student through writing curricula and interventions.

These practitioners and chapters offer roadmaps for doing this work in ethical, justice-oriented, empirical, and sustainable ways. Then again, there are also moments where the whole process or method needs to be scrutinized and replaced. Going back to the drawing board, or failed assessments, as these chapters show, are critical parts of this work and should not be scuttled away before they are discussed. We need a postmortem on the work we do, even when it fails.

There are, of course, other throughlines in this collection including the ways in which the COVID-19 pandemic has upended how we do assessment (and placement or writing work) and, also, how community has been impacted by fallout from the pandemic. Because we are located at small residential communities, which are built on deep and profound connections between students and faculty, we need to rethink what community means in our kinda sorta post-pandemic moment. Some of this work can come through bringing in students to the research and assessment process, as contributors here have done. But we also need to rethink what kinds of assessment are viable in this moment and what we are assessing. Perhaps some of our pre-pandemic preoccupations have shifted and new ones have arisen.

Finally, we hope to inspire a new generation of SLAC WPA and WCD researchers to take risks, to consider social justice and linguistic inclusion, and to be OK with "failure" as they undertake their own assessments at their institutions and, perhaps, collaboratively across SLACs. Where the previous book on SLAC WPA work was instructive in overviewing the field, these chapters and this collection offer a deep dive into what is possible, but there is still more work to be done.

Please join us.

Contributors

Hannah Bellwoar is a professor of English and the director of general education and writing at Juniata College. In her scholarship, she has focused on reciprocity in collaborative mentoring relationships through research on mentoring undergraduate researchers in writing studies and through her co-authoring of four publications with five of her undergraduate students. You can read this work in *Harlot*, *One Shot*, *Composition Studies*, and the *Naylor Report on Undergraduate Research in Writing Studies* (2020).

Holly Blakely is an associate professor of English and the writing center director at Cedarville University in Cedarville, Ohio. Her research interests include writing cognition, intercultural rhetoric, and the use of digital media in writing pedagogy.

George Cusack is a senior lecturer in English and the director of writing across the curriculum at Carleton College. His scholarship on writing instruction (co-written with Nathan Grawe) has most recently appeared in the edited volume *Teaching Principles of Microeconomics* (Edward Elgar, 2023).

Bridget Draxler teaches writing and directs the writing center at St. Olaf College in Northfield, MN. She is the co-author of *Engaging the Age of Jane Austen: Humanities in Practice* (with Danielle Spratt; University of Iowa Press, 2018) and *How to Be a Peer Research Consultant* (with Maggie Epstein; Association of College and Research Libraries, 2021).

Kim Fahle Peck is the director of the academic success center at York College of Pennsylvania, where she oversees the writing and communication studio as well as content tutoring and academic coaching. Her research focuses on online writing instruction, labor and professional development in writing centers, and undergraduate research. Her work has been published in *Computers and Composition*, *WLN: A Journal of Writing Center Scholarship*, *FORUM: Issues about Part-time and Contingent Faculty*, and several edited collections. She is also one of the current co-editors of *Young Scholars in Writing*.

Matthew Fledderjohann is the writing center director at Le Moyne College in Syracuse, New York. His research interests include writing administration and composition practices, apocalyptic rhetoric, revision, and endings. His work has been published in *The Cormac McCarthy Journal, Enculturation, Praxis*, and the edited collection *Preserving Emotion in Student Writing.*

Crystal N. Fodrey is an associate professor of English and director of the CCCC Writing Program Certificate of Excellence award-winning writing at Moravian program at Moravian University in Bethlehem, Pennsylvania. Her work appears in *Across the Disciplines*, the *WAC Journal, Composition Forum*, and in various edited collections.

Bridget Fullerton is director of student writing and lecturer in the humanities at Bates College, where she and her colleagues received the 2022 SLAC-WPA Martinson Innovation Award. In 2018, an article she co-wrote with three of her peers, an earlier version of which won the 2015 CWPA Graduate Student Writing Award, appeared in *WPA: Writing Program Administration*.

N. Claire Jackson is Assistant Professor of Writing Studies at SUNY Geneseo, where she teaches courses in academic writing, feminist and queer theories, and transgender studies. Her scholarship focuses on how institutional texts shape possibilities for agency and how individuals use writing to resist or rewrite dominant institutional discourses.

Sarah Kosel Agnihotri is an education specialist at Wayne State University. She previously worked as a writing center coordinator and adjunct writing instructor at Madonna University. Her work has been published in *WLN: A Journal of Writing Center Scholarship, Currents in Pharmacy Teaching and Learning,* and the edited collection *Teaching Writing in the Health Professions.*

Diane LeBlanc is a professor of English and director of writing at St. Olaf College. She is the author of five poetry collections and co-author of *Playing for Equality: Oral Histories of Women Leaders in the Early Year of Title IX*. Recent essays and poems appear in *Writing on the Edge, Inside Higher Ed, Southern Humanities Review*, and *Bellevue Literary Review*.

Bryan A. Lutz is an assistant professor of rhetoric and composition and the director of writing across the curriculum at Ohio Northern University. Dr. Lutz has published in the journals *Computers and Composition Online, The Journal of Critical Thought and Praxis*, and *The Journal of Interactive Technology and Pedagogy*, and serves as a communications consultant with both non-profit groups and private businesses.

Abby Madar graduated from Juniata College in 2022 with a Bachelor of Arts in English. During her time at Juniata, she worked as a writing tutor and as the assessment and project coordinator for general education. She collaborated with Hannah Bellwoar to present and write about their research together.

Gabriel Morrison is the associate director of the center for writing at the College of the Holy Cross. Gabriel's work has appeared in *WPA: Writing Program Administration* as well as various edited collections.

Julie Nelson Christoph is professor of English and director of the center for writing and learning at the University of Puget Sound, where she served formerly as dean of faculty affairs. Her work has been published in *College English, Research in the Teaching of English, Written Communication*, and several edited volumes.

Sarah E. Polo is an assistant professor of English and first-year writing seminar coordinator at Cottey College, a women's college in Missouri. Her work appears in *The Journal of Multimodal Rhetorics, Peitho*, and various edited collections.

Justine Post is a learning designer and consultant. She was an associate professor of rhetoric and composition at Ohio Northern University who spent seven years directing the university's writing center and three years coordinating first-year writing. Her research has been published in *Composition Studies, Applied Linguistics,* and the *Journal of English for Academic Purposes.*

Kristina Reardon is the director of intensive writing and senior lecturer in English and education studies at Amherst College, where she also serves as director of summer humanities and social science in the summer bridge program. Her work has appeared in *The Journal of Writing Assessment, The Writing Center Journal, Journal of Response to Writing, WLN: A Writing Center Journal, Journal of Education for Teaching* and others, as well as the edited collection *Critical Reading and Writing in the Era of Fake News* (2020).

Hayley C. Stefan is a lecturer in the Montserrat program and department of English at the College of the Holy Cross, where she focuses on the relationship between disability and race in American contemporary, children's, and young adult literature and media, and across the digital humanities. You can read her recent work in *American Literature, Disability Studies Quarterly*, and on her website: www.hayleystefan.org.

Nicole Weaver is the director of writing and a professor of practice in the English department at Le Moyne College. She serves as the administrator of the first-year writing program. Her research interests include first-year writing curriculum, assessment, and change, as well as the role of code-meshing in the first-year writing classroom.

Kara Wittman is associate teaching professor of English at the University of California, Berkeley. From 2016-2023 she served as assistant professor of English and director of college writing at Pomona College, where she was also the founding director of the center for speaking, writing, and the image. Her work has appeared in *College Composition and Communication*; *WLN: A Journal of Writing Center Scholarship*; *Workplace: A Journal for Academic Labor*; and various edited volumes. She is the editor, with Evan Kindley, of the *Cambridge Companion to the Essay* (Cambridge University Press, 2022).

Index

Abbot, Sophia, 127, 135, 136
Abby Madar, xxv, xxix, 119
academic advising, 286
academic dishonesty, 157, 160, 163
academic freedom, 8ç9, 30
academic writing, xxvii, 72, 78, 179, 184, 197, 211, 217, 224, 259, 284–285
accessibility, 24
accessible teaching, 27, 183
accountability, xii, 11, 15, 17, 33, 295
accreditation, ix–xii, xx–xxi, 6–8, 30, 79, 139, 230
Ackley-Holbrook, Elizabeth, 136
Adams, Meredith J. D., 282–283, 291
adjunct faculty, 76–77, 88, 100, 108, 114
Adler-Kassner, Linda, 27, 34
agency: student, 185, 210
Agnihotri, Sarah Kosel, xi, xxx, 273
AI-assisted writing, 158, 163
Aldohon, Hatem, 70, 73, 82, 85, 87, 91
Alexander, Joel E., 210
Allan, Elizabeth G., 237, 248
alliance building, xxix
Aloysius Cogan, John, xxxii
American Association of Colleges and Universities (AAC&U), 13, 18, 45, 54, 56, 136, 211, 234
Amherst College, xxiii, 255, 263, 265
analytical thinking, 141–142, 146
Anderson, Paul V., xxxi, 18, 35, 55, 91, 116, 135, 136, 191, 219, 248, 277, 292–294
annual reports, 256–258, 260, 264

Anson, Chris M., 23, 25, 31, 34–36, 70, 90–91
antiracism, xi, xxvii, xxix, 27, 36
anti-racist: assessment, xx, 176, 202, 207; pedagogy, xxviii, 202, 204
anxiety, 108, 177, 243, 282, 284–285
apprenticeship model, 124–125
argument, 76–77, 79, 80, 86, 93–94, 128–129, 141–142, 144–147, 149, 151, 179, 198, 209, 220, 279
artifact scoring, 202, 216
artifacts, xxvi, 9–12, 14, 19, 24, 30–32, 77, 156, 172, 175, 202, 205, 207–208, 211, 216–218, 232, 235–242
assessment, *passim*; indirect, 11, 87, 158; institutional, xi, xvi, 122, 190, 211, 289; methodologies, xxx; methods of, xi, xvii, xxvi, 32, 89, 102, 158, 187; practices, ix, xv, xx, xxviii, 23, 27, 39–40, 48, 61, 98, 102, 104, 114, 173–175, 177, 179, 186–187, 189–190, 205, 217, 290, 291; qualitative, xxii, xxiv, xxvi, 11, 32, 80, 84, 98, 100, 109, 111, 119, 121–123, 125, 128, 130–133, 135, 145, 229, 237, 242;
attendance, x, 44, 177, 180–182, 266–267, 268–271
audience awareness, 211, 214
autonomy, ix, xxviii, 6, 8, 25, 28, 30, 33, 71, 175–176, 190, 229–230, 236, 238–239, 241

Babcock, Rebecca Day, 275, 292
Bailey, Moya, 184–185, 190
Baker-Bell, April, 164, 168
Ballif, Michelle, 35

Banks, William P., 174–175, 189, 192
Bates College, xxiii, 229, 231
Bawarshi, Anis, 35
Bean, John C., 211, 219
Beaufort, Anne, 27, 34
Belanoff, Pat, 99, 115–116
Bell, Katrina, xxviii, xxx
Bellwoar, Hannah, xxv, xxix, 119–121, 127, 135–136
benchmarking, 205
BIPOC students, xxviii, 171, 202
Bizzell, Patricia, 175, 178, 191
Black, Laurel, xxi, xxxi, 31, 36, 41, 116, 168, 176
Blakely, Holly, xi, 273
Blanchard, Annelise, 183, 192
Blimling, Gregory S., 256, 271
Blum, Susan Debra, 167–168, 188, 191, 198
Blumer, Herbert, 101, 115
Borgman, Jessie, 192
Bovill, Catherine, 125, 135
Boyer, Ernest, 261, 272
brainstorming, 84, 89, 114, 142, 146, 288
Brent, Doug, 40, 55
Brereton, John C., 191
Britt-Smith, Laurie Ann, 257
Bromley, Pam, xix, xxx
Brookter, Josye, 99, 104, 115
Browning, Ella R., 27, 34
Brunk-Chavez, Beth, 55
Bullerjahn, Margaret, 70, 73, 89, 91
Bumstead, Andrew, 280, 292
Butler, Lisa D., 165, 168
Butterfield, Kenneth D., 157, 169

Camp, Roberta, 106, 115
campus culture, 53, 174
Campus, The, 158
career readiness, 126
Carello, Janice, 165, 168
Carillo, Ellen, 27, 34, 177, 181, 191, 199

Carleton College, xxii, 229, 231
Carr, Allison, 26, 30, 36
Carrick Hedges, Denise, 48
Caswell, Nicole I., 174–175, 189, 192, 292
character traits, 58
Charmaz, Kathy, 100, 101, 115
Chase, Geoffrey, 110, 114–115
ChatGPT, 158–159, 165
cheating, 157–163, 167
Cheatle, Joseph, 70, 73, 89, 91, 274, 292
Chegg (app), 165
Chen, Meiyi, 203
Cheung, Jessica, 160, 168
citation practices, 73, 78, 84, 156, 161, 167
civic engagement, xxii–xxiii
CLA+ (Collegiate Learning Assessment, 209, 213–214
Clark, Irene Lurkis, 165, 168
class engagement, xi–xii, xviii, xxii–xxiii, 8–12, 14, 22, 41, 56, 156–160, 165, 168, 172, 175, 177, 179–182, 184, 188, 193–194, 197–198, 202, 204, 209, 213–214, 223, 241, 274, 276, 287
class size: small, xviii, xxiv, 8
closing the loop, 12–13, 17, 132
code compliance, 156, 158, 171
collaboration, ix–x, 5, 27, 48, 52–54, 70–72, 74, 76, 88, 122–123, 125–126, 128, 132–134, 137, 156, 162, 165–166, 184, 189, 230, 241, 274, 289
Colton, Aaron, 282, 292
Columbine, 166
common essay, 110–113, 117
common reader, 46–48, 53–54, 56
community engagement, xxvii, 158
community-building, xi, 39–40, 45, 52–54, 159, 183–184
competition, 156, 165

Index 303

composition, xv–xvi, xix, 6, 36, 76, 102, 104, 108, 129, 146, 165, 178–179, 186–187, 200–201, 262, 278–279, 286
Condon, Frankie, xxviii, xxxi, 276, 292
Condon, William, 11, 18
contract grading, 176, 184, 186, 188, 190, 197
Cook-Sather, Alison, 125, 135
Corbin, Juliet, 100, 116
Cottey College, xxiii, xxviii, 39–46, 48–55, 59, 62, 64
Council of Writing Program Administrators (CWPA), x, xix, 44, 55, 98, 219
counterarguments, 113, 131–132, 145, 147–148, 151
course outcomes, 69–70, 75, 78, 81–83, 105
COVID-19, xxi, 41, 44, 51, 54, 61, 76, 79, 103, 109, 174, 183, 186, 191, 231, 259, 296
Cox, Michelle, 211, 220, 225
Craig, Sherri, 176, 189, 191
Creme, Phyllis, 238–239, 241, 248
Crimmins, Cynthia, 286, 292
critical thinking, xviii, 105–106, 140–141, 144, 184, 209, 211, 213–214
Cruz, Sor Juana Inés de la, 247, 249
curriculum, x, xvi, xviii, xx, xxiii, xxv, xxix, 4–5, 7, 9–10, 17, 21, 23–26, 33, 35–37, 40, 45, 47, 51–52, 72–77, 88, 105–106, 108, 121, 129, 145, 167, 179, 185–187, 189, 202–206, 213, 215, 218, 229, 232, 236, 238; shared, 47
Cusack, George, xi, xx, xxviii, xxx, 229

Daiker, Donald A., 116
data: analysis, 19, 70, 100–101, 209; collection, 24, 70, 79–80, 113, 158, 242, 260, 264–266, 288

data-driven methods, 70, 74
de Bie, Alise, 120, 123, 135
deficiency rubric, 107, 110
DelliCarpini, Dominic, 136, 286, 292
demographics, 145, 258
Denny, Harry, 276, 279, 292–293
Denton, David, 238, 248
Dickinson College, xxxii
direct measures, 70–71, 80, 89, 91, 121
directed self-placement, xxvi
disability, 164, 177, 183–185, 197
disability studies, 177
disciplinary writing, 7, 9–11
diversity, xi, xxi, 49, 90, 167, 229, 233, 244, 280, 295
documentary film, 48
documentation style, 81, 83, 95
Downs, Douglas, xxiii, xxxi–xxxii
Draxler, Bridget, xi, xx, xxv, xxviii, xxx, 202, 204
Driscoll, Dana Lynn, 237, 248, 275, 292
Dunn, Dana S., 26, 30, 36
Durst, Russel K., 99, 116

editing, 125, 131, 141, 144, 146, 220–221, 284
Elbow, Peter, 99, 116
elitism, xxix–xxx, 186, 189–190
Elliot, Norbert, 106, 116, 207, 220
Elliott, Alicia, 46, 56
Emery, Daniel L., 23, 35
empathy, 56, 58, 163, 183, 242, 245
engagement, xi–xii, xviii, xxii–xxiii, 8–12, 14, 22, 41, 56, 156–160, 165, 168, 172, 175, 177, 179–182, 184, 188, 193–194, 197–198, 202, 204, 209, 213–214, 223, 241, 274, 276, 287
enrollment, xxiv, 41, 278
Eodice, Michele, 23, 31, 35

equity, xvii, xxi, xxvi, xxviii–xxx, 7, 24, 31, 90, 114, 119–123, 125, 129, 133–134, 176, 189–190, 204, 206–207, 215, 217–218, 295
Estrem, Heidi, 55
ethics, xxiii, xxvii, 113–114, 140, 184, 208
evaluation, x, 23, 47, 86, 137–138, 145, 197, 205, 219, 255–259, 261–266, 269, 271, 283
exams: proficiency, 98–115, 117
Excel (app), 139, 172, 204, 266

faculty, *passim*; development, xvii, xxiv, 5–6, 8–9, 32–33, 52, 175, 178–179, 186, 188, 231, 237, 257; engagement, 5, 10–11, 13, 171, 230
Fahle Peck, Kim, xi, 273
Faison, Wonderful, xxviii, xxxi, 276, 292
Farruggia, Susan P., xxxii
feedback, 23, 46, 49, 51, 62–65, 73, 78–88, 99, 110, 118, 126, 130–134, 145, 150, 162, 171–172, 180, 184–185, 195–196, 198, 205, 216–217, 219–221, 223, 242, 258–259, 262–263, 277; live, 130–131, 133, 147, 150
Felten, Peter, 125, 135
Ferganchick-Neufang, Julia, 128, 135
Fine, Michelle, 129, 135
first-year composition, xi, xxiv–xxv, xxviii, xxx, 7, 26–28, 38–39, 41, 62, 69–71, 75, 78, 80, 83, 87, 98–102, 105, 109, 111, 113–117, 122, 125–126, 128–129, 131, 142–143, 146–147, 178, 202–206, 209, 212–213, 220, 238
first-year experience, 132, 145, 183
first-year seminars, xv, xxvi–xxvii, xxix, 5–6, 126, 129, 156, 178, 202–203, 215, 229–231, 238
Fishman, Jenn, 136
Fitz Gibbon, Heather, 135

Fitzgerald, Lauren, 72–73, 280, 292
Flash, Pamela, 22, 25, 28, 34–36, 91
Fledderjohann, Matthew, xi, 273
Florida, xx, xxvi, 3, 5
focus groups, 11, 31, 172, 202, 205, 207, 209–210, 215, 218, 222–223
Fodrey, Crystal N., xx, xxii, xxv–xxvi, xxix, xxxi, 21, 23, 25–27, 30, 34–35, 70, 73–74, 77, 91
formative assessment, 82
Fralix, Brandon, xxv, 70, 74, 91
Freire, Paolo, 164, 168
Fullerton, Bridget, xi, 229

Galin, Jeffrey R., 26, 33, 35
Gannett, Cinthia, 191
García, Romeo, xxviii, xxxi
Geller, Anne Ellen, 276, 293
general education, xxiv, xxvi, 5, 9, 13–14, 22, 24, 26, 28–29, 41–42, 51, 120–122, 124–126, 128–129, 132, 134, 139, 145, 202–203, 205, 209–210, 218–219, 281
Giaimo, Genie, xix–xxi, xxviii–xxix, xxxi, 18, 70, 91, 155, 274, 293, 295
Gillam, Alice, 293
Gillespie, Paula, 274, 293
Gilliland, Betsy, 199
Girl Who Smiled Beads, The, 46, 56
Gladstein, Jill M., ix–x, xv, xxi–xxii, xxiv–xxv, xxxi, 6–7, 18, 21, 25, 30, 35, 39, 42–44, 55, 70–71, 74, 89, 91, 114, 116, 121–122, 124, 135, 178, 191, 230, 248, 295
global awareness, 42, 45, 47, 49–50, 53, 58
Goldblatt, Eli, 120
Gomes, Mathew, 177, 180–181, 191
Goucher College, 22, 35
Grable, Jeffrey T., 192
grade inflation, 173–175
grading, xvii, xx–xxi, xxvi, xxviii, xxx, 23, 44, 103, 147, 150, 175–190, 193, 197–198, 201, 217,

238–240, 245; agreements, 189; contracts, 176–177, 180, 186, 189; engagement-based, 179–180, 193; nontraditional, 187; specifications, 184, 187, 197
grammar, 79, 82, 87, 102, 113
Grammarly (app), 11, 165
Grann, David, 46, 55
Green, Neisha-Anne S, 164, 168
Greenberg, Susan H., 159–160, 168
Greer, Jane, 136
Grineski, Sara, 127, 136
Grinnell College, xxxii
Grobman, Laurie, 292
Grossman, Robert, 237, 248
Grouling, Jennifer, 175, 191
Grutsch McKinney, Jackie, 277, 282, 292–293
guiding documents, 44–45
Gutierrez, Victoria, 203

Hall, Eric E., 127, 135–136
Hall, R. Mark, 276, 293
Haltiwanger Morrison, Talisha, xxviii, xxxi
Halverson, Kelsey, 203
Hamedani, MarYam G., 232, 237, 249
Hamraie, Aimi, 183, 191
Han, Ceon-Woo, xxxii
Harmston, Matt, 213, 220
Harris, Muriel, 165, 169
Hassay, Chris, xxxi, 23, 30, 34, 70, 73–74, 77, 91
Haswell, Richard H., 275, 293
Hauptman, Robert, 157, 169
Haverford College, 156, 169
help-seeking behavior, 155, 162–163, 216, 219
Hewerdine, Jennifer, xxviii, xxx
Hobart and William Smith College, 22
Hodkin, Zeke, 161, 169

holistic scoring, 207–208, 210, 216, 218
Holly-Wells, Jennifer, 70–72, 76, 85, 91
Holmes, Ashley J., 27, 35
Holy Cross (College of the), xxii, 173–174, 178–179, 183–184, 186, 188, 191, 198, 255–256, 259–263, 265, 272
honor codes, xx–xxi, xxviii, xxx, 155–168, 171–172
Hope, Mia, 177, 180–181, 191
Horner, Bruce, 275, 293
House, Veronica, 27, 35, 293
Howard, Rebecca Moore, 156, 169
human subjects research, 260, 263–265
Huot, Brian, 107–108, 115–116

Ianetta, Melissa, 280, 292
Immortal Life of Henrietta Lacks, The, 46, 55
Inayatulla, Shereen, 246, 248
inclusion, xx–xxi, xxiii, xxviii–xxix, 90, 204, 217, 283, 295–296
inclusive excellence, 190
individualism, 122
inequity, xxix, 162, 187, 217, 233
infographics, 47–48, 172
information literacy, 6, 129, 144
Inoue, Asao B., xxviii, xxxi, 27, 31, 35, 164, 169, 177, 180, 182, 184, 186–189, 191, 199, 204–205, 207–208, 216–217, 219
Inside Higher Ed, 165, 168–169
institutional support, 28
institutions: change, 119, 121–123, 127–128, 134–135, 173, 189–190; culture, 8, 173, 212, 229, 232; data, 149, 202, 205, 207, 209, 211, 214–215; ethnography, xxii, xxvi, xxx; mission, xxii, xxvii, 5, 12; research, 6–7, 112, 122, 204, 230
integration, 13, 73

integrity, 58, 155–157, 159–160, 166–168
interdisciplinarity, 4, 8, 28, 70, 72, 122, 178, 188
International Network of WAC Programs (INWAC), 52–53, 55
interrater reliability, 208, 211
interviews, xxvi, 11, 70, 73, 76, 84, 89, 100, 106, 109, 133, 171–172, 210, 234–235, 242, 260, 262, 265, 270
IRB applications, 100, 109, 172, 208, 258–266, 272, 276, 282, 284, 287
iterative processes, 107

Jackson, N. Claire, xx–xxi, xxiii, xxvi, xxviii–xxix, 173, 277
Jackson, Rebecca, 292
Jamieson, Sandra, 70–72, 76, 85, 91, 156, 169
Jessee, Mary Catherine, 183, 192
Jesuit education, xxii, 173–175, 191, 255, 283
Johnson, Margaret J., 285, 294
Juana Inés de la Cruz, Sor, 247, 249
Juniata College, xxii, 119–129, 131–132, 134–135, 137–139, 142, 144, 146
junior seminar, 5
justice, xxii–xxiii, xxvii–xxviii, 31, 33, 121, 123, 134, 174, 184, 296

Kahneman, Daniel, 256–257, 272
Keohane, Charlie, 159, 161, 169
Ketcham, Caroline J., 126, 135
Killers of the Flower Moon (film), 46, 55
Kinkead, Joyce, 292–293
Kirsch, Gesa, 128–129, 136, 292
Kixmiller, Lori A. S., 18
Klotz, Sarah, 199, 271–272
Kodama, Corinne M., xxxii
Konrad, Annika, 199
Kristof, Nicholas D., 46, 55
Kryger, Kathleen, 177, 192
Kuh, George, 125, 136

labor, xv, xvii, xix–xx, xxv–xxvi, xxviii, xxx, 44, 70, 72–74, 82, 108, 114, 127, 129, 166, 175–182, 184–188, 190, 207–208, 237, 244, 255, 264, 274–275, 277, 283–284, 286, 290, 295; scholarly, 273, 290
labor conditions, xv, xx, xxv, 190
labor-based grading, xxviii, 176–177, 179–180, 184, 187
LaFerriere, Alissa, 177, 180–181, 191
Laflen, Angela, 188, 192
Langenhove, Luk Van, 115
Lape, Noreen, xix, xxxii, 18
Latham, Michael, xviii, xxxii
Le Moyne College, xxii, 283–284
leadership, xi, xvi, xix, xxii–xxiii, xxvi, 3–4, 6–7, 17, 27, 33, 42, 45, 48, 50, 53, 71–72, 74, 79, 89, 121, 124, 187, 204
Leahy, Richard, 285, 293
learning objectives, 105–106, 110, 112, 244
learning outcomes, 4, 12–13, 15, 26, 29, 37, 45, 49, 75, 77, 130–131, 139, 144–146, 162, 203–204, 206, 210–211, 215–218, 232, 234
Lebduska, Lisa, x
LeBlanc, Diane, xi, xx, xxv, xxviii, xxx, 202, 204
Lerner, Neal, 273, 291, 293
liberal arts, ix–x, xv, xvii–xxi, xxiii–xxv, xxvii, xxx, 3–4, 21, 26, 33, 39–40, 42, 70–72, 74, 98, 101, 119, 121, 123–124, 126, 155–156, 158, 165, 173–174, 178, 189, 202, 215, 229, 247, 255–256, 263, 266, 273, 278, 281
liberal arts colleges, ix–x, xv, xvii–xxi, xxvii, xxx, 3–4, 21, 26, 39, 70–71, 98, 101, 119, 121, 123, 126, 155–156, 158, 165, 173, 189,

202, 215, 229, 247, 255–256, 263, 266, 273
liberal arts education, xxiii, 74
libraries, 96, 142–143, 210, 215
linguistic: justice, xxvii, 164, 295; norms, 180
literacy, 40, 140, 246, 295
Lockett, Alexandria, xxviii, xxxii, 276, 293
lore, 15, 273–276, 289, 291
lower-order concerns, 79, 83–85, 87, 279
Lunsford, Andrea, 165, 169
Luqueño, Leslie Patricia, 135
Luskey, Matthew, 23, 35
Lutz, Bryan A., xi, xxv, xxix, 69

Macauley, William J., 294
mad studies, 183–184
Manning, Kathleen, 261–262, 271–272
Marks, Amanda, 158, 170
Marquis, Elizabeth, 135
Martinez, Aya Y., xxviii, xxxii
Martini, Rebecca Hallman, 276, 289–291, 293
Matsuda, Paul Kei, 211, 220, 225
Mattern, Krista, 213, 220
McArdle, Casey, 192
McBride, Maureen, 273, 293
McCabe, Donald L., 157–158, 165, 169
McCurrie, Matthew Kilian, xxxii
McLeod, Susan H., 18
Mellon Foundation, 204
Melville House, 56
Melzer, Dan, 26–27, 35, 99, 116
mental health, xxviii, 174, 177, 237, 242–244
mentoring, xviii, xxiv, 120, 122, 126–129, 132, 134–135; mutual, xviii, 120, 122, 126–129, 132, 134–135

metacognition, 219, 230–231, 233, 235–236, 238, 240–241, 245–246, 253
methodologies, xxix–xxx, 3, 11, 275–276, 290, 295
Middle States Commission on Higher Education, 23, 29, 38
Middlebury College, xxiii, xxvi, 155–156, 158–162, 169–170
Mikovits, Meg, xxxi, 27, 34–35
Miles, Libby, 192
Miley, Michelle, 18
Miller, Paul, ix, 135
Miraglia, Eric, 18
modifications, 74, 264–266
Montaigne, Michel de, 247, 249
Montserrat Programs, 178–179, 183–185, 191, 197
Moon, Gretchen Flesher, 40, 55
Moore, Cindy, 107–108, 116, 123, 126–128, 135–136, 169
Moore, Jessie L., 107–108, 116, 123, 126–128, 135–136
Morales, Danielle, 127, 136
Moravian University, xxii, xxvi, 21–23, 25–30, 32–33, 37–38
Morrison, xx, xxii–xxiii, xxvi, xxviii, xxx–xxxi, 173
Morrison, Gabriel, xx, xxii–xxiii, xxvi, xxviii, xxx–xxxi, 173
Moss, Tim, xxxii
multimodal, 26–27
multiple measures, 205, 213
Mundy, Robert, 293
Murphy, Christina, 294
mutual aid, 159, 163, 165, 167
Myers, Brittany, xxxii

Nanton, Talia O., xxviii, xxxi
National Census of Writing, xviii, xxv–xxvi, xxxi, 18
National Council of Teachers of English (NCTE), 18, 35, 292–293

National Survey of Student Engagement (NSSE), 149, 209, 214–215
Naydan, Liliana M., 293
Nickoson, Lee, xxxi
Nilson, Linda Burzotta, 187, 192
North Carolina State University, 21
North, Stephen M., 21, 275, 294
Northway, Kara, xix, xxx
Northwestern University, 232, 237

Ohio Northern University, xxii, 70
Okuma, Taryn, 70, 91
Okun, Tema, 164, 170
Olinger, Andrea R., 70, 92
Oliveri, Maria Elena, 35
O'Neill, Megan, xix, 3, 5, 13, 157, 295
outreach, 73, 179, 186, 275, 281–282, 288

P.E.O. sisterhood, 40
Pajares, Frank, 285, 294
pandemic, xxi, 22, 26, 28, 33, 41, 44, 51, 54, 61, 76, 79, 103, 109–111, 182–183, 186, 189, 208, 231, 233, 240, 246, 256, 259, 274, 296
paraphrase, 94
participation, 100, 112, 120, 131, 177, 180–181, 184, 194, 201, 209, 243, 283, 286
partnerships, xvi, xxv–xxvi, 119, 121–123, 125, 134–135, 273, 276, 288, 290–291; pedagogical, 119, 121, 123–124, 129, 134–135
Pavela, Gary, 157–158, 165, 169
Paz, Chiara C., xxxi
Peckham, Irvin, 106, 116, 207, 220
peer consultants, 256
peer review, 49, 51, 62–63, 131, 133, 144, 147, 156, 159, 162, 182, 195, 214, 244–245, 266
peer tutoring, 7, 75, 125, 162–163, 179, 256–257, 291
Pemberton, Michael A., 293

Perdue, Sherry Wynn, 275–276, 292
performance, 10, 103, 107, 137, 204, 209, 211, 213–215, 237, 261, 283
Perkins, D. N., 236, 249
personal growth, xxii, 230
Pfeiffer, Christian A., 157, 170
piloting, 52
placement, xx–xxi, xxviii, xxx, 104, 208, 296
plagiarism, 158, 160, 168
podcasts, 47
Poe, Mya, xxviii, xxxii, 35, 189, 191, 204, 207–208, 219
Polo, Sarah E., xxv, xxviii–xxix, 39, 62
Pomona College, xxii, 229, 231
Porter, James E., 190, 192, 283, 294
Porter, Stephen R., 190, 192, 283, 294
portfolios, 17, 31–32, 99, 110, 142, 230
Post, Justine, xi, xxv, xxix, 69, 96, 138–139, 195, 224–225
Powell, Roger, 273
Price, Margaret, 184–185, 192
professional development, xxi, xxv, 44, 53, 90, 107, 113–114, 120, 127–128, 205, 208, 211, 217–219, 245
proficiency narratives, 213–214
program history, 4
publication, xix, xxiii, xxvi, 56, 128, 172, 262, 271

racial justice, xxi
Radunzel, Justine, 213, 220
Rafoth, Ben, 285, 294
Randall, Jennifer, xxxii, 31, 35
reading process, 221
Reardon, Kristina, xx, xxx, 255, 259, 271–272
recruitment, xxviii, 43, 53–54, 164, 280

reflection, ix, xxii, 16, 47, 56, 99, 107, 125, 134, 173, 181–184, 189–190, 195, 204, 206, 209, 217–218, 224–225, 230–231, 237–239, 245–247, 253, 257, 264
reflective writing, xx, xxviii, 230–233, 235–240, 242–243, 245, 247, 253
Regaignon, Dara Rossman, x, xv, xxi–xxii, xxiv, xxxi, 6, 18, 21, 25, 30, 35, 39, 42–44, 55, 70–71, 91, 114, 116, 121–122, 124, 135, 178, 191, 230, 248, 295
Reiff, Mary Jo, 29, 35
Rentscher, Molly, 273, 293
reporting, xv, xix, 3–5, 11, 14–15, 17, 31, 75, 157, 160, 162, 215, 218, 257, 266, 268, 284
research, *passim*; qualitative, xxii, 119, 123, 125, 128, 131–133, 135; quantitative, 257; questions, 129, 206, 262, 264, 266; RAD (replicable, aggregable, data supported), 274–276, 291; undergraduate, xxiv, 27, 125–128, 275
resource allocation, 30
responsibility, 13, 59–60, 107, 125, 156, 160–161, 236
retention, xxviii, 4, 10, 26, 31, 54, 125, 202, 287
revision, 11, 22, 24–25, 28, 79, 84–89, 95, 144, 147, 150, 166, 184, 197; global, 79
rhetoric, xv–xvi, xviii–xix, xxv–xxvi, 6–7, 36, 74, 76, 102, 172, 178–179
rhetorical analysis, xxi, xxvi, xxx, 47, 156
rhetorical appeals, 62
rhetorical situation, 56, 62–63, 82
Richards, Rebecca, 203
Ritchie, Joy, 128–129, 136
Robertson, Liane, 232, 238, 249
Roemer, Marjorie, 99, 116

Roig, Miguel, 158, 170
Rose, Shirley K, 135
Rose, Tara A., 36
Royster, Jacqueline Jones, 129, 136
RStudio (software), 172
rubrics, xxvi, 10, 13–14, 18–20, 23–24, 28, 30–32, 38, 46, 49–50, 59–60, 69–70, 72, 75–78, 80–81, 83, 85–86, 103, 110–112, 117, 129, 131–132, 145, 148, 205, 207–208, 210–211, 216–217, 229, 234, 236–237, 239, 241–242, 246–247
Ruecker, Todd, 54–55
Rutz, Carol, 101, 109, 114, 116

Salem, Lori, 273–274, 279–280, 282, 285, 292, 294
Salomon, Gavriel, 236, 249
Sanyal, Maya, 70–72, 76, 85, 91
Scafe, Robert, 23, 31, 35
scaffolding, 23, 77
Schendel, Ellen, 290, 294
Schmidt, Katherine M., 210
Schonberg, Eliana, xix, xxx
Schultz, Lucille M., 99, 116
Scott, Tony, 239, 241, 245, 249
self-assessment, 235, 240, 245, 252
self-efficacy, 162, 210, 214–215, 236
self-evaluation, 137
self-governance, 160
Serenbetz Institute for Women's Leadership, Social Responsibility and Global Awareness, 48, 53
service, xxii, 6, 54, 71, 73–75, 88, 186, 210, 261
Sévère, Richard, 293
Severino, Carol, 165, 170
Shanahan, Jenny Olin, 126–127, 136
Shapiro, Shawna, xix, xxxii, 33, 36, 231, 249
shared governance, xviii, 71, 230
Sheridan, Mary P., xxxi
Sheriff, Stacey, 23, 36
Sicari, Anna, 293

Siegal, Meryl, 199
signal phrases, 97
Sims, Mikenna, 188, 192
simultaneity, 273, 290–291
Sins Invalid (project), 184, 192
Sjodin, Tony, 158, 170
Skloot, Rebecca, 46, 55
Slomp, David, 35
slow thinking, 256–260, 262–265, 268, 271
Smith College, 22, 36
Smith, Buffy, 236, 249
Smith, Jonathan A., 115
social justice, xv, xviii, xxiii, xxvii–xxx, 33, 174, 186, 295–296
social responsibility, 42, 45, 49–50, 59–60
Society of Jesus, 174
Sommers, Jeffrey, 116
Sommers, Nancy, 86, 217, 220
Souza, Jane Marie, 36
Soven, Margot, 18
SPSS (software), 172
Sriram, Rishi, 256–259, 272
St. Olaf College, xxii, 202–204, 206, 209, 213–214
Stage, Frances, 261–262, 271–272
stakeholders, xvi, xxii, xxiv–xxv, xxviii–xxix, 3, 10, 12, 15–17, 19, 29–30, 37, 73, 79, 90, 114, 158, 171, 186, 190, 290–291, 295
standardized English, 218
Stanley, Gabrielle M., 27, 36
STATA (software), 172
Stay, Byron, 277, 293–294
Stefan, Hayley C., xx, xxii–xxiii, xxvi, xxx, 173, 201
Stephens, Nicole M., 232, 236–237, 249
Stetson University, xxiii, xxvi, xxxii, 3, 5, 13–14, 18
Stevenson, Bryan, 46, 55
Stewart, Kearsley, 136

Stiles, Randall, xviii, xxxii
Stommel, Jesse, 199
Strauss, Anselm, 100, 116
student wellbeing, 186, 189
students: first-generation, xxviii, 31, 167; marginalized, 156, 159, 163, 171, 185; multicultural, 206
Stygall, Gail, 116
success, x, xxii, 10–12, 14, 49, 53–54, 57, 69–73, 79, 83, 89, 137, 175, 236–237, 257, 281, 291
Sue, Derald Wing, 188, 192
Sullivan, Patricia, 192
summaries, 15, 82, 84, 94, 97, 131, 256–257
surveillance, 166
surveys, xxiv, xxvi, 11, 23, 31–32, 48, 51, 69–70, 75–76, 78, 89, 125, 130–132, 142, 144–147, 149, 151, 158–159, 163, 171–172, 207, 210, 213–215, 217–218, 237, 256, 260–270, 275, 282–285; fatigue, 210, 282–283
Suskie, Linda A., 31, 36, 204, 207, 211, 220
sustainability, 21, 23, 90, 128
Swaak, Taylor, 70, 92
Swarthmore College, xxvi
syllabus, 11, 51, 110, 185, 201
Syracuse Writing Across the Curriculum program, 36

Taczak, Kara, 232, 238, 249
technology, 164
Temple University, 119
tenure, xii, xx, xxv–xxvi, 7, 30, 42–44, 74–77, 90, 109, 113, 273, 295
TerLouw, Mickey, 203
Thaiss, Christopher, 18
thesis statements, 9, 62–63, 79, 86, 93–94, 113, 145, 148, 203, 224, 253, 282
Thompson, Isabelle, 277, 294
threshold concepts, 27, 33

Tomusko, Emily, 282, 294
tone, 94
Torre, María Elena, 129, 135
Towle, Beth, 277, 294
tradition, xxii, 71, 98, 100–104, 106, 111, 175
training, xv–xvii, xxiv, 6, 44, 51–53, 62–65, 71–72, 84, 86, 164, 208, 216–217, 231, 233, 236, 238, 279–280, 286
transcription, 210, 265
transfer, 4, 10, 26–27, 32, 42, 210, 215, 236–238
transition to college, 231, 233, 237, 241–242
Traupman-Carr, Carol, 26, 30, 36
Trevino, Linda Klebe, 157, 169
trust, 163
tutoring, xix, xxvii, 69, 71–73, 75, 78–88, 162, 257, 280, 282
tutors, xxvii, 5, 69, 71–73, 78–90, 120, 147, 159, 163, 166, 179, 203, 205, 210, 215, 256, 279–280, 283, 285–286; embedded, 5, 72, 207, 210, 216; training, 5, 70, 79, 82, 84, 86–87, 284, 290

Umbach, Paul D., 282–283, 291
ungrading, xxi, xxviii, 186, 188, 199
University of Puget Sound, xxiii, 229, 231, 234
usage patterns, 275, 290
usage statistics, 256–257, 260
utilization, 52, 69–70, 73, 75, 80–82, 86

value rubrics, 211
values, xix, xxi, xxiii, xxviii–xxix, 31, 44, 54, 92, 114, 122, 128, 160, 163, 167, 171, 187, 197, 212, 230, 270
Vandermaas-Peeler, Maureen, 135
vertical writing, 26–27
voice, 6, 119–124, 128, 131–132, 135

Waldo, Mark, 280, 294
Walkington, Helen, 135–136
Wamariya, Clemantine, 46, 56
Wang, Cassie, 183, 192
Wardle, Elizabeth, xxiii, xxxi–xxxii, 27, 34, 236, 249
Washington Post, 168
Watson, Missy, 168, 170
Watts, Field, 136
Wayne State University, xxii
WC Online, 258–260, 265
Weaver, Nicole, xi, xx, xxii, xxv, xxviii–xxix, 98
Web 2.0, 164–165
Weil, Elizabeth, 46, 56
Weiser, Irwin, 135
Weisser, Christian, 35
Weitzer, William H., 283, 294
West-Puckett, Stephanie, 174–175, 192
Wetcher-Hendricks, Debra, 26, 30, 36
Whitcomb, Michael E., 283, 294
white language supremacy, 216–217
White, Edward M., 31, 35, 106, 116, 170, 204–205, 207–208, 219–220, 271
Whithaus, Carl, 199
Wikipedia, 164
Wilcox, Kaitlin, xviii, xxxii
Williams, Raymond, 121
Wittman, Kara, 229
Wolf, Margery, 128–129, 136
Womack, Anne-Marie, 183, 192
workload, xvii, 7, 23, 47, 75, 90, 150, 243, 245, 291, 295
Wright, Cassie A., 220
writing across the curriculum (WAC), ix, xx, xxv, xxxi, 4, 7, 11, 17–18, 22–25, 27, 34–36, 40, 44, 52–55, 70–73, 75, 91, 116, 122, 169, 186, 191–192, 199, 219

writing assessment, xi–xii, xv–xvii, xxi, xxvi, 8–17, 22, 26, 99, 101–102, 104–105, 108, 110–111, 113–114, 122, 180, 186, 205, 207, 210, 230, 236, 238
writing associates, 9, 119, 124–126, 130–131, 133–134, 143, 145, 147
writing center directors (WCD), xv–xvi, xxiv, 4, 6–8, 17, 90, 295–296
writing centers, xi–xii, xv–xvii, xix–xx, xxv–xxix, 3–13, 17, 27, 29, 53, 69–71, 73–76, 78–81, 89, 96, 119–120, 125, 130–131, 133, 147, 150, 156, 158–159, 161–164, 172, 181, 216, 255–256, 258, 261, 264, 273–291
writing content knowledge, 63–64
writing enhanced curriculum (WEC), 4, 7, 21–38, 73, 91
writing fellows, xxvii, 9, 17, 27, 29, 71–72, 125, 256, 259, 262–263, 266–267, 270–271
writing in the disciplines (WID), ix, xxv–xxvi, 7, 11, 22, 30, 32, 38, 186
writing instruction, xxii, 5, 9, 14, 21–22, 24, 32–33, 37, 46, 64, 71, 73, 89, 130, 144, 147, 164, 178–179, 186, 188, 219
writing pedagogy, xxviii, 44, 51, 165
writing plans, 22, 25, 29, 33
writing process, xi, 62–64, 80, 82, 88, 99, 130, 141–142, 144–145, 147, 149–150, 155–156, 158, 164, 216, 221, 237, 262
writing program administrators, ix–x, xi, xv–xvi, xviii–xx, xxiv, xxviii, xxx, xxxii, 4–7, 9–10, 16–17, 19, 21–22, 25, 27–28, 30, 33, 35, 40–41, 50, 53, 55, 69–71, 75, 79, 89–90, 98, 115, 135, 158, 163, 207, 229, 232, 240, 245, 295–296
writing programs: SLAC, xxviii, 6, 22, 101
writing samples, 11, 14, 23, 148, 205, 209
writing support, xviii, xxviii, 25, 72, 74, 76, 79, 159, 164, 166, 203, 256
writing-intensive courses, 5, 14, 18, 22, 27, 32, 181, 203, 282
writing-intensive courses (WI), xxiv, 5, 13
Wudunn, Sheryl, 55

Yancey, Kathleen Blake, 99, 114, 116, 232, 238, 249
York College, xxii, xxxi, 55–56, 166, 168, 191–192, 249, 272, 280, 283, 292–294
Young, Vershawn Ashanti, 27, 36
Yozell, Erica, xxxi, 34

Zimmerman, Griffin X., 177, 192

About the Editors

Dr. Genie Nicole Giaimo is an Associate Professor of Writing Studies and Rhetoric and Director of the Writing Center at Hofstra University. Prior to joining Hofstra, Genie was Assistant Professor of Writing and Rhetoric at Middlebury College. They have worked in several academic institutions, including a two-year college and a land grant institution. Their current research utilizes qualitative and quantitative models to answer a range of questions about behaviors and practices in and around writing centers and writing programs as well as labor issues in the profession. Their research has appeared in *Praxis, Writing Center Journal, TPR, Journal of Writing Research, Kairos, Journal of Writing Analytics, Journal of Multimodal Rhetorics, Composition Studies* and several other peer reviewed journals in rhetoric and composition. They are the author of three other books including: *Storying Writing Center Labor for Anti-Capitalist Futures* (2024) with Dan Lawson, *Unwell Writing Centers: Searching for Wellness in Neoliberal Educational Institutions and Beyond* (2023) (which earned the IWCA Outstanding Book Award in 2024) and *Wellness and Care in Writing Center Work* (2021). They are the 2021 recipient, along with Sam Turner, of the CWPA Outstanding Scholarship Award.

Photograph of Genie Nicole Giaimo. Used by permission.

Dr Megan O'Neill is a Professor of English and the Director of Writing at Stetson University. Megan has made a career at Stetson after three years at Creighton University, where she was the Director of First Year Writing and built interests in assessment, faculty development, and high impact pedagogy. At Stetson University since 1999, she has focused on transforming the general education curriculum around writing-intensive courses, including the enhancement of faculty development strategies, the creation of a WAC program that replaced the long-standing First Year English courses, and the establishment of a continuous process of writing assessment. She reported on this work in *Composition Studies* (2014) and has offered related workshops and conference presentations to a wide range of audiences (AAC&U, SLAC WPA, NCTE, and others), showcasing her interests in pedagogy, information literacy, and writing assessment. As the Director of the Quality Enhancement Plan and Executive Director for Liberal Learning at Stetson, Megan has been part of several significant curricular change initiatives, among them the AAC&U Institutes on General Education, Pedagogy, and Artificial Intelligence.

Photograph of Megan O'Neill. Used by permission.

Milton Keynes UK
Ingram Content Group UK Ltd.
UKHW031351011224
451755UK00004B/404